Improving Your Written and Oral Communication Skills

EDITION 10

Guffey/Loewy

Australia • Brazil • Japan • Korea • Mexico • Singapore • Spain • United Kingdom • United States

**Improving Your Written and Oral
Communication Skills
10 E**

For product information and technology assistance, contact us at
Cengage Learning Customer & Sales Support, 1-800-354-9706

For permission to use material from this text or product,
submit all requests online at **cengage.com/permissions**
Further permissions questions can be emailed to
permissionrequest@cengage.com

This book contains select works from existing Cengage Learning resources and was produced by Cengage Learning Custom Solutions for collegiate use. As such, those adopting and/or contributing to this work are responsible for editorial content accuracy, continuity and completeness.

Compilation © 2016 Cengage Learning

ISBN: 978-1-337-04128-7

Cengage Learning
20 Channel Center Street
Boston, MA 02210
USA

Cengage Learning is a leading provider of customized learning solutions with office locations around the globe, including Singapore, the United Kingdom, Australia, Mexico, Brazil, and Japan. Locate your local office at:
www.international.cengage.com/region.

Cengage Learning products are represented in Canada by Nelson Education, Ltd.

For your lifelong learning solutions, visit **www.cengage.com/custom.**

Visit our corporate website at **www.cengage.com.**

Printed at CLDPC, USA, 08-20

Brief Contents

Curator Biographies

Dr. Marylou Shockley is currently the Chair of the College of Business and the Professor of Management and International Business at CSUMB. She has been teaching at CSUMB since fall 2006. Professor Shockley was previously at Oxford University in the United Kingdom. Her focus is on management, leadership, diversity, and corporate governance from a social responsibility perspective. Her teaching interests include management, business communications, organization behavior, leadership and .international business.

She feels that student learning must be the core value of our culture in the college of business. Her teaching philosophy emphasizes student engagement through reinforcing conceptual skills, using real world examples.

Professor Shockley holds several degrees. In addition to attending Oxford University to obtain her doctoral degree at the Said School of Business, she also holds an M.S. degree in business from Stanford University as a Sloan Fellow. Dr. Shockley has also attended the University of Southern California for her MBA and the University of Hawaii for her BBA.

Calvin Carr has thirty years of successful marketing communications experience in high tech trade publishing. He has recently owned a marketing communications consultancy business where he helped high tech companies with their social media messaging content and strategies.

He has successfully managed sales, marketing, and operations teams. He is an accomplished builder and leader of motivated, results-oriented teams that have increased sales, enhanced profits and promoted rapid business growth.

Professor Carr recently completed his MS degree with honors in Journalism and Mass Communications at San Jose State University and also an Online Teaching Certification at UCSC Extension. He received his BA from St. Lawrence University.

He has taught at California State University, East Bay in the Communications Department and the Marketing/Entrepreneurship Department within the College of Business and Economics.

Also, he has taught in the Department of Communication Studies at CSU-Stanislaus and in the business school at UCSC Extension in both the classroom and online platforms.

Professor Carr has lived in Kenya, Italy, and Thailand and thrives in diverse ethnic, socioeconomic and cultural environments.

As a life-long learner, he is passionate about teaching and learning every day from his students. His teaching philosophy encourages the love of challenges, enjoying the effort, fostering curiosity, and being intrigued by mistakes.

Textbook Preface:

This custom text was created specifically for students enrolled in BUS 304 within the College of Business at CSU-Monterey Bay. This book represents the excellent work of two authors, Mary Ellen Guffey and Dana Loewy.

BUS 304 – Business Communications, Ethics, and Critical Thinking enables upper division students to acquire and demonstrate effective critical thinking and business writing and speaking skills. *Improving Your Written and Oral Communication Skills* complements BUS 304 learning outcomes and helps students to learn the essentials of business communications in our emerging digital age.

Improving Your Written and Oral Communication Skills has three goals:

- **Less is more.** Targeted chapters provide relevant content that addresses specific BUS 304 learning objectives.
- **Show, Don't Tell.** Graphic examples and learning activities help students engage with content and enhance comprehension.
- **Learn by Doing.** A variety of hands-on activities like Edit Challenges and Radical Rewrites provide clear, concrete and informative learning experiences.

This new edition includes real-world examples of written and oral communications utilizing digital technologies and mobile devices. With this custom text, students can learn, hone, and demonstrate written and oral communication skills, problem-recognition strategies, and analytical skills applicable to real-world business issues and events.

Appreciation for Support

No successful textbook reaches a No. 1 position without a great deal of help. We are exceedingly grateful to the reviewers and other experts who contributed their pedagogic and academic expertise in shaping *Essentials of Business Communication.*

We extend sincere thanks to many professionals at Cengage Learning, including Jack W. Calhoun, Senior Vice President; Erin Joyner, Vice President, General Manager; Michael Schenk, Product Director, Business, Management & Marketing; Michele Rhoades, Senior Product Manager; Kristen Hurd, Senior Brand Manager; John Rich, Senior Media Developer; Jeff Tousignant, Marketing Manager; Shirley Stacy, Senior Art Director; and Jana Lewis, Content Project Manager. We are also grateful to Crystal Bullen, DPS Associates, and Malvine Litten, LEAP Publishing Services, who ensured premier quality and excellent accuracy throughout the publishing process.

Our very special thanks go to Mary Emmons, Senior Content Developer, whose wise counsel, exceptional management skills, friendship, and unfailingly upbeat outlook have kept us sane and on track as she shepherded many editions of our books to market leadership.

Our heartfelt appreciation goes to the following for their expertise in creating superior instructor and student support materials: Jane Flesher, Chippewa Valley Technical College; Janet Mizrahi, University of California, Santa Barbara; Joyce Staples, Bellevue College; and Christina Turner, Des Moines Area Community College.

Mary Ellen Guffey
Dana Loewy

Grateful Thanks to the Following

Faridah Awang
Eastern Kentucky University

Joyce M. Barnes
Texas A & M University - Corpus Christi

Patricia Beagle
Bryant & Stratton Business Institute

Nancy C. Bell
Wayne Community College

Ray D. Bernardi
Morehead State University

Karen Bounds
Boise State University

Daniel Brown
University of South Florida

Cheryl S. Byrne
Washtenaw Community College

Jean Bush-Bacelis
Eastern Michigan University

Mary Y. Bowers
Northern Arizona University

Therese Butler
Long Beach City College

Derrick Cameron
Vance-Granville Community College

Brennan Carr
Long Beach City College

Steven V. Cates
Averett University

Irene Z. Church
Muskegon Community College

Lise H. Diez-Arguelles
Florida State University

Dee Anne Dill
Dekalb Technical Institute

Dawn Dittman
Dakota State University

Elizabeth Donnelly-Johnson
Muskegon Community College

Jeanette Dostourian
Cypress College

Nancy J. Dubino
Greenfield Community College

Donna N. Dunn
Beaufort County Community College

Cecile Earle
Heald College

Valerie Evans
Cuesta College

Bartlett J. Finney
Park University

Pat Fountain
Coastal Carolina Community College

Marlene Friederich
New Mexico State University – Carlsbad

Christine Foster
Grand Rapids Community College

JoAnn Foth
Milwaukee Area Technical College

Gail Garton
Ozarks Technical Community College

Nanette Clinch Gilson
San Jose State University

Robert Goldberg
Prince George's Community College

Margaret E. Gorman
Cayuga Community College

Judith Graham
Holyoke Community College

Lauren Gregory
South Plains College

Bruce E. Guttman
Katharine Gibbs School, Melville, New York

Susan E. Hall
University of West Georgia

April Halliday
Georgia Piedmont Technical College

Tracey M. Harrison
Mississippi College

Debra Hawhee
University of Illinois

L. P. Helstrom
Rochester Community College

Jack Hensen
Morehead State University

Rovena L. Hillsman
California State University, Sacramento

Karen A. Holtkamp
Xavier University

Michael Hricik
Westmoreland County Community College

Jodi Hoyt
Southeast Technical Institute

Sandie Idziak
University of Texas, Arlington

Karin Jacobson
University of Montana

Bonnie Jeffers
Mt. San Antonio College

Edna Jellesed
Lane Community College

Jane Johansen
University of Southern Indiana

Pamela R. Johnson
California State University, Chico

Edwina Jordan
Illinois Central College

Sheryl E. C. Joshua
University of North Carolina, Greensboro

Diana K. Kanoy
Central Florida Community College

Ron Kapper
College of DuPage

Jan Kehm
Spartanburg Community College

Karen Kendrick
Nashville State Community College

Lydia Keuser
San Jose City College

Linda Kissler
Westmoreland County Community College

Deborah Kitchin
City College of San Francisco

Frances Kranz
Oakland University

Keith Kroll
Kalamazoo Valley Community College

Rose Marie Kuceyeski
Owens Community College

Richard B. Larsen
Francis Marion University

Mary E. Leslie
Grossmont College

Ruth E. Levy
Westchester Community College

Gary R. Lewis
Southwest Florida College

Maryann Egan Longhi
Dutchess Community College

Nedra Lowe
Marshall University

Elaine Lux
Nyack College

Margarita Maestas-Flores
Evergreen Valley College

Jane Mangrum
Miami-Dade Community College

Maria Manninen
Delta College

Tim March
Kaskaskia College

Paula Marchese
State University of New York College at Brockport

Tish Matuszek
Troy University Montgomery

Kenneth R. Mayer
Cleveland State University

Victoria McCrady
University of Texas at Dallas

Karen McFarland
Salt Lake Community College

Pat McGee
Southeast Technical Institute

Bonnie Miller
Los Medanos College

Mary C. Miller
Ashland University

Willie Minor
Phoenix College

Nancy Moody
Sinclair Community College

Suman Mudunuri
Long Beach City College

Nancy Mulder
Grand Rapids Junior College

Paul W. Murphey
Southwest Wisconsin Technical College

Nan Nelson
University of Arkansas Phillips Community College

Lisa Nieman
Indiana Wesleyan University

Jackie Ohlson
University of Alaska – Anchorage

Richard D. Parker
Western Kentucky University

Martha Payne
Grayson County College

Catherine Peck
Chippewa Valley Technical College

Carol Pemberton
Normandale Community College

Carl Perrin
Casco Bay College

Jan Peterson
Anoka-Hennepin Technical College

Susan Peterson
Scottsdale Community College

Kay D. Powell
Abraham Baldwin College

Jeanette Purdy
Mercer County College

Carolyn A. Quantrille
Spokane Falls Community College

Susan Randles
Vatterott College

Diana Reep
University of Akron

Ruth D. Richardson
University of North Alabama

Carlita Robertson
Northern Oklahoma College

Vilera Rood
Concordia College

Rich Rudolph
Drexel University

Rachel Rutledge
Carteret Community College

Joanne Salas
Olympic College

Rose Ann Scala
Data Institute School of Business

Joseph Schaffner
SUNY College of Technology, Alfred

Susan C. Schanne
Eastern Michigan University

James Calvert Scott
Utah State University

Laurie Shapero
Miami-Dade Community College

Lance Shaw
Blake Business School

Cinda Skelton
Central Texas College

Estelle Slootmaker
Aquinas College

Margaret Smallwood
The University of Texas at Dallas

Clara Smith
North Seattle Community College

Nicholas Spina
Central Connecticut State University

Marilyn St. Clair
Weatherford College

Judy Sunayama
Los Medanos College

Dana H. Swensen
Utah State University

James A. Swindling
Eastfield College

David A. Tajerstein
SYRIT College

Marilyn Theissman
Rochester Community College

Zorica Wacker
Bellevue College

Lois A. Wagner
Southwest Wisconsin Technical College

Linda Weavil
Elan College

William Wells
Lima Technical College

Gerard Weykamp
Grand Rapids Community College

Beverly Wickersham
Central Texas College

Leopold Wilkins
Anson Community College

Anna Williams
College of Central Florida, Ocala

Charlotte Williams
Jones County Junior College

Donald Williams
Feather River College

Janice Willis
Bellevue College

Janice Willis
College of San Mateo

Almeda Wilmarth
State University of New York – Delhi

Barbara Young
Skyline College

About the Authors

Dr. Mary Ellen Guffey

A dedicated professional, Mary Ellen Guffey has taught business communication and business English topics for over thirty-five years. She received a bachelor's degree, *summa cum laude,* from Bowling Green State University; a master's degree from the University of Illinois, and a doctorate in business and economic education from the University of California, Los Angeles (UCLA). She has taught at the University of Illinois, Santa Monica College, and Los Angeles Pierce College.

Now recognized as the world's leading business communication textbook author, Dr. Guffey corresponds with instructors around the globe who are using her books. She is the founding author of the award-winning *Business Communication: Process and Product,* the leading business communication textbook in this country. She also wrote *Business English,* which serves more students than any other book in its field; *Essentials of College English*; and *Essentials of Business Communication,* the leading text/workbook in its market. Dr. Guffey is active professionally, serving on the review boards of the *Business and Professional Communication Quarterly* and the *Journal of Business Communication*, publications of the Association for Business Communication. She participates in national meetings, sponsors business communication awards, and is committed to promoting excellence in business communication pedagogy and the development of student writing skills.

Dr. Dana Loewy

Dana Loewy has been teaching business communication at California State University, Fullerton for the past eighteen years. She enjoys introducing undergraduates to business writing and honing the skills of graduate students in managerial communication. Most recently, she has also taught various German classes. Dr. Loewy is a regular guest lecturer at Fachhochschule Nürtingen, Germany. Having earned a PhD from the University of Southern California in English with a focus on translation, she is a well-published freelance translator, interpreter, brand-name consultant, and textbook author. Dr. Loewy has collaborated with Dr. Guffey on recent editions of *Business Communication: Process & Product* as well as on *Essentials of Business Communication.*

Fluent in several languages, among them German and Czech, her two native languages, Dr. Loewy has authored critical articles in many areas of interest—literary criticism, translation, business communication, and business ethics. Before teaming up with Dr. Guffey, Dr. Loewy published various poetry and prose translations, most notably *The Early Poetry* of Jaroslav Seifert and *On the Waves of TSF*. Active in the Association for Business Communication, Dr. Loewy focuses on creating effective teaching/learning materials for undergraduate and graduate business communication students.

Planning Business Messages

© LDprod/Shutterstock.com

OBJECTIVES
After studying this chapter, you should be able to

2-1
Discuss the five steps in the communication process.

2-2
Recognize the goals of business writing, summarize the 3-x-3 writing process, and explain how it guides a writer.

2-3
Analyze the purpose of a message, anticipate its audience, and select the best communication channel.

2-4
Employ adaptive writing techniques such as incorporating audience benefits, developing the "you" view, and using conversational but professional language.

2-5
Develop additional expert writing techniques including the use of a positive and courteous tone, bias-free language, plain language, and precise words.

2-1 Understanding the Communication Process

The digital revolution has profoundly changed the way we live our lives, do business, and communicate. People are sending more and more messages, and they are using exciting new media as the world becomes increasingly interconnected. However, even as we have become accustomed to e-mail, instant messaging, Facebook, Twitter, and other social media, the nature of communication remains unchanged. No matter how we create or send our messages, the basic communication process consists of the same five steps. It starts with an idea that must be transmitted.

In its simplest form, *communication* may be defined as "the transmission of information and meaning from a sender to a receiver." The crucial element in this definition is *meaning*. The process is successful only when the receiver understands an idea as the sender intended it. How does an idea travel from one person to another? It involves a sensitive process, shown in Figure 2.1. This process can be easily sidetracked resulting in miscommunication. It is successful when both the sender and the receiver understand the process and how to make it work. In our discussion we will be most concerned with professional communication in the workplace so that you can be successful as a business communicator in your career.

2-1a Sender Has Idea

The communication process begins when the sender has an idea. The form of the idea may be influenced by complex factors surrounding the sender. These factors

messages enable you to stay connected and express your feelings. In the workplace, however, you will want your writing to be:

- **Purposeful.** You will be writing to solve problems and convey information. You will have a definite strategy to fulfill in each message.
- **Economical.** You will try to present ideas clearly but concisely. Length is not rewarded.
- **Audience oriented.** You will concentrate on looking at a problem from the perspective of the audience instead of seeing it from your own.

These distinctions actually ease your task. You won't be searching your imagination for creative topic ideas. You won't be stretching your ideas to make them appear longer. Writing consultants and businesspeople complain that many college graduates entering industry have a conscious—or perhaps unconscious—perception that quantity enhances quality. Wrong! Get over the notion that longer is better. Whether you are presenting your message in an e-mail message, in a business report, or at a wiki site, conciseness and clarity are what count in business.

The ability to prepare purposeful, concise, and audience-centered messages does not come naturally. Very few people, especially beginners, can sit down and compose an effective e-mail message, letter, or report without training. However, following a systematic process, studying model messages, and practicing the craft can make nearly anyone a successful business writer or speaker.

2-2b Introducing the 3-x-3 Writing Process

Regardless of what you are writing, the process will be easier if you follow a systematic plan. The 3-x-3 writing process breaks the entire task into three phases: *prewriting*, *drafting*, and *revising*, as shown in Figure 2.2.

To illustrate the writing process, let's say that you own a popular local McDonald's franchise. At rush times, you face a problem. Customers complain about the chaotic multiple waiting lines to approach the service counter. You once saw two customers nearly get into a fistfight over cutting into a line. What's more, customers often are so intent on looking for ways to improve their positions in line that they fail to examine the menu. Then they are undecided when their turn arrives. You want to convince other franchise owners that a single-line (serpentine) system would work better. You could telephone the other owners. However, you want to present a serious argument with good points that they will remember and be willing to act on when they gather for their next district meeting. You decide to send a persuasive e-mail that you hope will win their support.

Prewriting. The first phase of the writing process prepares you to write. It involves *analyzing* the audience and your purpose for writing. The audience for your message will be other franchise owners, some highly educated and others not. Your purpose in writing is to convince them that a change in policy would improve customer service. You think that a single-line system, such as that used in banks, would reduce chaos and make customers happier because they would not have to worry about where they are in line.

Prewriting also involves *anticipating* how your audience will react to your message. You are sure that some of the other owners will agree with you, but others might fear that customers seeing a long single line might go elsewhere. In *adapting* your message to the audience, you try to think of the right words and the right tone that will win approval.

Drafting. The second phase involves researching, organizing, and then drafting the message. In *researching* information for this message, you would probably investigate other kinds of businesses that use single lines for customers. You might check your competitors. What are Wendy's and Burger King doing? You might do some calling to see whether other franchise owners are concerned about chaotic

OFFICE INSIDER

"Writing in the Harvard Business Review, *David Silverman blasts "an educational system that rewards length over clarity." Students learn to overwrite, he says, in hopes that at least some of their sentences "hit the mark." Once on the job, they continue to act as if they were paid by the word, a perception that must be unlearned."*

—David Silverman, businessman, entrepreneur, and blogger

Figure **2.2** The 3-x-3 Writing Process

1 Prewriting

Analyze

- What is your purpose?
- What do you want the receiver to do or believe?
- What channel should you choose: face-to-face conversation, group meeting, e-mail, memo, letter, report, blog, wiki, tweet, etc.

Anticipate

- Profile the audience.
- What does the receiver already know?
- Will the receiver's response be neutral, positive, or negative? How will this affect your organizational strategy?

Adapt

- What techniques can you use to adapt your message to its audience?
- How can you promote feedback?
- Strive to use positive, conversational, and courteous language.

2 Drafting

Research

- Gather data to provide facts.
- Search company files, previous correspondence, and the Internet.
- What do you need to know to write this message?
- How much does the audience already know?

Organize

- Organize direct messages with the big idea first, followed by an explanation in the body and an action request in the closing.
- For persuasive or negative messages, use an indirect, problem-solving strategy.

Draft

- Prepare a first draft, usually quickly.
- Focus on short, clear sentences using the active voice.
- Build paragraph coherence by repeating key ideas, using pronouns, and incorporating appropriate transitional expressions.

3 Revising

Edit

- Edit your message to be sure it is clear, concise, conversational, readable.
- Revise to eliminate wordy fillers, long lead-ins, redundancies, and trite business phrases.
- Develop parallelism.
- Consider using headings and numbered and bulleted lists for quick reading.

Proofread

- Take the time to read every message carefully.
- Look for errors in spelling, grammar, punctuation, names, and numbers.
- Check to be sure the format is consistent.

Evaluate

- Will this message achieve your purpose?
- Does the tone sound pleasant and friendly rather than curt?
- Have you thought enough about the audience to be sure this message is appealing?
- Did you encourage feedback?

---

lines. Before writing to the entire group, you might brainstorm with a few owners to see what ideas they have for solving the problem.

Once you have collected enough information, you would focus on *organizing* your message. Should you start out by offering your solution? Or should you work up to it slowly, describing the problem, presenting your evidence, and then ending with the solution? The final step in the second phase of the writing process is actually *drafting* the letter. At this point many writers write quickly, realizing that they will polish their ideas when they revise.

Revising. The third phase of the process involves editing, proofreading, and evaluating your message. After writing the first draft, you will spend considerable time *editing* the message for clarity, conciseness, tone, and readability. Could parts of it be rearranged to make your point more effectively? This is the time when you look for ways to improve the organization and tone of your message. Next, you will spend time *proofreading* carefully to ensure correct spelling, grammar, punctuation, and format. The final phase involves *evaluating* your message to decide whether it accomplishes your goal.

2-2c Pacing the Writing Process

The time you spend on each phase of the writing process varies depending on the complexity of the problem, the purpose, the audience, and your schedule. On

Figure 2.3 Scheduling the Writing Process

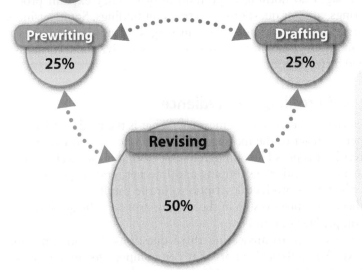

Prewriting 25%

Drafting 25%

Revising 50%

Although the writing process looks like a linear set of steps, it actually is recursive, enabling writers to revise their work continually as they progress. However, careful planning can avoid wasted time and frustration caused by rethinking and reorganizing during drafting.

average, you should expect to spend about 25 percent of your time prewriting, 25 percent drafting, and 50 percent revising, as shown in Figure 2.3.

These are rough guides, yet you can see that good writers spend most of their time on the final phase of revising and proofreading. Much depends, of course, on your project, its importance, and your familiarity with it. What is critical to remember, though, is that revising is a major component of the writing process even if the message is short.

It may appear that you perform one step and progress to the next, always following the same order. Most business writing, however, is not that rigid. Although writers perform the tasks described, the steps may be rearranged, abbreviated, or repeated. Some writers revise every sentence and paragraph as they go. Many find that new ideas occur after they have begun to write, causing them to back up, alter the organization, and rethink their plan. Beginning business writers often follow the writing process closely. With experience, though, they will become like other good writers and presenters who alter, compress, and rearrange the steps as needed.

2-3 Analyzing and Anticipating the Audience

LEARNING OBJECTIVE 3
Analyze the purpose of a message, anticipate its audience, and select the best communication channel.

Surprisingly, many people begin writing and discover only as they approach the end of a message what they are trying to accomplish. If you analyze your purpose before you begin, you can avoid backtracking and starting over. The remainder of this chapter covers the first phase of the writing process: analyzing the purpose for writing, anticipating how the audience will react, and adapting the message to the audience.

2-3a Determining Your Purpose

As you begin to compose a workplace message, ask yourself two important questions: (a) Why am I sending this message? and (b) What do I hope to achieve? Your responses will determine how you organize and present your information.

Your message may have primary and secondary purposes. For college work your primary purpose may be merely to complete the assignment; secondary purposes might be to make yourself look good and to earn an excellent grade. The primary purposes for sending business messages are typically to inform and to persuade. A secondary purpose is to promote goodwill. You and your organization want to look good in the eyes of your audience.

Many business messages do nothing more than *inform*. They explain procedures, announce meetings, answer questions, and transmit findings. Some business messages, however, are meant to *persuade*. These messages sell products, convince managers, motivate employees, and win over customers. Persuasive and informative messages are developed differently.

2-3b Anticipating and Profiling the Audience

A good writer anticipates the audience for a message: What is the reader or listener like? How will that person react to the message? Although one can't always know exactly who the receiver is, it is possible to imagine some of that person's characteristics. A copywriter at Lands' End, the shopping and Internet retailer, pictures his sister-in-law whenever he writes product descriptions for the catalog.

Profiling your audience is a pivotal step in the writing process. The questions in Figure 2.4 will help you profile your audience.

How much time you devote to answering these questions depends on your message and its context. An analytical report that you compose for management or an oral presentation that you deliver to a big group would, of course, demand considerable audience anticipation. An e-mail message to a coworker or a message to a familiar supplier might require only a few moments of planning.

Preparing a blog on an important topic to be posted to a company website would require you to think about the people in local, national, and international audiences who might read that message. Similarly, posting brief messages at social media sites such as Facebook, Twitter, and Tumblr should make you think about who will read the messages. How much of your day and life do you want to share? Will customers and business partners be reading your posts?

No matter how short your message, though, spend some time thinking about the audience so that you can tailor your words to your readers. Remember that they will be thinking, *What's in it for me (WIIFM)?* One of the most important writing tips you can take away from this book is recognizing that every message you write should begin with the notion that your audience is thinking *WIIFM?*

Figure **2.4** Asking the Right Questions to Profile Your Audience

Primary Audience

- Who is my primary reader or listener?
- What are my personal and professional relationships with this person?
- What position does this person hold in the organization?
- How much does this person know about the subject?
- What do I know about this person's education, beliefs, culture, and attitudes?
- Should I expect a neutral, positive, or negative response to my message?

Secondary Audience

- Who might see or hear this message in addition to the primary audience?
- How do these people differ from the primary audience?
- Do I need to include more background information?
- How must I reshape my message to make it understandable and acceptable to others to whom it might be forwarded?

2-3c Making Choices Based on the Audience Profile

Profiling your audience helps you make decisions about shaping the message. You will discover what language is appropriate, whether you are free to use specialized technical terms, whether you should explain the background, and so on. Profiling the audience helps you decide whether your tone should be formal or informal and whether the receiver is likely to feel neutral, positive, or negative about your message.

Another advantage of profiling your audience is considering the possibility of a secondary audience. For example, let's say you start to write an e-mail message to your supervisor, Sheila, describing a problem you are having. Halfway through the message you realize that Sheila will probably forward this message to her boss, the vice president. Sheila will not want to summarize what you said; instead she will take the easy route and merely forward your e-mail. When you realize that the vice president will probably see this message, you decide to back up and use a more formal tone. You remove your inquiry about Sheila's family, you reduce your complaints, and you tone down your language about why things went wrong. Instead, you provide more background information, and you are more specific in explaining issues with which the vice president is unfamiliar. Analyzing the task and anticipating the audience help you adapt your message so it is effective for both primary and secondary receivers.

2-3d Selecting the Best Channel

After identifying the purpose of your message, you'll want to select the most appropriate communication channel. In this digital age, the number of channels continues to expand, as shown in Figure 2.5. Whether to send an e-mail message, schedule a

Figure 2.5 Comparing Rich and Lean Communication Channels

Ten Levels of Richness in Today's Workplace Communication Channels—Richest to Leanest

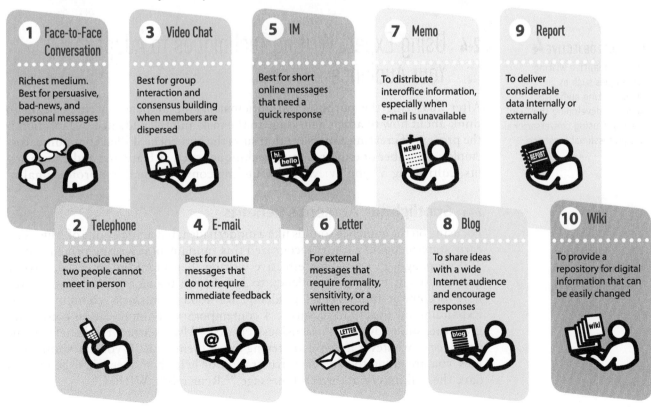

1 Face-to-Face Conversation — Richest medium. Best for persuasive, bad-news, and personal messages

2 Telephone — Best choice when two people cannot meet in person

3 Video Chat — Best for group interaction and consensus building when members are dispersed

4 E-mail — Best for routine messages that do not require immediate feedback

5 IM — Best for short online messages that need a quick response

6 Letter — For external messages that require formality, sensitivity, or a written record

7 Memo — To distribute interoffice information, especially when e-mail is unavailable

8 Blog — To share ideas with a wide Internet audience and encourage responses

9 Report — To deliver considerable data internally or externally

10 Wiki — To provide a repository for digital information that can be easily changed

video conference, or have a face-to-face conversation or group meeting depends on some of the following factors:

- Importance of the message
- Amount and speed of feedback and interactivity required
- Necessity of a permanent record
- Cost of the channel
- Degree of formality desired
- Confidentiality and sensitivity of the message
- Receiver's preference and level of technical expertise

In addition to these practical issues, you will also consider how *rich* the channel is. The *richness* of a channel involves the extent to which it recreates or represents all the information available in the original message. A richer medium, such as a face-to-face conversation, permits more interactivity and feedback. A leaner medium, such as a letter or an e-mail, presents a flat, one-dimensional message. Richer media enable the sender to provide more verbal and visual cues, as well as allow the sender to tailor the message to the audience.

Choosing the wrong medium can result in the message being less effective or even misunderstood. If, for example, marketing manager Connor must motivate the sales force to increase sales in the fourth quarter, he is unlikely to achieve his goal if he merely posts an announcement on the office bulletin board, writes a memo, or sends an e-mail. He could be more persuasive with a richer channel such as individual face-to-face conversations or a group meeting to stimulate sales. For sales reps on the road, a richer medium would be a videoconference. Keep in mind the following tips for choosing a communication channel:

- Use the richest media available.
- Employ richer media for more persuasive or personal communications.

LEARNING OBJECTIVE 4

Employ adaptive writing techniques such as incorporating audience benefits, developing the "you" view, and using conversational but professional language.

2-4 Using Expert Writing Techniques to Adapt to Your Audience

After analyzing the purpose and anticipating the audience, writers begin to think about how to adapt a message to the task and the audience. Adaptation is the process of creating a message that suits the audience. Skilled communicators employ a number of expert writing techniques such as featuring audience benefits, cultivating a "you" view, and sounding conversational but professional.

2-4a Spotlighting Audience Benefits

Focusing on the audience sounds like a modern idea, but actually one of America's early statesmen and authors recognized this fundamental writing principle over 200 years ago. In describing effective writing, Ben Franklin observed, "To be good, it ought to have a tendency to benefit the reader."[1] These wise words have become a fundamental guideline for today's business communicators. Expanding on Franklin's counsel, a contemporary communication consultant gives this solid advice to his business clients: "Always stress the benefit to the audience of whatever it is you are trying to get them to do. If you can show them how you are going to save them frustration or help them meet their goals, you have the makings of a powerful message."[2] Remember, WIIFM!

Adapting your message to the receiver's needs means putting yourself in that person's shoes. It's called *empathy*. Empathic senders think about how a receiver will decode a message. They try to give something to the receiver, solve the receiver's problems, save the receiver's money, or just understand the feelings and position of that person. Which version of each of the following messages is more appealing to the audience?

DON'T SENDER FOCUS	DO✓ AUDIENCE FOCUS
✗ All employees are instructed herewith to fill out the enclosed questionnaire so that we can allocate our training funds to employees.	✓ By filling out the enclosed questionnaire, you can be one of the first employees to sign up for our training funds.
✗ Our warranty becomes effective only when we receive an owner's registration.	✓ Your warranty begins working for you as soon as you return your owner's registration.

2-4b Developing the "You" View

In concentrating on audience benefits, skilled communicators naturally develop the "you" view. They emphasize second-person pronouns (*you, your*) instead of first-person pronouns (*I/we, us, our*). Whether your goal is to inform, persuade, or promote goodwill, the catchiest words you can use are *you* and *your*. Compare the following examples.

DON'T "I/WE" VIEW	DO✓ "YOU" VIEW
✗ We are requiring all employees to respond to the attached survey about health benefits.	✓ Because your ideas count, please complete the attached survey about health benefits.
✗ I need your account number before I can do anything.	✓ Please give me your account number so that I can locate your records and help you solve this problem.

Although you want to focus on the reader or listener, don't overuse or misuse the second-person pronoun *you*. Readers and listeners appreciate genuine interest; on the other hand, they resent obvious attempts at manipulation. The authors of some sales messages, for example, are guilty of overkill when they include *you* dozens of times in a direct-mail promotion. What's more, the word can sometimes create the wrong impression. Consider this statement: *You cannot return merchandise until you receive written approval.* The word *you* appears twice, but the reader may feel singled out for criticism. In the following version, the message is less personal and more positive: *Customers may return merchandise with written approval.*

Another difficulty in emphasizing the "you" view and de-emphasizing *we/I* is that it may result in overuse of the passive voice. For example, to avoid writing *We will give you* (active voice), you might write *You will be given* (passive voice). The active voice in writing is generally preferred because it identifies who is doing the acting. You will learn more about active and passive voice in Chapter 3.

Workplace in Focus

GLOBAL STRENGTHS

Jeff Kowalsky/Bloomberg/Getty Images

While addressing a panel at the 2014 Consumer Electronics Show, Ford marketing chief Jim Farley stirred controversy in comments meant to showcase the automaker's advanced GPS features. Instead of selling consumers on the benefits of in-dash computers, Farley confirmed their worst suspicions: "We know everyone who breaks the law, and we know when you're doing it," he said. "We have GPS in your car, so we know what you're doing." The remark startled listeners and violated nearly every rule of audience-focused communication. Ford quickly denounced the comments. How might automakers adopt the "you" view to emphasize the benefits of in-dash navigation services to customers?[4]

In recognizing the value of the "you" view, however, you don't have to sterilize your writing and totally avoid any first-person pronouns or words that show your feelings. You can convey sincerity, warmth, and enthusiasm by the words you choose. Don't be afraid of phrases such as *I'm happy* or *We're delighted*, if you truly are. When speaking face-to-face, you can show sincerity and warmth with nonverbal cues such as a smile and a pleasant voice tone. In letters, e-mail messages, memos, and other digital messages, however, only expressive words and phrases can show your feelings. These phrases suggest hidden messages that say, *You are important, I hear you*, and *I'm honestly trying to please you*.

2-4c Sounding Conversational but Professional

Most business messages replace conversation. That's why they are most effective when they convey an informal, conversational tone instead of a formal, pretentious tone. Just how informal you can be depends greatly on the workplace. At Google, casual seems to be preferred. In a short message to users describing changes in its privacy policies, Google recently wrote, "we believe this stuff matters."[3] In more traditional organizations, that message probably would have been more formal. The dilemma for you, then, is knowing how casual to be in your writing. We suggest that you strive to be conversational but professional, especially until you learn what your organization prefers.

E-mail, instant messaging, chat, Twitter, and other short messaging channels enable you and your coworkers to have spontaneous conversations. Don't, however, let your messages become sloppy, unprofessional, or even dangerous. You will learn more about the dangers of e-mail and other digital channels later. At this point, though, we focus on the tone of the language.

To project a professional image, you want to sound educated and mature. Overuse of expressions such as *totally awesome, you know*, and *like*, as well as a reliance on unnecessary abbreviations (*BTW* for *by the way*), make a business-person sound like a teenager. Professional messages do not include texting-style abbreviations, slang, sentence fragments, and chitchat. We urge you to strive for a warm, conversational tone that avoids low-level diction. Levels of diction, as shown in Figure 2.6, range from unprofessional to formal.

Your goal is to convey a warm, friendly tone that sounds professional. Although some writers are too casual, others are overly formal. To impress readers and listeners, they use big words, long sentences, legal terminology, and third-person constructions. Stay away from expressions such as *the undersigned, the writer*, and *the affected party*. You will sound friendlier with familiar pronouns such as *I, we*, and *you*. The following examples illustrate a professional yet conversational tone:

DON'T UNPROFESSIONAL	DO✔ PROFESSIONAL
✕ Hey, boss, Gr8 news! Firewall now installed!! BTW, check with me b4 announcing it.	✓ Mr. Smith, our new firewall software is now installed. Please check with me before announcing it.
✕ Look, dude, this report is totally bogus. And the figures don't look kosher. Show me some real stats. Got sources?	✓ Because the figures in this report seem inaccurate, please submit the source statistics.

DON'T OVERLY FORMAL	DO✔ CONVERSATIONAL
✕ All employees are herewith instructed to return the appropriately designated contracts to the undersigned.	✓ Please return your contracts to me.
✕ Pertaining to your order, we must verify the sizes that your organization requires prior to consignment of your order to our shipper.	✓ We will send your order as soon as we confirm the sizes you need.

Figure 2.6 Levels of Diction

Unprofessional (Low-level diction) 😦	Conversational (Middle-level diction) 😄	Formal (High-level diction) 😐
badmouth	criticize	denigrate
guts	nerve	courage
pecking order	line of command	dominance hierarchy
ticked off	upset	provoked
rat on	inform	betray
rip off	steal	expropriate
If we just hang in there, we'll snag the contract.	If we don't get discouraged, we'll win the contract.	If the principals persevere, they will secure the contract.

2-5 Developing Additional Expert Writing Techniques

LEARNING OBJECTIVE 5
Develop additional expert writing techniques including the use of a positive and courteous tone, bias-free language, plain language, and precise words.

As you continue to improve your writing skills, you can use additional expert techniques that improve the clarity, tone, and effectiveness of a message. These skillful techniques include using a positive and courteous tone, bias-free language, simple expression, and precise words. Take a look at Figure 2.7 to see how a writer can improve an e-mail message by applying numerous expert writing techniques.

2-5a Being Positive Rather Than Negative

One of the best ways to improve the tone of a message is to use positive rather than negative language. Positive language generally conveys more information than negative language does. Moreover, positive messages are uplifting and pleasant to read. Positive wording tells what *is* and what *can be done* rather than what *isn't* and what *can't be done*. For example, *Your order cannot be shipped by January 10*

Figure 2.7 Applying Expert Writing Techniques to Improve an E-Mail Message

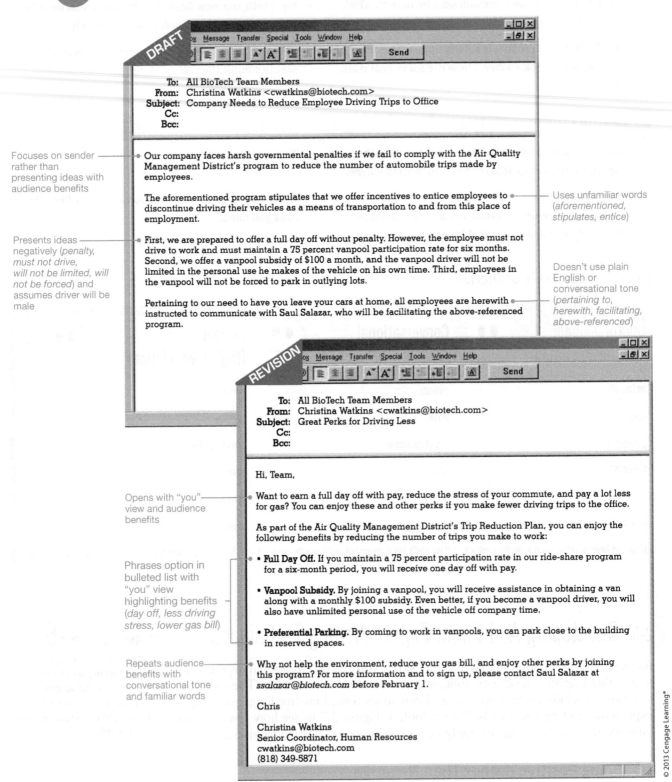

Focuses on sender rather than presenting ideas with audience benefits

Presents ideas negatively (*penalty, must not drive, will not be limited, will not be forced*) **and assumes driver will be male**

DRAFT

Message Transfer Special Tools Window Help

Send

To: All BioTech Team Members
From: Christina Watkins <cwatkins@biotech.com>
Subject: Company Needs to Reduce Employee Driving Trips to Office
Cc:
Bcc:

Our company faces harsh governmental penalties if we fail to comply with the Air Quality Management District's program to reduce the number of automobile trips made by employees.

The aforementioned program stipulates that we offer incentives to entice employees to discontinue driving their vehicles as a means of transportation to and from this place of employment.

First, we are prepared to offer a full day off without penalty. However, the employee must not drive to work and must maintain a 75 percent vanpool participation rate for six months. Second, we offer a vanpool subsidy of $100 a month, and the vanpool driver will not be limited in the personal use he makes of the vehicle on his own time. Third, employees in the vanpool will not be forced to park in outlying lots.

Pertaining to our need to have you leave your cars at home, all employees are herewith instructed to communicate with Saul Salazar, who will be facilitating the above-referenced program.

Uses unfamiliar words (*aforementioned, stipulates, entice*)

Doesn't use plain English or conversational tone (*pertaining to, herewith, facilitating, above-referenced*)

REVISION

Message Transfer Special Tools Window Help

Send

To: All BioTech Team Members
From: Christina Watkins <cwatkins@biotech.com>
Subject: Great Perks for Driving Less
Cc:
Bcc:

Hi, Team,

Want to earn a full day off with pay, reduce the stress of your commute, and pay a lot less for gas? You can enjoy these and other perks if you make fewer driving trips to the office.

As part of the Air Quality Management District's Trip Reduction Plan, you can enjoy the following benefits by reducing the number of trips you make to work:

• **Full Day Off.** If you maintain a 75 percent participation rate in our ride-share program for a six-month period, you will receive one day off with pay.

• **Vanpool Subsidy.** By joining a vanpool, you will receive assistance in obtaining a van along with a monthly $100 subsidy. Even better, if you become a vanpool driver, you will also have unlimited personal use of the vehicle off company time.

• **Preferential Parking.** By coming to work in vanpools, you can park close to the building in reserved spaces.

Why not help the environment, reduce your gas bill, and enjoy other perks by joining this program? For more information and to sign up, please contact Saul Salazar at *ssalazar@biotech.com* before February 1.

Chris

Christina Watkins
Senior Coordinator, Human Resources
cwatkins@biotech.com
(818) 349-5871

Opens with "you" view and audience benefits

Phrases option in bulleted list with "you" view highlighting benefits (*day off, less driving stress, lower gas bill*)

Repeats audience benefits with conversational tone and familiar words

---

is not nearly as informative as *Your order will be shipped January 15*. An office supply store adjacent to an ice cream parlor in Portland, Maine, posted a sign on its door that reads: *Please enjoy your ice cream before you enjoy our store*. That sounds much more positive and inviting than *No food allowed!*[5]

Using positive language also involves avoiding negative words that create ill will. Some words appear to blame or accuse your audience. For example, opening a letter to a customer with *You claim that* suggests that you don't believe the customer. Other loaded words that can get you in trouble are *complaint, criticism, defective, failed, mistake,* and *neglected.* Also avoid phrases such as *you apparently are unaware of* or *you did not provide* or *you misunderstood* or *you don't understand.* Often you may be unaware of the effect of these words. Notice in the following examples how you can revise the negative tone to create a more positive impression.

DON'T NEGATIVE	**DO** POSITIVE
✗ This plan definitely cannot succeed if we don't obtain management approval.	✓ This plan definitely can succeed if we obtain management approval.
✗ You failed to include your credit card number, so we can't mail your order.	✓ We look forward to completing your order as soon as we receive your credit card number.
✗ Your letter of May 2 claims that you returned a defective headset.	✓ Your May 2 letter describes a headset you returned.
✗ Employees cannot park in Lot H until April 1.	✓ Employees may park in Lot H starting April 1.

2-5b Expressing Courtesy

Maintaining a courteous tone involves not just guarding against rudeness but also avoiding words that sound demanding or preachy. Expressions such as *you should, you must,* and *you have to* cause people to instinctively react with *Oh, yeah?* One remedy is to turn these demands into rhetorical questions that begin with *Will you please. . . .* Giving reasons for a request also softens the tone.

Even when you feel justified in displaying anger, remember that losing your temper or being sarcastic will seldom accomplish your goals as a business communicator: to inform, to persuade, and to create goodwill. When you are irritated, frustrated, or infuriated, keep cool and try to defuse the situation. In dealing with customers in telephone conversations, use polite phrases such as these: *I would be happy to assist you with that, Thank you for being so patient,* and *It was a pleasure speaking with you.*

DON'T LESS COURTEOUS	**DO** MORE COURTEOUS AND HELPFUL
✗ Can't you people get anything right? This is the second time I've written!	✓ Please credit my account for $340. My latest statement shows that the error noted in my letter of May 15 has not yet been corrected.
✗ Stewart, you must complete all performance reviews by Friday.	✓ Stewart, will you please complete all performance reviews by Friday.
✗ Am I the only one who can read the operating manual?	✓ Let's review the operating manual together so that you can get your documents to print correctly next time.

2-5c Employing Bias-Free Language

In adapting a message to its audience, be sure your language is sensitive and bias-free. Few writers set out to be offensive. Sometimes, though, we all say things that we never thought could be hurtful. The real problem is that we don't think about the words that stereotype groups of people, such as *the boys in the mail room* or *the girls in the front office*. Be cautious about expressions that might be biased in terms of gender, race, ethnicity, age, and disability.

Generally, you can avoid gender-biased language by choosing alternate language for words involving *man* or *woman*, by using plural nouns and pronouns, or by changing to a gender-free word (*person* or *representative*). Avoid the *his or her* option whenever possible. It's wordy and conspicuous. With a little effort, you can usually find a construction that is graceful, grammatical, and unself-conscious.

Specify age only if it is relevant, and avoid expressions that are demeaning or subjective (such as *spry old codger*). To avoid disability bias, do not refer to an individual's disability unless it is relevant. When necessary, use terms that do not stigmatize people with disabilities. The following examples give you a quick look at a few problem expressions and possible replacements. The real key to bias-free communication, though, lies in your awareness and commitment. Be on the lookout to be sure that your messages do not exclude, stereotype, or offend people.

DON'T GENDER BIASED	DO✔ BIAS FREE
✗ female doctor, woman attorney, cleaning woman	✓ doctor, attorney, cleaner
✗ waiter/waitress, authoress, stewardess	✓ server, author, flight attendant
✗ mankind, man-hour, man-made	✓ humanity, working hours, artificial
✗ office girls	✓ office workers
✗ the doctor . . . he	✓ doctors . . . they
✗ the teacher . . . she	✓ teachers . . . they
✗ executives and their wives	✓ executives and their spouses
✗ foreman, flagman, workman, craftsman	✓ lead worker, flagger, worker, artisan
✗ businessman, salesman	✓ businessperson, sales representative
✗ Each employee had his picture taken.	✓ Each employee had a picture taken.
	All employees had their pictures taken.
	Each employee had his or her picture taken.

DON'T RACIALLY OR ETHNICALLY BIASED	DO✔ BIAS FREE
✗ An Indian accountant was hired.	✓ An accountant was hired.
✗ James Lee, an African-American, applied.	✓ James Lee applied.

DON'T AGE BIASED	DO✔ BIAS FREE
✗ The law applied to old people.	✓ The law applied to people over sixty-five.
✗ Sally Kay, 55, was transferred.	✓ Sally Kay was transferred.
✗ a sprightly old gentleman	✓ a man
✗ a little old lady	✓ a woman

DON'T DISABILITY BIASED	DO ✔ BIAS FREE
✗ afflicted with arthritis, crippled by arthritis	✔ has arthritis
✗ confined to a wheelchair	✔ uses a wheelchair

2-5d Preferring Plain Language and Familiar Words

In adapting your message to your audience, use plain language and familiar words that you think audience members will recognize. Don't, however, avoid a big word that conveys your idea efficiently and is appropriate for the audience. Your goal is to shun pompous and pretentious language. Instead, use GO words. If you mean *begin*, don't say *commence* or *initiate*. If you mean *pay*, don't write *compensate*. By substituting everyday, familiar words for unfamiliar ones, as shown here, you help your audience comprehend your ideas quickly.

DON'T UNFAMILIAR	DO ✔ FAMILIAR
✗ commensurate	✔ equal
✗ interrogate	✔ question
✗ materialize	✔ appear
✗ obfuscate	✔ confuse
✗ remuneration	✔ pay, salary
✗ terminate	✔ end

At the same time, be selective in your use of jargon. *Jargon* describes technical or specialized terms within a field. These terms enable insiders to communicate complex ideas briefly, but to outsiders they mean nothing. Human resources professionals, for example, know precisely what's meant by *cafeteria plan* (a benefits option program), but most of us would be thinking about lunch. Geologists refer to *plate tectonics*, and physicians discuss *metastatic carcinomas*. These terms mean little to most of us. Use specialized language only when the audience will understand it. In addition, don't forget to consider secondary audiences: Will those potential receivers understand any technical terms used?

2-5e Using Precise, Vigorous Words

Strong verbs and concrete nouns give receivers more information and keep them interested. Don't overlook the thesaurus (also available online or on your computer) for expanding your word choices and vocabulary. Whenever possible, use precise, specific words, as shown here:

DON'T IMPRECISE, DULL	DO ✔ MORE PRECISE
✗ a change in profits	✔ a 25 percent hike in profits a 10 percent plunge in profits
✗ to say	✔ to promise, confess, understand to allege, assert, assume, judge
✗ to think about	✔ to identify, diagnose, analyze to probe, examine, inspect

OFFICE INSIDER

"Simple changes can have profound results. . . . Plain talk isn't only rewriting. It's rethinking your approach and really personalizing your message to the audience and to the reader."

—Janet Shimabukuro, manager, Taxpayers Services, Department of Revenue, Washington State

SUMMARY OF LEARNING OBJECTIVES

2-1 Discuss the five steps in the communication process.
- A sender encodes (selects) words or symbols to express an idea in a message.
- The message travels over a channel (such as an e-mail, website, tweet, letter, or smartphone call).
- "Noise" (loud sounds, misspelled words, or other distractions) may interfere with the transmission.
- The receiver decodes (interprets) the message and may respond with feedback.

2-2 Recognize the goals of business writing, summarize the 3-x-3 writing process, and explain how it guides a writer.
- Business writing should be purposeful, economical, and audience oriented.
- The 3-x-3 writing process helps writers create efficient and effective messages.
- Phase 1 (prewriting): analyze the message, anticipate the audience, and consider how to adapt the message to the audience.
- Phase 2 (drafting): research the topic, organize the material, and draft the message.
- Phrase 3 (revising): edit, proofread, and evaluate the message.

2-3 Analyze the purpose of a message, anticipate its audience, and select the best communication channel.
- Before composing, decide what you hope to achieve.
- Select the appropriate channel to inform, persuade, or convey goodwill.
- After identifying the purpose, visualize both the primary and secondary audiences.
- Remember that receivers will usually be thinking, *What's in it for me (WIIFM)?*
- Select the best channel by considering (a) the importance of the message, (b) the amount and speed of feedback required, (c) the necessity of a permanent record, (d) the cost of the channel, (e) the degree of formality desired, (f) the confidentiality and sensitivity of the message, and (g) the receiver's preference and level of technical expertise.

2-4 Employ adaptive writing techniques such as incorporating audience benefits, developing the "you" view, and using conversational but professional language.
- Look for ways to shape the message from the receiver's, not the sender's, view.
- Apply the "you" view without attempting to manipulate.
- Use conversational but professional language.

2-5 Develop additional expert writing techniques including the use of a positive and courteous tone, bias-free language, plain language, and precise words.
- Use positive language that tells what can be done rather than what can't be done
  (*The project will be successful with your support* rather than *The project won't be successful without your support*).
- Be courteous rather than rude, preachy, or demanding.
- Provide reasons for a request to soften the tone of a message.
- Avoid biased language that excludes, stereotypes, or offends people (*lady lawyer, spry old gentleman, confined to a wheelchair*).
- Strive for plain language (*equal* instead of *commensurate*), familiar terms (*end* instead of *terminate*), and precise words (*analyze* instead of *think about*).

CHAPTER REVIEW

1. Define *communication*. When is it successful? (Obj. 1)

2. List the five steps in the communication process. (Obj. 1)

3. In what ways is business writing different from school essays and private messages? (Obj. 2)

4. Describe the components in each stage of the 3-x-3 writing process. Approximately how much time is spent on each stage? (Obj. 2)

5. What does *WIIFM* mean? Why is it important to business writers? (Obj. 3)

6. What seven factors should writers consider in selecting an appropriate channel to deliver a message? (Obj. 3)

7. What is the "you" view? When can the use of the pronoun *you* backfire? (Obj. 4)

8. How can a business writer sound conversational but also be professional? (Obj. 4)

9. Why is positive wording more effective in business messages than negative wording? (Obj. 5)

10. What are three ways to avoid biased language? Give an original example of each. (Obj. 5)

CRITICAL THINKING

11. Has digital transmission changed the nature of communication? (Obj. 1)

12. Why do you think employers prefer messages that are not written like high school and college essays? (Obj. 2)

13. Why should business writers strive to use short, familiar, simple words? Does this "dumb down" business messages? (Obj. 5)

14. A wise observer once said that bad writing makes smart people look dumb. Do you agree or disagree, and why? (Objs. 1–5)

15. In a letter to the editor, a teacher criticized an article in *USA Today* on autism because it used the term *autistic child* rather than *child with autism*. She championed *people-first* terminology, which avoids defining individuals by their ability or disability.[6] For example, instead of identifying someone as a *disabled person*, one would say, *she has a disability*. What does *people-first language* mean? Can language change perceptions? (Obj. 5)

WRITING IMPROVEMENT EXERCISES

Audience Benefits and the "You" View (Obj. 4)

YOUR TASK. Revise the following sentences to emphasize the perspective of the audience and the "you" view.

16. We have prepared the enclosed form that may be used by victims to report identity theft to creditors.

17. To help us process your order with our new database software, we need you to go to our website and fill out the customer information required.

18. We are now offering RapidAssist, a software program we have developed to provide immediate technical support through our website to your employees and customers.

19. We find it necessary to restrict parking in the new company lot to those employee vehicles with "A" permits.

20. To avoid suffering the kinds of customer monetary losses experienced in the past, our credit union now prohibits the cashing of double-endorsed checks presented by our customers.

21. Our warranty goes into effect only when we have received the product's registration card from the purchaser.

22. Unfortunately, you will not be able to use our computer and telephone systems on Thursday afternoon because of upgrades to both systems.

23. As part of our company effort to be friendly to the environment, we are asking all employees to reduce paper consumption by communicating by e-mail and avoiding printing.

Conversational but Professional (Obj. 4)

YOUR TASK. Revise the following to make the tone conversational yet professional.

24. Per your recent e-mail, the undersigned takes pride in informing you that we are pleased to be able to participate in the Toys for Tots drive.

25. Pursuant to your message of the 15th, please be advised that your shipment was sent August 14.

26. Yo, Jeff! Look, dude, I need you to sweet talk Ramona so we can drop this budget thingy in her lap.

27. BTW, Danika was totally ticked off when the manager accused her of ripping off office supplies. She may split.

28. He didn't have the guts to badmouth her 2 her face.

29. The undersigned respectfully reminds affected individuals that employees desirous of changing their health plans must do so before November 1.

Positive and Courteous Expression (Obj. 5)

YOUR TASK. Revise the following statements to make them more positive.

30. Employees are not allowed to use instant messaging until a company policy is established.

31. We must withhold authorizing payment of your consultant's fees because our CPA claims that your work is incomplete.

32. Plans for the new health center cannot move forward without full community support.

33. This is the last time I'm writing to try to get you to record my October 3 payment of $359.50 to my account! Anyone who can read can see from the attached documents that I've tried to explain this to you before.

34. Although you apparently failed to read the operator's manual, we are sending you a replacement blade for your food processor. Next time read page 18 carefully so that you will know how to attach this blade.

35. Everyone in this department must begin using new passwords as of midnight, June 15. Because of flagrant password misuse, we find it necessary to impose this new rule so that we can protect your personal information and company records.

Bias-Free Language (Obj. 5)

YOUR TASK. Revise the following sentences to reduce gender, racial, ethnic, age, and disability bias.

36. Every employee must wear his photo identification on the job.

37. The conference will offer special excursions for the wives of executives.

38. Does each salesman have his own smartphone loaded with his special sales information?

39. A little old lady returned this item.

40. Serving on the panel are a lady veterinarian, an Indian CPA, two businessmen, and a female doctor.

41. Each nurse is responsible for her patient's medications.

Plain Language and Familiar Words (Obj. 5)

YOUR TASK. Revise the following sentences to use plain language and familiar words.

42. The salary we are offering is commensurate with remuneration for other managers.

43. To expedite ratification of this agreement, we urge you to vote in the affirmative.

44. In a dialogue with the manager, I learned that you plan to terminate our contract.

45. Did your car's braking problem materialize subsequent to our recall effort?

46. Pursuant to your invitation, we will interrogate our agent.

Precise, Vigorous Words (Obj. 5)

YOUR TASK. From the choices in parentheses, select the most precise, vigorous words.

47. Government economists (say, hypothesize, predict) that employment will (stabilize, stay the same, even out) next year.

48. The growing number of (people, consumers, buyers) with (devices, gadgets, smartphones) provides an (idea, indicator, picture) of economic growth.

49. Although international trade can (get, offer, generate) new profits and (affect, lower) costs, it also introduces a (different, higher, new) level of risk and complexity.

50. The World Bank sees international trade as a (good, fine, vital) tool for (decreasing, changing, addressing) poverty.

RADICAL REWRITES ⊠

In most chapters you will find Radical Rewrite cases, poorly written messages that invite you to apply the writing techniques you have been learning. Rewriting is an excellent way to help you build writing skills. It enables you to focus on revising and not on supplying a context or generating imaginary facts. Your instructor's feedback regarding your strengths and challenges will speed your growth as a business communicator.

Note: Radical Rewrites are provided at **www.cengagebrain.com** for you to download and revise. Your instructor may show a suggested solution.

2.1 Radical Rewrite: Watch Your Tone! (Objs. 4, 5)

The following demanding message to be sent by the vice president to all employees suffers from many writing faults, requiring a radical rewrite.

YOUR TASK. Analyze the message and list at least five writing faults. Pay special attention to its tone. Your instructor may ask you to revise the message so that it reflects some of the expert writing techniques you learned in this chapter. How can you make this message more courteous, positive, and precise? In addition, think about using familiar words and developing the "you" view.

To:	All Staff
From:	Sybil Montrose <smontrose@syracuse.com>
Subject:	Problematic Online Use by Employees
Cc:	
Bcc:	
Attached:	E-Mail and Internet Policy

Once again I have the decidedly unpleasant task of reminding all employees that you may NOT utilize company computers or the Internet other than for work-related business and essential personal messages. Effective immediately a new policy must be implemented.

Our guys in IT tell me that our bandwidth is now seriously compromised by some of you boys and girls who are using company computers for Facebooking, blogging, shopping, chatting, gaming, and downloading streaming video. Yes, we have given you the right to use e-mail responsibly for essential personal messages. That does **not**, however, include checking your Facebook or other social accounts during work hours or downloading shows or sharing music.

We distributed an e-mail policy a little while ago. We have now found it necessary to amplify and extrapolate that policy to include use of the Internet. If our company fails to control its e-mail and Internet use, you will continue to suffer slow downloads and virus intrusions. You may also lose the right to use e-mail altogether. In the past every employee has had the right to send a personal e-mail occasionally, but he must use that right carefully. We don't want to prohibit the personal use of e-mail entirely. Don't make me do this!

You will be expected to study the attached E-Mail and Internet policy and return the signed form with your agreement to adhere to this policy. You must return this form by March 1. No exceptions!

List at least five specific writing faults and include examples.

ACTIVITIES

2.2 Channel Selection: Various Business Scenarios (Obj. 3)

YOUR TASK. Using Figure 2.5 on page 43, suggest the best communication channels for the following messages. Assume that all channels shown are available, ranging from face-to-face conversations to instant messages, blogs, and wikis. Be prepared to justify your choices based on the richness of each channel.

a. As part of a task force to investigate cell phone marketing, you need to establish a central location where each team member can see general information about the task as well as add comments for others to see. Task force members are located throughout the country.

b. You're sitting on the couch in the evening watching TV when you suddenly remember that you were supposed to send Jeremy some information about a shared project. Should you text him right away before you forget?

c. As an event planner, you have been engaged to research sites for a celebrity golf tournament. What is the best channel for conveying your findings to your boss or planning committee?

d. You want to persuade your manager to change your work schedule.

e. As a sales manager, you want to know which of your sales reps in the field are available immediately for a quick teleconference meeting.

f. You need to know whether Amanda in Reprographics can produce a rush job for you in two days.

g. Your firm must respond to a notice from the Internal Revenue Service announcing that the company owes a penalty because it underreported its income in the previous fiscal year.

GRAMMAR/MECHANICS CHECKUP—2

Pronouns

Review Sections 1.07–1.09 in the Grammar/Mechanics Handbook. Then study each of the following statements. In the space provided, write the word that completes the statement correctly and the number of the G/M principle illustrated. When you finish, compare your responses with those provided near the end of the book. If your responses differ, study carefully the principles in parentheses.

its _____ _1.09d_ **EXAMPLE** The Employee Development Committee will make (its, their) recommendation soon.

_____ 1. The manager said that Elena would call. Was it (she, her) who left the message?

_____ 2. Every member of the men's soccer team must have (his, their) medical exam completed by Monday.

_____ 3. Even instant messages sent between the CEO and (he, him) were revealed in the court case.

_____ 4. (Who, Whom) have you hired to create cutting-edge ads for us?

_____ 5. It looks as if (yours, your's) is the only report that cites electronic sources correctly.

_____ 6. Mark asked Catherine and (I, me, myself) to help him complete his research.

_____ 7. My friend and (I, me, myself) were interviewed for the same job.

_____ 8. To park the car, turn (it's, its) wheels to the left.

_____ 9. Give the budget figures to (whoever, whomever) asked for them.

_____ 10. Everyone except the interviewer and (I, me, myself) noticed the alarm.

_____ 11. No one knows that case better than (he, him, himself).

_____ 12. A proposed budget was sent to (we, us) owners before the vote.

_____ 13. One of the female travelers left (their, her) smartphone on the seat.

_____ 14. Neither the glamour nor the excitement of the Vegas job had lost (its, it's, their) appeal.

_____ 15. If neither Cory nor I receive confirmation of our itinerary, (him and me, him and I, he and I) cannot make the trip.

EDITING CHALLENGE—2

To fine-tune your grammar and mechanics skills, in every chapter you will be editing a message. This e-mail message is a short report about beverage sweeteners from a researcher to his boss. However, the message suffers from proofreading, spelling, grammar, punctuation, and other writing faults that require correction. Study the guidelines in the Grammar/Mechanics Handbook. as well as the lists of Confusing Words and Frequently Misspelled Words at the end of the book to sharpen your skills.

YOUR TASK. Edit the following message (a) by correcting errors in your textbook or on a photocopy using proofreading marks from Appendix A or (b) by downloading the message from **www.cengagebrain.com** and correcting at your computer. Your instructor may show you a possible solution.

To:	Vicky Miranda <v.miranda@dino.com>
From:	Aliriza Kasra <a.kasra@dino.com>
Subject:	Sending Information on Beverage Sweeteners
Cc:	
Bcc:	

Vicky,

Per your request, herewith is a short report of the investigation you assigned to Oliver Orenstein and I pertaining to sweeteners. As you probaly already know, Coca-Cola co. and PepsiCo inc. market many drinks using sweeteners that are new to the market. Totally awesome!

Coca-Cola brought out Sprite Green, a reduced calorie soft drink that contains Truvia. Which it considers a natural sweetener because it is derived from an herb. The initial launch focused on locations and events oriented to teenagers and young adults. According to inside information obtained by Ollie and I, this product was tested on the shelfs of grocerys, mass merchants, and conveience stores in 5 citys in Florida.

PepsiCo has it's own version of the herbal sweetener, however it was developed in collaboration with Green earth sweetener co. Its called Pure Via. The first products that contained the sweetener were 3 flavors of zero-calorie SoBe Lifewater. It may also be used in a orange-juice drink with half the calorys and sugar of orange juice. Another new sweetener is Nectresse, marketed by Splenda. It comes from the monk fruit. Which has been cultivated for centurys, and only recently rediscovered as a source of natural sweetness.

BTW, approval by the Food and drug administration did not materialize automatically for these new sweeteners. FDA approval was an issue because studys conducted in the early 1990s suggested that their was possible adverse health effects from the use of stevia-based products. However the herb has been aproved for use in 12 countrys.

Both companys eventually received FDA approval and there products are all ready on the market. We cannot submit our full report until October 15.

Al

Aliriza Kasra
a.kasra@dino.com
Research and Development
Office: (927) 443-9920
Cell: (927) 442-2310

COMMUNICATION WORKSHOP

Get Ready for Critical Thinking, Problem Solving, and Decision Making!

Gone are the days when management expected workers to check their brains at the door and do only as told. Today, you will be expected to use your brain and think critically. You will be solving problems and making decisions. Much of this book is devoted to helping you solve problems and communicate those decisions to management, fellow workers, clients, the government, and the public. Faced with a problem or an issue, most of us do a lot of worrying before identifying the issues or making a decision. You can convert all that worrying to directed thinking by channeling it into the following procedure:

- **Identify and clarify the problem.** Your first task is to recognize that a problem exists. Some problems are big and unmistakable, such as failure of an air-freight delivery service to get packages to customers on time. Other problems may be continuing annoyances, such as regularly running out of toner for an office copy machine. The first step in reaching a solution is pinpointing the problem.

- **Gather information.** Learn more about the problem situation. Look for possible causes and solutions. This step may mean checking files, calling suppliers, or brainstorming with fellow workers. For example, the air-freight delivery service would investigate the tracking systems of the commercial airlines carrying its packages to determine what is going wrong.

- **Evaluate the evidence.** Where did the information come from? Does it represent various points of view? What biases could be expected from each source? How accurate is the information gathered? Is it fact or opinion? For example, it is a fact that packages are missing; it is an opinion that they are merely lost and will turn up eventually.

- **Consider alternatives and implications.** Draw conclusions from the gathered evidence and pose solutions. Then weigh the advantages and disadvantages of each alternative. What are the costs, benefits, and consequences? What are the obstacles, and how can they be handled? Most important, what solution best serves your goals and those of your organization? Here is where your creativity is especially important.

- **Choose the best alternative and test it.** Select an alternative, and try it out to see if it meets your expectations. If it does, put your decision it into action. If it doesn't, rethink your alternatives. The freight company decided to give its unhappy customers free delivery service to make up for the lost packages and downtime. Be sure to continue monitoring and adjusting the solution to ensure its effectiveness over time.

CAREER APPLICATION. Let's return to the McDonald's problem (discussed on page 39) in which customers and some franchise owners are unhappy with the multiple lines for service. Customers don't seem to know where to stand to be the next served. Tempers flare when aggressive customers cut in line, and other customers spend so much time protecting their places in line that they are not ready to order. As a franchise owner, you want to solve this problem. Any new procedures, however, must be approved by a majority of McDonald's owners in your district. You know that McDonald's management feels that the multi-line system accommodates higher volumes of customers more quickly than a single-line system does. In addition, customers are turned off when they see a long line.

YOUR TASK

- Individually or with a team, use the critical-thinking steps outlined here. Begin by clarifying the problem.

- Where could you gather information? Would it be wise to see what your competitors are doing? How do banks handle customer lines? Airlines?

- Evaluate your findings and consider alternatives. What are the pros and cons of each alternative?

- With your team, choose the best alternative. Present your recommendation to your class and give your reasons for choosing it.

ENDNOTES

[1] Arnold, V. (1986, August). Benjamin Franklin on writing well. *Personnel Journal*, p. 17.

[2] Bacon, M. (1988, April). Quoted in Business writing: One-on-one speaks best to the masses. *Training*, p. 95.

[3] Google (personal communication with Mary Ellen Guffey, January 30, 2012).

[4] Photo essay based on Henkel, K. and Shepardson, D. (2014, January 9). Ford exec apologizes for saying company tracks customers with GPS. *The Detroit News*. Retrieved from http://www.detroitnews.com /article/20140109/AUTO0102/301090127

[5] Be positive. (2009, March). *Communication Briefings*, p. 5. Adapted from Brandi, J. Winning at customer retention at http://www .customercarecoach.com

[6] Link, S. (2012, May 2). Use "person first" language. [Letter to editor]. *USA Today*, p. 6A.

ACKNOWLEDGMENTS

p. 39 Office Insider based on Silverman, D. (2009, February 10). Why is business writing so bad? *Harvard Business Review*. Retrieved from http://blogs.hbr.org /silverman/2009/02/why-is-business-writing-so-bad.html

p. 45 Office Insider based on Clark, B. (n.d.). The two most important words in blogging. Copyblogger. Retrieved from http://www.copyblogger.com /the-two-most-important-words-in-blogging

p. 46 Workplace in Focus based on Henkel, K. and Shepardson, D. (2014, January 9). Ford exec apologizes for saying company tracks customers with GPS. *The Detroit News*. Retrieved from http://www.detroitnews.com/article/20140109/AUTO0102/301090127

p. 49. Office Insider based on Blake, G. (2002, November 4). Insurers need to upgrade their employees' writing skills. *National Underwriter Life & Health- Financial Services Edition, 106*(44), 35.

p. 53. Office Insider based on Shimabukuro, J. (2006, December 11). Quoted in Wash. state sees results from 'plain talk' initiative. *USA Today*, p. 18A.

Organizing and Drafting Business Messages

© nopporn/Shutterstock.com.

3-1 Drafting Workplace Messages

Who me? Write on the job? Not a chance! With today's advances in technology, lots of people believe they will never be required to write on the job. The truth is, however, that business, technical, and professional people in this digital age are exchanging more messages than ever before. The more quickly you can put your ideas down and the more clearly you can explain what needs to be said, the more successful and happy you will be in your career.

Being able to write clearly is also critical to promotions. That's why we devote three chapters to teaching you a tried-and-true writing process, summarized in Figure 3.1 This process guides you through the steps necessary to write rapidly but, more important, clearly. Instead of struggling with a writing assignment and not knowing where to begin or what to say, you can use this effective process both in school and on the job.

Chapter 2 focused on the prewriting stage of the writing process. You studied the importance of using a conversational tone, positive language, plain and courteous expression, and familiar words. This chapter addresses the second stage of the process, which involves gathering information, organizing it into outlines, and drafting messages.

LEARNING OBJECTIVE 1

Apply Phase 2 of the 3-x-3 writing process, which begins with formal and informal research to collect background information.

3-1a Getting Started Requires Researching Background Information

No smart businessperson would begin drafting a message before gathering background information. We call this process research, a rather formal-sounding term. For our purposes, however, *research* simply means "collecting information about a certain topic." This is an important step in the writing process because that information helps the writer shape the message. Discovering significant information after a message is half completed often means having to start over and reorganize. To avoid frustration and inaccurate messages, writers collect information that answers several questions:

- What does the receiver need to know about this topic?
- What is the receiver to do?
- How is the receiver to do it?
- When must the receiver do it?
- What will happen if the receiver doesn't do it?

Whenever your communication problem requires more information than you have in your head or at your fingertips, you must conduct research. This research may be informal or formal.

3-1b Informal Research Methods

Many routine tasks—such as drafting e-mails, memos, letters, informational reports, and oral presentations—require information that you can collect informally. Where can you find information before starting a project? The following techniques are useful in informal research:

- **Search your company's files.** If you are responding to an inquiry or drafting a routine message, you often can find background information such as previous correspondence in your own files or those of the company. You might consult the company wiki or other digital and manual files. You might also consult colleagues.
- **Talk with the boss.** Get information from the individual making the assignment. What does that person know about the topic? What slant should you take? What other sources would that person suggest?
- **Interview the target audience.** Consider talking with individuals at whom the message is aimed. They can provide clarifying information that tells

Figure **3.1**   The 3-x-3 Writing Process

1 Prewriting

Analyze: Decide on the message purpose. What do you want the receiver to do or believe?

Anticipate: What does the audience already know? How will it receive this message?

Adapt: Think about techniques to present this message most effectively. Consider how to elicit feedback.

2 Drafting

Research: Gather background data by searching files and the Internet.

Organize: Arrange direct messages with the big idea first. For persuasive or negative messages, use an indirect, problem-solving strategy.

Draft: Prepare the first draft, using active-voice sentences, coherent paragraphs, and appropriate transitional expressions.

3 Revising

Edit: Eliminate wordy fillers, long lead-ins, redundancies, and trite business phrases. Strive for parallelism, clarity, conciseness, and readability.

Proofread: Check carefully for errors in spelling, grammar, punctuation, and format.

Evaluate: Will this message achieve your purpose? Is the tone pleasant? Did you encourage feedback?

you what they want to know and how you should shape your remarks. Suggestions for conducting more formal interviews are presented in Chapter 10.

- **Conduct an informal survey.** Gather unscientific but helpful information through questionnaires, telephone surveys, or online surveys. In preparing a report predicting the success of a proposed company fitness center, for example, circulate a questionnaire asking for employee reactions.

- **Brainstorm for ideas.** Alone or with others, discuss ideas for the writing task at hand, and record at least a dozen ideas without judging them. Small groups are especially fruitful in brainstorming because people spin ideas off one another.

3-1c Formal Research Methods

Long reports and complex business problems generally require formal research methods. Let's say you are part of the management team for an international retailer such as Forever 21 and you have been asked to help launch a new store in Canada. Or, let's assume you must write a term paper for a college class. Both tasks require more data than you have in your head or at your fingertips. To conduct formal research, consider the following research options:

- **Access electronic sources.** College and public libraries provide digital retrieval services that permit access to a wide array of books, journals, magazines, newspapers, and other online literature. In this information age, you also could conduct an online Google search turning up thousands of hits, which can be overwhelming. Expect to be deluged with torrents of information, presenting a troubling paradox: research seems to be far more difficult to conduct in the digital age than in previous times.[2] With so much data drowning today's researchers, they struggle to sort through it all, trying to decide what is current, relevant, and credible. Help is on the way, however! You'll learn more about researching and using electronic sources effectively in Chapter 10.

- **Search manually.** Valuable background and supplementary information is available through manual searching of resources in public and college libraries. These traditional paper-based sources include books and newspaper, magazine, and journal articles. Other sources are encyclopedias, reference books, handbooks, dictionaries, directories, and almanacs.

- **Investigate primary sources.** To develop firsthand, primary information for a project, go directly to the source. In helping to launch a new Forever 21 outlet in Canada, you might travel to possible sites and check them out. If you need information about how many shoppers pass by a location or visit a shopping

Workplace in Focus

© wavebreakmedia/Shutterstock.com

At Jump Associates, a San Francisco growth strategy firm, brainstorming may devolve into a kind of competitive-idea tennis match. One "Jumpster" starts with the first idea, and the next Jumpster says, "Yes, and?" which leads to another "Yes, and?" bouncing around its Black Box idea room. Once a storytelling method, this technique became an effective collaboration procedure and a core element of scrum, a daily standing meeting where the same "yes, and" principle is applied in improv games that prepare the company for its unique approach to brainstorming. For its megaclient Target, Jump helped create a product called "Kitchen in a Box," which became a phenomenal success. How does the "Yes, and" concept improve brainstorming?[1]

center, you might conduct a traffic count. If you need information about consumers, you could search blogs, Twitter, wikis, and Facebook fan pages. To learn more about specific shoppers, you could use questionnaires, interviews, or focus groups. Formal research often includes scientific sampling methods that enable investigators to make accurate judgments and valid predictions.

- **Conduct scientific experiments.** Another source of primary data is experimentation. Instead of merely asking for the target audience's opinion, scientific researchers present choices with controlled variables. Assume, for example, that the management team at Forever 21 wants to know at what price and under what circumstances consumers would purchase jeans from Forever 21 instead of from Abercrombie & Fitch. Instead of jeans, let's say that management wants to study the time of year and type of weather conditions that motivate consumers to begin purchasing sweaters, jackets, and cold-weather gear. The results of such experimentation would provide valuable data for managerial decision making. Because formal research techniques are particularly necessary for reports, you will study resources and techniques more extensively in Unit 4.

3-2 Organizing Information to Show Relationships

Once you have collected data, you must find some way to organize it. Organizing includes two processes: grouping and strategizing. Well-organized messages group similar items together; ideas follow a sequence that helps the reader understand relationships and accept the writer's views. Unorganized messages proceed free-form, jumping from one thought to another. Such messages fail to emphasize important points. Puzzled readers can't see how the pieces fit together, and they become frustrated and irritated. Many communication experts regard poor organization as the greatest failing of business writers. Two simple techniques can help you organize data: the scratch list and the outline.

Some writers make a quick scratch list of the topics they wish to cover in a message. They then compose the message on a computer directly from the scratch list. Most writers, though, need to organize their ideas—especially if the project is complex—into a hierarchy such as an outline. The beauty of preparing an outline is that it gives you a chance to organize your thinking before you get bogged down in word choice and sentence structure. Figure 3.2 shows an outline format.

Direct Strategy for Receptive Audiences. After preparing a scratch list or an outline, think about how the audience will respond to your ideas. When you expect the reader to be pleased, mildly interested, or, at worst, neutral—use the direct strategy. That is, put your main point—the purpose of your message—in the first or second sentence. Dianna Booher, renowned writing consultant, pointed out that typical readers begin any message by thinking, "So what am I supposed to do with this information?" In business writing you have to say, "Reader, here is my point!"[3] As quickly as possible, tell why you are writing. Compare the direct and indirect strategies in the following e-mail openings. Notice how long it takes to get to the main idea in the indirect opening.

DON'T INDIRECT OPENING	DO✔ DIRECT OPENING
✗ Our company has been concerned with attracting better-qualified prospective job candidates. For this reason, the Management Council has been gathering information about an internship program for college students. After considerable investigation, we have voted to begin a pilot program starting next fall.	✓ The Management Council has voted to begin a college internship pilot program next fall.

Figure **3.2** Format for an Outline

Title: Major Idea or Purpose

I. First major component
    A. First subpoint
        1. Detail, illustration, evidence
        2. Detail, illustration, evidence
        3. Detail, illustration, evidence
    B. Second subpoint
        1.
        2.
II. Second major component
    A. First subpoint
        1.
        2.
    B. Second subpoint
        1.
        2.
        3.

Tips for Making Outlines
- Define the main topic in the title.
- Divide the main topic into major components or classifications (preferably three to five).
- Break the components into subpoints.
- Don't put a single item under a major component; if you have only one subpoint, integrate it with the main item above it or reorganize.
- Strive to make each component exclusive (no overlapping).
- Use details, illustrations, and evidence to support subpoints.

Explanations and details follow the direct opening. What's important is getting to the main idea quickly. This direct method, also called *frontloading*, has at least three advantages:

- **Saves the reader's time.** Many of today's businesspeople can devote only a few moments to each message. Messages that take too long to get to the point may lose their readers along the way.

- **Sets a proper frame of mind.** Learning the purpose up front helps the reader put the subsequent details and explanations in perspective. Without a clear opening, the reader may be thinking, "Why am I being told this?"

- **Reduces frustration.** Readers forced to struggle through excessive verbiage before reaching the main idea can become frustrated and begin to resent the writer. Poorly organized messages create a negative impression of the writer.

Typical business messages that follow the direct strategy include routine requests and responses, orders and acknowledgments, nonsensitive memos, e-mails, informational reports, and informational oral presentations. All these tasks have one element in common: none has a sensitive subject that will upset the reader. It should be noted, however, that some business communicators prefer to use the direct strategy for nearly all messages.

Indirect Strategy for Unreceptive Audiences. When you expect the audience to be uninterested, unwilling, displeased, or perhaps even hostile, the indirect strategy is more appropriate. In this strategy you reveal the main idea only after you have offered an explanation and evidence. This approach works well with three kinds of messages: (a) bad news, (b) ideas that require persuasion, and (c) sensitive news, especially when being transmitted to superiors. The indirect strategy has these benefits:

- **Respects the feelings of the audience.** Bad news is always painful, but the trauma can be lessened by preparing the receiver for it.

- **Facilitates a fair hearing.** Messages that may upset the reader are more likely to be read when the main idea is delayed. Beginning immediately with a piece of

US Air Force Photo/Alamy

When Hurricane Sandy slammed the East Coast of the United States, the superstorm flooded thousands of homes and left citizens displaced, especially in New Jersey and New York. In the weeks that followed, devastated homeowners contacted insurance companies for help rebuilding their lives—only to discover that standard homeowner policies do not cover flood losses. Sympathetic claims adjusters struggled to break the bad news, and heartbroken policyholders expressed anger and disbelief as their claims were denied. "It's traumatic to lose your house and everything you own," said one survivor. "On top of this, you find out your insurance is not helping you." How should claims administrators organize messages when denying claims to disaster victims?[4]

bad news or a persuasive request, for example, may cause the receiver to stop reading or listening.

- **Minimizes a negative reaction.** A reader's overall reaction to a negative message is generally improved if the news is delivered gently.

Typical business messages that could be developed indirectly include e-mails, memos, and letters that refuse requests, deny claims, and disapprove credit. Persuasive requests, sales letters, sensitive messages, and some reports and oral presentations may also benefit from the indirect strategy. You will learn more about using the indirect strategy in Chapters 7 and 8.

In summary, business messages may be organized directly (with the main idea first) or indirectly. How you expect the audience to respond determines which strategy to use, as illustrated in Figure 3.3. Although these two strategies cover many communication problems, they should be considered neither universal nor inviolate. Every business transaction is distinct. Some messages are mixed: part good news, part bad; part goodwill, part persuasion. In upcoming chapters you will practice applying the direct and indirect strategies in typical situations. Then, you will have the skills and confidence to evaluate communication problems and vary these strategies depending on the goals you wish to achieve.

Figure **3.3** Audience Response Determines Direct or Indirect Strategy

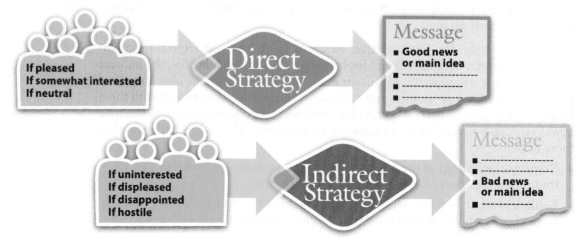

3-3 Composing the First Draft With Effective Sentences

LEARNING OBJECTIVE 3

Compose the first draft of a message using a variety of sentence types while avoiding sentence fragments, run-on sentences, and comma splices.

Once you have researched your topic, organized the data, and selected a strategy, you're ready to begin drafting. Many writers have trouble getting started, especially if they haven't completed the preparatory work. Organizing your ideas and working from an outline are very helpful in overcoming writer's block. Composition is also easier if you have a quiet environment in which to concentrate, if you set aside time to concentrate, and if you limit interruptions.

As you begin writing, think about what style fits you best. Some experts suggest that you write quickly (*freewriting*). Get your thoughts down now and refine them in later versions. As you take up each idea, imagine that you are talking to the reader. Don't let yourself get bogged down. If you can't think of the right word, insert a substitute or type *find perfect word later*. Freewriting works well for some writers, but others prefer to move more slowly and think through their ideas more deliberately. Whether you are a speedy or a deliberate writer, keep in mind that you are writing the first draft. You will have time later to revise and polish your sentences.

3-3a Achieving Variety With Four Sentence Types

Messages that repeat the same sentence pattern soon become boring. To avoid monotony and to add spark to your writing, use a variety of sentence types. You have four sentence types from which to choose: simple, compound, complex, and compound-complex.

Simple Sentence

Contains one complete thought (an independent clause) with a subject and predicate verb:

   The *entrepreneur* *saw* an opportunity.

Compound Sentence

Contains two complete but related thoughts. May be joined by (a) a conjunction such as *and*, *but*, or *or*; (b) a semicolon; or (c) a conjunctive adverb such as *however*, *consequently*, and *therefore*:

   The *entrepreneur* *saw* an opportunity, and *she* *responded* immediately.

   The *entrepreneur* *saw* an opportunity; *she* *responded* immediately.

   The *entrepreneur* *saw* an opportunity; consequently, *she* *responded* immediately.

Complex Sentence

Contains an independent clause (a complete thought) and a dependent clause (a thought that cannot stand by itself). Dependent clauses are often introduced by words such as *although, since, because, when*, and *if*. When dependent clauses precede independent clauses, they always are followed by a comma:

   When the *entrepreneur* *saw* the opportunity, *she* *responded* immediately.

Compound-Complex Sentence

Contains at least two independent clauses and one dependent clause:

   When the *entrepreneur* *saw* the opportunity, *she* *responded* immediately; however, *she* *needed* capital.

3-3b Avoiding Three Common Sentence Faults

As you craft your sentences, beware of three common traps: fragments, run-on (fused) sentences, and comma-splice sentences. If any of these faults appears in a business message, the writer immediately loses credibility.

One of the most serious errors a writer can make is punctuating a fragment as if it were a complete sentence. A *fragment* is usually a broken-off part of a complex sentence. Fragments often can be identified by the words that introduce them—words such as *although, as, because, even, except, for example, if, instead of, since, such as, that, which,* and *when.* These words introduce dependent clauses, as italicized in the following fragment examples. They should not be punctuated as sentences. Make sure such clauses always connect to independent clauses, as shown in the revisions.

DON'T FRAGMENT	DO ✔ REVISION
✗ *Because most transactions require a permanent record.* Good writing skills are critical.	✔ Because most transactions require a permanent record, good writing skills are critical.
✗ The recruiter requested a writing sample. *Even though the candidate seemed to communicate well.*	✔ The recruiter requested a writing sample even though the candidate seemed to communicate well.

A second serious writing fault is the **run-on (fused) sentence.** A sentence with two independent clauses must be joined by a coordinating conjunction (*and, or, nor, but*) or by a semicolon (;) or separated into two sentences. Without a conjunction or a semicolon, a run-on sentence results.

DON'T RUN-ON SENTENCE	DO ✔ REVISION
✗ Many job seekers prepare traditional résumés some also use websites as electronic portfolios.	✔ Many job seekers prepare traditional résumés. Some also use websites as electronic portfolios.
✗ One candidate sent an e-mail résumé another sent a link to her Web portfolio.	✔ One candidate sent an e-mail résumé; another sent a link to her Web portfolio.

A third sentence fault is a **comma splice.** It results when a writer joins (splices together) two independent clauses with a comma. Independent clauses may be joined with a coordinating conjunction (*and, or, nor, but*) or a conjunctive adverb (*however, consequently, therefore,* and others). Notice that clauses joined by a coordinating conjunctions require only a comma. Clauses joined by a conjunctive adverb require a semicolon and a comma. To rectify a comma splice, try one of the possible revisions shown here:

DON'T COMMA SPLICE	DO ✔ REVISIONS
✗ Some employees prefer their desktop computers, others prefer their tablets.	✔ Some employees prefer their desktop computers, but others prefer their tablets.
	✔ Some employees prefer their desktop computers; however, others prefer their tablets.
	✔ Some employees prefer their desktop computers; others prefer their tablets.

3-3c Favoring Short Sentences

Because your goal is to communicate clearly, you should strive for sentences that average 20 words. Some sentences will be shorter; some will be longer. The American Press Institute reports that reader comprehension drops off markedly as sentences become longer.[5] Therefore, in crafting your sentences, think about the relationship between sentence length and comprehension.

Sentence Length	Comprehension Rate
8 words	100%
15 words	90%
19 words	80%
28 words	50%

Instead of stringing together clauses with *and, but,* and *however,* break some of those complex sentences into separate segments. Business readers want to grasp ideas immediately. They can do that best when thoughts are separated into short sentences. On the other hand, too many monotonous short sentences will sound "grammar schoolish" and may bore or even annoy the reader. Strive for a balance between longer sentences and shorter ones. Your grammar-checker and spell-checker can show you readability statistics that flag long sentences and give you an average sentence length.

3-4 Developing Business Writing Techniques

Business writers can significantly improve their messages by working on a few writing techniques. In this section we focus on emphasizing and de-emphasizing ideas and using active and passive voice strategically.

3-4a Developing Emphasis

When you are talking with someone, you can emphasize your main ideas by saying them loudly or by repeating them slowly. You could even pound the table if you want to show real emphasis! Another way you could signal the relative importance of an idea is by raising your eyebrows or by shaking your head or whispering in a low voice. But when you write, you must rely on other means to tell your readers which ideas are more important than others. Emphasis in writing can be achieved primarily in two ways: mechanically and stylistically.

Achieving Emphasis Through Mechanics. To emphasize an idea in print, a writer may use any of the following devices:

Underlining	<u>Underlining</u> draws the eye to a word.
Italics and boldface	Using *italics* or **boldface** conveys special meaning.
Font changes	Selecting a large, small, or different font draws interest.
All caps	Printing words in ALL CAPS is like shouting them.
Dashes	Dashes—used sparingly—can be effective.
Tabulation	Listing items vertically makes them stand out:

1. First item
2. Second item
3. Third item

LEARNING OBJECTIVE 4

Improve your writing by emphasizing important ideas, employing the active and passive voice effectively, using parallelism, and preventing dangling and misplaced modifiers.

Other means of achieving mechanical emphasis include the arrangement of space, color, lines, boxes, columns, titles, headings, and subheadings. Today's software and color printers provide a wonderful array of capabilities for setting off ideas. More tips on achieving emphasis are coming in Chapter 4, in which we cover document design.

Achieving Emphasis Through Style. Although mechanical devices are occasionally appropriate, more often a writer achieves emphasis stylistically. That is, the writer chooses words carefully and constructs sentences skillfully to emphasize main ideas and de-emphasize minor or negative ideas. Here are four suggestions for emphasizing ideas stylistically:

Use vivid, not general, words. Vivid words are emphatic because the reader can picture ideas clearly.

DON'T GENERAL	DO✔ VIVID
✗ The way we seek jobs has changed.	✓ The Internet has dramatically changed how job hunters search for positions.
✗ Someone will contact you as soon as possible.	✓ Ms. Rivera will telephone you before 5 p.m. tomorrow, May 3.

Label the main idea. If an idea is significant, tell the reader.

DON'T UNLABELED	DO✔ LABELED
✗ Consider looking for a job online, but also focus on networking.	✓ Consider looking for a job online; but, *most important*, focus on networking.
✗ We shop here because of the customer service and low prices.	✓ We like the customer service, but the *primary reason* for shopping here is the low prices.

Place the important idea first or last. Ideas have less competition from surrounding words when they appear first or last in a sentence. Observe how the concept of *productivity* can be emphasized by its position in the sentence:

DON'T MAIN IDEA LOST	DO✔ MAIN IDEA EMPHASIZED
✗ Profit-sharing plans are more effective in increasing *productivity* when they are linked to individual performance rather than to group performance.	✓ *Productivity* is more likely to be increased when profit-sharing plans are linked to individual performance rather than to group performance.

Give the important idea the spotlight. Don't dilute the effect of the main idea by making it share the stage with other words and clauses. Instead, put it in a simple sentence or in an independent clause.

<table>
<tr><td colspan="2">

DON'T MAIN IDEA LOST

</td><td colspan="2">

DO MAIN IDEA CLEAR

</td></tr>
</table>

DON'T — MAIN IDEA LOST	**DO ✓ — MAIN IDEA CLEAR**
✗ Although you are the first trainee we have hired for this program, we had many candidates and expect to expand the program in the future. (The main idea is lost in a dependent clause.)	✓ You are the first trainee we have hired for this program. (Simple sentence)

De-emphasizing When Necessary. To de-emphasize an idea, such as bad news, try one of the following stylistic devices:

Use general words.

DON'T — EMPHASIZES HARSH STATEMENT	**DO ✓ — DE-EMPHASIZES HARSH STATEMENT**
✗ Our records indicate that you were recently fired.	✓ Our records indicate that your employment status has recently changed.

Place the bad news in a dependent clause connected to an independent clause that contains something positive. In sentences with dependent clauses, the main emphasis is always on the independent clause.

DON'T — EMPHASIZES BAD NEWS	**DO ✓ — DE-EMPHASIZES BAD NEWS**
✗ We cannot issue you credit at this time, but we have a special plan that will allow you to fill your immediate needs on a cash basis.	✓ Although credit cannot be issued at this time, you can fill your immediate needs on a cash basis with our special plan.

3-4b Using the Active and Passive Voice Effectively

In active-voice sentences, the subject, the actor, performs the action. In passive-voice sentences, the subject receives the action. Active-voice sentences are more direct because they reveal the performer immediately. They are easier to understand and usually shorter. Most business writing should be in the active voice. However, passive voice is useful to (a) emphasize an action rather than a person, (b) de-emphasize negative news, and (c) conceal the doer of an action.

Active Voice	Passive Voice
Actor → Action Justin must submit a tax return.	Receiver ← Action The tax return was submitted [by Justin].
Actor → Action Officials reviewed all tax returns.	Receiver ← Action All tax returns were reviewed [by officials].
Actor → Action We cannot make cash refunds.	Receiver ← Action Cash refunds cannot be made.
Actor → Action Our CPA made a big error in the budget.	Receiver ← Action A big error was made in the budget.

3-4c Developing Parallelism

Parallelism is a skillful writing technique that creates balanced writing. Sentences written so that their parts are balanced, or parallel, are easy to read and understand.

To achieve parallel construction, use similar structures to express similar ideas. For example, the words *computing, coding, recording*, and *storing* are parallel because the words all end in *-ing*. To express the list as *computing, coding, recording*, and *storage* is disturbing because the last item is not what the reader expects. Try to match nouns with nouns, verbs with verbs, and clauses with clauses. Avoid mixing active-voice verbs with passive-voice verbs. Your goal is to keep the wording balanced in expressing similar ideas.

DON'T LACKS PARALLELISM	DO ✓ ILLUSTRATES PARALLELISM
✗ The policy affected all vendors, suppliers, and *those involved with consulting.*	✓ The policy affected all vendors, suppliers, and *consultants.* (Matches nouns.)
✗ Our primary goals are to increase productivity, reduce costs, and *the improvement of product quality.*	✓ Our primary goals are to increase productivity, reduce costs, and *improve product quality.* (Matches verbs.)
✗ We are scheduled to meet in Atlanta on January 5, *we are meeting in Montreal on the 15th of March*, and in Chicago on June 3.	✓ We are scheduled to meet in Atlanta on January 5, *in Montreal on March 15*, and in Chicago on June 3. (Matches phrases.)
✗ Shelby audits all accounts lettered A through L; accounts lettered M through Z are audited by Andrew.	✓ Shelby audits all accounts lettered A through L; Andrew audits accounts lettered M through Z. (Matches clauses.)
✗ Our Super Bowl ads have three objectives: 1. We want to increase product use. 2. Introduce complementary products. 3. Our corporate image will be enhanced.	✓ Our Super Bowl ads have three objectives: 1. Increase product use 2. Introduce complementary products 3. Enhance our corporate image (Matches verbs in listed items.)

3-4d Escaping Dangling and Misplaced Modifiers

For clarity, modifiers must be close to the words they describe or limit. A modifier dangles when the word or phrase it describes is missing from its sentence—for example, *After working overtime, the report was finally finished*. This sentence says that the report was working overtime. Revised, the sentence contains a logical subject: *After working overtime, we finally finished the report*.

A modifier is misplaced when the word or phrase it describes is not close enough to be clear—for example, *Firefighters rescued a dog from a burning car that had a broken leg*. Obviously, the car did not have a broken leg. The solution is to position the modifier closer to the word(s) it describes or limits: *Firefighters rescued a dog with a broken leg from a burning car*.

Introductory verbal phrases are particularly dangerous; be sure to follow them immediately with the words they logically describe or modify. Try this trick for detecting and remedying many dangling modifiers. Ask the question *Who?* or *What?* after any introductory phrase. The words immediately following should tell the reader who or what is performing the action. Try the *Who?* test on the first three danglers here:

DANGLING OR MISPLACED MODIFIER	CLEAR MODIFICATION
✗ Skilled at graphic design, the contract went to DesignOne.	✓ Skilled at graphic design, DesignOne won the contract.
✗ Working together as a team, the project was finally completed.	✓ Working together as a team, we finally completed the project.
✗ To meet the deadline, your Excel figures must be sent by May 1.	✓ To meet the deadline, you must send your Excel figures by May 1.
✗ The recruiter interviewed candidates who had excellent computer skills in the morning.	✓ In the morning the recruiter interviewed candidates with excellent computer skills.
✗ As an important customer to us, we invite you to our spring open house.	✓ As you are an important customer to us, we invite you to our spring open house. *OR*:
	✓ As an important customer to us, you are invited to our spring open house.

3-5 Drafting Well-Organized, Effective Paragraphs

LEARNING OBJECTIVE 5

Draft well-organized paragraphs that incorporate (a) topic sentences, (b) support sentences, and (c) transitional expressions to build coherence.

Good business writers develop well-organized paragraphs by focusing on a single main idea. The sentences in their paragraphs cohere, or stick together, by using transitional expressions.

3-5a Crafting Topic Sentences

A paragraph is unified when it develops a single main idea. That idea is usually expressed in a topic sentence, which may appear at the beginning, in the middle, or at the end of the paragraph. Business writers generally place the topic sentence first in the paragraph. It tells readers what to expect and helps them understand the paragraph's central thought immediately.

3-5b Developing Support Sentences

Support sentences illustrate, explain, or strengthen the topic sentence. One of the hardest things for beginning writers to remember is that all support sentences in the paragraph must relate to the topic sentence. Any other topics should be treated separately. Support sentences provide specific details, explanations, and evidence. The following example starts with a topic sentence about flexible work scheduling and is followed by three support sentences that explain how flexible scheduling could work. Transitional expressions are italicized:

Topic sentence: Flexible work scheduling could immediately increase productivity and enhance employee satisfaction in our organization.

Support sentences: Managers would maintain their regular hours. For many other employees, *however*, flexible scheduling provides extra time to manage family responsibilities. Feeling less stress, employees are able to focus their attention better at work; *therefore*, they become more relaxed and more productive.

3-5c Building Paragraph Coherence

Paragraphs are coherent when ideas are linked—that is, when one idea leads logically to the next. Well-written paragraphs take the reader through a number of

Figure 3.4 Transitional Expressions to Build Coherence

To Add or Strengthen	To Show Time or Order	To Clarify	To Show Cause and Effect	To Contradict	To Contrast
additionally	after	for example	accordingly	actually	as opposed to
accordingly	before	for instance	as a result	but	at the same time
again	earlier	I mean	consequently	however	by contrast
also	finally	in other words	for this reason	in fact	conversely
beside	first	put another way	hence	instead	on the contrary
indeed	meanwhile	that is	so	rather	on the other hand
likewise	next	this means	therefore	still	previously
moreover	now	thus	thus	yet	similarly

steps. When the author skips from Step 1 to Step 3 and forgets Step 2, the reader is lost. Several techniques allow the reader to follow the writer's ideas:

- **Repeat a key idea by using the same expression or a similar one:** *Employees treat guests as VIPs. These VIPs are never told what they can or cannot do.*

- **Use pronouns to refer to previous nouns:** *All new employees receive a two-week orientation. They learn that every staffer has a vital role.*

- **Show connections with transitional expressions:** *Hospitality is our business; consequently, training is critical.* (Use transitions such as *consequently, however, as a result,* and *meanwhile.* For a complete list, see Figure 3.4.)

3-5d Controlling Paragraph Length

Although no rule regulates the length of paragraphs, business writers recognize the value of short paragraphs. Paragraphs with eight or fewer printed lines look inviting and readable. Long, solid chunks of print appear formidable. If a topic can't be covered in eight or fewer printed lines (not sentences), consider breaking it into smaller segments.

SUMMARY OF LEARNING OBJECTIVES

3-1 Apply Phase 2 of the 3-x-3 writing process, which begins with formal and informal research to collect background information.

- Apply the second phase of the writing process (prewriting) by researching, organizing, and drafting.
- Collect information by answering questions about what the receiver needs to know and what the receiver is to do.
- Conduct informal research for routine tasks by looking in the company's digital and other files, talking with the boss, interviewing the target audience, organizing informal surveys, and brainstorming for ideas
- Conduct formal research for long reports and complex problems by searching electronically or manually, investigating primary sources, and organizing scientific experiments.

3-2 Organize information into strategic relationships.

- For simple messages, make a quick scratch list of topics; for more complex messages, create an outline.
- To prepare an outline, divide the main topic into three to five major components.

- Break the components into subpoints consisting of details, illustrations, and evidence.
- Organize the information using the **direct strategy** (with the main idea first) when audiences will be pleased, mildly interested, or neutral.
- Organize information using the **indirect strategy** (with explanations preceding the main idea) for audiences that will be unwilling, displeased, or hostile.

3-3 Compose the first draft of a message using a variety of sentence types while avoiding sentence fragments, run-on sentences, and comma splices.
- Decide whether to compose quickly (*freewriting*) or to write more deliberately—but remember that you are writing a first draft.
- Employ a variety of sentence types including simple (one independent clause), complex (one independent and one dependent clause), compound (two independent clauses), and compound-complex (two independent clauses and one dependent clause).
- Avoid fragments (broken-off parts of sentences), run-on sentences (two clauses fused improperly), and comma splices (two clauses joined improperly with a comma).
- Remember that sentences are most effective when they are short (20 or fewer words).

3-4 Improve your writing by emphasizing important ideas, employing the active and passive voice effectively, using parallelism, and preventing dangling and misplaced modifiers.
- Emphasize an idea mechanically by using underlining, italics, boldface, font changes, all caps, dashes, tabulation, and other devices.
- Emphasize an idea stylistically by using vivid words, labeling it, making it the sentence subject, placing it first or last, and removing competing ideas.
- For most business writing, use the active voice by making the subject the doer of the action (*the company hired the student*).
- Use the passive voice (*the student was hired*) to de-emphasize negative news, to emphasize an action rather than the doer, or to conceal the doer of an action.
- Employ parallelism for balanced construction (*jogging, hiking, and biking* rather than *jogging, hiking, and to bike*).
- Avoid dangling modifiers (*sitting at my computer, the words would not come*) and misplaced modifiers (*I have the report you wrote in my office*).

3-5 Draft well-organized paragraphs that incorporate (a) topic sentences, (b) support sentences, and (c) transitional expressions to build coherence.
- Build well-organized, unified paragraphs by focusing on a single idea.
- Always include a topic sentence that states the main idea of the paragraph.
- Develop support sentences to illustrate, explain, or strengthen the topic sentence.
- Build coherence by repeating a key idea, using pronouns to refer to previous nouns, and showing connections with transitional expressions (*however, therefore, consequently*).
- Control paragraph length by striving for eight or fewer lines.

CHAPTER REVIEW

1. What is *research*, and how do informal and formal research methods differ? (Obj. 1)

2. Before drafting a message, what questions should writers ask as they collect information? (Obj. 1)

3. Why do writers need to outline complex projects before beginning? (Obj. 2)

4. What business messages are better organized directly, and which are better organized indirectly? (Obj. 2)

5. What are the four sentence types? Provide an original example of each. (Obj. 3)

6. What is the relationship between sentence length and comprehension? (Obj. 3)

7. How is a sentence fragment different from a comma splice? (Obj. 3)

8. What is the difference between active-voice and passive-voice sentences? Give an original example of each. When should business writers use each? (Obj. 4)

9. How are topic sentences different from support sentences? (Obj. 5)

10. Name three techniques for building paragraph coherence. (Obj. 5)

CRITICAL THINKING

11. What trends in business and developments in technology are forcing workers to write more than ever before? (Obj. 1)

12. Molly, a twenty-three-year-old college graduate with a 3.5 GPA, was hired as an administrative assistant. She was a fast learner on all the software, but her supervisor had to help her with punctuation. On the ninth day of her job, she resigned, saying: "I just don't think this job is a good fit. Commas, semicolons, spelling, typos—those kinds of things just aren't all that important to me. They just don't matter."[6] For what kind of job is Molly qualified? (Objs. 1–5)

13. Why is audience analysis so important in the selection of the direct or indirect organization strategy for a business message? (Obj. 2)

14. How are speakers different from writers in the way they emphasize ideas? (Obj. 4)

15. Now that you have studied the active and passive voice, what do you think when someone in government or business says, "Mistakes were made"? Is it unethical to use the passive voice to avoid specifics?

WRITING IMPROVEMENT EXERCISES

Sentence Type (Obj. 3)

For each of the following sentences, select the letter that identifies its type:

    a. Simple sentence   c. Complex
    b. Compound sentence   d. Compound-complex

_____ 16. Many companies are now doing business in international circles.

_____ 17. If you travel abroad on business, you may bring gifts for business partners.

_____ 18. In Latin America a knife is not a proper gift; it signifies cutting off a relationship.

_____ 19. When Arabs, Middle Easterners, and Latin Americans talk, they often stand close to each other.

_____ 20. Unless they are old friends, Europeans do not address each other by first names; consequently, businesspeople should not expect to do so.

_____ 21. In the Philippines men wear a long embroidered shirt called a *barong*, and women wear a dress called a *terno*.

Sentence Faults (Obj. 3)

In each of the following sentences, identify the sentence fault (fragment, run-on, comma splice). Then revise it to remedy the fault.

22. Because 90 percent of all business transactions involve written messages. Good writing skills are critical.

23. Darcy agreed to change her password. Even though she thought her old one was just fine.

24. Major soft-drink companies considered a new pricing strategy, they tested vending machines that raise prices in hot weather.

25. Thirsty consumers may think that variable pricing is unfair they may also refuse to use the machine.

26. About half of Pizza Hut's 7,600 outlets make deliveries, the others concentrate on walk-in customers.

27. McDonald's sold its chain of Chipotle Mexican Grill restaurants the chain's share price doubled on the next day of trading.

Emphasis (Obj. 4)

For each of the following sentences, circle (a) or (b). Be prepared to justify your choice.

28. Which is more emphatic?
    a. Our dress code is fine.
    b. Our dress code reflects common sense and good taste.

29. Which is more emphatic?
    a. A budget increase would certainly improve hiring.
    b. A budget increase of $70,000 would enable us to hire two new people.

30. Which is more emphatic?
    a. The committee was powerless to act.
    b. The committee was unable to take action.

31. Which de-emphasizes the refusal?
    a. Although our resources are committed to other projects this year, we hope to be able to contribute to your worthy cause next year.
    b. We can't contribute to your charity this year.

32. Which sentence places more emphasis on the date?
    a. The deadline is November 30 for health benefit changes.
    b. November 30 is the deadline for health benefit changes.

33. Which is *less* emphatic?
    a. One division's profits decreased last quarter.
    b. Profits in beauty care products dropped 15 percent last quarter.

34. Which sentence *de-emphasizes* the credit refusal?
    a. We are unable to grant you credit at this time, but we welcome your cash business and encourage you to reapply in the future.
    b. Although credit cannot be granted at this time, we welcome your cash business and encourage you to reapply in the future.

35. Which sentence gives more emphasis to *leadership*?
    a. Jason has many admirable qualities, but most important is his leadership skill.
    b. Jason has many admirable qualities, including leadership skill, good judgment, and patience.

36. Which is more emphatic?
    a. We notified three departments: (1) Marketing, (2) Accounting, and (3) Distribution.
    b. We notified three departments:
       1. Marketing
       2. Accounting
       3. Distribution

Active Voice (Obj. 4)

Business writing is more forceful when it uses active-voice verbs. Revise the following sentences so that verbs are in the active voice. Put the emphasis on the doer of the action.

Passive: Antivirus software was installed by Craig on his computer.
Active: Craig installed antivirus software on his computer.

37. Employees were given their checks at 4 p.m. every Friday by the manager.

38. New spices and cooking techniques were tried by McDonald's to improve its hamburgers.

39. Our new company logo was designed by my boss.

40. The managers with the most productive departments were commended by the CEO.

Passive Voice (Obj. 4)

Revise the following sentences so that they are in the passive voice.

41. The auditor discovered a computational error in the company's tax figures.

42. We discovered the error too late to correct the balance sheet.

43. Stacy did not submit the accounting statement on time.

44. The Federal Trade Commission targeted deceptive diet advertisements by weight-loss marketers.

Parallelism (Obj. 4)

Revise the following sentences so that their parts are balanced.

45. (**Hint:** Match adjectives.) To be hired, an applicant must be reliable, creative, and show enthusiasm.

46. (**Hint:** Match active voice.) If you have decided to cancel our service, please cut your credit card in half and the pieces should be returned to us.

47. (**Hint:** Match verbs.) Guidelines for improving security at food facilities include inspecting incoming and outgoing vehicles, restriction of access to laboratories, preventing workers from bringing personal items into food-handling areas, and inspection of packaging for signs of tampering.

48. (**Hint:** Match adjective-noun expressions.) The committee will continue to monitor merchandise design, product quality, and check the feedback of customers.

49. (**Hint:** Match verb clauses.) To use the fax copier, insert your meter, the paper trays must be loaded, indicate the number of copies needed, and your original sheet should be inserted through the feeder.

50. (**Hint:** Match *ing* verbs.) Sending an e-mail establishes a more permanent record than to make a telephone call.

Dangling and Misplaced Modifiers (Obj. 4)

Revise the following sentences to avoid dangling and misplaced modifiers.

51. After leaving the midtown meeting, Angela's car would not start.

52. Walking up the driveway, the Hummer parked in the garage was immediately spotted by the detectives.

53. To complete the project on time, a new deadline was established by the team.

54. Acting as manager, several new employees were hired by Mr. Lopez.

55. Michelle Mitchell presented a talk about workplace drug problems in our boardroom.

Organizing Paragraph Sentences (Obj. 5)

In a memo to the college president, the athletic director argues for a new stadium scoreboard. One paragraph will describe the old scoreboard and why it needs to be replaced. Study the following list of ideas for that paragraph.

1. *The old scoreboard is a tired warhorse that was originally constructed in the 1970s.*
2. *It is now hard to find replacement parts when something breaks.*
3. *The old scoreboard is not energy efficient.*
4. *Coca-Cola has offered to buy a new sports scoreboard in return for exclusive rights to sell soda pop on campus.*
5. *The old scoreboard should be replaced for many reasons.*
6. *It shows only scores for football games.*
7. *When we have soccer games or track meets, we are without a functioning scoreboard.*

_____ 56. Which sentence should be the topic sentence?

_____ 57. Which sentence(s) should be developed in a separate paragraph?

_____ 58. Which sentences should become support sentences?

Building Coherent Paragraphs (Obj. 5)

59. Use the information from the preceding sentences to write a coherent paragraph about replacing the sports scoreboard. Strive to use three devices to build coherence: (a) repetition of key words, (b) pronouns that clearly refer to previous nouns, and (c) transitional expressions.

60. Revise the following paragraph. Add a topic sentence and improve the organization. Correct problems with pronouns, parallelism, wordiness, and misplaced or dangling modifiers. Add transitional expressions if appropriate.

You may be interested in applying for a new position within the company. The Human Resources Department has a number of jobs available immediately. The positions are at a high level. Current employees may apply immediately for open positions in production, for some in marketing, and jobs in administrative support are also available. To make application, these positions require immediate action. Come to the Human Resources Department. We have a list showing the open positions, what the qualifications are, and job descriptions are shown. Many of the jobs are now open. That's why we are sending this now. To be hired, an interview must be scheduled within the next two weeks.

61. Revise the following paragraph. Add a topic sentence and improve the organization. Correct problems with pronouns, parallelism, wordiness, and misplaced or dangling modifiers.

As you probably already know, this company (Lasertronics) will be installing new computer software shortly. There will be a demonstration April 18, which is a Tuesday. You are invited. We felt this was necessary because this new software is so different from our previous software. It will be from 9 to 12 a.m. in the morning. This will show employees how the software programs work. They will learn about the operating system, and this should be helpful to nearly everyone. There will be information about the new word processing program, which should be helpful to administrative assistants and product managers. For all you people who work with payroll, there will be information about the new database program. We can't show everything the software will do at this one demo, but for these three areas there will be some help at the Tuesday demo. Presenting the software, the demo will feature Paula Roddy. She is the representative from Quantum Software.

62. From the following information, develop a coherent paragraph with a topic and support sentences. Strive for conciseness and coherence.

- Car dealers and lenders offer a variety of loan terms.
- To get the best deal, shop around when buying a new or used car.
- You have two payment options: you may pay in full or finance over time.
- You should compare offers and be willing to negotiate the best deal.
- If you are a first-time buyer—or if your credit isn't great—be cautious about special financing offers.
- Buying a new or used car can be challenging.
- Financing increases the total cost of the car because you are also paying for the cost of credit.
- If you agree to financing that carries a high interest rate, you may be taking a big risk. If you decide to sell the car before the loan expires, the amount you get from the sale may be far less than the amount you need to pay off the loan.
- If money is tight, you might consider paying cash for a less expensive car than you originally had in mind.

Note: Radical Rewrites are provided at **www.cengagebrain.com** for you to download and revise. Your instructor may provide a suggested solution.

3.1 Radical Rewrite: Seattle Health Club Offers Ailing E-Mail Message (Objs. 2–5)

In Seattle the 24-Hour Gym promises to strengthen bodies. However, its weak e-mail to its clients needs a radical rewrite to improve its effectiveness.

YOUR TASK. The following e-mail suffers from numerous writing faults such as dangling modifiers, overuse of the passive voice, and fragments. Notice that small superscript numbers identify each sentence or group of words. Individually or in a group, analyze this message and list the faulty sentences or groups of words. Be sure your group agrees on its analysis. Your instructor may ask you to revise the message to remedy its faults.

To: Tyler.Long <tlong@cox.org>
From: Janice Rivera <jrivera@24hourgym.com>
Subject: Expanding Your Workouts at 24-Hour Gym
Cc:
Bcc:

Dear Mr. Long,

[1]24-Hour Gym here in Seattle was probably selected by you because it is one of the top-rated gyms in the Northwest. [2]Our principal goal has always been making your workouts productive. [3]To continue to provide you with the best equipment and programs, your feedback is needed.

[4]An outstanding program with quality equipment and excellent trainers has been provided by 24-Hour Gym. [5]However, more individual attention could be given by us to our customers if our peak usage time could be extended. [6]You have probably noticed that attendance at the gym increases from 4 p.m. to 8 p.m. [7]We wish it were possible to accommodate all our customers on their favorite equipment during those hours. [8]Although we can't stretch an hour. [9]We would like to make better use of the time between 8 p.m. and 11 p.m. [10]If more members came later, the gym would have less crush from 4 p.m. to 8 p.m.

[11]To encourage you to stay later, security cameras for our parking area are being considered by my partner and me. [12]Cameras for some inside facilities may also be added. [13]This matter has been given considerable thought. [14]Although 24-Hour Gym has never had an incident that endangered a member.

[15]Please fill in the attached interactive questionnaire. [16]Which will give us instant feedback about scheduling your workouts. [17]By completing this questionnaire, your workouts and training sessions can be better planned so that you can enjoy exactly the equipment and trainers you prefer.

Cordially,

What three sentences have dangling modifiers?
What eight sentences exhibit passive voice?
Which three groups of words represent fragments?

GRAMMAR/MECHANICS CHECKUP—3

Verbs

Review Sections 1.10–1.15 in the Grammar Review section of the Grammar/Mechanics Handbook. Then study each of the following statements. Underline any verbs that are used incorrectly. In the space provided, write the correct form (or C if correct) and the number of the G/M principle illustrated. When you finish, compare your responses with those provided near the end of the book. If your responses differ, study carefully the principles in parentheses.

has _____ (1.10c) **EXAMPLE** Every one of the top-ranking executives <u>have</u> been insured.

_____ 1. Are you convinced that Google's database of customers' messages and private information are secure?

_____ 2. Google's data team have been carefully studying how to shield users from unwarranted government intrusion.

_____ 3. Wells-Fargo, along with most other large national banks, offer a variety of savings plans.

_____ 4. In the next building is the administrative staff and our marketing people.

_____ 5. The city council have unanimously approved the parking fee hike.

_____ 6. If you was in my position, you might agree with my decision.

_____ 7. Everyone except the temporary workers employed during the past year has become eligible for health benefits.

_____ 8. All employees should have went to the emergency procedures demonstration.

_____ 9. The reports have laid on his desk for 11 days and are now overdue.

_____ 10. Either of the flight times are fine with me.

_____ 11. Some of the jury members believes that the prosecution's evidence is not relevant.

In the space provided, write the letter of the sentence that illustrates consistency in subject, voice, tense, and mood.

_____ 12. a. By carefully following the instructions, much time can be saved.
b. By carefully following the instructions, you can save much time.

_____ 13. a. All employees must fill out application forms; only then will you be insured.
b. All employees must fill out application forms; only then will they be insured.

_____ 14. a. First, advertise the position; then, evaluate applications.
b. First, advertise the position; then, applications must be evaluated.

_____ 15. a. Our manager was a computer whiz who was always ready to help.
b. Our manager was a computer whiz who is always ready to help.

EDITING CHALLENGE—3

To fine-tune your grammar and mechanics skills, in every chapter you will be editing a message. This message is from a financial planner answering an inquiry about eBay profits. However, the message suffers from proofreading, spelling, grammar, punctuation, wordiness, and other writing faults that require correction. Study the guidelines in the Grammar/Mechanics Handbook.

YOUR TASK. Edit the following message (a) by correcting errors in your textbook or on a photocopy using proofreading marks from Appendix A or (b) by downloading the message from **www.cengagebrain.com** and correcting at your computer. Your instructor may show you a possible solution.

ANDALUZ FINANCIAL PLANNING
CERTIFIED FINANCIAL PLANNERS
2230 GIBSON BOULEVARD SE
ALBUQUERQUE, NM 87108
505.256.1002
marcy.martinez@andaluz.com

September 12, 2016

Ms. Stephanie Jimenez
2509 Blake Road NW
Albuquerque, NM 87110

Dear Stephany:

I just wanted to let you know that, as your Financial Planner, I'm happy to respond to your request for more information and clarification on the Tax status of eBay profits.

As you in all probability are all ready aware of, you can use eBay to clean out your closets or eBay can be used to run a small business. Your smart to enquire about your tax liability. Although there is no clear line that separates fun from profit or a hobby from a business. One thing is certin, the IRS taxs all income.

There are a number of factors that help determine whether or not your hobby should or should not be considered a business. To use eBay safely, the following questions should be considered:

1. Do you run the operation in a businesslike manner? Do you keep records, is your profit and loss tracked, and how about keeping a seperate checking account?

2. Do you devote alot of time and effort to eBay? If you spend eighteen hours a day selling on eBay the IRS would tend to think your in a business.

3. Some people depend on the income from their eBay activitys for their livelihood.

Are you selling items for more then they cost you? If you spend five dollars for a Garage Sale vase and sell it for fifty dollars the IRS would probably consider this a business transaction.

All profits is taxable. Even for eBay sellers who are just playing around. If you wish to discuss this farther please call me at 256-1002.

Sincerely,

Marcy Martinez

Marcy Martinez
Certified Financial Planner

COMMUNICATION WORKSHOP

Guidelines for Safe Social Networking

More and more people are becoming accustomed to communicating and sharing information, both business and personal, on Facebook, Twitter, Instagram, Tumblr, and other social media sites. As the popularity of these social networks grows, so do the risks. Savvy business communicators can protect themselves by employing smart practices such as the following:

- **Establish boundaries.** Don't share information, images, and media online that you would not be comfortable sharing openly in the office.

- **Be cautious in clicking links.** Treat links on social media sites with the same caution you use with e-mail messages. Cyber criminals are eager for you to "like" them or open their links.

- **Remember that Big Data is watching you.** Whether you are making business contacts or visiting fun sites, you are leaving a digital trail.

- **Distrust privacy settings.** Even privacy settings don't guarantee complete protection from prying eyes. Facebook has repeatedly come under fire for changing privacy settings and opening unwitting users' profiles for the world to see.

- **Beware of oversharing.** If your employer visits your Facebook page and notices a flurry of activity while you should be working, you might land on the hot seat. If you report that you're sick and then your Facebook location shows you posting from the local movie theater, this could reveal that you're playing hooky.

- **Doubt suspicious messages.** Even if a strange message looks as if it's from a friend, remember that hackers may have broken into that person's account. Use an alternate method to reach your friend to find out.

- **Rein in your friends.** One of your 500 Facebook friends may tag you in an inappropriate photograph. Tags make pictures searchable, so that an embarrassing college incident may resurface years later. Always ask before tagging someone.

- **Expect the unexpected.** Recruiters now routinely check applicants' online presence. Some employers have gone so far as to demand that candidates disclose their Facebook login information. Facebook and lawmakers have criticized the practice.

- **Beware of "friending."** Don't reject friend requests from some coworkers while accepting them from others. Snubbed workers may harbor ill feelings. Don't friend your boss unless he or she friends you first. Send friend requests only once.

CAREER APPLICATION. Office workers and businesspeople are using more and more technology to complete their work. Best practices and netiquette rules are still evolving. We've presented nine tips here for smart use of social media.

YOUR TASK. In teams discuss the tips presented here. From your own experience, add more suggestions that can make social media users safer. What risky behavior have you experienced or learned about? What violations of netiquette have you seen? Prepare a list of additional helpful tips. Show them using the format shown here, with each statement a command. Submit your list to your instructor and discuss it in class.

ENDNOTES

[1] Photo essay based on Segal, D. (2010, December 16). In pursuit of the perfect brainstorm. *The New York Times*. Retrieved from http://www.nytimes.com

[2] Head, A., & Eisenberg, M. (2009, February 4). What today's college students say about conducting research in the digital age. Project Information Literacy Progress Report, University of Washington. Retrieved from http://www.educause.edu/library/resources/what-today%E2%80%99s-college-students-say-about-conducting-research-digital-age

[3] Rindegard, J. (1999, November 22). Use clear writing to show you mean business. *InfoWorld*, p. 78.

[4] Photo essay based on Beeson, E. (2013, January 20). Hurricane Sandy to spawn storm of insurance lawsuits. *The Star-Ledger*. Retrieved from http://www.nj.com/business/index.ssf/2013/01/hurricane_sandy_to_spawn_storm.html

[5] Goddard, R. W. (1989, April). Communication: Use language effectively. *Personnel Journal*, 32.

[6] Booher, D. (2007). *The voice of authority*. New York: McGraw-Hill, p. 93.

ACKNOWLEDGMENTS

p. 64 Office Insider based on Tucci, J. M. (2004, September 1). Quoted in the National Writing Project, Writing: A ticket to work . . . or a ticket out. Retrieved from http://www.nwp.org/cs/public/print/resource/2154

p. 70 Office Insider based on Wiens, K. (2012, July 20). I won't hire people who use poor grammar. Here's why. *Harvard Business Review* blog. Retrieved from http://blogs.hbr.org/cs/2012/07/i_wont_hire_people_who_use_poo.html

p. 71 Office Insider based on Johnson, L. G. (2011, January 12). Avoid this simple "comma splice" error. Retrieved from http://www.businesswritingblog.com/business_writing/2011/01/avoid-this-simple-comma-splice-error.html

p. 74 Office Insider based on O'Conner, P. (1996). *Woe is I*. New York: Putnam, p. 161.

p. 88 Communication Workshop based on the following: Horn, L. (2013, June 14). What Emily Post can't teach us about 'netiquette.' Retrieved from http://gizmodo.com/what-emily-post-cant-teach-us-about-netiquette-513423651; Palmer, M. (2012, February 6). The netiquette of working life. Retrieved from http://www.ft.com/intl/cms/s/0/94239bbe-4dae-11e1-b96c-00144feabdc0.html#axzz2ccxWuyPJ;
Zwilling, M. (2013, August 17). 7 steps to productive business use of social media. Retrieved from http://www.forbes.com/sites/martinzwilling/2013/08/17/7-steps-to-productive-business-use-of-social-media; Naish, J. (2009, August 11). Is multi-tasking bad for the brain? Experts reveal hidden perils of juggling too many jobs. Retrieved from http://www.dailymail.co.uk/health/article-1205669/Is-multi-tasking-bad-brain-Experts-reveal-hidden-perils-juggling-jobs.html

Revising Business Messages

© Sergey Nivens/Shutterstock.com

4-1
Complete business messages by revising for conciseness, which includes eliminating flabby expressions, long lead-ins, *there is/are* and *it is/was* fillers, redundancies, and empty words, as well as condensing for microblogging.

4-2
Improve clarity in business messages by keeping the ideas simple, dumping trite business phrases, dropping clichés, avoiding slang and buzzwords, rescuing buried verbs, controlling exuberance, and choosing precise words.

4-3
Enhance readability by understanding document design including the use of white space, margins, typefaces, fonts, numbered and bulleted lists, and headings.

4-4
Recognize proofreading problem areas, and apply effective techniques to catch mistakes in both routine and complex documents.

4-5
Evaluate a message to judge its effectiveness.

4-1 Taking Time to Revise: Applying Phase 3 of the Writing Process

In this digital age of e-mailing, texting, and tweeting, the idea of stopping to revise a message seems almost alien to productivity. What? Stop to proofread? Crazy idea! No time! However, sending quick but sloppy business messages not only fails to enhance productivity but also often produces the opposite result. Those rushed messages can be confusing and frustrating. They often set into motion a maddening series of back-and-forth queries and responses seeking clarification. To avoid messages that waste time, create confusion, and reduce your credibility, take time to slow down and revise—even for short messages.

The final phase of the 3-x-3 writing process focuses on editing, proofreading, and evaluating. Editing means improving the content and sentence structure of your message. Proofreading involves correcting its grammar, spelling, punctuation, format, and mechanics. Evaluating is the process of analyzing whether your message achieves its purpose.

Rarely is the first or even second version of a message satisfactory. Only amateurs expect writing perfection on the first try. The revision stage is your chance to make sure your message says what you mean and makes you look good. Many professional writers compose the first draft quickly without worrying about language, precision, or correctness. Then they revise and polish extensively. Other writers, however, prefer to revise as they go—particularly for shorter business documents.

Whether you revise immediately or after a break, you will want to examine your message critically. You should be especially concerned with ways to improve its conciseness, clarity, and readability.

4-1a Tightening Your Message by Revising for Conciseness

In business, time is indeed money. Translated into writing, this means that concise messages save reading time and, thus, money. In addition, messages that are written directly and efficiently are easier to read and comprehend. In the revision process, look for shorter ways to say what you mean. Examine every sentence that you write. Could the thought be conveyed in fewer words? Your writing will be more concise if you eliminate flabby expressions, drop unnecessary introductory words, get rid of redundancies, and purge empty words.

Eliminating Flabby Expressions. As you revise, focus on eliminating flabby expressions. This takes conscious effort. As one expert copyeditor observed, "Trim sentences, like trim bodies, usually require far more effort than flabby ones."[1] Turning out slim sentences and lean messages means that you will strive to "trim the fat." For example, notice the flabbiness in this sentence: *Due to the fact that sales are booming, profits are strong.* It could be said more concisely: *Because sales are booming, profits are strong.* Many flabby expressions can be shortened to one concise word as shown here and illustrated in Figure 4.1. Notice in this figure how you can revise digital documents with strikethrough formatting and color. If you are revising print documents, use proofreading marks.

DON'T FLABBY	DO ✓ CONCISE
✗ as a general rule	✓ generally
✗ at a later date	✓ later
✗ at this point in time	✓ now, presently
✗ despite the fact that	✓ although
✗ due to the fact that, inasmuch as, in view of the fact that	✓ because
✗ feel free to	✓ please
✗ for the period of, for the purpose of	✓ for
✗ in addition to the above	✓ also
✗ in all probability	✓ probably
✗ in the event that	✓ if
✗ in the near future	✓ soon
✗ in very few cases	✓ seldom, rarely
✗ until such time as	✓ until

LEARNING OBJECTIVE 1

Complete business messages by revising for conciseness, which includes eliminating flabby expressions, long lead-ins, *there is/are* and *it is/was* fillers, redundancies, and empty words, as well as condensing for microblogging.

Limiting Long Lead-Ins. Another way to create concise sentences is to delete unnecessary introductory words. Consider this sentence: *I am sending you this e-mail to announce that a new manager has been hired.* A more concise and more direct sentence deletes the long lead-in: *A new manager has been hired.* The meat of the sentence often follows the long lead-in.

Figure **4.1** Revising Digital and Print Documents

Revising Digital Documents Using Strikethrough and Color

~~This is a short note to let you know that, as~~ As you requested, I ~~made an~~ ~~investigation of~~ investigated several of our competitors' websites. Attached ~~hereto~~ is a summary of my findings ~~of my investigation.~~ I was ~~really~~ most interested in ~~making a comparison of the employment of~~ ~~strategies for~~ comparing marketing strategies as well as ~~the use of~~ navigational graphics ~~used~~ to guide visitors through the sites. ~~In view of~~ ~~the fact that~~ Because we will be revising our own website ~~in the near~~ ~~future~~ soon, I was ~~extremely~~ intrigued by the organization, ~~kind of~~ marketing tactics, and navigation at each ~~and every~~ site I visited.

> When revising digital documents, you can use simple word processing tools such as strikethrough and color. In this example, strikethroughs in red identify passages to be deleted. The strikethrough function is located on the Font **tab.** We used blue to show inserted words, but you may choose any color you prefer.

Revising Printed Documents Using Proofreading Symbols

When revising printed documents, use standard symbols to manually show your revisions.

~~This is a short note to let you know that,~~ as you requested, I ~~made an~~ investigat~ed~ ~~of~~ several of our competitors' websites. Attached ~~hereto~~ is a summary of my findings ~~of my investigation.~~ I was ~~really~~ most interested in ~~making a comparison of the employment of~~ strategies ~~for marketing~~ as well as ~~the use of~~ navigational graphics ~~used~~ to guide visitors through the sites. ~~In view of the fact that~~ Because we will be revising our own website ~~in the near~~ ~~future,~~ soon I was ~~extremely~~ intrigued by the organization, ~~kind of~~ marketing tactics, and navigation at ~~each and~~ every site I visited.

Popular Proofreading Symbols

Delete	ℒ
Capitalize	≡
Insert	∧
Insert comma	⋏
Insert period	⊙
Start paragraph	¶

DON'T **WORDY**	**DO ✓** **CONCISE**
✕ We are sending this announcement to let everyone know that we expect to change Internet service providers within six weeks.	✓ We expect to change Internet service providers within six weeks.
✕ This is to inform you that you may find lower airfares at our website.	✓ You may find lower airfares at our website.
✕ I am writing this letter because Professor Brian Wilson suggested that your organization was hiring trainees.	✓ Professor Brian Wilson suggested that your organization was hiring trainees.

Dropping Unnecessary *There is/are* and *It is/was* Fillers. In many sentences the expressions *there is/are* and *it is/was* function as unnecessary fillers. In addition to taking up space, these fillers delay getting to the point of the sentence. Eliminate them by recasting the sentence. Many—but not all—sentences can be revised so that fillers are unnecessary.

DON'T WORDY	DO✓ CONCISE
✗ *There are* more women than men enrolled in college today.	✓ More women than men are enrolled in college today.
✗ *There* is an aggregator that collects and organizes blogs.	✓ An aggregator collects and organizes blogs.
✗ *It was* a Facebook post that revealed the news.	✓ A Facebook post revealed the news.

Rejecting Redundancies. Expressions that repeat meaning or include unnecessary words are redundant. Saying *unexpected surprise* is like saying *surprise surprise* because *unexpected* carries the same meaning as *surprise*. Excessive adjectives, adverbs, and phrases often create redundancies and wordiness. Redundancies do not add emphasis, as some people think. Instead, they identify a writer as inexperienced. As you revise, look for redundant expressions such as the following:

DON'T REDUNDANT	DO✓ CONCISE
✗ absolutely essential	✓ essential
✗ adequate enough	✓ adequate
✗ basic fundamentals	✓ fundamentals *or* basics
✗ big in size	✓ big
✗ combined together	✓ combined
✗ exactly identical	✓ identical
✗ each and every	✓ each *or* every
✗ necessary prerequisite	✓ prerequisite
✗ new beginning	✓ beginning
✗ refer back	✓ refer
✗ repeat again	✓ repeat
✗ true facts	✓ facts

Purging Empty Words. Familiar phrases roll off the tongue easily, but many contain expendable parts. Be alert to these empty words and phrases: *case, degree, the fact that, factor, instance, nature,* and *quality*. Notice how much better the following sentences sound when we remove all the empty words:

In the case of Facebook, it increased users but lost share value.

Because of the degree of support from upper management, the plan worked.

We are aware of the fact that sales of new products soar when pushed by social networking.

Except for the instance of Toyota, Japanese imports sagged.

She chose a career in a field that was analytical in nature. [OR: She chose a career in an analytical field.]

Student writing in that class is excellent in quality.

Also avoid saying the obvious. In the following examples, notice how many unnecessary words we can omit through revision:

~~When it arrived,~~ I cashed your check immediately. *(Announcing the check's arrival is unnecessary. That fact is assumed in its cashing.)*

As consumers learn more about ingredients ~~and as they become more knowledgeable~~, they are demanding fresher foods. *(Avoid repeating information.)*

Look carefully at clauses beginning with *that*, *which*, and *who*. They can often be shortened without loss of clarity. Search for phrases such as *it appears that*. These phrases often can be reduced to a single adjective or adverb such as *apparently*.

Changing the name of a~~∧~~company ~~that is successful~~ is always risky.
                              successful

All employees ~~who are among those~~ completing the course will be reimbursed.

Our~~∧~~proposal, ~~which was~~ slightly altered ~~in its final form~~, was approved.
      final

We plan to schedule~~∧~~meetings ~~on a weekly basis~~.
                        weekly

4-1b Writing Concisely for Microblogging and Posting on Social Media Networks

Concise expression is especially important in microblogging. As its name suggests, *microblogging* consists of short messages exchanged on social media networks such as Twitter, Facebook, and Tumblr. Many businesses are eagerly joining these microblogging networks to hear what's being said about them and their products. When they hear complaints, they can respond immediately and often solve customer problems. Companies are also using microblogging to make announcements, promote goodwill, and sell their products.

Microblogging may be public or private. Twitter and similar social networks are predominantly public channels with messages broadcast externally to the world. Twitter limits each post ("tweet") to 140 characters, including spaces, punctuation, and links. Recognizing the usefulness of microblogging but desiring more confidentiality and security, some companies prefer to keep their messaging internal. IBM, for example, employs Blue Twit, a tool that enables IBMers to share real-time news and get help from colleagues without going outside the organization. BlueTwit extends the length of messages to 400 characters.

Regardless of the microblogging network, conciseness is critical. Your messages must be short—without straying too far from conventional spelling, grammar, and punctuation. Sound difficult? It is, but it can be done, as shown in the following 140-character examples of workplace tweets:

Sample Response to Customer Complaint
@complainer Our manual can be confusing about that problem. Call me at 800-123-4567 or see http://bit.ly/xx for easy fix. Thanks, Henry[2]

Zappos CEO Announces Meeting
Livestreaming the Zappos Family quarterly all hands meeting 1-5 PM Pacific today! Tune in: http://on.fb.me/allhandslive[3]

Southwest Airlines Explains
Southwest Airlines responds to loss of pressurization event on flight from PHX to SMF [with a link to a Southwest statement about the event][4]

Starbucks Thanks Customers
Throughout April, you contributed 231,000+ hours of community service in 34 countries across five continents. Thank You! #monthofservice[5]

When microblogging, (a) include only main ideas, (b) choose descriptive but short words, (c) personalize your message if possible, and (d) be prepared to write several versions striving for conciseness, clarity, and, yes, even correctness. It's like playing a game: can you get your message across in only 140 characters?

4-2 Making Your Message Clear

A major revision task involves assessing the clarity of your message. A clear message is one that is immediately understood. Employees, customers, and investors increasingly want to be addressed in a clear and genuine way. Fuzzy, long-winded, and unclear writing prevents comprehension. Readers understand better when information is presented clearly and concisely, as a Dartmouth study about drug facts illustrates in Figure 4.2. Three techniques can improve the clarity of your writing: applying the KISS formula (Keep It Short and Simple), dumping trite business phrases, and avoiding clichés and slang.

4-2a Keep It Short and Simple

To achieve clarity, resist the urge to show off or be fancy. Remember that your goal is not to impress a reader. As a business writer, your goal is to *express*, not *impress*. One way to achieve clear writing is to apply the familiar KISS formula. Use active-voice sentences that avoid indirect, pompous language.

LEARNING OBJECTIVE 2

Improve clarity in business messages by keeping the ideas simple, dumping trite business phrases, dropping clichés, avoiding slang and buzzwords, rescuing buried verbs, controlling exuberance, and choosing precise words.

DON'T WORDY AND UNCLEAR	**DO** ✔ IMPROVED
✗ Employees have not been made sufficiently aware of the potentially adverse consequences regarding the use of these perilous chemicals.	✔ Warn your employees about these dangerous chemicals.
✗ In regard to the matter of obtaining optimal results, it is essential that employees be given the implements that are necessary for jobs to be completed satisfactorily.	✔ To get the best results, give employees the tools they need to do the job.

Figure **4.2** Conciseness Aids Clarity in Understanding Drug Facts

72%

People who correctly quantified a heart drug's benefits after reading concise fact box.

9%

People who correctly quantified a heart drug's benefits after reading the company's long ad.

Consumers understand drug effects better when the information is presented concisely and clearly. A Dartmouth University study revealed that concise fact boxes were superior to the tiny-type, full-page DTC (direct-to-consumer) advertisements that drug manufacturers usually publish.

4-2b Dumping Trite Business Phrases

To sound "businesslike," some business writers repeat the same stale expressions that others have used over the years. Your writing will sound fresher and more vigorous if you eliminate these trite phrases or find more original ways to convey the idea.

DON'T TRITE PHRASE	DO ✔ IMPROVED
✗ as per your request	✓ as you request
✗ pursuant to your request	✓ at your request
✗ enclosed please find	✓ enclosed is
✗ every effort will be made	✓ we'll try
✗ in accordance with your wishes	✓ as you wish
✗ in receipt of	✓ have received
✗ please do not hesitate to	✓ please
✗ respond forthwith	✓ respond immediately
✗ thank you in advance	✓ thank you
✗ under separate cover	✓ separately
✗ with reference to	✓ about

4-2c Dropping Clichés

Clichés are expressions that have become exhausted by overuse. Many cannot be explained, especially to those who are new to our culture. Clichés lack not only freshness but also clarity. Instead of repeating clichés such as the following, try to find another way to say what you mean.

below the belt	last but not least
better than new	make a bundle
beyond a shadow of a doubt	pass with flying colors
easier said than done	quick as a flash
exception to the rule	shoot from the hip
fill the bill	step up to the plate
first and foremost	think outside the box
good to go	true to form

4-2d Avoiding Slang and Buzzwords

Slang is composed of informal words with arbitrary and extravagantly changed meanings. Slang words quickly go out of fashion because they are no longer appealing when everyone begins to understand them. If you want to sound professional, avoid expressions such as *snarky, lousy, blowing the budget, bombed, getting burned*, and other slangy expressions.

Buzzwords are technical expressions that have become fashionable and often are meant to impress rather than express. Business buzzwords include empty terms such as *optimize, incentivize, innovative, leveraging, right-size,* and *paradigm shift.* Countless businesses today use vague rhetoric in the form of phrases such as *cost effective, positioned to perform, solutions-oriented,* and *value-added services with end-to-end fulfillment.*

Consider the following statement of a government official who had been asked why his department was dropping a proposal to lease offshore oil lands: *The Administration has an awful lot of other things in the pipeline, and this has more wiggle room so they just moved it down the totem pole.* He added, however, that the proposal might be offered again since *there is no pulling back because of hot-potato factors.* What exactly does this mean?

4-2e Rescuing Buried Verbs

Buried verbs are those that are needlessly converted to wordy noun expressions. Verbs such as *acquire, establish,* and *develop* are made into nouns such as *acquisition, establishment,* and *development.* Such nouns often end in *-tion, -ment,* and *-ance.* Sometimes called *zombie nouns* because they cannibalize and suck the life out of active verbs,[6] these nouns increase sentence length, slow the reader, and muddy the thought. Notice how you can make your writing cleaner and more forceful by avoiding buried verbs and zombie nouns:

DON'T BURIED VERBS	DO ✔ UNBURIED VERBS
✕ conduct a discussion of	✔ discuss
✕ create a reduction in	✔ reduce
✕ engage in the preparation of	✔ prepare
✕ give consideration to	✔ consider
✕ make an assumption of	✔ assume
✕ make a discovery of	✔ discover
✕ perform an analysis of	✔ analyze
✕ reach a conclusion that	✔ conclude
✕ take action on	✔ act

4-2f Controlling Exuberance

Occasionally, we show our exuberance with words such as *very, definitely, quite, completely, extremely, really, actually,* and *totally.* These intensifiers can emphasize and strengthen your meaning. Overuse, however, makes your writing sound unbusinesslike. Control your enthusiasm and guard against excessive use.

DON'T EXCESSIVE EXUBERANCE	DO ✔ BUSINESSLIKE
✕ The manufacturer was *extremely* upset to learn that its smartphones were *definitely* being counterfeited.	✔ The manufacturer was upset to learn that its smartphones were being counterfeited.
✕ We *totally* agree that we *actually* did not give his proposal a *very* fair trial.	✔ We agree that we did not give his proposal a fair trial.

"If you could taste words, most corporate websites, brochures, and sales materials would remind you of stale, soggy rice cakes: nearly calorie free, devoid of nutrition, and completely unsatisfying. . . . Unfortunately, years of language dilution by lawyers, marketers, executives, and HR departments have turned the powerful, descriptive sentence into an empty vessel optimized for buzzwords, jargon, and vapid expressions."

—Jason Fried, software developer and cofounder of the company 37signals

Workplace in Focus

Ever heard of Internet content that is "snackable"? Do you prefer Web sites that deliver an "immersive experience"? Have you seen the latest pet photos that have "gone viral" because of their "clickability"? Do you know what any of this means? You do if you work in the world of digital marketing, according to technology blog Mashable, which included these words in a list of the most overused buzzwords in the digital media profession. While people use buzzwords to sound smart or trendy, such words are inappropriate in most—but not all—business settings. In what situations should communicators avoid using buzzwords and slang?[7]

©iStockphoto.com/RapidEye

4-2g Choosing Clear, Precise Words

As you revise, make sure your words are precise so that the audience knows exactly what you mean. Clear writing creates meaningful images in the mind of the reader. Such writing is sparked by specific verbs, concrete nouns, and vivid adjectives. Foggy messages are marked by sloppy references that may require additional inquiries to clarify their meaning.

DON'T — LESS PRECISE	DO ✔ — MORE PRECISE
✗ She requested that everyone help out.	✓ Our manager begged each team member to volunteer.
✗ They will consider the problem soon.	✓ Our steering committee will consider the recruitment problem on May 15.
✗ We received many responses.	✓ The Sales Division received 28 job applications.
✗ Someone called about the meeting.	✓ Russell Vitello called about the June 12 sales meeting

LEARNING OBJECTIVE 3

Enhance readability by understanding document design including the use of white space, margins, typefaces, fonts, numbered and bulleted lists, and headings.

4-3 Enhancing Readability Through Document Design

Well-designed documents improve your messages in two important ways. First, they enhance readability and comprehension. Second, they make readers think you are a well-organized and intelligent person. In the revision process, you have a chance to adjust formatting and make other changes so that readers grasp your main points quickly. Significant design techniques to improve readability include the appropriate use of white space, margins, typefaces, fonts, numbered and bulleted lists, and headings for visual impact.

4-3a Employing White Space

Empty space on a page is called *white space*. A page crammed full of text or graphics appears busy, cluttered, and unreadable. To increase white space, use headings, bulleted or numbered lists, and effective margins. Remember that short sentences (20 or fewer words) and short paragraphs (eight or fewer printed lines) improve readability and comprehension. As you revise, think about shortening long sentences. Consider breaking up long paragraphs into shorter chunks.

4-3b Understanding Margins and Text Alignment

Margins determine the white space on the left, right, top, and bottom of a block of type. They define the reading area and provide important visual relief. Business letters and memos usually have side margins of 1 to 1.5 inches.

Your word processing program probably offers four forms of margin alignment: (a) lines align only at the left, (b) lines align only at the right, (c) lines align at both left and right (*justified*), and (d) lines are centered. Nearly all text in Western cultures is aligned at the left and reads from left to right. The right margin may be either *justified* or *ragged right*. The text in books, magazines, and other long works is often justified on the left and right for a formal appearance.

Justified text, however, may require more attention to word spacing and hyphenation to avoid awkward empty spaces or "rivers" of spaces running through a document. When right margins are *ragged*—that is, without alignment or justification—they provide more white space and improve readability. Therefore, you are best served by using left-justified text and ragged-right margins without justification. Centered text is appropriate for headings and short invitations but not for complete messages.

4-3c Choosing Appropriate Typefaces

Business writers today may choose from a number of typefaces on their word processors. A typeface defines the shape of text characters. A wide range of typefaces, as shown in Figure 4.3, is available for various purposes. Some are decorative and useful for special purposes. For most business messages, however, you should choose from *serif* or *sans serif* categories.

Figure 4.3 Typefaces With Different Personalities for Different Purposes

All-Purpose Sans Serif	Traditional Serif	Happy, Creative Script/Funny	Assertive, Bold Modern Display	Plain Monospaced
Arial	Century	Brush Script	Britannic Bold	Courier
Calibri	Garamond	Comic Sans	Broadway	Letter Gothic
Helvetica	Georgia	Gigi	Elephant	Monaco
Tahoma	Goudy	Jokerman	Impact	Prestige Elite
Univers	Palatino	Lucinda	Bauhaus 93	
Verdana	Times New Roman	Kristen	SHOWCARD	

Serif typefaces have small features at the ends of strokes. The most common serif typeface is Times New Roman. Other popular serif typefaces are Century, Georgia, and Palatino. Serif typefaces suggest tradition, maturity, and formality. They are frequently used for body text in business messages and longer documents. Because books, newspapers, and magazines favor serif typefaces, readers are familiar with them.

Sans serif typefaces include Arial, Calibri, Gothic, Tahoma, Helvetica, and Univers. These clean characters are widely used for headings, signs, and material that does not require continuous reading. Web designers often prefer sans serif typefaces for simple, pure pages. For longer documents, however, sans serif typefaces may seem colder and less appealing than familiar serif typefaces.

For less formal messages or special decorative effects, you might choose one of the "happy" fonts such as Comic Sans or a bold typeface such as Impact. You can simulate handwriting with a script typeface. Despite the wonderful possibilities available on your word processor, don't get carried away with fancy typefaces. All-purpose sans serif and traditional serif typefaces are most appropriate for your business messages. Generally, use no more than two typefaces within one document.

4-3d Capitalizing on Type Fonts and Sizes

Font refers to a specific style within a typeface family. Here are examples of font styles in the Verdana font family:

CAPITALIZATION	underline
SMALL CAPS	Outline
boldface	Shadow
italics	Emboss

Font styles are a mechanical means of adding emphasis to your words. ALL CAPS, SMALL CAPS, and **bold** are useful for headings, subheadings, and single words or short phrases in the text. ALL CAPS, HOWEVER, SHOULD **NEVER** BE USED FOR LONG STRETCHES OF TEXT BECAUSE ALL THE LETTERS ARE THE SAME HEIGHT. This makes it difficult for readers to differentiate words. In addition, excessive use of all caps feels like shouting and irritates readers.

Boldface, *italics*, and underlining are effective for calling attention to important points and terms. Be cautious, however, when using fancy or an excessive number of font styles. Don't use them if they will confuse, annoy, or delay readers.

As you revise, think about type size. Readers are generally most comfortable with 10- to 12-point type for body text. Smaller type enables you to fit more words into a space. Tiny type, however, makes text look dense and unappealing. Slightly larger type makes material more readable. Overly large type (14 points or more) looks amateurish and out of place for body text in business messages. Larger type, however, is appropriate for headings.

4-3e Numbering and Bulleting Lists for Quick Comprehension

One of the best ways to ensure rapid comprehension of ideas is through the use of numbered or bulleted lists. Lists provide high "skim value." This means that readers can browse quickly and grasp main ideas. By breaking up complex information into smaller chunks, lists improve readability, understanding, and retention. They also force the writer to organize ideas and write efficiently.

When revising, look for ideas that could be converted to lists, and follow these techniques to make your lists look professional:

- **Numbered lists:** Use for items that represent a sequence or reflect a numbering system.
- **Bulleted lists:** Use to highlight items that don't necessarily show a chronology.
- **Capitalization:** Capitalize the initial word of each line.
- **Punctuation:** Add end punctuation only if the listed items are complete sentences.
- **Parallelism:** Make all the lines consistent; for example, start each with a verb.

In the following examples, notice that the list on the left presents a sequence of steps with numbers. The bulleted list does not show a sequence of ideas; therefore, bullets are appropriate. Also notice the parallelism in each example. In the numbered list, each item begins with a verb. In the bulleted list, each item follows an adjective/noun sequence. Business readers appreciate lists because they focus attention. Be careful, however, not to use so many that your messages look like grocery lists.

Numbered List	Bulleted List
Our recruiters follow these steps when hiring applicants:	To attract upscale customers, we feature the following:
1. Examine the application.	• Quality fashions
2. Interview the applicant.	• Personalized service
3. Check the applicant's references.	• Generous return policy

4-3f Adding Headings for Visual Impact

Headings are an effective tool for highlighting information and improving readability. They encourage the writer to group similar material together. Headings help the reader separate major ideas from details. They enable a busy reader to skim familiar or less important information. They also provide a quick preview or review. Headings appear most often in reports, which you will study in greater detail in Chapters 9 and 10. However, headings can also improve readability in e-mails, memos, and letters. In the following example, notice how *category headings* highlight the listings:

Our company focuses on the following areas in the employment process:

- **Attracting applicants.** We advertise for qualified applicants, and we also encourage current employees to recommend good people.
- **Interviewing applicants.** Our specialized interviews include simulated customer encounters as well as scrutiny by supervisors.
- **Checking references.** We investigate every applicant thoroughly. We contact former employers and all listed references.

In Figure 4.4 the writer converts a dense, unappealing e-mail message into an easier-to-read version by applying professional document design. Notice that the all-caps font shown earlier makes its meaning difficult to decipher. Justified margins and lack of white space further reduce readability. In the revised version, the writer changed the all-caps font to upper- and lowercase and also used ragged-right margins to enhance visual appeal. One of the best document design techniques in this message is the use of headings and bullets to help the reader see

Figure 4.4 Document Design Improves Readability

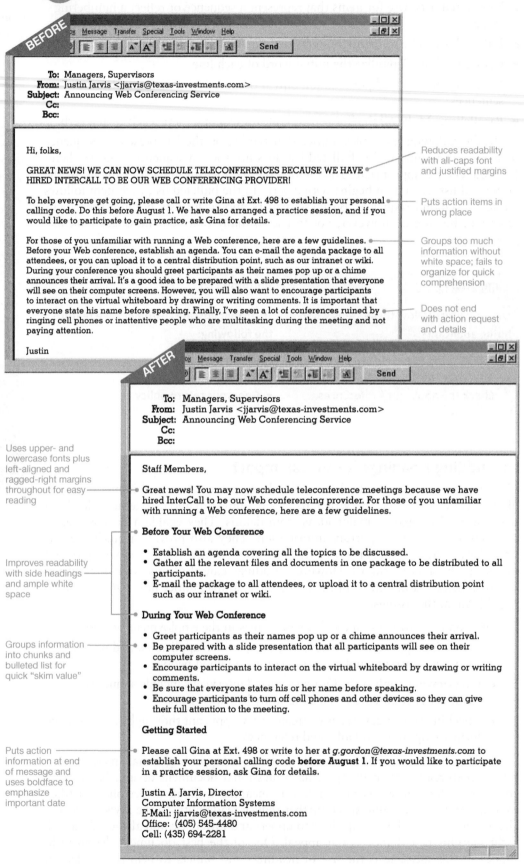

BEFORE

To: Managers, Supervisors
From: Justin Jarvis <jjarvis@texas-investments.com>
Subject: Announcing Web Conferencing Service
Cc:
Bcc:

Hi, folks,

GREAT NEWS! WE CAN NOW SCHEDULE TELECONFERENCES BECAUSE WE HAVE HIRED INTERCALL TO BE OUR WEB CONFERENCING PROVIDER!

To help everyone get going, please call or write Gina at Ext. 498 to establish your personal calling code. Do this before August 1. We have also arranged a practice session, and if you would like to participate to gain practice, ask Gina for details.

For those of you unfamiliar with running a Web conference, here are a few guidelines. Before your Web conference, establish an agenda. You can e-mail the agenda package to all attendees, or you can upload it to a central distribution point, such as our intranet or wiki. During your conference you should greet participants as their names pop up or a chime announces their arrival. It's a good idea to be prepared with a slide presentation that everyone will see on their computer screens. However, you will also want to encourage participants to interact on the virtual whiteboard by drawing or writing comments. It is important that everyone state his name before speaking. Finally, I've seen a lot of conferences ruined by ringing cell phones or inattentive people who are multitasking during the meeting and not paying attention.

Justin

- Reduces readability with all-caps font and justified margins
- Puts action items in wrong place
- Groups too much information without white space; fails to organize for quick comprehension
- Does not end with action request and details

AFTER

To: Managers, Supervisors
From: Justin Jarvis <jjarvis@texas-investments.com>
Subject: Announcing Web Conferencing Service
Cc:
Bcc:

Staff Members,

Great news! You may now schedule teleconference meetings because we have hired InterCall to be our Web conferencing provider. For those of you unfamiliar with running a Web conference, here are a few guidelines.

Before Your Web Conference

- Establish an agenda covering all the topics to be discussed.
- Gather all the relevant files and documents in one package to be distributed to all participants.
- E-mail the package to all attendees, or upload it to a central distribution point such as our intranet or wiki.

During Your Web Conference

- Greet participants as their names pop up or a chime announces their arrival.
- Be prepared with a slide presentation that all participants will see on their computer screens.
- Encourage participants to interact on the virtual whiteboard by drawing or writing comments.
- Be sure that everyone states his or her name before speaking.
- Encourage participants to turn off cell phones and other devices so they can give their full attention to the meeting.

Getting Started

- Please call Gina at Ext. 498 or write to her at *g.gordon@texas-investments.com* to establish your personal calling code **before August 1**. If you would like to participate in a practice session, ask Gina for details.

Justin A. Jarvis, Director
Computer Information Systems
E-Mail: jjarvis@texas-investments.com
Office: (405) 545-4480
Cell: (435) 694-2281

- Uses upper- and lowercase fonts plus left-aligned and ragged-right margins throughout for easy reading
- Improves readability with side headings and ample white space
- Groups information into chunks and bulleted list for quick "skim value"
- Puts action information at end of message and uses boldface to emphasize important date

chunks of information in similar groups. All of these improvements are made in the revision process. You can make any message more readable by applying the document design techniques presented here.

4-4 Proofreading to Catch Errors

LEARNING OBJECTIVE 4

Recognize proofreading problem areas, and apply effective techniques to catch mistakes in both routine and complex documents.

Alas, none of us is perfect, and even the best writers sometimes make mistakes. The problem, however, is not making the mistakes; the real problem is not finding and correcting them. Documents with errors affect your credibility and the success of your organization, as illustrated in Figure 4.5.

Once the message is in its final form, it's time to proofread. Don't proofread earlier because you may waste time checking items that eventually will be changed or omitted. Important messages—such as those you send to management or to customers or turn in to instructors for grades—deserve careful revision and proofreading. When you finish a first draft, plan for a cooling-off period. Put the document aside and return to it after a break, preferably after 24 hours or longer. Proofreading is especially difficult because most of us read what we thought we wrote. That's why it's important to look for specific problem areas.

4-4a What to Watch for in Proofreading

Careful proofreaders check for problems in the following areas:

- **Spelling.** Now is the time to consult the dictionary. Is *recommend* spelled with one or two *c*'s? Do you mean *affect* or *effect*? Use your computer spell-checker, but don't rely on it totally.

- **Grammar.** Locate sentence subjects; do their verbs agree with them? Do pronouns agree with their antecedents? Review the principles in the Grammar/Mechanics Handbook if necessary. Use your computer's grammar-checker, but be suspicious. It's not always correct.

- **Punctuation.** Make sure that introductory clauses are followed by commas. In compound sentences put commas before coordinating conjunctions *(and, or, but, nor)*. Double-check your use of semicolons and colons.

- **Names and numbers.** Compare all names and numbers with their sources because inaccuracies are not always visible. Especially verify the spelling of the names of individuals receiving the message. Most of us immediately dislike someone who misspells our name.

- **Format.** Be sure that your document looks balanced on the page. Compare its parts and format with those of standard documents shown in Appendix B. If you indent paragraphs, be certain that all are indented and that their spacing is consistent.

Figure 4.5 Why Proofread?

WHY PROOFREAD? IN BUSINESS, ACCURACY MATTERS

A survey of business professionals revealed the following:

100% said that writing errors influenced their opinions about a business.

57% will stop considering a company if its print brochure has one writing error.

77% have eliminated a prospective company from consideration in part because of writing errors.

75% thought misspelled words were inexcusable.

30% of Web visitors will leave if a website contains writing errors.

© Goodluz/Shutterstock.com; © 2016 Cengage Learning®

4-4b How to Proofread Routine Documents

Most routine documents require a light proofreading. If you read on screen, use the down arrow to reveal one line at a time. This focuses your attention at the bottom of the screen. A safer proofreading method, however, is reading from a printed copy. Regardless of which method you use, look for typos and misspellings. Search for easily confused words, such as *to* for *too* and *then* for *than*. Read for missing words and inconsistencies. For handwritten or printed messages, use standard proofreading marks, shown briefly in Figure 4.6 or completely in Appendix A. For digital documents and collaborative projects, use the simple word processing tools also shown in Figure 4.1 or use the **Comment** and **Track Changes** functions discussed in the Communication Workshop at the end of this chapter.

4-4c How to Proofread Complex Documents

Long, complex, or important documents demand careful proofreading. Apply the previous suggestions but also add the following techniques:

- Print a copy, preferably double-spaced, and set it aside for at least a day. You will be more alert after a breather.

- Allow adequate time to proofread carefully. A common excuse for sloppy proofreading is lack of time.

- Be prepared to find errors. One student confessed, "I can find other people's errors, but I can't seem to locate my own." Psychologically, we don't expect to find errors, and we don't want to find them. You can overcome this obstacle by anticipating errors and congratulating, not criticizing, yourself each time you find one.

- Read the message at least twice—once for word meanings and once for grammar and mechanics. For very long documents (book chapters and long articles or reports), read a third time to verify consistency in formatting.

- Reduce your reading speed. Concentrate on individual words rather than ideas.

Figure 4.6 Most Common Proofreading Marks

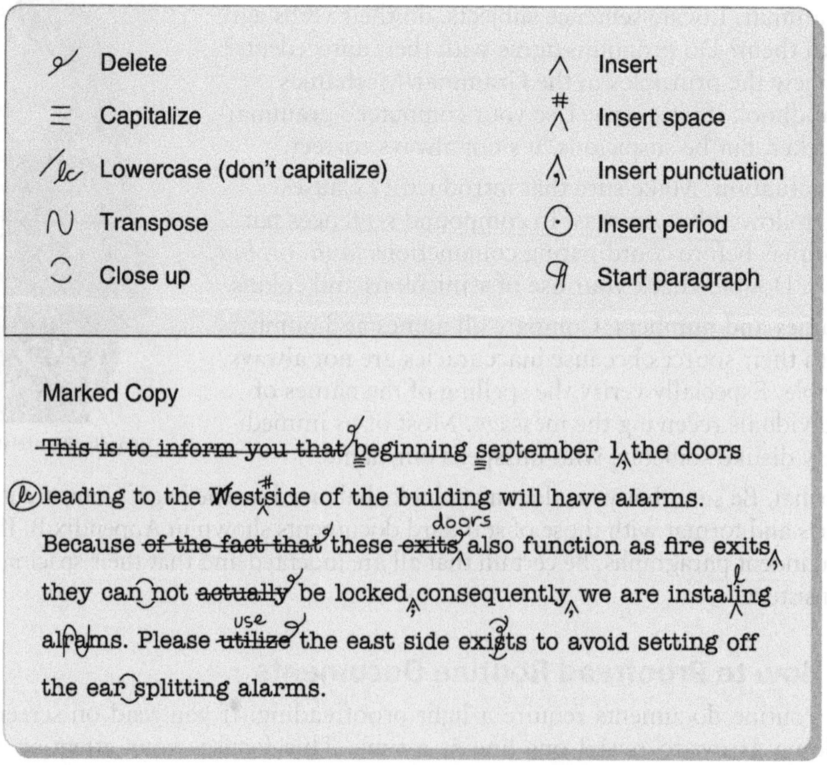

- For documents that must be perfect, enlist a proofreading buddy. Have someone read the message aloud, spelling names and difficult words, noting capitalization, and reading punctuation.
- Use the standard proofreading marks shown in Appendix A to indicate changes.

Many of us struggle with proofreading our own writing because we are seeing the same information over and over. We tend to see what we expect to see as our eyes race over the words without looking at each one carefully. We tend to know what is coming next and glide over it. To change the appearance of what you are reading, you might print it on a different colored paper or change the font. If you are proofing on screen, enlarge the page view or change the background color of the screen.

4-5 Evaluating the Effectiveness of Your Message

LEARNING OBJECTIVE 5
Evaluate a message to judge its effectiveness.

As you apply finishing touches, take a moment to evaluate your writing. Remember that everything you write, whether for yourself or someone else, takes the place of a personal appearance. If you were meeting in person, you would be certain to dress appropriately and professionally. The same standard applies to your writing. Evaluate what you have written to be sure that it attracts the reader's attention. Is it polished and clear enough to convince the reader that you are worth listening to? How successful will this message be? Does it say what you want it to? Will it achieve its purpose? How will you know whether it succeeds?

The best way to judge the success of your communication is through feedback. For this reason you should encourage the receiver to respond to your message. This feedback will tell you how to modify future efforts to improve your communication technique.

Your instructor will also be evaluating some of your writing. Although any criticism is painful, try not to be defensive. Look on these comments as valuable advice tailored to your specific writing weaknesses—and strengths. Many businesses today spend thousands of dollars bringing in communication consultants to improve employee writing skills. You are getting the same training in this course. Take advantage of this chance—one of the few you may have—to improve your skills. The best way to improve your skills, of course, is through instruction, practice, and evaluation.

In this class you have all three elements: instruction in the writing process, practice materials, and someone to guide you and evaluate your efforts. Those three elements are the reasons this book and this course may be the most valuable in your entire curriculum. Because it's almost impossible to improve your communication skills alone, take advantage of this opportunity.

SUMMARY OF LEARNING OBJECTIVES

4-1 Complete business messages by revising for conciseness, which includes eliminating flabby expressions, long lead-ins, *there is/are* and *it is/was* fillers, redundancies, and empty words, as well as condensing for microblogging.
- Revise for conciseness by eliminating flabby expressions (*as a general rule, at a later date, at this point in time*).
- Exclude opening fillers (*there is, there are*), redundancies (*basic essentials*), and empty words (*in the case of, the fact that*).
- In microblogging messages, include only main ideas, choose descriptive but short words, personalize your message if possible, and be prepared to write several versions striving for conciseness, clarity, and correctness.

4-2 Improve clarity in business messages by keeping the ideas simple, dumping trite business phrases, dropping clichés, avoiding slang and buzzwords, rescuing buried verbs, controlling exuberance, and choosing precise words.

- To be sure your messages are clear, apply the KISS formula: Keep It Short and Simple.
- Avoid foggy, indirect, and pompous language.
- Do not include trite business phrases (*as per your request, enclosed please find, pursuant to your request*), clichés (*better than new, beyond a shadow of a doubt, easier said than done*), slang (*snarky, lousy, bombed*), and buzzwords (*optimize, paradigm shift, incentivize*).
- Avoid burying nouns (*to conduct an investigation* rather than *to investigate, to perform an analysis* rather than *to analyze*).
- Don't overuse intensifiers that show exuberance (*totally, actually, very, definitely*) but sound unbusinesslike.
- Choose precise words (*the report was well-organized* rather than *the report was great*).

4-3 Enhance readability by understanding document design including the use of white space, margins, typefaces, fonts, numbered and bulleted lists, and headings.

- Enhance readability and comprehension by using ample white space, appropriate side margins, and ragged-right (not justified) margins.
- Use serif typefaces (fonts with small features at the ends of strokes, such as Times New Roman, Century, and Palatino) for body text; use sans serif typefaces (clean fonts without small features, such as Arial, Helvetica, and Tahoma) for headings and signs.
- Choose appropriate font styles and sizes for business messages.
- Provide high "skim value" with numbered and bulleted lists.
- Include headings to add visual impact and aid readability in business messages as well as in reports.

4-4 Recognize proofreading problem areas, and apply effective techniques to catch mistakes in both routine and complex documents.

- In proofreading be especially alert to spelling, grammar, punctuation, names, numbers, and document format.
- Proofread routine documents immediately after completion by reading line by line on the computer screen or, better yet, from a printed draft.
- Proofread more complex documents after a breather.
- Allow adequate time, reduce your reading speed, and read the document at least three times—for word meanings, for grammar and mechanics, and for formatting.

4-5 Evaluate a message to judge its effectiveness.

- Encourage feedback from the receiver so that you can determine whether your communication achieved its goal.
- Welcome any advice from your instructor on how to improve your writing skills.

CHAPTER REVIEW

1. What's involved in the revision process? Is revision still necessary in a digital age when workplace messages fly back and forth in split seconds? (Obj. 1)

2. What's wrong with a message that begins, *I am writing this announcement to let everyone know that . . .* ? (Obj. 1)

3. What is microblogging, and why is conciseness especially important in microblogging messages and social media posts? (Obj. 1)

4. What's wrong with familiar business phrases such as *as per your request* and *enclosed please find*? (Obj. 2)

5. Why should writers avoid expressions such as *first and foremost* and *think outside the box?* (Obj. 2)

6. What are buried verbs and zombie nouns? Give an original example of each. Why should they be avoided? (Obj. 2)

7. How do bulleted and numbered lists improve readability? (Obj. 3)

8. In proofreading, why is it difficult for writers to find their own errors? How could they overcome this barrier? (Obj. 4)

9. What are five items to check in proofreading? Be ready to discuss methods you find useful in spotting these errors. (Obj. 4)

10. How can you overcome defensiveness when your writing is criticized constructively? (Obj. 5)

CRITICAL THINKING

11. In this digital age of rapid communication, how can you justify the time it takes to stop and revise a message? (Objs. 1–5)

12. Assume you have started a new job in which you respond to customers by using boilerplate (previously constructed) paragraphs. Some of them contain clichés such as *pursuant to your request* and *in accordance with your wishes*. Other paragraphs are wordy and violate the principle of using concise and clear writing that you have learned. What should you do? (Obj. 2)

13. Because business writing should have high "skim value," why not write everything in bulleted lists? (Obj. 3)

14. Conciseness is valued in business. However, can messages be too short? (Obj. 1)

15. What advice would you give in this ethical dilemma? Brittani is serving as interim editor of the company newsletter. She receives an article written by the company president describing, in abstract and pompous language, the company's goals for the coming year. Brittani thinks the article will need considerable revising to make it readable. Attached to the president's article are complimentary comments by two of the company vice presidents. What action should Brittani take?

WRITING IMPROVEMENT EXERCISES

Flabby Expressions (Obj. 1)

YOUR TASK. Revise the following sentences to eliminate flabby expressions.

16. We are sending a revised proposal at this point in time due to the fact that building costs have jumped at a considerable rate.

17. In the normal course of events, we would seek additional funding; however, in view of the fact that rates have increased, we cannot.

18. In very few cases has it been advisable for us to borrow money for a period of 90 or fewer days.

19. Inasmuch as our Web advertising income is increasing in a gradual manner, we might seek a loan in the amount of $50,000.

20. Despite the fact that we have had no response to our bid, we are still available in the event that you wish to proceed with your building project.

Long Lead-Ins (Obj. 1)

YOUR TASK. Revise the following to eliminate long lead-ins.

21. This is an announcement to tell you that all computer passwords must be changed every six months for security purposes.

22. We are sending this memo to notify everyone that anyone who wants to apply for telecommuting may submit an application immediately.

23. I am writing this letter to inform you that your new account executive is Edward Ho.

24. This is to warn you that cyber criminals use sophisticated tools to decipher passwords rapidly.

25. This message is to let you know that social media services can position your company at the forefront of online marketing opportunities.

There is/are and *It is/was* Fillers (Obj. 1)

YOUR TASK. Revise the following to avoid unnecessary *there is/are* and *it is/was* fillers.

26. There is a password-checker that is now available that can automatically evaluate the strength of your password.

27. It is careless or uninformed individuals who are the most vulnerable to computer hackers.

28. There are computers in Internet cafes, at conferences, and in airport lounges that should be considered unsafe for any personal use.

29. A computer specialist told us that there are keystroke-logging devices that gather information typed on a computer, including passwords.

30. If there are any questions that you have about computer safety, please call us.

Redundancies (Obj. 1)

YOUR TASK. Revise the following to avoid redundancies.

31. Because his laptop was small in size, he could carry it everywhere.

32. A basic fundamental of computer safety is to avoid storing your password on a file in your computer because criminals will look there first.

33. The manager repeated again his warning that we must use strong passwords.

34. Although the two files seem exactly identical, we should proofread each and every page.

35. The computer specialist combined together a PowerPoint presentation and a handout.

Empty Words (Obj. 1)

YOUR TASK. Revise the following to eliminate empty words.

36. Are you aware of the fact that social media can drive brand awareness and customer loyalty?

37. Except for the instance of MySpace, social networking sites are booming.

38. If you seek to build an online community that will support your customers, social media services can help.

39. With such a degree of active participation in Facebook and Twitter, it's easy to understand why businesses are flocking to social media sites.

40. We plan to schedule online meetings on a monthly basis.

Condensing for Microblogging (Obj. 1)

YOUR TASK. Read the following real Twitter messages and write a 140-character microblog reply to each. Be selective in what you include. Your instructor may show you the actual responses that the company wrote.

41. **@HTWilson94 asks whether grocer Whole Foods stocks Whole Trade–certified flowers all year long.**[8] Prepare a response (140 or fewer characters) based on the following information: Yes, at Whole Foods stores we do indeed offer Whole Trade–certified flowers the entire year. We strongly advocate and support the Whole Trade movement, which strives to promote quality, premium price to the producer, better wages and working conditions, and the environment. However, we can't tell you exactly which certified flowers will be available at our stores and when. You would have to check with your local store for its specific selection.

42. **@AmyJean64 sent Bank of America a tweet saying she was frustrated with a real estate short sale. "Have a contract on a house and cannot get them to return calls to finalize."**[9] Prepare a response based on the following information: You work for Bank of America, and you would very much like to help her, but you can't without certain information. You need her to send you the property address along with her name and phone number so that you can call to see how you can help. She should probably DM (direct message) you with this crucial information.

43. **@VickiK wrote to JetBlue: "I have booked a flt in July, CA-VT. Wondering about flying my wedding dress w/me. Is there a safe place to hang it on the plane?"**[10] Prepare a response based on the following information: We congratulate you on your coming wedding! We bet your wedding dress is beautiful. We don't have special closets on our planes and certainly nothing big enough for a wedding dress. But here's a suggestion: Have you considered having it shipped ahead of time? All the best wishes on your upcoming happy event!

44. **@ChrisC sent a message to Southwest Airlines saying, "This is extremely frustrating, how is it possible for your website to be down the entire day?"**[11] Prepare a response based on the following information: Southwest is very, very sorry! It's extremely frustrating to us also. We realize that you are accustomed to using this site to book flights. Our IT people tell us that the website functionality is getting better. We are not sure exactly what that means in terms of availability, but we are very hopeful that customers will be able to book their flights soon.

45. **@JamesR. sent a message to the delivery service UPS complaining, "Holy XXX. It's after 6 pm and UPS still hasn't delivered my pkg yet."** Prepare a response based on the following information: UPS makes every effort to deliver all packages promptly. For packages destined for offices, we must deliver by 3 p.m. However, for packages going to residences, our goal is to deliver by 7 p.m. But we can't always make it, so our drivers can sometimes run later. We're sorry about the wait.

46. **@calinelb sent a message to H&R Block: "YOU SUCK! I've been waiting for my return more than 3.5 months."**[12] Prepare a response based on the following: We are sorry that you feel that way. We certainly can't understand the reason for this long delay. We would like to look into the matter, but before we can respond, we need you to send a DM (direct message) to our customer service desk at @HRBlockAnswers. We will definitely check on this and get back to you.

Trite Business Phrases (Obj. 2)

YOUR TASK. Revise the following sentences to eliminate trite business phrases.

47. Pursuant to your request, I will submit your repair request immediately.

48. Enclosed please find the list of customers to be used in our promotion.

49. As per your request, we are sending the contract under separate cover.

50. Every effort will be made to proceed in accordance with your wishes.

51. If we may help in any way, please do not hesitate to call.

Clichés, Slang, Buzzwords, and Wordiness (Obj. 2)

YOUR TASK. Revise the following sentences to avoid confusing clichés, slang, buzzwords, and wordiness.

52. Our manager insists that we must think outside the box in promoting our new kitchen tool.

53. Although we got burned in the last contract, you can be sure we will stand our ground this time.

54. Beyond the shadow of a doubt, our lousy competitor will make another snarky claim that is below the belt.

55. If you refer back to our five-year plan, you will see that there are provisions for preventing blowing the budget.

56. BTW, have you heard the latest buzz about hackers ripping off customer info from Best Buy?

Buried Verbs (Obj. 2)

YOUR TASK. Revise the following sentences to recover buried verbs.

57. After making an investigation, the fire department reached the conclusion that the blaze was set intentionally.

58. Our committee made a promise to give consideration to your proposal at its next meeting.

59. When used properly, zero-based budgeting can bring about a reduction in overall costs.

60. Did our department put in an application for increased budget support?

61. The budget committee has not taken action on any projects yet.

62. Homeowners must make a determination of the total value of their furnishings.

Lists, Bullets, and Headings (Obj. 3)

YOUR TASK. Revise the following poorly written sentences and paragraphs. Use lists, bullets, and category headings, if appropriate. Improve parallel construction and reduce wordiness.

63. **Three Best Twitter Practices**. There are three simple ways you can build an online following, drive your reputation, and develop customers' trust by using these uncomplicated and simple Twitter practices. First off, share some of your photos and information about your business from behind the scenes. Sharing is so important! Next, listen. That is, you should regularly monitor the comments about your company, what's being said about your brand, and any chatter about your products. And, of course, you should respond. In real time it is necessary to respond to statements that are compliments and just general feedback.

64. Revise the following by incorporating a numbered list.

    Computer passwords are a way of life at this point in time. In the creation of a strong password, you should remember a few things. First, you should come up with an eight-word phrase that is easy to remember, such as this: *my goal is a degree in 4 years*. Then take each of those words and the first letter should be selected, such as this: *mgiadi4y*. The last step for creating a really strong password is to exchange—that is, swap out—some of those letters for characters and capital letters: *Mgia$in4Y*.

65. Revise the following paragraph by incorporating a bulleted list with category headings. Eliminate all the wordiness.

    In response to your inquiry with questions about how credit scores are made, this is to let you know that there are four important factors that make up your credit score. Because you say you are interested in improving your score so that it reaches the highest level, you will be interested in this. One of the most important items lenders consider before approving anyone for a loan is your payment history. It is important that you have a long history of making payments on time. Almost as important is the amount of available credit that you have. If you are close to maxing out your accounts, you are a higher risk and will have a lower score. How long you have had accounts is also important. Accounts that have been open for ten years will help your credit score. Finally, if you are opening lots of new accounts, you can lower your credit score.

RADICAL REWRITES

Note: Radical Rewrites are provided at **www.cengagebrain.com** for you to download and revise. Your instructor may show a suggested solution.

4.1 Radical Rewrite: Information E-Mail—Wretched Invitation (Objs. 1–5)

The following wordy, inefficient, and disorganized message invites department managers to three interviewing sessions to select student interns. However, to be effective, this message desperately needs a radical rewrite.

YOUR TASK. Study the message and list at least five weaknesses. Then revise to avoid excessive wordiness and repetition. Also think about how to develop an upbeat tone and improve readability. Can you reduce this sloppy 15-sentence message to 6 efficient sentences plus a list—and still convey all the necessary information?

To:	List - Department Managers
From:	Aaron Alexander <aalexander@vasco.com>
Subject:	Upcoming Interviews
Cc:	
Bcc:	

For some time our management team has been thinking about hiring several interns. We decided to offer compensation to the interns in our internship program because in two fields (computer science and information systems) interns are usually paid, which is the norm. However, you may be disappointed to learn that we can offer only three internships.

In working with our nearby state university, we have narrowed the field to six excellent candidates. These six candidates will be interviewed. This is to inform you that you are invited to attend three interviewing sessions for these student candidates. Your presence is required at these sessions to help us avoid making poor selections.

Mark your calendars for the following three times. The first meeting is May 3 in the conference room. The second meeting is May 5 in Office 22 (the conference room was scheduled). On May 9 we can finish up in the conference room. All of the meetings will start at 2 p.m. In view of the fact that your projects need fresh ideas and talented new team members, I should not have to urge you to attend and be well prepared.

Please examine all the candidates' résumés and send me your ranking lists.

Aaron Alexander

[Full contact information]

List at least five weaknesses.

Adjectives and Adverbs

Review Sections 1.16 and 1.17 of the Grammar/Mechanics Handbook. Then study each of the following statements. Underscore any inappropriate forms. In the space provided, write the correct form (or *C* if correct) and the number of the G/M principle illustrated. You may need to consult your dictionary for current practice regarding some compound adjectives. When you finish, compare your responses with those provided at the end of the book. If your answers differ, carefully study the principles in parentheses.

cost-effective   (1.17e)   **EXAMPLE** We need a <u>cost effective</u> solution for this continuing problem.

_____ 1. The newly opened restaurant offered many tried and true menu items.

_____ 2. Amazingly, most of the ten year old equipment is still working.

_____ 3. Although purchased ten years ago, the equipment still looked brightly.

_____ 4. Global messages today are exchanged so quick that international business moves more rapidly than ever.

_____ 5. The president's veto of the tax plan couldn't have sent a more clearer message.

_____ 6. You may submit only work related expenses to be reimbursed.

_____ 7. Amanda and Max said that they're planning to open there own business next year.

_____ 8. Haven't you ever made a spur of the moment decision?

_____ 9. Not all decisions that are made on the spur of the moment turn out badly.

_____ 10. The committee offered a well thought out plan to revamp online registration.

_____ 11. You must complete a change of address form when you move.

_____ 12. Each decision will be made on a case by case basis.

_____ 13. I could be more efficient if my printer were more nearer my computer.

_____ 14. If you reject his offer to help, Kurt will feel badly.

_____ 15. The truck's engine is running smooth after its tune-up.

This message transmits a suggestion from an employee to her boss. However, the message suffers from proofreading, wordiness, spelling, punctuation, and other writing faults that require correction.

YOUR TASK. Edit the following message (a) by correcting errors in your textbook or on a photocopy using proofreading marks from Appendix A or (b) by downloading the message from the premium website at **www.cengagebrain.com** and correcting at your computer. Your instructor may show you a possible solution.

To: Daniel R. Kesling <daniel.kesling@federalsavings.com>
From: Misty McKenney<misty.mckenney@federalsavings.com>
Subject: My Idea
Cc:
Bcc:

Mr. Kesling,

Due to the fact that you recently asked for ideas on how to improve customer relations I am submitting my idea. This message is to let you know that I think we can improve customer satisfaction easy by making a change in our counters.

Last June glass barriers were installed at our branch. There are tellers on one side and customers on the other. The barriers, however, do have air vents to be able to allow we tellers to carry on communication with our customers. Management thought that these bullet proof barriers would prevent and stop thiefs from jumping over the counter.

I observed that there were customers who were surprised by these large glass partitions. Communication through them is really extremely difficult and hard. Both the customer and the teller have to raise there voices to be heard. Its even more of a inconvenience when you are dealing with an elderly person or someone who happens to be from another country. Beyond a shadow of a doubt, these new barriers make customers feel that they are being treated impersonal.

I made an effort to research the matter of these barriers and made the discovery that we are the only bank in town with them. There are many other banks that are trying casual kiosks and open counters to make customers feel more at home.

Although it may be easier said than done, I suggest that we actually give serious consideration to the removal of these barriers as a beginning and initial step toward improving customer relations.

Misty McKenney

E-mail: misty.mckenney@federalsavings.com
Support Services
(316) 448-3910

COMMUNICATION WORKSHOP

Revising and Editing Documents in MS Word

Collaborative writing and editing projects are challenging. Fortunately, Microsoft Word offers many useful tools to help team members edit and share documents electronically. Three simple but useful editing tools are **text highlight color, font color**, and **strikethrough**, which you learned about earlier in this chapter. These tools enable reviewers to point out editing changes. Complex projects, however, may require more advanced editing tools such as **Track Changes** and Insert **Comments**, as illustrated in Figure 4.7.

TRACK CHANGES. To suggest specific editing changes to other team members, **Track Changes** is handy. When this command is in effect, all changes to a document are recorded in a different color, with one color for each reviewer. New text is underlined, and a vertical line appears in the margin to show where changes were made. Text that has been deleted is crossed out. Suggested revisions offered by different team members are identified and dated. The original writer may accept or reject these changes. In Word 2007, 2010, and 2013, you will find **Track Changes** on the **Review** menu.

INSERT COMMENTS. By using **Insert Comments**, you can point out problematic passages or errors, ask or answer questions, and share ideas without changing or adding text. When more than one person adds comments, the comments appear in different colors and are identified by the individual writers' names and date/time stamps.

CAREER APPLICATION. On the job, you will likely be working with others on projects that require written documents. During employment interviews, employers may ask whether you have participated in team projects using collaborative software. To be able to answer that question favorably, take advantage of this opportunity to work on a collaborative document using some of the features described here.

YOUR TASK. Divide into two-person teams to edit the Editing Challenge document. One partner downloads the file from **www .cengagebrain.com** or retypes it from the textbook. That partner makes all necessary changes using font color, strikethrough, and the **Comment** feature and then saves the file with a file name such as *PartnerName-Editing4*. The first partner then sends an e-mail to the second partner with the attached file and asks the partner to make further edits. The receiving partner prints a copy of the sending partner's file before editing the message further using font color, strikethrough, and the **Comment** feature. The second partner approves or rejects the first partner's edits and then submits the edited copy along with a copy of the message with both partners' edits. Be sure to name each file distinctly. Your instructor will decide whether to require hard copies or e-mail copies.

Figure **4.7** Track Changes and Comment Features Aid Revision Process

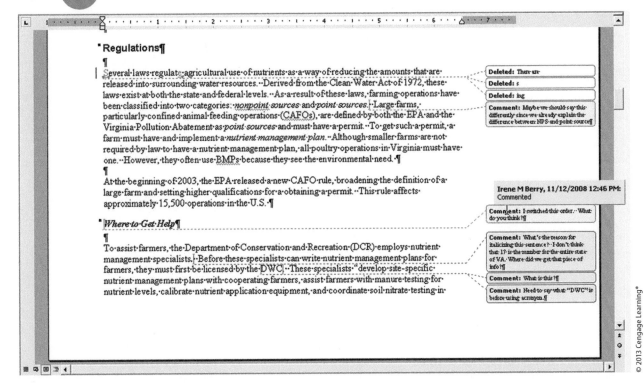

© 2013 Cengage Learning®

ENDNOTES

[1] Cook, C. (1985). *Line by line*. Boston: Houghton Mifflin, p. 17.

[2] Glassman, N. (2010, November 29). 6 tips for brands on responding to customer complaints on Twitter. Retrieved from http://socialtimes.com/responding-customer-complaints-twitter_b29179

[3] Hsieh, T. (2011, May 11). Twitter. Retrieved from http://twitter.com/#!/zappos

[4] Holmes, E. (2011, December 9). Tweeting without fear. Wall Street Journal Online. Retrieved from http://online.wsj.com/article/SB10001424052970204319004577086140865075800.html

[5] Starbucks. (2012, May 30). Retrieved from http://twitter.com/#!/Starbucks

[6] Sword, H. (2012, July 25). Zombie nouns. Retrieved from http://www.3quarksdaily.com/3quarksdaily/2012/07/zombie-nouns.html

[7] Photo essay based on Al-Greene, B. (2013, May 23). 30 overused buzzwords in digital marketing. Mashable. Retrieved from http://mashable.com/2013/05/23/buzzword-infographic/

[8] Based on Van Grove, J. (2009, January 21). 40 of the best twitter brands and the people behind them. Retrieved from http://mashable.com/2009/01/21/best-twitter-brands

[9] Based on Bank of America Twitter Help. (2012, June 3). @AmyJo 63Owen. Twitter. Retrieved from https://twitter.com/#!/BofA_Help

[10] Based on JetBlue Twitter Help. (2012, June 4). VictoriaKlim @vikiybubbles. Twitter. Retrieved from https://twitter.com/#!/JetBlue

[11] Based on Southwest Airlines Twitter. (2012, May 15). Chris Cichon@cichonship. Twitter. Retrieved from https://twitter.com/#!/SouthwestAir

[12] Based on H&R Block. (2012, June 4). Carlos Noriega@calinelbarbaro. Twitter. Retrieved from https://twitter.com/#!/hrblock

ACKNOWLEDGMENTS

p. 91 Office Insider based on Powell, E. (2003, November/December). Ten tips for better business writing. *Office Solutions*, *20*(6), 36.

p. 93 Office Insider based on Zinsser, W. (2006). *On writing well* (7th ed.). New York: HarperCollins.

p. 95 Office Insider based on Shankman, P. (2011, May 20). I will never hire a "social media expert," and neither should you. Retrieved from http://shankman.com/i-will-never-hire-a-social-media-expert-and-neither-should-you

p. 96 Office Insider based on Adams, S. (2011, April 9-10). How to get a real education. *The Wall Street Journal*, pp. C1–C2.

p. 97 Office Insider based on Fried, J. (2010, May 1). Why is business writing so awful? *Inc.* magazine. Retrieved from http://www.inc.com/magazine/20100501/why-is-business-writing-so-awful.html

p. 101 Office Insider based on Levitt, A. (2011, April 2). A word to Wall Street: 'Plain English,' please. Retrieved from Wall Street Journal Online at http://online.wsj.com/article/SB10001424052748704471904576231002037599510.html

© Alexander Raths/Shutterstock.com

Proposals and Formal Reports

OBJECTIVES
After studying this chapter,
you should be able to

10-1
Understand the importance,
purpose, and components
of informal and formal
proposals.

10-2
Describe the steps in writing
and editing formal business
reports.

10-3
Conduct research using
primary and secondary
sources, and understand
how to assess the credibility
of resources.

10-4
Identify the purposes and
techniques of documenting
and citing sources in
business reports.

10-5
Convert report data into
meaningful visual aids and
graphics.

10-6
Describe the components of
typical formal reports.

10-1 Preparing Business Proposals

A *proposal* is a written offer to solve problems, provide services, or sell products. Proposals can mean life or death for a business. Why are they so important? Multimillion-dollar aerospace and engineering firms depend on proposals to compete for business. People running smaller businesses—such as electricians, contractors, plumbers, and interior designers—also depend on proposals to sell their services and products.

10-1a Types of Business Proposals

Writers prepare proposals for various reasons, such as asking for funds or promoting products and services to customers. Some proposals are brief; some are lengthy and complex. A proposal recipient could be a manager inside your company or a potential client outside your company. All types of proposals share two significant characteristics: (a) they use easy-to-understand language, and (b) they show the value and benefits of the product or services being recommended. Proposals may be classified as (a) informal or formal, (b) internal or external, and (c) solicited or unsolicited.

Informal or Formal. Informal proposals are short reports, often formatted as memos or letters. Proposal sections can vary, but an informal proposal might include the following parts: (a) an introduction or description of the problem, (b)

LEARNING OBJECTIVE **1**

Understand the importance, purpose, and components of informal and formal proposals.

pertinent background information or a statement of need, (c) the proposal benefits and schedule for completion, (d) the staffing requirements, (e) a budget analysis, and (f) a conclusion that may include an authorization request. Figure 10.2 shows an informal letter proposal to a Florida dentist who sought to improve patient satisfaction. The research company submitting the proposal describes the benefits of a patient survey to gather data about the level of patient satisfaction. As you can see, the proposal contains the basic components of an informal proposal.

Formal proposals are more complex and may range from 5 to 200 or more pages. In addition to the six basic parts of informal proposals, formal proposals may contain some or all of these additional parts: (a) a copy of a request for proposal (RFP), (b) a letter of transmittal, (c) an abstract or executive summary, (d) a title page, (e) a table of contents, (f) a list of figures, and (g) an appendix. Figure 10.1 shows the typical sections included in informal and formal proposals.

Internal or External. Proposal writers may submit internal proposals to management when they see benefits in changing a company policy, purchasing equipment, or adding new products and services. A company decision maker will review the proposal and accept or reject the idea. Internal proposals may resemble justification and recommendation reports, as discussed in Chapter 9. Most proposals, however, are external and addressed to clients and customers outside the company. An external sales proposal to a client would show how the company's goods or services would solve a problem or benefit the client.

Another type of external proposal is a grant request, written to obtain funding from agencies that support worthwhile causes. For example, Project C.U.R.E. submitted a successful grant request to Ronald McDonald House Charities to help reduce infant mortality in remote locations around the world.

Figure **10.1** Components of Informal and Formal Proposals

Informal Proposals

| Introduction |
| Background, problem, purpose |
| Proposal, plan, schedule |
| Staffing |
| Budget |
| Conclusion and authorization |

Formal Proposals

| Copy of RFP (optional) |
| Letter of transmittal |
| Abstract or executive summary |
| Title page |
| Table of contents |
| List of figures |
| Introduction |
| Background, problem, purpose |
| Proposal, plan, schedule |
| Staffing |
| Budget |
| Authorization |
| Appendix |

Following the glitch-ridden launch of Healthcare.gov in 2013, the U.S. government fired the site's chief programmer and awarded the $91 million e-commerce contract to Accenture, a Chicago-based technology company familiar with the government services sector. While the change was welcome news for millions of Americans needing health care, doubts arose after the public learned that Accenture won the contract through a noncompetitive "no bid" process. Confidence eroded even further when watchdog groups discovered a Justice Department investigation in which Accenture was accused of rigging bids and receiving financial "kickbacks." The U.S. Postal Service Inspector General's Office even urged terminating Accenture's government contracts due to ethics questions. What bidding process helps organizations award contracts fairly and judiciously?[1]

Solicited (RFP) or Unsolicited. When government organizations or businesses have a specific need, they prepare a *request for proposal (RFP)*, a document that specifies their requirements. Government agencies as well as private businesses use RFPs to solicit competitive bids from vendors. RFPs ensure that bids are comparable and that funds are awarded fairly. For example, the city of Las Vegas, Nevada, prepared a 30-page RFP seeking bids for a parking initiative from public and private funding sources.[2] Companies responding to these solicited proposals are careful to follow the RFP instructions explicitly, which might include following a specific proposal format.

Enterprising companies looking for work or special projects might submit unsolicited proposals. For example, the world-renowned architect who designed the Louvre Museum pyramid in Paris, I. M. Pei, was so intrigued by the mission of the Buck Institute for Age Research that he submitted an unsolicited proposal to design the biomedical research facility in Novato, California.[3] Pei's proposal must have impressed the decision makers, because the research facility now features his geometric elements and floating staircases.

Both large and small companies are likely to use RFPs to solicit bids on their projects. This enables them to compare prices from various companies on their projects. Not only do they want a good price from their project bidders, but they also want the legal protection offered by proposals, which are considered legal contracts.

When writing proposals, remember that they must be persuasive, not merely mechanical descriptions of what you can do. Like the persuasive sales messages discussed in Chapter 8, effective proposals must (a) get the reader's attention, (b) emphasize how your methods and products will benefit the reader, (c) showcase your expertise and build credibility, and (d) present ideas clearly and logically, making it easy for the reader to understand.

10-1b Components of Informal Proposals

The titles, or headings, of the components of informal proposals may vary, but the goals of the components are standard. Each of the following components of a typical informal proposal serves a purpose and contributes to its overall success.

Figure **10.2** Informal Letter Proposal

1 Prewriting

Analyze: The purpose of this letter proposal is to persuade the reader to accept this proposal.

Anticipate: The reader expects this proposal but must be convinced that this survey project is worth its hefty price.

Adapt: Because the reader will be resistant at first, use a persuasive approach that emphasizes benefits.

2 Drafting

Research: Collect data about the reader's practice and other surveys of patient satisfaction.

Organize: Identify four specific purposes (benefits) of this proposal. Specify the survey plan. Promote the staff, itemize the budget, and ask for approval.

Draft: Prepare a first draft, expecting to improve it later.

3 Revising

Edit: Revise to emphasize benefits. Improve readability with functional headings and lists. Remove jargon and wordiness.

Proofread: Check spelling of client's name. Verify dates and calculation of budget figures. Recheck all punctuation.

Evaluate: Is this proposal convincing enough to sell the client?

3250 West Bay Street | phone 904.457.7332
Jacksonville, FL 32202 | fax 904.457.8614
email: info@momentum.com

May 30, 2016

Valerie Stevens, D.D.S.
490 Houston Street, Suite 301
Green Cove Springs, FL 32043

Dear Dr. Stevens:

Grabs attention with "hook" that focuses on key benefit

Understanding the views of your patients is the key to meeting their needs. Momentum Research is pleased to propose a plan to help you become even more successful by learning what patients expect of your practice, so that you can improve your services.

Uses opening paragraph to focus on key benefits

Background and Goals

We know that you have been incorporating a total quality management approach in your practice. Although you have every reason to believe that your patients are pleased with your services, you may want to give them an opportunity to share what they like and suggest areas of improvement. Specifically, your goals are to survey your patients to (a) determine the level of their satisfaction with you and your staff, (b) collect and analyze their suggestions for improvement, (c) learn more about how they discovered you, and (d) compare the responses of your "preferred" and "standard" patients.

Identifies four purposes of survey

Proposed Plan

Announces heart of proposal

On the basis of our experience in conducting many local and national customer satisfaction surveys, Momentum proposes the following plan:

Survey. We will develop a short but thorough questionnaire that will collect the data you desire. Although the survey instrument will include both open-ended and closed questions, it will concentrate on the latter. Closed questions enable respondents to answer easily; they also facilitate systematic data analysis. The questionnaire will gauge patients' views of staff courtesy, professionalism, accuracy of billing, office atmosphere, and waiting time. After you approve it, the questionnaire will be sent to a carefully selected sample of 300 patients whom you have designated as "preferred" and "standard."

Describes procedure for solving problem and achieving goals

Divides proposed plan into logical, readable segments

Analysis. Survey data will be analyzed by demographic segments, such as patient type, age, and gender. Using state-of-the-art statistical tools, our team of seasoned experts will study (a) satisfaction levels, (b) the reasons for satisfaction or dissatisfaction, and (c) the responses of your "preferred" compared to "standard" patients. Moreover, our team will give you specific suggestions for making patient visits more pleasant.

Report. You will receive a final report with the key findings clearly spelled out, Dr. Stevens. Our expert staff will draw conclusions based on the results. The report will include tables summarizing all responses, divided into preferred and standard patients.

Figure **10.2** (Continued)

Dr. Valerie Stevens   Page 2   May 30, 2016

Includes second-page heading

Uses past-tense verbs to show that work has already started on the project

Schedule. With your approval, the following schedule has been arranged for your patient satisfaction survey:

Questionnaire development and mailing	August 1–6
Deadline for returning questionnaire	August 24
Data tabulation and processing	August 24–26
Completion of final report	September 1

Staffing

Promotes credentials and expertise of key people

Momentum is a nationally recognized, experienced research consulting firm specializing in survey investigation. I have assigned your customer satisfaction survey to Dr. Joseph Hales, PhD, our director of research. Dr. Hales was trained at Emory University and has successfully supervised our research program for the past nine years. Before joining Momentum, he was a marketing analyst with T-Mobile.

Builds credibility by describing outstanding staff and facilities

Assisting Dr. Hales will be a team headed by Lesha Barber, our vice president for operations. Ms. Barber earned a BS degree in computer science and an MA degree in marketing from the University of Florida. She supervises our computer-aided telephone interviewing system and manages our 30-person professional staff.

Budget

Itemizes costs carefully because a proposal is a contract offer

	Estimated Hours	Rate	Total
Professional and administrative time			
Questionnaire development	3	$175/hr.	$ 525
Questionnaire mailing	4	50/hr.	200
Data processing and tabulation	12	50/hr.	600
Analysis of findings	15	175/hr.	2,625
Preparation of final report	5	175/hr.	875
Mailing costs			
300 copies of questionnaire			150
Postage and envelopes			300
Total costs			$5,275

Conclusion and Authorization

Makes response easy

We are convinced, Dr. Stevens, that our professionally designed and administered patient satisfaction survey will provide beneficial data for improving your practice. Momentum Research can have specific results for you by September 1 if you sign the enclosed duplicate copy of this letter and return it to us with a retainer of $2,500 so that we may begin developing your survey immediately. The rates in this offer are in effect only until October 1.

Closes by repeating key qualifications and main benefits

Provides deadline

Sincerely,

Vincent Diaz

Vincent Diaz, President

VD:mem
Enclosure

Introduction. The proposal's introduction states the reasons for the proposal and highlights the writer's qualifications. To grab attention and be more persuasive, the introduction should strive to provide a "hook," such as the following:

- Hint at extraordinary results with details to be revealed shortly.

- Promise low costs or speedy results.

- Mention a remarkable resource (well-known authority, new computer program, and well-trained staff) available exclusively to you.

- Identify a serious problem (worry item) and promise a solution, to be explained later.

- Specify a key issue or benefit that you feel is the heart of the proposal.

Before writing the proposal shown in Figure 10.2 on page 302, Vincent Diaz analyzed the request of Florida dentist, Valerie Stevens, and decided that she was most interested in improving service to her patients. Vincent focused on this issue in the opening sentence and offered his company's assistance in meeting Dr. Stevens' needs. The writer confidently proposes a plan to promote success in this strong introductory paragraph. In longer proposals the introduction may also describe the scope and limitations of the project.

Background, Problem, and Purpose. The background section identifies the problem and discusses the goals or purposes of the project. In an unsolicited proposal, your goal is to convince the reader that a problem exists. Therefore, you must present the problem in detail, discussing such factors as revenue losses, failure to comply with government regulations, or decreased customer satisfaction.

In a solicited proposal, your aim is to persuade the reader that you understand the reader's issues and that you have a realistic solution. If an RFP is involved, follow its requirements precisely and use the company's language in your description of the problem. For example, if the RFP asks for *the design of a maintenance program for wireless communication equipment,* do not call it a *customer service program for wireless products.* The background section might include segments titled *Statement of Need, Basic Requirements, Most Critical Tasks,* or *Important Secondary Problems.*

Proposal, Plan, and Schedule. In the proposal section itself, you would explain your plan for solving the problem. In some proposals this is tricky because you want to disclose enough of your plan to secure the contract, while being cautious about providing so much information that your services will not be needed. Without specifics, though, your proposal has little chance, so you must decide how much to reveal.

The proposal section often includes an implementation plan. If research is involved, state what methods you will use to gather the data. Remember to be persuasive by showing how your methods and products will benefit the reader. For example, show how the initial investment will pay off later. The proposal might even promise specific *deliverables*—tangible things your project will produce for the customer. A proposal deliverable might be a new website design or an online marketing plan. To add credibility, also specify how the project will be managed and audited. Most writers also include a schedule or timetable of activities showing the proposal's benchmarks for completion.

Staffing. The staffing section of a proposal describes the staff qualifications for implementation of the proposal as well as the credentials and expertise of the project leaders. In other words, this section may include the size and qualifications of the support staff. This section is a good place to endorse and promote your staff. The client sees that qualified people will be on board to implement the project. Even résumés may be included in this section. Experts, however, advise proposal writers against including generic résumés that have not been revised to mirror the RFP's requirements. Only well-tailored résumés will inspire the kind of trust in a team's qualifications that is necessary if a proposal is to be accepted.[4]

Budget. A central item in most proposals is the budget, a list of proposed project costs. Some proposal writers title this section *Statement of Costs.* You need to prepare this section carefully because it represents a contract; you cannot raise the project costs later—even if your costs increase.

In the proposal shown in Figure 10.2, Vincent Diaz decided to justify the budget for his firm's patient satisfaction survey by itemizing the costs. Whether the costs in a proposal are itemized or treated as a lump sum depends on the reader's needs and the proposal's goals.

Conclusion and Authorization. The closing section should remind the reader of the proposal's key benefits and make it easy for the reader to respond. It might also include a project completion date as well as a deadline date beyond which the proposal offer will no longer be in effect. Writers of informal proposals often refer to this as a request for approval or authorization. The conclusion of the proposal in Figure 10.2 mentions a key benefit as well as a deadline for approval.

10-2 Writing and Editing Formal Business Reports

LEARNING OBJECTIVE **2**
Describe the steps in writing and editing formal business reports.

A formal report may be defined as a document in which a writer analyzes findings, draws conclusions, and makes recommendations intended to solve a problem. Formal business reports are similar to formal proposals in length, organization, and tone. However, instead of solving problems, proposing changes, or responding to an RFP, formal reports present findings and recommendations based on research and data analysis. Report writers then present the recommendations to decision makers in the fields of business, industry, government, and education.

10-2a Steps for Writing Formal Business Reports

Writing a formal report is a difficult task. It requires planning, researching, and organizing. Because this is a complex process, writers are most successful when they follow specific steps, as outlined in the following sections.

Determine the Purpose and Scope of the Report. Like proposals and informal reports, formal reports begin with a purpose statement. Preparing a written purpose statement is helpful because it defines the focus of the report and provides a standard that keeps the project on target. Study the following purpose statement and notice the use of action words (*adding*, *writing*, and *establishing*):

> **Simple purpose statement:** *To recommend adding three positions to our sales team, writing a job description for the sales team leader, and establishing recruitment guidelines for sales team hiring.*

You can determine the scope of the report by defining the problem or problems that will be researched and analyzed. Then examine your limitations by considering these questions: How much time do you have to complete the report? How accessible is the data you need? How thorough should your research be, and what boundaries will help you limit the scope of this report? If interviews or surveys are appropriate, how many people should you contact, and what questions should you ask?

Anticipate the Needs of the Audience. Report writers know the information their readers want and need. Keep in mind that the audience may or may not be familiar with the topic. Your goal is to present key findings that are relevant to your audience. If you were reporting to a targeted audience of human resources managers, the following facts gathered from an employee survey would be considered relevant: *According to the company survey completed by 425 of our 515 employees, 72 percent of employees are currently happy with their health benefits package.* A good report writer considers the needs of the audience every step of the way.

Decide on a Work Plan and Appropriate Research Methods. A work plan is a tentative plan that guides the investigation. This plan includes a clear problem statement, a purpose statement, and a description of the research methods to be used. A good work plan also involves a tentative outline of the report's major sections and a logical work schedule for completion of major tasks, as illustrated in Figure 10.3.

Figure 10.3 Work Plan for a Formal Report

Statement of Problem

Many women between the ages of 18 and 34 have trouble finding jeans that fit. Lee Jeans hopes to remedy that situation with its One True Fit line. We want to demonstrate to Lee that we can create a word-of-mouth campaign that will help it reach its target audience.

Defines purpose, scope, limits, and significance of report

Statement of Purpose

The purpose of this report is to secure an advertising contract from Lee Jeans. We will examine published accounts about the jeans industry and Lee Jeans in particular. In addition, we will examine published results of Lee's current marketing strategy. We will conduct focus groups of women in our company to generate campaign strategies for our pilot study of 100 BzzAgents. The report will persuade Lee Jeans that word-of-mouth advertising is an effective strategy to reach women in this demographic group and that BzzAgent is the right company to hire. The report is significant because an advertising contract with Lee Jeans would help our company grow significantly in size and stature.

Research Strategy (Sources and Methods of Data Collection)

Describes primary and secondary data

We will gather information about Lee Jeans and the product line by examining published marketing data and conducting focus group surveys of our employees. In addition, we will gather data about the added value of word-of-mouth advertising by examining published accounts and interpreting data from previous marketing campaigns, particularly those targeted toward similar age groups. Finally, we will conduct a pilot study of 100 BzzAgents in the target demographic.

Tentative Outline

I. How effectively has Lee Jeans marketed to the target population?
   A. Historically, who has typically bought Lee Jeans products? How often? Where?
   B. How effective are the current marketing strategies for the One True Fit line?
II. Is this product a good fit for our marketing strategy and our company?
   A. What do our staff members and our sample survey of BzzAgents say about this product?
   B. How well does our pool of BzzAgents correspond to the target demographic in terms of age and geographic distribution?
III. Why should Lee Jeans engage BzzAgent to advertise its One True Fit line?
   A. What are the benefits of word of mouth in general and for this demographic in particular?
   B. What previous campaigns have we engaged in that demonstrate our company's credibility?

Factors problem into manageable chunks

Work Schedule

Investigate Lee Jeans and One True Fit line's current marketing strategy	July 15–25
Test product using focus groups	July 15–22
Create campaign materials for BzzAgents	July 18–31
Run a pilot test with a selected pool of 100 BzzAgents	August 1–21
Evaluate and interpret findings	August 22–25
Compose draft of report	August 26–28
Revise draft	August 28–30
Submit final report	September 1

Estimates time needed to complete report tasks

Conduct Research Using Primary and Secondary Sources. Formal report writers conduct most of their research using *secondary sources*—that is, information that has been previously analyzed and compiled. Books, articles, Web documents, podcasts, correspondence, and annual reports are examples of secondary sources. In contrast, writers may conduct some of their research using primary sources—information and data gathered from firsthand experience. Interviews, observations, surveys, questionnaires, and meetings are examples of primary research. Research methods are discussed in the section "Conducting Primary and Secondary Research" later in this chapter.

Organize, Analyze, and Draw Conclusions. Formal report writers should organize their information logically and base their recommendations on solid facts to impress decision makers. They should analyze the findings and make sure they are relevant to the report's purpose.

When organizing your ideas, place your main topics and subtopics into an outline format as shown in Figure 10.4.

As you sort through your information, decide what information is substantiated and credible. Give readers only the information they need. Then arrange that information using one of the strategies shown in Figure 10.5. For example, if a company wants to design its own online surveys, management may request a report that compares the best survey software solutions. In this case, the compare/contrast strategy helps the report writer organize the data and compare the features and costs of each survey tool.

Conclude the report by summarizing your findings, drawing conclusions, and making recommendations. The way you conclude depends on the purpose of your report and what the reader needs. A well-organized report with conclusions based on solid data will impress management and other decision makers.

Design Graphics to Clarify the Report's Message. Presenting numerical or quantitative data visually helps your reader understand information readily. Trends, comparisons, and cycles are easier to comprehend when they are expressed graphically. These visual elements in reports draw attention, add interest, and

Figure **10.4** Outline Format

FORMS OF BUSINESS OWNERSHIP

I. **Sole proprietorship**
    A. Advantages of sole proprietorship
        1. Minimal capital requirements
        2. Control by owner
    B. Disadvantages of sole proprietorship
        1. Unlimited liability
        2. Limited management talent
II. **Partnership**
    A. Advantages of partnership
        1. Access to capital
        2. Management talent
        3. Ease of formation
    B. Disadvantages of partnership
        1. Unlimited liability
        2. Personality conflicts

Figure **10.5** Strategies for Organizing Report Findings

Strategy Type	Data Arrangement	Useful Application
Chronological	Arrange information in a time sequence to show history or development of topic.	Useful in showing time relationships, such as five-year profit figures or a series of events leading to a problem
Geographical	Organize information by geographic regions or locations.	Appropriate for topics that are easily divided into locations, such as East Coast, Northwest, etc.
Topic/Function	Arrange by topics or functions. May use a prescribed, conventional format.	Works well for topics with established categories or for recurring reports
Compare/Contrast	Present problem and show alternative solutions. Use consistent criteria. Show how the solutions are similar and different.	Best used for "before and after" scenarios or when comparing alternatives
Importance	Arrange from least to most important, lowest to highest priority, or lowest to highest value, etc.	Appropriate when persuading the audience to take a specific action or change a belief
Simple/Complex	Proceed from simple to more complex concepts or topics.	Useful for technical or abstract topics
Best Case/Worst Case	Describe the best and the worst possible scenarios.	Useful when dramatic effect is needed to achieve results; helpful when audience is uninterested or uninformed

often help readers gain information quickly. Visuals include drawings, graphs, maps, charts, photographs, tables, and infographics. This topic is covered in more depth in the section "Incorporating Meaningful Visual Aids and Graphics" later in this chapter.

10-2b What to Review When Editing Formal Business Reports

The final step in preparing a formal business report involves editing and proofreading. Because the reader is the one who determines the report's success, review the report as if you were the intended audience. Pay particular attention to the following elements:

- **Format.** Look at the report's format and assess the report's visual appeal.
- **Consistency.** Review the report for consistency in margins, page numbers, indents, line spacing, and font style.
- **Graphics.** Make sure all graphics have meaningful titles, are clear, and are placed in the report near the words that describe them.
- **Heading levels.** Check the heading levels for consistency in font style and placement. Headings and subheadings should be meaningful and help the reader follow the report's logic.
- **Accuracy.** Review the content for accuracy and clarity. Make sure all facts are documented.
- **Mechanics.** Correct all grammar, punctuation, capitalization, and usage errors. These errors will damage your credibility and might cause the reader to mistrust the report's content.

LEARNING OBJECTIVE **3**
Conduct research using primary and secondary sources, and understand how to assess the credibility of resources.

10-3 Conducting Primary and Secondary Research

Research, or the gathering of information, is one of the most important steps in writing a report. Because a report is only as good as its data, you will want to spend considerable time collecting data before you begin writing.

As you analyze a report's purpose and audience, think about your research strategy and what data you will need to support your argument or explain your topic. Will the audience need a lot of background or contextual information? Will your readers appreciate statistics, case studies, or expert opinions? Will your data collection involve interviews or surveys?

Data sources fall into two broad categories, primary and secondary. Primary data result from gathering original data from firsthand experience, from interviews and surveys, or from direct observation. Secondary data result from reading what others have published, experienced, or observed. The makers of the energy drink Red Bull, for example, produce primary data when they give away samples, conduct interviews in the streets, and record the reactions of consumers. These same sets of data become secondary after they have been published in a newspaper article about the growing popularity of caffeinated energy drinks.

Secondary data sources are easier and cheaper to gather than primary data sources, which might involve interviewing large groups or sending out questionnaires. When considering primary and secondary sources, report writers usually focus first on secondary sources because most of their information will come from those sources.

10-3a Secondary Research Sources

Reviewing secondary sources can save time and effort. Find out first what has already been written about your topic. Most secondary material is available either in print or online. Common secondary research sources are journals, magazines, newspapers, and Web documents. You can find print resources such as books and periodicals in libraries. You can also find relevant information by searching online databases and reliable Web sources.

Print Resources. Although most report writers first look online for resource material, they should not underestimate libraries. In fact, libraries feature print resources that might not be available online.

If you are an infrequent library user, talk with a reference librarian about your writing project. Librarians will steer you in the right direction and help you understand their computer cataloging and retrieval systems.

Books. Although quickly outdated, books provide excellent historical, in-depth data. Like most contemporary sources, books can be located using the library's automated online catalog system.

Periodicals. Magazines, pamphlets, and journals are called *periodicals* because of their recurrent, or periodic, publication. Journals are compilations of scholarly articles. Articles in journals and other periodicals are extremely useful because they are concise, limited in scope, and current. Current publications are also digitized and available in full text online, often as PDF documents.

Indexes. University libraries offer online access to *The Readers' Guide to Periodical Literature*, a comprehensive index of popular, important periodicals. This index is now offered by EBSCO, a multidisciplinary resource composed of research databases, e-books, and e-journals. Contemporary business writers rely mostly on electronic indexes and research databases such as EBSCO to locate references, abstracts, and full-text articles from magazines, journals, and newspapers, such as *The New York Times*. When using Web-based online indexes, follow the on-screen instructions or ask a librarian for assistance.

Online Databases. As a writer of business reports, you will probably begin your secondary research with electronic resources. Online databases have become the staple of secondary research as they are fast and easy to use.

A *database* is a collection of information stored digitally so that it is accessible by computers or mobile electronic devices. Databases provide bibliographic information (titles of documents and brief abstracts) and full-text documents. Various databases contain a rich array of magazine, newspaper, and journal articles, as well as newsletters, business reports, company profiles, government data, reviews, and directories. The five databases most useful to business writers are ABI/INFORM (ProQuest), Business Source Premier (powered by EBSCOhost), JSTOR Business, Factiva (Dow Jones), and LexisNexis Academic. Figure 10.6 shows the ABI/INFORM Trade & Industry results page for a search on sustainable development and energy efficiency.

Efficient search strategies take time to master. Therefore, get advice from a librarian. Remember that college and public libraries as well as some employers offer free access to several commercial databases, sparing you the high cost of individual subscriptions.

The Web. Like most adults, you probably use the Web for entertainment, news, shopping, making travel arrangements, getting help with work projects, playing online games, or finding answers to questions. You may actively participate on Facebook, LinkedIn, Twitter, Instagram, or Pinterest. You have probably looked up directions on Google Maps and may have bid on or sold items on eBay. In short, you rely on the Internet daily for information and entertainment. The Web is also an effective research tool when you need valid information quickly.

Web Search Tools. Finding what you are looking for on the Web is less frustrating when you know about specialized search tools. Search engines, such as Google, Bing, and Yahoo Search, are popular tools that look for Web pages that match the keywords you enter. Another search tool is a Web directory, such as the Open Directory Project and WWW Virtual Library. Directories have human editors

Figure 10.6 ABI/INFORM (ProQuest) Search Result Page

ABI/INFORM (ProQuest) is a comprehensive business research database that delivers more than 6,800 publications, nearly 80 percent of which are in full text. Users can access diverse publication types, including annual reports, newspapers, magazines, dissertations, scholarly journals, and business cases. Figure 10.6 shows that the search terms *sustainable development* and *energy efficiency* brought up 912 full-text search results.

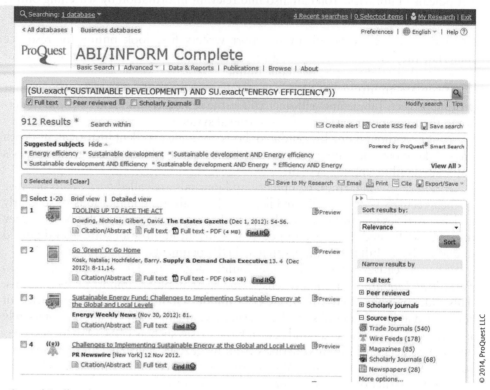

Source: http://search.proquest.com

that select and organize Web pages into subject categories. Metasearch engines, such as InfoSpace and WebCrawler, search through multiple search engines and summarize the results.

Both search engines and subject directories will help you find specific information. Figure 10.7 shows Business.com, a business search engine and subject directory in one. For best results, researchers should use various search tools and compare the quality of the search results.

Web Search Operators. When searching the Web, researchers might use a string of keywords with search operators to filter the results. Others may prefer using a search engine's Advance Search filters. Search operators help you narrow your search and find what you need. People who search regularly are familiar with the Boolean search operators, AND, OR, and NOT. You can narrow or broaden your search when you place these operators between words or groups of words. Check the Help section found on a search engine's website to see which search operators they recommend.

Google, undeniably one of the most popular search engines in the world, helps users search effectively on its pages titled Basic Search Tips and How to Search on Google. Google's Search Operators page gives tips for limiting results, and the Advanced Search page allows you to choose one or more filters to find the most relevant information. Google's search operators, some of which are shown in Figure 10.8, will help you search like an expert.

Web Encyclopedias. Encyclopedias are considered good sources of baseline information on most topics. The well-known general Web encyclopedia, Wikipedia, may provide helpful background information on topics that require more in-depth research. Because Wikipedia is written by amateurs, however, some schools and universities do not consider it a reliable source of information for research papers. Because anyone can contribute to or alter an article in Wikipedia,

Figure 10.7 Business.com

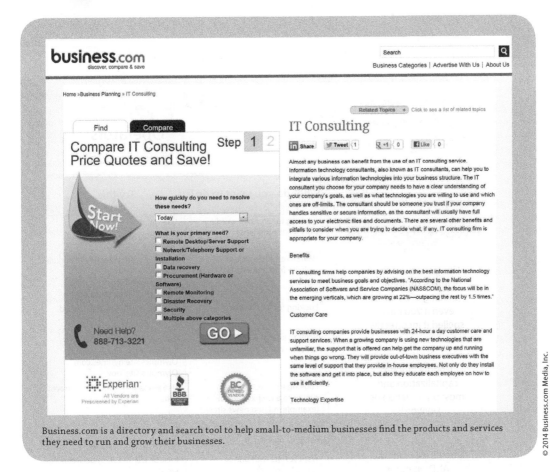

Business.com is a directory and search tool to help small-to-medium businesses find the products and services they need to run and grow their businesses.

the information might not be accurate or verifiable. In fact, Wikipedia's own disclaimer reminds readers that it cannot guarantee the validity of its information. However, this information-packed wiki site often provides its own references (bibliographies) so that you can locate the original sources of information and use them in your research.

Web Resources and Their Credibility. When searching the Web, you need to check the credibility and accuracy of the information you find. Anyone can publish on the Web, and credibility is sometimes difficult to determine. Wikis and unmoderated discussion forums are a case in point. The authorship may be unverifiable, and the credibility of the information may be questionable.

To assess the credibility of a Web page, you must scrutinize what you find and consider the following criteria:

- **Currency.** What is the date of the Web page? If the information is time sensitive and the site has not been updated recently, the site is probably not reliable.

- **Authority.** Who publishes or sponsors this Web page? Is information about the author or sponsoring organization available on the About Us page? Can the author be contacted? Be skeptical about data and assertions from individuals and organizations whose credentials are not verifiable.

- **Content.** Is the purpose of the page to entertain, inform, convince, or sell? Is the purpose readily apparent? Who is the intended audience, based on content, tone, and style? Evaluate the overall value of the content and see how it compares with other resources on this topic.

Figure **10.8** Google Search Operators

Search Smart with Google Operators

SEARCH OPERATORS
symbols or words that give you control over the results you see

How Google Looks at Keyword Searches

Google returns the most common spelling of a word, even if you have spelled it incorrectly.

Google ignores capitalization and most punctuation of keywords.

Google assumes the AND operator between all keywords, so no need to use AND or +.

What do you want to do?	Try this.
Looking for an exact word, phrase, or song lyric?	Use quotes "top-level domains" "over the rainbow"
Want to exclude a word or a website from your results?	Add a space-[hyphen] (-) to exclude that word. Jaguar speed -car Pandas -site:Wikipedia.org
Looking for a definition?	Put define in front of any word. define loquacious
Want to search within a specific website or domain?	Include site: in your query (no spaces). Olympics site:nytimes.com Olympics site:.gov
Looking for sites that are similar to a well-known URL? (example: related news sites)	Use related: in front of the known URL. related:nytimes.com
Looking for an unknown word or term? (wildcard)	Use an asterisk (*). "A * saved is a * earned"
Want results with one of several choices?	Include OR (in CAPS) between words. world cup winner 2013 OR 2014
Want to see schedules and game scores of your favorite team?	Enter your team's name. Real Madrid

- **Accuracy.** Do the facts that are presented seem reliable? Do you find errors in spelling, grammar, or usage? Do you see any evidence of bias? Are references provided? Do the external links work? Errors and missing references should alert you that the data may be questionable.

10-3b Primary Research Sources

Although you will start nearly every business report assignment by sifting through secondary sources, you will probably need primary data to add credibility and show the bigger picture. Business reports that solve specific current problems typically rely on primary, firsthand data. If, for example, management wants to discover the cause of increased employee turnover in its Seattle office, it might investigate employment trends in Seattle, prepare an employee survey about job satisfaction, and interview management for another perspective. Providing answers to business problems often means generating primary data through surveys, interviews, observation, or experimentation.

Surveys. Surveys collect data from groups of people. Before developing new products, for example, companies often survey consumers to learn about their preferences. Surveys gather data economically and efficiently from large groups of recipients. Moreover, people responding to surveys have time to consider their answers, which may improve the accuracy of the data.

Mailed or e-mailed surveys, of course, have disadvantages. Response rates may be low, and the returns may not represent an accurate sampling. Another disadvantage has to do with truthfulness. Some respondents may simply not respond accurately. In preparing print or electronic surveys, consider these suggestions:

- **Select the survey population carefully.** Many surveys question a small group of people (a *sampling*) and project the findings to a larger population. Let's say that a survey of your class reveals that the majority prefer *phờ*, the Vietnamese meat and rice noodle soup. Can you then say that all students on other campuses prefer pho? For important surveys you will want to learn sampling techniques. As for pho, in a Sodexo survey the soup ranked among the top three comfort foods favored by American college students.[5] This comment implies that the researchers had a large sampling response from many college campuses.

- **Explain why the survey is necessary.** In a brief message, describe the need for the survey. Suggest how the responses will benefit a cause. If appropriate, offer to send recipients a copy of the findings.

- **Consider incentives.** If the survey is long and time-consuming, consider offering money (such as a $1 bill), coupons, gift certificates, or other incentives to encourage a response.

- **Limit the number of questions.** Resist the temptation to ask for too much. Request only information you will use. Don't, for example, include demographic questions (income, gender, age, and so forth) unless that information serves a purpose.

- **Use questions that produce quantifiable answers.** Check-off, multiple-choice, yes/no, and scale (or rank-order) questions, illustrated in Figure 10.9, provide quantifiable results that are easily tabulated. These *close-ended questions* require participants to choose from a limited number of responses determined by the researcher. Responses to *open-ended questions* (*What should the bookstore do about plastic bags?*) reveal interesting, but difficult-to-quantify, perceptions.[6] To obtain workable data, give survey participants a list of possible responses, as shown in items 1 through 4 of Figure 10.9, a college bookstore student survey. For scale and multiple-choice questions, try to present all the possible answer choices. Add an *Other* or *Don't know* category in case the choices seem insufficient to the respondent. Many surveys use scale questions because they capture degrees of feelings. Typical scale headings are *Strongly agree, Somewhat agree, Neutral* (or *No opinion*), *Somewhat disagree*, and *Strongly disagree*.

- **Avoid leading or ambiguous questions.** The wording of a question can dramatically affect responses to it.[7] When respondents were asked, "Are we spending too much, too little, or about the right amount on *assistance to the poor?*" 13 percent responded *Too much*. When the same respondents were asked, "Are we spending too much, too little, or about the right amount on *welfare?*" 44 percent responded *Too much*. Because words have different meanings for different people, you must strive to use objective language and pilot test your questions with typical respondents. Ask neutral questions (*Do CEOs earn too much, too little, or about the right amount?*). Also, avoid queries that ask two or more things (*Should the salaries of CEOs be reduced or regulated by government legislation?*). Instead, break them into separate questions (*Should the salaries of CEOs be reduced by government legislation? Should the salaries of CEOs be regulated by government legislation?*).

Figure 10.9 College Bookstore Student Survey

Shoreline College Bookstore
STUDENT SURVEY

The Shoreline College Bookstore wants to do its part in protecting the environment. Each year we give away 45,000 plastic bags for students to carry off their purchases. We are considering changing from plastic to cloth bags or some other alternative, but we need your views.

Please place checks below to indicate your responses.

1. How many units are you presently carrying?   ___ Male
   ___ 15 or more units   ___ Female
   ___ 9 to 14 units
   ___ 8 or fewer units

2. How many times have you visited the bookstore this semester?
   ___ 0 times ___ 1 time ___ 2 times ___ 3 times ___ 4 or more times

3. Indicate your concern for the environment.
   ___ Very concerned ___ Concerned ___ Unconcerned

4. To protect the environment, would you be willing to change to another type of bag when buying books?
   ___ Yes
   ___ No

Indicate your feeling about the following alternatives.

	Agree	Undecided	Disagree
For major purchases the bookstore should			
5. Continue to provide plastic bags.	___	___	___
6. Provide no bags; encourage students to bring their own bags.	___	___	___
7. Provide no bags; offer cloth bags at reduced price (about $3).	___	___	___
8. Give a cloth bag with each major purchase, the cost to be included in registration fees.	___	___	___
9. Consider another alternative, such as_____			

_____

Please return the completed survey form to your instructor or to the survey box at the Shoreline College Bookstore exit. Your opinion counts.

Thanks for your help!

Margin annotations:

Uses groupings that do not overlap (not *9 to 15* and *15 or more*)

Allows respondent to add an answer in case choices provided seem insufficient

Explains need for survey (use cover letter for longer surveys)

Uses scale questions to channel responses into quantifiable alternatives, as opposed to open-ended questions

Tells how to return survey form

- **Make it easy for respondents to return the survey.** If surveys are mailed, researchers often provide prepaid self-addressed envelopes to encourage a higher response rate. Since most people now have Internet access, Web surveys have grown in popularity because of their low cost, convenience, and quick response rate. Web-based survey companies such as SurveyMonkey and Zoomerang help users develop simple, template-driven surveys with a feature that allows them to collect the data and see real-time results.

- **Conduct a pilot study.** When considering a pilot study, try the questionnaire with a small group so that you can make needed adjustments. For example, the survey shown in Figure 10.9 revealed that female students generally favored cloth shopping bags and were willing to pay for them. Male students opposed purchasing cloth bags. By adding a gender category, researchers could verify this finding. The pilot study also revealed the need to ensure an appropriate representation of male and female students in the survey.

Personal Interviews. Excellent report information can come from personal interviews, particularly on topics about which little has been written. Interview those both inside and outside your company when gathering information for business reports. Scheduling and conducting personal interviews requires preparation and professionalism. See Figure 10.10 for a brief review of how to schedule and conduct an interview.

Observation and Experimentation. Some data can be obtained only through firsthand observation and investigation. If your study requires observation, the data you collect must be reliable. For example, a manager may want to learn how to improve customer service by sitting on the sales floor, observing interactions, and taking notes. The data-gathering observations must occur at regular intervals over a period of time in order for the data to be considered valid and reliable. Perhaps a customer service survey and personal interviews would also be part of this data collection.

If firsthand observation involves recording the session, secure permissions beforehand. Arrive early enough to introduce yourself and set up any equipment. Sometimes drop-in visits by company leaders result in firsthand information. Starbucks chief Howard Schultz frowns on research, advertising, and customer surveys. Instead of relying on sophisticated marketing research, Schultz visits 25 Starbucks locations a week to learn about his customers.[8]

Experimentation produces data suggesting causes and effects. Informal experimentation might be as simple as providing an optional customer service training course for employees and then observing whether the newly trained employees had fewer customer complaints than the untrained employees. Scientists would call the untrained employees the control group and the trained employees the experimental group. Informal experimentation has some merit if what you are trying to prove is relevant and valid.

Figure **10.10** Gathering Information Through Personal Interviews

How to Schedule and Conduct an Interview

- **Locate an expert.** Interview knowledgeable individuals who are experts in their field.

- **Prepare for the interview.** Read all you can about the topic you will discuss so you can converse intelligently. Learn the name and background of the individual you are interviewing. Be familiar with the terminology of the topic. Let's say you are interviewing a corporate communication expert about the advantages of creating a corporate blog. You ought to be familiar with terms such as *brand management, RSS feeds, traffic,* and *damage control.*

- **Maintain a professional attitude.** Call before the interview to confirm the appointment, and arrive on time. You'll also want to be professional in your dress, language, and behavior.

- **Ask objective and open-ended questions.** Adopt a courteous, respectful attitude when asking questions. Open-ended questions encourage a variety of responses. Do not debate any issues and do not interrupt. You are there to listen, not to talk.

- **Watch the time.** Tell interviewees in advance how much time you'll need. Watch the clock and keep the interview discussion on track.

- **End graciously.** Conclude graciously with a general question, such as *Is there anything you would like to add?* Express your appreciation, and ask permission to contact the interviewee later if necessary.

LEARNING OBJECTIVE **4**

Identify the purposes and techniques of documenting and citing sources in business reports.

10-4 Documenting and Citing Sources in Business Reports

In writing business reports, you will often build on the ideas and words of others. In Western culture, whenever you "borrow" the ideas or words of others, you must give credit to your information sources. This is called *documentation*. You can learn more about common documentation (or citation) styles in Appendix C.

10-4a Documentation Guidelines

Whether you quote or paraphrase another's words, you must document the source. To use the ideas of others skillfully and ethically, you need to know why, what, and how to document.

Why Document. As a careful writer, you should take pains to document report data properly for the following reasons:

- **To strengthen your argument and add credibility.** Including good data from reputable sources will convince readers of your credibility and the logic of your reasoning.
- **To protect yourself against charges of plagiarism.** Acknowledging your sources keeps you honest. *Plagiarism*, which is not only unethical but in some cases illegal, is the act of using others' ideas without proper documentation.
- **To help the reader learn more about the topic.** Citing references enables readers to pursue a topic further and make use of the information themselves.
- **To provide proper credit in an ever-changing world.** The world of business moves so quickly that words and ideas are often borrowed—which is acceptable when you give credit to your sources.

What to Document. When you write reports, you are continually dealing with other people's ideas. You are expected to conduct research, synthesize ideas, and build on the work of others. However, you must give proper credit for borrowed material. To avoid plagiarism, give credit whenever you use the following:[9]

- Another person's ideas, opinions, examples, or theory
- Any facts, statistics, graphs, and drawings that are not common knowledge
- Quotations of another person's actual spoken or written words
- Paraphrases of another person's spoken or written words
- Visuals, images, and any kind of electronic media

Information that is common knowledge requires no documentation. For example, the statement *The Wall Street Journal is a popular business newspaper* would require no citation. Statements that are not common knowledge, however, must be documented. For example, *Texas is home to two of the nation's top ten fastest-growing cities (100,000 or more population): Austin and San Antonio.* This statement requires a citation.

How to Paraphrase. In writing reports and using the ideas of others, you will probably rely heavily on *paraphrasing*, which means restating an original passage in your own words and in your own style. To do a good job of paraphrasing, follow these steps:

1. Read the original material intently to comprehend its full meaning.
2. Write your own version without looking at the original.

3. Avoid repeating the grammatical structure of the original and merely replacing words with synonyms.

4. Reread the original to be sure you covered the main points but did not borrow specific language.

To better understand the difference between plagiarizing and paraphrasing, study the following passages. Notice that the writer of the plagiarized version uses the same grammatical construction as the source and often merely replaces words with synonyms. Even the acceptable version, however, requires a reference to the source author.

Source
We have seen, in a short amount of time, the disappearance of a large number of household brands that failed to take sufficient and early heed of the software revolution that is upending traditional brick-and-mortar businesses and creating a globally pervasive digital economy.[10]

Plagiarized version
Many trusted household name brands disappeared very swiftly because they did not sufficiently and early pay attention to the software revolution that is toppling traditional physical businesses and creating a global digital economy. (Saylor, 2012)

Acceptable paraphrase
Digital technology has allowed a whole new virtual global economy to blossom and very swiftly wiped out some formerly powerful companies that responded too late or inadequately to the disruptive force that has swept the globe. (Saylor, 2012)

When and How to Quote. On occasion, you will want to use the exact words of a source, but beware of overusing quotations. Documents that contain pages of spliced-together quotations suggest that writers have few ideas of their own. Wise writers and speakers use direct quotations for three purposes only:

- To provide objective background data and establish the severity of a problem as seen by experts
- To repeat identical phrasing because of its precision, clarity, or aptness
- To duplicate exact wording before making critical statements

When you must use a long quotation, try to summarize and introduce it in your own words. Readers want to know the gist of a quotation before they tackle it. For example, to introduce a quotation discussing the shrinking staffs of large companies, you could precede it with your words: *In predicting employment trends, Charles Waller believes the corporation of the future will depend on a small core of full-time employees.* To introduce quotations or paraphrases, use wording such as the following:

According to Waller. . . .

Waller argues that. . . .

In his recent study, Waller reported. . . .

Use quotation marks to enclose exact quotations, as shown in the following: *"The current image," says Charles Waller, "of a big glass-and-steel corporate headquarters on landscaped grounds directing a worldwide army of tens of thousands of employees may soon be a thing of the past" (2013, p. 51).*

10-4b Copyright and Fair Use

The Copyright Act of 1976 protects authors—literary, dramatic, and artistic— of published and unpublished works. The word *copyright* refers to "the right to copy," and a key provision is fair use. Under *fair use*, individuals have limited use of copyrighted material without requiring permission. These uses are for criticism, comment, news reporting, teaching, scholarship, and research. Unfortunately, the distinctions between fair use and infringement are not clearly defined.

Four-Factor Test to Assess Fair Use. What is fair use? Actually, it is a shadowy territory with vague and often disputed boundaries—now even more so with the addition of cyberspace. Courts use four factors as a test in deciding disputes over fair use:

- **Purpose and character of the use, particularly whether for profit.** Courts are more likely to allow fair use for nonprofit educational purposes than for commercial ventures.
- **Nature of the copyrighted work.** When information is necessary for the public good—such as medical news—courts are more likely to support fair use.
- **Amount and substantiality of the portion used.** Copying a 200-word passage from a 200,000-word book might be allowed but not 200 words from a 1,000-word article or a substantial part of a shorter work. A total of 300 words is mistakenly thought by many to be an acceptable limit for fair use, but courts have not upheld this figure.
- **Effect of the use on the potential market.** If use of the work may interfere with the author's potential profit from the original, fair use copying would not be allowed.

How to Avoid Copyright Infringement. Whenever you borrow words, charts, graphs, photos, music, and other media—in short, any *intellectual property*—be sure you know what is legal and acceptable. The following guidelines will help:

- **Assume that all intellectual property is copyrighted.** Nearly everything created privately and originally after 1989 is copyrighted and protected whether or not it has a copyright notice.
- **Realize that Internet items and resources are NOT in the public domain.** No contemporary intellectual or artistic creation is in the public domain (free to be used by anyone) unless the owner explicitly says so.
- **Observe fair-use restrictions.** Be aware of the four-factor test. Avoid appropriating large amounts of outside material.
- **Ask for permission.** You are always safe if you obtain permission. Write to the source, identify the material you wish to include, and explain where it will be used. Expect to pay for permission.
- **Don't assume that a footnote is all that is needed.** Including a footnote to a source prevents plagiarism but not copyright infringement. Anything copied beyond the boundaries of fair use requires permission.

10-4c Common Citation Formats

You can direct readers to your sources with parenthetical notes inserted into the text and with bibliographies. Figure 10.11 shows the most common citation formats presented by the Modern Language Association (MLA), the American Psychological Association (APA), and the Chicago Manual of Style (CMS). Learn more about using MLA and APA formats in Appendix C.

10-5 Incorporating Meaningful Visual Aids and Graphics

After collecting and interpreting information, you need to consider how best to present it. If your report contains complex data, you will want to display the information graphically in tables, charts, graphs, or even infographics. Graphics clarify

Figure **10.11** Comparing Bibliographic Citation Formats: MLA, APA, CMS

Figure 10.11 Comparing Bibliographic Citation Formats: MLA, APA, CMS

Modern Language Association (MLA) Works Cited

Saylor, M. The Mobile Wave: How Mobile Intelligence Will Change Everything. New York: Vanguard Press, 2012. Print.

Pazos, Pilar, Jennifer M. Chung, and Marina Micari. "Instant Messaging as a Task-Support Tool in Information Technology Organizations." *Journal of Business Communication* 50.1 (2013): 68–86. Print. doi:10.1177/0021943612465181

American Psychological Association (APA) References

Saylor, M. (2012). *The mobile wave: How mobile intelligence will change everything.* New York: Vanguard Press, p. ix.

Pazos, P., Chung J. M., & Micari, M. (2013, January). Instant messaging as a task-support tool in information technology organizations. *Journal of Business Communication, 50*(1), 68–86. doi:10.1177/0021943612465181

Chicago Manual of Style (CMS) Bibliography

Saylor, M. *The Mobile Wave: How Mobile Intelligence Will Change Everything.* New York: Vanguard Press, 2012.

Pazos, Pilar, Jennifer M. Chung, and Marina Micari. 2013. Instant Messaging as a Task-Support Tool in Information Technology Organizations. *Journal of Business Communication* 50:68–86. doi:10.1177/0021943612465181

data, add visual interest, and make complex data easy to understand. When incorporating graphics into your report, think about what type of graphic will display the information most effectively.

10-5a Matching Graphics and Objectives

When selecting a graphic, consider your objective. If your objective is to show changes over time, you may choose a line chart to display your data. Report writers select graphics (e.g., tables, bar charts, pie charts, or pictures) that will convey their information most effectively. Figure 10.12 summarizes appropriate uses for each type of graphic.

10-5b Using Tables, Charts, and Infographics

Why are graphics important? Report writers know that readers grasp meaning from visuals more quickly than they do from text. Therefore, they prefer to use tables and various types of charts and infographics to show data, relationships,

Figure **10.12** Matching Graphics to Objectives

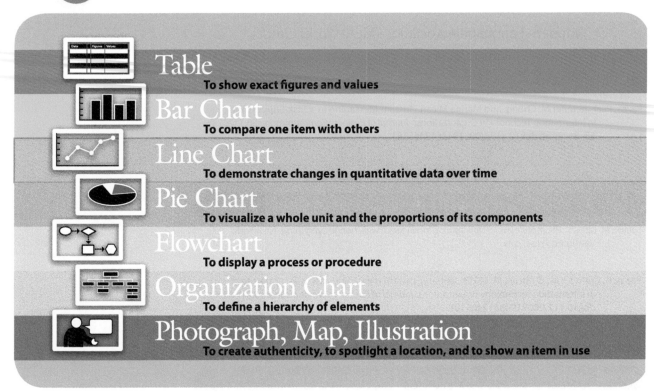

Table
To show exact figures and values

Bar Chart
To compare one item with others

Line Chart
To demonstrate changes in quantitative data over time

Pie Chart
To visualize a whole unit and the proportions of its components

Flowchart
To display a process or procedure

Organization Chart
To define a hierarchy of elements

Photograph, Map, Illustration
To create authenticity, to spotlight a location, and to show an item in use

trends, and comparisons. Adding photographs, maps, illustrations, and diagrams also heightens visual interest and adds clarity to report information.

Tables. One of the most frequently used report graphics is the table. Because a *table* presents quantitative or verbal information in systematic columns and rows, it can clarify large quantities of data in small spaces. Here are tips for creating good tables, an example of which is shown in Figure 10.13.

- Add a meaningful title at the top of the table.
- Arrange items in a logical order (alphabetical, chronological, highest to lowest), depending on what you need to emphasize.
- Provide bold headings for rows and columns.
- Identify the units in which figures are given (percentages, dollars, hours) in the table title, in the column or row heading, in the first item of a column, or in a note at the bottom.
- Use *N/A* (*not available*) for missing data rather than leaving a cell empty.
- Make long tables easier to read by shading alternate lines or by leaving a blank line between groups of five.
- Place tables as close as possible to the place where they are mentioned in the text.

The table in Figure 10.13 presents data about the MPM Entertainment Company over several years, making it easy to compare several divisions over time. Notice that the year 2015 shows a projected income based on revenue growth during the years 2011 through 2014.

Bar Charts. *Bar charts* make visual comparisons by using horizontal or vertical bars of varying lengths. Bar charts are useful for comparing related items, illustrating

Figure **10.13** Table Summarizing Precise Data

			DVDs &	
Figure 1 MPM ENTERTAINMENT COMPANY Income by Division (in millions of dollars)				
	Theme Parks	**Motion Pictures**	**Blu-ray Discs**	**Total**
2012	$15.8	$39.3	$11.2	$66.3
2013	18.1	17.5	15.3	50.9
2014	23.8	21.1	22.7	67.6
2015	32.2	22.0	24.3	78.5
2016 (projected)	35.1	21.0	26.1	82.2

Source: *Industry Profiles* (New York: DataPro, 2015) 225

changes in data over time, and showing segments as a part of a whole. Figures 10.16 and 10.17 need legends to explain the colors used in the chart. Note how the bar charts in Figures 10.14 to 10.17 display information in different ways.

Many techniques for constructing tables also hold true for bar charts. Here are a few additional tips:

- Keep the length and width of each bar and segment proportional.
- Include a total figure on the bar if it adds clarity for the reader and does not clutter the chart.
- Always start dollar or percentage amounts at zero.

Line Charts. Line charts show changes over time, thus indicating trends. The vertical axis is typically the dependent variable; the horizontal axis is the independent variable. Simple line charts (Figure 10.18) show just one variable. Multiple line charts (Figure 10.19) compare two or more data sets and require a legend to explain them. Here are some reminders when preparing line charts:

- Begin with a rectangular grid showing a vertical and horizontal axis.
- Place the time component (usually years) horizontally across the bottom.
- Label the vertical and horizontal axes (if needed) for clarification.

Segmented Area (Surface) Charts. Segmented area, or surface, charts (Figure 10.20) illustrate how the components of a whole change over time. If you want to stack the revenue increments for each division as shown in Figure 10.20, the top line indicates the total of the three division revenues. Area charts require a legend for clarity.

Pie Charts. Pie charts, or circle graphs, enable readers to see how the components, or wedges, relate to the whole. Pie charts are useful for showing percentages, as Figure 10.21 illustrates. For the most effective pie charts, follow these suggestions:

- Place the largest wedge near the top of the circle and arrange the others in descending order.
- Include the actual percentage for each wedge.
- Use four to six segments for best results; smaller wedges can be grouped in a segment labeled *Other*.

Flowcharts. Procedures are simplified and clarified in a flowchart, as shown in Figure 10.22. Whether you need to describe the procedure for handling a customer's purchase, highlight steps in solving a problem, or display a problem with a process,

Figure **10.14** Vertical Bar Chart

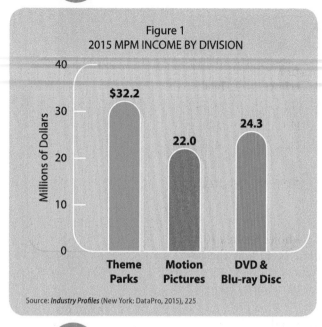

Figure 1
2015 MPM INCOME BY DIVISION

Source: *Industry Profiles* (New York: DataPro, 2015), 225

Figure **10.15** Horizontal Bar Chart

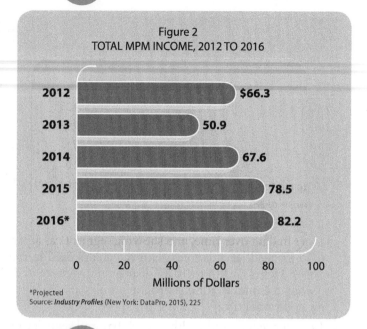

Figure 2
TOTAL MPM INCOME, 2012 TO 2016

*Projected
Source: *Industry Profiles* (New York: DataPro, 2015), 225

Figure **10.16** Grouped Bar Chart

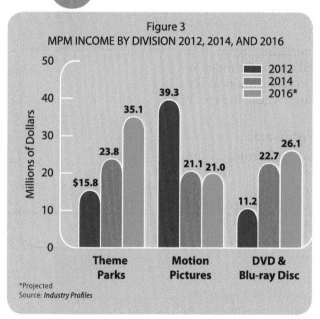

Figure 3
MPM INCOME BY DIVISION 2012, 2014, AND 2016

*Projected
Source: *Industry Profiles*

Figure **10.17** Segmented 100 Percent Bar Chart

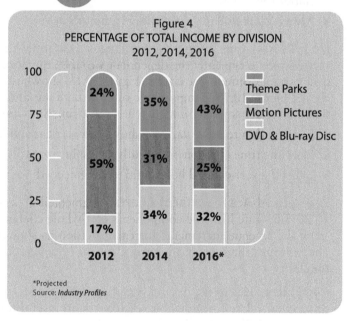

Figure 4
PERCENTAGE OF TOTAL INCOME BY DIVISION
2012, 2014, 2016

*Projected
Source: *Industry Profiles*

flowcharts help the reader visualize the process. Traditional flowcharts use the following symbols:

- Ovals to designate the beginning and end of a process
- Diamonds to designate decision points
- Rectangles to represent major activities or steps

Infographics. An *infographic* is a visual representation of complex information in a format that is easy to understand. Compelling infographics tell a story by combining images and graphic elements, such as charts and diagrams. Because these data visualizations tend to be long, they are commonly shared in online environments.

Figure **10.18** Simple Line Chart

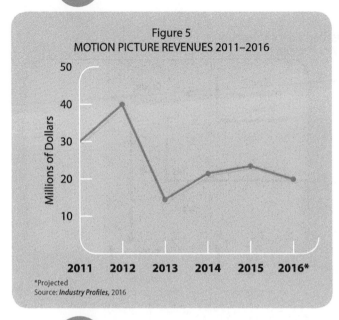

Figure 5
MOTION PICTURE REVENUES 2011–2016

*Projected
Source: *Industry Profiles*, 2016

Figure **10.19** Multiple Line Chart

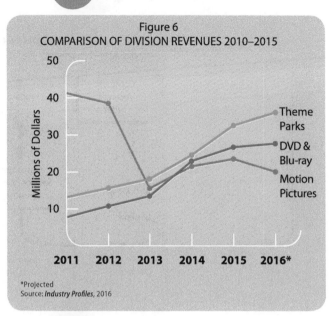

Figure 6
COMPARISON OF DIVISION REVENUES 2010–2015

*Projected
Source: *Industry Profiles*, 2016

Figure **10.20** Segmented Area (Surface) Chart

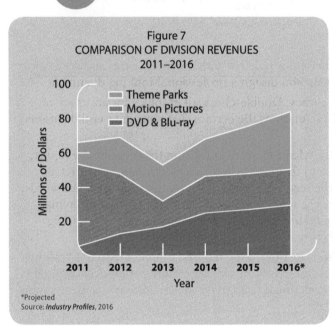

Figure 7
COMPARISON OF DIVISION REVENUES
2011–2016

*Projected
Source: *Industry Profiles*, 2016

Figure **10.21** Pie Chart

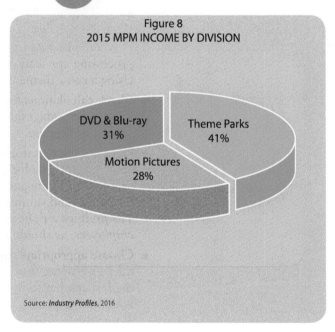

Figure 8
2015 MPM INCOME BY DIVISION

Source: *Industry Profiles*, 2016

10-5c Incorporating Graphics in Reports

Used appropriately, graphics make reports more interesting and easier to understand. When inserting graphics into your reports, follow these suggestions:

- **Consider the audience.** Will your graphics help the reader understand and retain the information? How many graphics are necessary? Longer technical reports may use more graphics than shorter informal reports do.

- **Use color wisely.** Colors used in graphics add visual appeal to a report. Warm colors such as yellow, orange, and red tend to advance on the page. In contrast, cool colors such as green, blue, and purple tend to recede. Most word

Figure **10.22** Flowchart

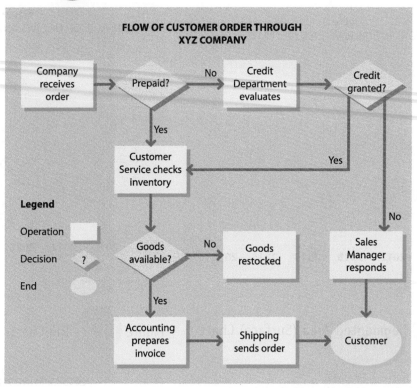

FLOW OF CUSTOMER ORDER THROUGH XYZ COMPANY

processing applications offer color palettes with a mix of warm and cool colors. Using a color theme will help you design a professional-looking document.

- **Check calculations for accuracy.** Double-check all graphics for accuracy of figures, percentages, and calculations. Be certain that your data visualizations are not misleading.

- **Place graphics strategically.** Mention every graphic in the text of your report, and place the graphic close to the point where it is mentioned. When referring to the graphic, help the reader understand its significance. In other words, be specific and summarize the main point of the graphic. Instead of saying, *The findings are shown in Figure 3*, say this: *Two thirds of the responding employees, as shown in Figure 3, favor a flextime schedule.*

- **Choose appropriate captions or titles.** Like reports, graphics may use "talking" titles or generic, functional titles. Talking titles are more persuasive; they tell the reader what to think. Functional titles make general references using nouns without interpreting the data.

Talking Title	Functional Title
Rising Workplace Drug Testing Unfair and Inaccurate	Workplace Drug Testing
College Students' Diets Clogged With Fat	College Students and Nutrition

Amateur designers can create captivating infographics using free online tools at sites such as Infogr.am, Piktochart, and Visual.ly. A few innovative companies have even turned reports and executive summaries into infographics. Another popular application of infographics is designing visual résumés, as shown in Figure 10.23.

Figure **10.23** Infographic Résumé

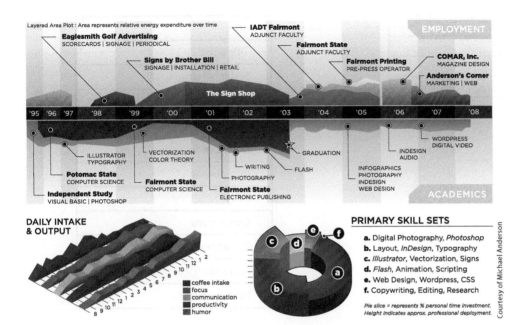

Michael Anderson
RÉSUMÉ / INFOGRAPHICS

theportfolio.ofmichaelanderson.com
lunyboy@yahoo.com | 304-382-5145
HC 63 BOX 2340 | ROMNEY, WV 26757

10-6 Understanding Report Components

LEARNING OBJECTIVE **6**
Describe the components of typical formal reports.

Because formal business reports can be long and complex, they usually include more sections than routine informal business reports do. Figure 10.24 shows the components of informal and formal business reports. These components are standard and conventional; that is, the audience expects to see them in a professional report. You will find most of the components addressed here in Figure 10.25, a formal analytical report studying the economic impact of an industrial park on Flagstaff, Arizona.

10-6a Front Matter Components

The front matter of a formal report refers to the preliminary sections before the body section. Some front matter components are optional, but they typically appear in the following order: (a) report cover (optional), (b) title page, (c) letter or memo of transmittal (optional), (d) table of contents, (e) list of figures or tables (optional), and (f) executive summary. Writers often number these sections with lowercase Roman numerals; the title page, however, is normally not numbered. These components make it easy for the reader to find specific information quickly.

Title Page. The format of title pages may vary, but title pages often include the same elements. The report title page shown in Figure 10.25 follows MLA style and includes the following elements:

- Name of the report, often in uppercase letters (no underscore and no quotation marks)

- *Prepared for* (or *Submitted to*) followed by the name, title, and organization of the individual receiving the report

Figure **10.24** Components of Informal and Formal Reports

Informal Business Reports

| Introduction |
| Body |
| Conclusions |
| Recommendations (if requested) |

Formal Business Reports

| Cover |
| Title page |
| Letter of transmittal |
| Table of contents |
| List of figures |
| Executive summary |
| Introduction |
| Body |
| Conclusions |
| Recommendations (if requested) |
| Appendix |
| References |

- *Prepared by* (or *Submitted by*) followed by the author's name and title
- Date of submission

Letter or Memo of Transmittal. Generally written on organization stationery, a letter or memorandum of transmittal may introduce a formal report. A transmittal letter or memo uses the direct strategy and is usually less formal than the report itself. The transmittal document typically (a) announces the topic of the report and tells how it was authorized; (b) briefly describes the project; (c) highlights the report's findings, conclusions, and recommendations; and (d) closes with appreciation for the assignment or instruction for follow-up actions. If a report is going to various readers, you would prepare a special transmittal letter or memo for each reader.

Table of Contents. The table of contents shows the main sections in the report and their page numbers. The proper title is *Contents* or *Table of Contents*. The table of contents includes front matter items, the body section's main headings and subheadings, and back matter sections, such as the appendix. Major headings are left-aligned, and leaders (spaced dots) help guide the eye to the page numbers.

List of Figures. For reports with many figures or tables, you may wish to list the figures to help readers locate them easily. This list may appear on the same page as the table of contents, space permitting. For each figure or table, include a title and page number. Some writers prepare separate lists for tables and figures. Because the model report in Figure 10.25 has few illustrations, the writer labeled them all *figures*.

Executive Summary. The purpose of an executive summary is to present an overview of the longer report for people who may not have time to read the entire document. Generally, an executive summary is prepared by the author of the report. However, you might be asked to write an executive summary of a published report or article written by someone else. In either case, the writer's goal is to summarize the report's major sections, such as the purpose, background, conclusions, and recommendations. Readers often go straight to the executive summary and look for the recommendations before glancing at the full report.

The one-page executive summary in Figure 10.25 includes headings that help direct the reader to the main sections. The format and headings of an executive summary may vary according to the organization's preferences.

10-6b Body Components

Body components of formal reports typically include the introduction and body sections. In the introduction, the writer briefly describes the report's contents. In the body, the longest and most substantive section, the writer discusses the problem and findings, before presenting conclusions and recommendations. Extensive and bulky materials that don't fit in the body belong in the appendix.

Introduction. Formal reports begin with an introduction to announce the topic and to set the stage for the reader. A good report introduction typically covers the following elements, although not necessarily in this order:

- **Background:** Events leading up to the problem or need
- **Problem or purpose:** Explanation of the problem or need that motivated the report
- **Significance:** Account of the importance of the report topic, which may include quotes from experts, journals, or Web resources
- **Scope:** Boundaries of the report, defining what will be included or excluded
- **Organization:** A road map or structure of the report

Workplace in Focus

While casino gaming is harmless fun for most people, a 95-page report published by British Columbia's public health chief found that gaming is a serious problem for an increasing number of Canadians. According to the report, the number of British Columbians with a severe gambling habit rose from 13,000 to 31,000 over a five-year period, presenting a grave public health risk. To help regulators address the crisis, the report offered 17 recommendations, such as raising the gambling age, eliminating high-risk electronic gaming machines, and reducing the number of ATMs in casinos. Where can readers expect to find such important recommendations in lengthy formal reports? [10]

Jack Sullivan/Alamy

Beyond these minimal introductory elements, consider adding any of the following information that may be relevant to your readers:

- **Authorization:** The name of whoever commissioned the report and its intended audience
- **Literature review:** A summary of other publications on this topic
- **Sources and methods:** A description of secondary sources (periodicals, books, databases) and methods of collecting primary data
- **Key terms:** Definitions of important and unfamiliar terms used in the report

Report Body. The body is the principal section in a formal report. It discusses, analyzes, interprets, and evaluates the research findings or solution to the initial problem. This is where you show the evidence that justifies your conclusions. Organize the body into main categories following your original outline.

The body section contains clear headings that explain each major section. Headings may be functional or talking. Functional heads (such as *Results of the Survey, Analysis of Findings*, or *Discussion*) help readers identify the general purpose of the section. Such headings are useful for routine reports or for sensitive topics that may upset readers. Talking heads (for example, *Findings Reveal Revenue and Employment Benefits*) are more descriptive and informative.

Conclusions and Recommendations. Writers know that the conclusions and recommendations section is most important to a reader. This section tells what the findings mean, particularly in terms of solving the original problem. Some writers prefer to intermix their conclusions with the analysis of the findings. Other writers place the conclusions before the body so that busy readers can examine them immediately. Still other writers combine the conclusions and recommendations. Most writers, though, present the conclusions after the body because readers expect this sequence. To improve readability, you may present the conclusions in a numbered or bulleted list.

10-6c Back Matter Components

The back matter of most reports includes a reference section and one or more appendixes. The reference section includes a bibliography of sources, and the appendix contains supplemental information or source documents. In organizing the back matter sections, use standard Arabic numerals to number the pages.

Works Cited, References, or Bibliography. If you use the MLA (Modern Language Association) referencing format, list all sources of information alphabetically in a section titled *Works Cited*. If you use the APA (American Psychological Association) format, list your sources in a section called *References*. Your listed sources must correspond to in-text citations in the report whenever you are borrowing words or ideas from published and unpublished resources.

10-6d Model Formal Report With MLA Format Plus Alternate APA Reference List

Formal reports in business generally aim to study problems and recommend solutions. In the formal report shown in Figure 10.25, Martha Montoya, senior research consultant with Sedona Development Company, examined the economic impact of a local industrial park on the city of Flagstaff, Arizona, resulting in this formal report.

Martha's report illustrates many of the points discussed in this chapter. Although it is a good example of the typical report format and style, it should not be viewed as the only way to present a report. This model report illustrates MLA in-text citations and references ("Works Cited"). The model also shows the report references in APA format ("References") so that you can compare the citation styles.

Figure **10.25** Model Formal Report With MLA Citation Format and Alternate APA Reference List

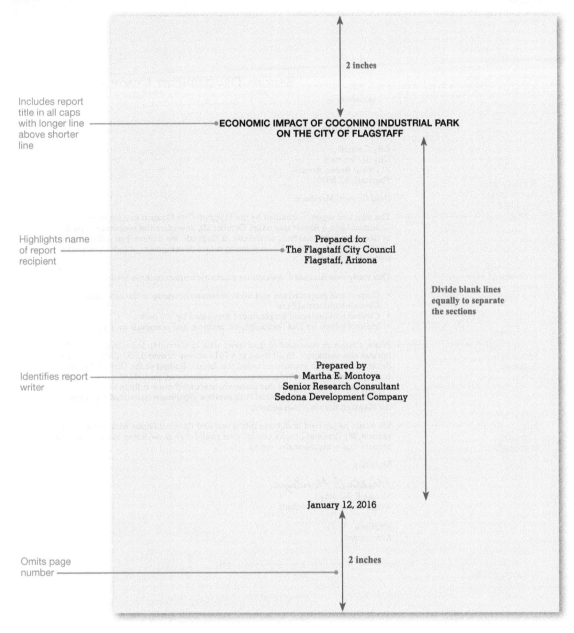

Includes report title in all caps with longer line above shorter line

2 inches

ECONOMIC IMPACT OF COCONINO INDUSTRIAL PARK ON THE CITY OF FLAGSTAFF

Highlights name of report recipient

Prepared for
The Flagstaff City Council
Flagstaff, Arizona

Divide blank lines equally to separate the sections

Identifies report writer

Prepared by
Martha E. Montoya
Senior Research Consultant
Sedona Development Company

January 12, 2016

Omits page number

2 inches

The title page is usually arranged in four evenly balanced areas. If the report is to be bound on the left, move the left margin and center point 0.25 inch to the right. Notice that no page number appears on the title page, although it is counted as page i. In designing the title page, be careful to avoid anything unprofessional—such as too many type fonts, italics, oversized print, and inappropriate graphics. Keep the title page simple and professional. This model report uses MLA documentation style. However, it does not illustrate double-spacing, the recommended format for research papers using MLA style. Instead, this model uses single-spacing, which saves space and is more appropriate for business reports.

Figure 10.25 (Continued) Letter of Transmittal

SEDONA DEVELOPMENT COMPANY
426 Saddle Rock Circle
Sedona, Arizona 86340
www.sedonadevco.com
928.450.3348

January 12, 2016

City Council
City of Flagstaff
211 West Aspen Avenue
Flagstaff, AZ 86001

Dear Council Members:

Announces report and identifies authorization

The attached report, requested by the Flagstaff City Council in a letter to Goldman-Lyon & Associates dated October 20, describes the economic impact of Coconino Industrial Park on the city of Flagstaff. We believe you will find the results of this study useful in evaluating future development of industrial parks within the city limits.

Gives broad overview of report purposes

This study was designed to examine economic impact in three areas:

• Current and projected tax and other revenues accruing to the city from Coconino Industrial Park
• Current and projected employment generated by the park
• Indirect effects on local employment, income, and economic growth

Describes primary and secondary research

Primary research consisted of interviews with 15 Coconino Industrial Park (CIP) tenants and managers, in addition to a 2014 survey of over 5,000 CIP employees. Secondary research sources included the Annual Budget of the City of Flagstaff, county and state tax records, government publications, periodicals, books, and online resources. Results of this research, discussed more fully in this report, indicate that Coconino Industrial Park exerts a significant beneficial influence on the Flagstaff metropolitan economy.

Offers to discuss report; expresses appreciation

We would be pleased to discuss this report and its conclusions with you at your request. My firm and I thank you for your confidence in selecting our company to prepare this comprehensive report.

Sincerely,

Martha E. Montoya

Martha E. Montoya
Senior Research Consultant

MEM:coe
Attachment

Uses Roman numerals for prefatory pages ——————————————— ii

A letter or memo of transmittal announces the report topic and explains who authorized it. It briefly describes the project and previews the conclusions, if the reader is supportive. Such messages generally close by expressing appreciation for the assignment, suggesting follow-up actions, acknowledging the help of others, or offering to answer questions. The margins for the transmittal should be the same as for the report, about 1 to 1.25 inches for side margins. The dateline is placed 2 inches from the top, and the margins should be left-justified. A page number is optional.

Figure **10.25** (Continued) Table of Contents and List of Figures

TABLE OF CONTENTS

LIST OF FIGURES

iii

Because the table of contents and the list of figures for this report are small, they are combined on one page. Notice that the titles of major report parts are in all caps, while other headings are a combination of upper- and lowercase letters. This duplicates the style within the report. Advanced word processing capabilities enable you to generate a contents page automatically, including leaders and accurate page numbering—no matter how many times you revise. Notice that the page numbers are right-justified.

Figure **10.25** (Continued) Executive Summary

EXECUTIVE SUMMARY

Opens directly with major research findings

The city of Flagstaff can benefit from the development of industrial parks like the Coconino Industrial Park. Both direct and indirect economic benefits result, as shown by this in-depth study conducted by Sedona Development Company. The study was authorized by the Flagstaff City Council when Goldman-Lyon & Associates sought the City Council's approval for the proposed construction of a G-L industrial park. The City Council requested evidence demonstrating that an existing development could actually benefit the city.

Identifies data sources

Our conclusion that the city of Flagstaff benefits from industrial parks is based on data supplied by a survey of 5,000 Coconino Industrial Park employees, personal interviews with managers and tenants of CIP, city and state documents, and professional literature.

Summarizes organization of report

Analysis of the data revealed benefits in three areas:

- **Revenues.** The city of Flagstaff earned over $3 million in tax and other revenues from the Coconino Industrial Park in 2014. By 2020 this income is expected to reach $5.4 million (in constant 2014 dollars).

- **Employment.** In 2014, CIP businesses employed a total of 7,035 workers, who earned an average wage of $56,579. By 2020, CIP businesses are expected to employ directly nearly 15,000 employees who will earn salaries totaling over $998 million.

- **Indirect benefits.** Because of the multiplier effect, by 2020 Coconino Industrial Park will directly and indirectly generate a total of 38,362 jobs in the Flagstaff metropolitan area.

Condenses recommendations

On the basis of these findings, it is recommended that development of additional industrial parks be encouraged to stimulate local economic growth. The city would increase its tax revenues significantly, create much-needed jobs, and thus help stimulate the local economy in and around Flagstaff.

iv

For readers who want a quick overview of the report, the executive summary presents its most important elements. Executive summaries focus on the information the reader requires for making a decision related to the issues discussed in the report. The summary may include some or all of the following elements: purpose, scope, research methods, findings, conclusions, and recommendations. Its length depends on the report it summarizes. A 100-page report might require a 10-page summary. Shorter reports may contain 1-page summaries, as shown here. Unlike letters of transmittal (which may contain personal pronouns and references to the writer), the executive summary of a long report is formal and impersonal. It uses the same margins as the body of the report. See Chapter 9 for additional discussion of executive summaries.

Figure 10.25 (Continued) Page 1

Uses a bulleted list for clarity and ease of reading

Lists three problem questions

Describes authorization for report and background of study

Includes APA citation with author name and date

INTRODUCTION: COCONINO AND THE LOCAL ECONOMY

This study was designed to analyze the direct and indirect economic impact of Coconino Industrial Park on the city of Flagstaff. Specifically, the study seeks answers to these questions:

- What current tax and other revenues result directly from this park? What tax and other revenues may be expected in the future?

- How many and what kinds of jobs are directly attributable to the park? What is the employment picture for the future?

- What indirect effects has Coconino Industrial Park had on local employment, incomes, and economic growth?

BACKGROUND: THE ROLE OF CIP IN COMMERCIAL DEVELOPMENT

The development firm of Goldman-Lyon & Associates commissioned this study of Coconino Industrial Park at the request of the Flagstaff City Council. Before authorizing the development of a proposed Goldman-Lyon industrial park, the city council requested a study examining the economic effects of an existing park. Members of the city council wanted to determine to what extent industrial parks benefit the local community, and they chose Coconino Industrial Park as an example.

For those who are unfamiliar with it, Coconino Industrial Park is a 400-acre industrial park located in the city of Flagstaff about 4 miles from the center of the city. Most of the land lies within a specially designated area known as Redevelopment Project No. 2, which is under the jurisdiction of the Flagstaff Redevelopment Agency. Planning for the park began in 1999; construction started in 2001.

The original goal for Coconino Industrial Park was development for light industrial users. Land in this area was zoned for uses such as warehousing, research and development, and distribution. Like other communities, Flagstaff was eager to attract light industrial users because such businesses tend to employ a highly educated workforce, are relatively quiet, and do not pollute the environment (Cohen C1). The city of Flagstaff recognized the need for light industrial users and widened an adjacent highway to accommodate trucks and facilitate travel by workers and customers coming from Flagstaff.

1

The first page of a formal report generally contains the title printed 2 inches from the top edge. Headings for major parts of a report are centered in all caps. In this model document we show functional heads, such as *PROBLEM, BACKGROUND, FINDINGS,* and *CONCLUSIONS.* However, most business reports would use talking heads or a combination such as *FINDINGS REVEAL REVENUE AND EMPLOYMENT BENEFITS.* First-level headings (such as *Revenues* on page 2) are printed with bold upper- and lowercase letters. Second-level headings (such as *Distribution* on page 3) begin at the side, are bolded, and are written in upper- and lowercase letters. See Figure 9.6 for an illustration of heading formats. This business report is shown with single-spacing, although some research reports might be double-spaced. Always check with your organization to learn its preferred style.

Figure **10.25** (Continued) Page 2

The park now contains 14 building complexes with over 1.25 million square feet of completed building space. The majority of the buildings are used for office, research and development, marketing and distribution, or manufacturing uses. Approximately 50 acres of the original area are yet to be developed.

Provides specifics for data sources ●——— Data for this report came from a 2014 survey of over 5,000 Coconino Industrial Park employees; interviews with 15 CIP tenants and managers; the annual budget of the city of Flagstaff; county and state tax records; and current books, articles, journals, and online resources. Projections for future revenues resulted from analysis of past trends and "Estimates of Revenues for Debt Service Coverage, Redevelopment Project Area 2" (Miller 79).

Uses combination heads ●——— **DISCUSSION: REVENUES, EMPLOYMENT, AND INDIRECT BENEFITS**

Previews organization of report ●——— The results of this research indicate that major direct and indirect benefits have accrued to the city of Flagstaff and surrounding metropolitan areas as a result of the development of Coconino Industrial Park. The research findings presented here fall into three categories: (a) revenues, (b) employment, and (c) indirect benefits.

Revenues

Coconino Industrial Park contributes a variety of tax and other revenues to the city of Flagstaff, as summarized in Figure 1. Current revenues are shown, along with projections to the year 2020. At a time when the economy is unstable, revenues from an industrial park such as Coconino can become a reliable income stream for the city of Flagstaff.

Places figure close to textual reference ●——— Figure 1

REVENUES RECEIVED BY THE CITY OF FLAGSTAFF
FROM COCONINO INDUSTRIAL PARK

Current Revenues and Projections to 2020

	2014	2020
Sales and use taxes	$1,966,021	$3,604,500
Revenues from licenses	532,802	962,410
Franchise taxes	195,682	220,424
State gas tax receipts	159,420	211,134
Licenses and permits	86,213	201,413
Other revenues	75,180	206,020
Total	$3,015,318	$5,405,901

Source: Arizona State Board of Equalization Bulletin. Phoenix: State Printing Office, 2014, p. 28.

2

Notice that this formal report is single-spaced. Many businesses prefer this space-saving format. However, some organizations prefer double-spacing, especially for preliminary drafts. If you single-space, don't indent paragraphs. If you double-space, do indent the paragraphs. Page numbers may be centered 1 inch from the bottom of the page or placed 1 inch from the upper right corner at the margin. Your word processor can insert page numbers automatically. Strive to leave a minimum of 1 inch for top, bottom, and side margins. References follow the parenthetical citation style (or in-text citation style) of the Modern Language Association (MLA). Notice that the author's name and a page reference are shown in parentheses. The complete bibliographic entry for any in-text citation appears at the end of the report in the works-cited section.

Figure 10.25 (Continued) Page 3

Continues
interpreting
figures in table

Sales and Use Revenues

As shown in Figure 1, the city's largest source of revenues from CIP is the sales and use tax. Revenues from this source totaled $1,966,021 in 2014, according to figures provided by the Arizona State Board of Equalization (28). Sales and use taxes accounted for more than half of the park's total contribution to the total income of $3,015,318.

Other Revenues

Other major sources of city revenues from CIP in 2014 include alcohol licenses, motor vehicle in lieu fees, trailer coach licenses ($532,802), franchise taxes ($195,682), and state gas tax receipts ($159,420). Although not shown in Figure 1, other revenues may be expected from the development of recently acquired property. The U.S. Economic Development Administration has approved a grant worth $975,000 to assist in expanding the current park eastward on an undeveloped parcel purchased last year. Revenues from leasing this property may be sizable.

Projections

Total city revenues from CIP will nearly double by 2020, producing an income of $5.4 million. This estimate is based on an annual growth rate of 0.65 percent, as projected by the Bureau of Labor Statistics.

Employment

Sets stage for
next topic to be
discussed

One of the most important factors to consider in the overall effect of an industrial park is employment. In Coconino Industrial Park the distribution, number, and wages of people employed will change considerably in the next six years.

Distribution

A total of 7,035 employees currently work in various industry groups at Coconino Industrial Park. The distribution of employees is shown in Figure 2. The largest number of workers (58 percent) is employed in manufacturing and assembly operations. The next largest category, computer and electronics, employs 24 percent of the workers. Some overlap probably exists because electronics assembly could be included in either group. Employees also work in publishing (9 percent), warehousing and storage (5 percent), and other industries (4 percent).

Although the distribution of employees at Coconino Industrial Park shows a wide range of employment categories, it must be noted that other industrial parks would likely generate an entirely different range of job categories.

3

Only the most important research findings are interpreted and discussed for readers. The depth of discussion depends on the intended length of the report, the goal of the writer, and the expectations of the reader. Because the writer wants this report to be formal in tone, she avoids *I* and *we* in all discussions.

As you type a report, avoid widows and orphans (ending a page with the first line of a paragraph or carrying a single line of a paragraph to a new page). Strive to start and end pages with at least two lines of a paragraph, even if a slightly larger bottom margin results.

Figure **10.25** (Continued) Page 4

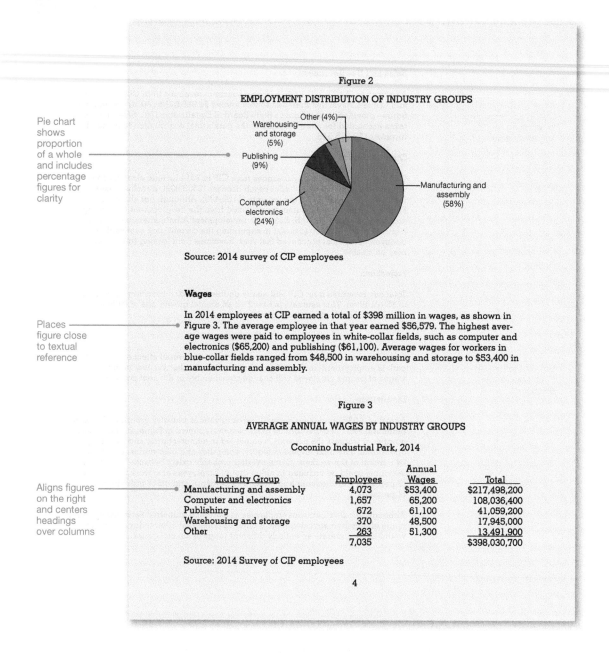

Pie chart shows proportion of a whole and includes percentage figures for clarity

Figure 2

EMPLOYMENT DISTRIBUTION OF INDUSTRY GROUPS

Other (4%)

Warehousing and storage (5%)

Publishing (9%)

Computer and electronics (24%)

Manufacturing and assembly (58%)

Source: 2014 survey of CIP employees

Wages

Places figure close to textual reference

In 2014 employees at CIP earned a total of $398 million in wages, as shown in Figure 3. The average employee in that year earned $56,579. The highest average wages were paid to employees in white-collar fields, such as computer and electronics ($65,200) and publishing ($61,100). Average wages for workers in blue-collar fields ranged from $48,500 in warehousing and storage to $53,400 in manufacturing and assembly.

Figure 3

AVERAGE ANNUAL WAGES BY INDUSTRY GROUPS

Coconino Industrial Park, 2014

Aligns figures on the right and centers headings over columns

Industry Group	Employees	Annual Wages	Total
Manufacturing and assembly	4,073	$53,400	$217,498,200
Computer and electronics	1,657	65,200	108,036,400
Publishing	672	61,100	41,059,200
Warehousing and storage	370	48,500	17,945,000
Other	263	51,300	13,491,900
	7,035		$398,030,700

Source: 2014 Survey of CIP employees

4

If you use figures or tables, be sure to introduce them in the text (for example, *as shown in Figure 3*). Although it isn't always possible, try to place them close to the spot where they are first mentioned. To save space, you can print the title of a figure at its side. Because this report contains few tables and figures, the writer named them all "Figures" and numbered them consecutively.

Figure **10.25** (Continued) Page 5

Clarifies
information
and tells what
it means in
relation to
original
research
questions

Projections

By 2020 Coconino Industrial Park is expected to more than double its number of employees, bringing the total to over 15,000 workers. The total payroll in 2020 will also more than double, producing over $998 million (using constant 2014 dollars) in salaries to CIP employees. These projections are based on a 9 percent growth rate (Miller 78), along with anticipated increased employment as the park reaches its capacity.

Future development in the park will influence employment and payrolls. One CIP project manager stated in an interview that much of the remaining 50 acres is planned for medium-rise office buildings, garden offices, and other structures for commercial, professional, and personal services (Novak interview). Average wages for employees are expected to increase because of an anticipated shift to higher-paying white-collar jobs. Industrial parks often follow a similar pattern of evolution (Badri, Rivera, and Kusak 41). Like many industrial parks, CIP evolved from a warehousing center into a manufacturing complex.

Combines
conclusions
and recommen-
dations

CONCLUSIONS AND RECOMMENDATIONS

Analysis of tax revenues, employment data, personal interviews, and professional literature leads to the following conclusions and recommendations about the economic impact of Coconino Industrial Park on the city of Flagstaff:

Uses a
numbered
list for clarity
and ease of
reading

1. Sales tax and other revenues produced over $3 million in income to the city of Flagstaff in 2014. By 2020 sales tax and other revenues are expected to produce $5.4 million in city income.

2. CIP currently employs 7,035 employees, the majority of whom are working in manufacturing and assembly. The average employee in 2014 earned $56,579.

3. By 2020 CIP is expected to employ more than 15,000 workers producing a total payroll of over $998 million.

4. Employment trends indicate that by 2020 more CIP employees will be engaged in higher-paying white-collar positions.

On the basis of these findings, we recommend that the City Council of Flagstaff authorize the development of additional industrial parks to stimulate local economic growth. The direct and indirect benefits of Coconino Industrial Park strongly suggest that future commercial development would have a positive impact on the Flagstaff community and the surrounding region as population growth and resulting greater purchasing power would trigger higher demand.

As the Coconino example shows, gains in tax revenue, job creation, and other direct and indirect benefits would follow the creation of additional industrial parks in and around Flagstaff.

5

After discussing and interpreting the research findings, the writer articulates what she considers the most important conclusions and recommendations. Longer, more complex reports may have separate sections for conclusions and resulting recommendations. In this report they are combined. Notice that it is unnecessary to start a new page for the conclusions.

Figure 10.25 MLA Works Cited

Works Cited

Arizona State Board of Equalization. *Bulletin.* Phoenix State Printing Office, 2014, 26-29. Print.

Badri, Joseph, H. Jose Rivera, and Michael E. Kusak. "A Comparison of Sustainability and Economic Development in Urban Industrial Parks." *Journal of Industrial Ecology,* 24.4 (2011): 233-268. Print. doi 10.1078/0366-6133.25.335

Cohen, Andrew P. "Industrial Parks Invade Suburbia." *The New York Times* 14 Dec. 2014: C1. Print.

Fighting Poverty and Protecting the Environment: Development of a Sustainable Technologies Industrial Park, (n.d.). Web. 7 June 2015.

Miller, Aaron M. *Redevelopment Projects: Future Prospects.* New York: Rincon Press. Print.

Pearson, Sophie. "Travel to Work Characteristics for the 50 Largest Metropolitan Areas by Population in the United States." *The Wall Street Journal* 30 June 2013. Web. 3 July 2013.

U.S. Department of Labor, Bureau of Labor Statistics. *Overview of the 2010-2020 Projections.* 2014: n pag. Web. 5 June 2015.

On this page the writer lists all references cited in the text as well as others that she examined during her research. The writer lists these citations following the MLA referencing style. Notice that all entries are arranged alphabetically. The *MLA Handbook for Writers of Research Papers,* Seventh Edition, 2009, requires italics for titles of books, magazines, newspapers, journals, and Web sites. For electronic sources, the following sequence is suggested: author or editor names; article name in quotation marks; title of website, project, or book in italics; any version numbers available; publisher information, including the publisher name and publishing date; page numbers, if available; medium of publication (such as *Web, Print,* or PDF); access date; and URL if necessary for retrieval or required by your instructor.

This works-cited page is shown with single-spacing, which is preferable for business reports. However, MLA style recommends double-spacing for research reports, including the works-cited page.

Figure  Alternate References Shown in APA Style

Arranges references in alphabetical order

References

Brochure —————— Arizona State Board of Equalization Bulletin. (2014). Phoenix: State Printing Office, 26-29.

Journal with doi —————— Badri, J., Rivera, H., & Kusak, M. (2011) A comparison of sustainability and economic development in urban industrial parks. *Journal of Industrial Ecology, 24*(4), 233-268. doi: 10.1078/0366-6133.25.335

Newspaper article —————— Cohen, A. P. (2014, December 14). Industrial parks invade suburbia. *The New York Times,* p. C1.

Website without author or date —————— Fighting poverty and protecting the environment: Development of a sustainable technologies industrial park. Retrieved from http://www.smart-communities .ncat.org/success/northam.shtml

Book —————— Miller, A. M. (2013). *Redevelopment projects: Future prospects.* New York: Rincon Press.

Online article —————— Pearson, S. (2013, June 30). Travel to work characteristics for the 50 largest metropolitan areas by population in the United States. Retrieved from http://www.wsj.com /article 130630

Government publication —————— U.S. Department of Labor, Bureau of Labor Statistics. (2014). *Overview of the 2010-2020 Projections.* Retrieved from http://www.bls.gov/ooh/About/Projections-Overview .htm

If this formal report had used APA referencing style, the references would appear as shown here. The writer lists all references cited in the text as well as the writer lists all references cited in the text as well as others that she examined during her research. The writer lists these citations following the APA referencing style. Notice that all entries are arranged alphabetically. Book and periodical titles are italicized, but they could be underlined. When referring to online items, she shows the full name of the citation and then identifies the URL as well as the date on which she accessed the electronic reference. This references page is shown with single-spacing, which is preferable for business reports. However, APA style recommends double-spacing for research reports, including the references page.

SUMMARY OF LEARNING OBJECTIVES

10-1 Understand the importance, purpose, and components of informal and formal proposals.
- Proposals are written offers that solve problems, provide services, or sell products.
- Proposals may be solicited (requested by an organization) or unsolicited (written to offer a service, request funding, or solve a problem).
- Components of informal proposals often include an introduction; a background and purpose statement; a proposal, plan, and schedule; staffing requirements; a budget showing project costs; and a conclusion.
- Formal proposals often include additional components, such as a letter of transmittal, a title page, a table of contents, and an appendix.

10-2 Describe the steps in writing and editing formal business reports.
- Writers begin formal reports with a statement of purpose that defines the focus of the report.
- Report writers focus on their readers' needs and wants in order to present relevant findings.
- Researchers gather information from primary sources (firsthand observation, interviews, and surveys) and secondary sources (books, articles, journals, and the Web).
- Writers proofread and edit formal reports by reviewing the format, spacing and font consistency, graphics placement, heading levels, data accuracy, and mechanics.

10-3 Conduct research using primary and secondary sources, and understand how to assess the credibility of resources.

- Writers gather most of their research from secondary sources by reading what others have published in books, scholarly journals, magazines, and Web documents.
- Web researchers find the information they want by using search operators and advanced search features to filter the results.
- Good writers assess the credibility of each Web resource by evaluating its currency (last update), author or sponsoring organization, content, purpose, and accuracy.
- Report writers gather data from primary sources by distributing surveys, conducting interviews, and collecting data from firsthand observation.

10-4 Identify the purposes and techniques of documenting and citing sources in business reports.

- Documenting sources means giving credit to information sources to avoid plagiarism.
- Copyright refers to "the right to copy"; under fair use, individuals have limited use of copyrighted material without requiring permission.
- Writers should assume that all intellectual property (words, charts, photos, music, and media) is copyrighted and protected whether or not it has a copyright notice.
- Common citation formats include the Modern Language Association (MLA), the American Psychological Association (APA), and the Chicago Manual of Style (CMS).

10-5 Convert report data into meaningful visual aids and graphics.

- Graphics clarify data, add visual interest, and make complex data easy to understand; they should be placed close to where they are referenced.
- Tables show quantitative information in systematic tables and rows; they require meaningful titles, bold column headings, and a logical data arrangement (alphabetical, chronological, etc.)
- Bar charts and line charts show visual comparisons using horizontal or vertical bars or lines of varying lengths; pie charts show a whole and the proportion of its components; flowcharts diagram processes and procedures.
- Infographics, popular in online environments, combine images and graphic elements to illustrate information in an easy-to-understand format.

10-6 Describe the components of typical formal reports.

- Front matter components of formal reports often include the following: title page, letter or memo of transmittal, table of contents, list of figures, and executive summary.
- Body components of formal reports include the introduction, the body, and the conclusions and recommendations.
- The body is the principal section of a formal report and discusses, analyzes, interprets, and evaluates the research findings before drawing conclusions.
- Back matter components of a formal report include a bibliography, which may be a works-cited or reference page, and any appendixes.

CHAPTER REVIEW

1. For what reasons do writers prepare proposals? (Obj. 1)

2. For what reasons would government agencies and other firms use requests for proposals (RFPs)? Name an example of a project that might require an RFP. (Obj. 1)

3. What is the purpose of providing a "hook" in the introduction of a proposal? Give three examples. (Obj. 1)

4. What sources are considered secondary sources, and where can they be found? (Obj. 3)

5. What is the difference between an open-ended and close-ended survey question? Give an example of each. (Obj. 3)

6. Why should report writers document their sources? (Obj. 4)

7. Define the term *fair use*. When might using copyrighted material be considered fair use? (Obj. 4)

8. Why do report writers include visuals and graphics in reports? (Obj. 5)

9. What should the introduction to a formal business report include? (Obj. 6)

10. What information might be included in an appendix at the end of a formal report? (Obj. 6)

CRITICAL THINKING

11. In what ways is a proposal similar to a persuasive sales message? (Obj. 1)

12. Some people say that business reports should not contain footnotes. If you were writing your first business report and did considerable research, what would you do about documenting your sources? (Objs. 3, 4, and 6)

13. Why do researchers often trust the reliability of information obtained from scholarly journals, major newspapers, and well-known magazines? Why should researchers use caution when accessing information from Wikipedia, online forums, and blogs? (Obj. 3)

14. Starbucks chief Howard Schultz frowns on research, advertising, and customer surveys. He conducts his own informal primary research by visiting 25 store locations a week and talking with his baristas, managers, and customers in person. This kind of observation, he insists, provides the information he needs most.[12] What are the pros and cons of such informal research to gather primary data? (Obj. 3)

15. Information graphics, also called *infographics*, are wildly popular, especially in online environments. Why do you think infographics continue to receive so much attention? How could infographics be useful in your field? (Obj. 5)

ACTIVITIES AND CASES

10.1 Proposal: Expanding the Use of Social Media (Objs. 1, 2)

> E-mail   Social Media   Web

Businesses both large and small are flocking to social media platforms to engage consumers in conversations and also to drive sales through deals and coupons. Small businesses have found that social media and the Internet help them to level the playing field. They can foster closer relationships with clients and identify potential customers. Flirty Cupcakes owner Tiffany Kurtz says that Facebook and Twitter greatly helped her with product innovation, market expansion, and customer service.[13] Many other entrepreneurs are using social media to launch and expand their businesses. As an employee in a small business, you see opportunities to expand the use of social media. You want to first see how other companies are using social networks and then recommend the platforms you believe would be most useful to your business.

YOUR TASK. Search for small businesses that have used social media to expand their market share and promote their products and services. Select three businesses to study, and analyze their use of social media. What do they have in common? In what social media platforms are they engaged? What results have they seen? In an e-mail or memo to your instructor, describe briefly the three companies you selected. Explain how each company is using social media to promote and grow its business. Then write the introduction to a proposal that promotes expanding your company's use of social media. Include a brief description of the reasons for the proposal, specify the key benefits of using social networks, and state how the three companies you studied are using social media. Then recommend which social media platforms you believe would benefit your business.

10.2 Proposal: Workplace Problems Requiring Minor Expenditures (Obj. 1)

The ability to spot problems before they turn into serious risks is prized by most managers. Think about your current or past internship and work experiences. Do you see problems that could be solved with a small to moderate financial investment? Consider issues such as creating space for badly needed lunch and break rooms; offering stress-reducing health initiatives such as wellness programs and gym club memberships; replacing high-emission, gas-guzzling company vehicles; or increasing recycling efforts.

YOUR TASK. Discuss with your instructor the workplace problem that you have identified. Make sure you choose a relatively weighty problem that can be lessened or eliminated with a minor expenditure. Be sure to include a cost–benefit analysis. Address your unsolicited letter or memo proposal to your current or former boss and copy your instructor.

10.3 Proposal: Starting Your Own Business (Objs. 1, 3)

> Web

Perhaps you have dreamed about one day owning your own company, or maybe you have already started a business. Proposals are offers to a very specific audience with whom you hope to do business. Think of a product or service that you like or know something about. On the Web or in electronic databases, research the market so that you understand going rates, prices, and costs. Search the Small Business Administration's website for valuable tips on how to launch and manage a business.

YOUR TASK. Choose a product or service you would like to offer to a particular audience, such as an upholstery business, a bakery featuring your favorite pastries or cakes, a photography business, a new Asian or European hair care line, massage therapy, or landscaping services. Discuss products and services as well as target audiences with your instructor. Write an informal letter addressed to a potential investor, Mr. Simon Lipton, 7430 Fondren Road, Houston, TX 77074. Keep the letter short and don't mention financing, as your goal is to first generate interest.

10.4 Proposal Writing Resources: Offering Assistance in Writing a Proposal (Objs. 1, 3)

> Web

Many new companies with services or products to sell would like help writing unsolicited or solicited proposals. Your friend Teresa has started her own designer uniform company and has asked you for help. Her goal is to offer her colorful yet functional uniforms to hospitals and clinics. Before writing a proposal, however, she wants to learn more about the proposal-writing process.

YOUR TASK. Search the Web and find two sites that offer proposal writing advice. Avoid sites that want you to register or buy templates and books. Prepare a memo to Teresa in which you do the following:
a. Suggest two excellent sites where Teresa can learn the how-tos of creating an effective proposal.
b. Suggest headings for each section of Teresa's unsolicited proposal to promote her hospital/clinic uniforms.
c. Suggest two sites where Teresa can find free proposal templates.
d. Write a suggested introduction for Teresa's proposal.

10.5 Proposal: Informal Letter Proposing a Business Writing Workshop (Obj. 1)

Business employees understand more than ever the importance of improving their writing skills. Whether e-mailing status updates to team members, writing a Web article, preparing meeting agendas, or corresponding with potential customers, employees must write concise, coherent, clear, error-free documents and messages. As the founder of Business Writing Solutions, you offer one- and two-day business writing workshops for businesses and organizations. Your website features writing tips, workshop descriptions, and your contact information. These workshops are presented on-site in corporate training rooms.

You received an e-mail inquiry from Human Resources Director Janet Somerfield, who is considering a one-day, on-site business writing workshop for employees in her midsized advertising agency. Janet is looking at several seminar companies who offer writing training. She asks about pricing, optimal class size, and course content. She also wants to know whether you can offer feedback on writing samples. Because Janet is considering other training options, you decide to respond with an informal proposal. Your goal is to meet her needs and win the contract.

Review the components of an informal proposal and include the appropriate components, which may include the following: an introduction, a statement of your goals and purpose, the proposed seminar details (time requirements, optimal class size, costs, location, schedule), and a conclusion. Organize the proposal, write meaningful headings, and choose a readable font. Decide where it is appropriate to mention the following advantages of improving writing skills in business environments:

- Excellent writing skills help build trusting relationships, improve one's professional image, and add to the credibility of an organization.
- Business associates appreciate clarity, conciseness, and results-focused messages.
- Better writing skills help employees advance their careers, which in turn improves retention.

The one-day workshop is offered in two 4-hour blocks in the client's training room. The course includes the following topics: (a) writing results-oriented e-mail messages; (b) structuring routine, persuasive, and negative news messages; (c) reviewing the most common grammar errors; and (d) designing documents for readability. You will also offer feedback on brief writing samples furnished by the participants. Employees who attend the workshop will earn a certificate of completion.

The cost of the writing workshop is $175 per person. If 15 employees participate, the cost would be $2,625. The cost includes workbooks and writing supplies for each participant.

YOUR TASK. Write an informal letter proposal promoting a one-day business writing workshop to Janet Somerfield, Director, Human Resources, Faulkner Advertising, 420 Fowler Avenue, Tampa, FL 33620.

10.6 Researching and Analyzing Findings: Service Learning Projects (Obj. 3)

Your school may be one that encourages service learning, a form of experiential learning. You could receive credit for a project that bridges academic and nonacademic communities. Because writing skills are in wide demand, you may have an opportunity to simultaneously apply your skills, contribute to the community, and expand your résumé. The National Service-Learning Clearinghouse describes service learning as "a teaching and learning strategy that integrates meaningful community service with instruction and reflection to enrich the learning experience, teach civic responsibility, and strengthen communities."[14] The Web offers many sites devoted to examples of students engaging in service learning projects.

YOUR TASK. Research possible service learning projects in this class or another. Your instructor may ask you to submit a memo or e-mail message analyzing your findings. Describe at least four completed service learning projects that you found on the Web. Draw conclusions about what made them successful or beneficial. What kinds of similar projects might be possible for you or for others in your class? Your instructor may use this as a research project or turn it into a hands-on project by having you find a service organization in your community in need of trained writers.

10.7 Executive Summary: Reviewing Articles and Summarizing Findings (Objs. 3, 5)

Many managers and executives are too rushed to read long journal articles, but they are eager to stay current in their fields. Assume your boss has asked you to help him stay abreast of research in the field by submitting one executive summary every month on an article of interest.

YOUR TASK. In your field of study, select a professional journal, such as the *Journal of Management*. Using ProQuest, Factiva, EBSCO, or some other database, look for articles in your target journal. Select an article that is at least five pages long and is interesting to you. Write an executive summary in a memo format. Include an introduction that might begin with *The following executive summary of the* *article titled "(title of article)" is from (source and date of publication).* Then preview the main idea and summarize the most important findings of the study or article. Use descriptive, or "talking," headings rather than functional headings. Also summarize any recommendations made. Your boss would also like a concluding statement indicating your reaction to the journal article. Address your memo summary to Marcus E. Solomon.

10.8 Unsolicited Proposal: Requesting Funding for Your Campus Business Club (Obj. 1)

Professional associations often have student-organized chapters on college campuses. Let's say you are a member of a campus business club, such as the Society for the Advancement of Management (SAM), the American Marketing Association (AMA), the American Management Association (AMA), the Accounting Society (AS), the International Association of Administrative Professionals (IAAP), or the Association of Information Technology Professionals (AITP). Your club or association has managed its finances well, and therefore, it is able to fund monthly activities. However, membership dues are insufficient to cover any extras. You see the need for a special one-time seminar with a panel of experts or a keynote speaker that would benefit many business students. For example, you see value in inviting a panel of recruiters to come and discuss current job requirements and hiring processes. You must now request funding for this event.

YOUR TASK. Write an unsolicited letter or memo proposal to your program chair or business division dean to request one-time funding to cover the costs associated with this event. Identify your need or problem, provide the details of the event, mention the ways this event will benefit the attendees, support your claims with evidence, and provide a budget. Think ahead about costs associated with printing, appreciation gifts for the presenters, food and beverage needs, and other miscellaneous expenses.

10.9 Primary Research: Designing an Online Customer Service Survey (Obj. 3)

Web

Companies use surveys to continually improve their products and services. As a sales manager in a store selling wireless devices and electronics, you are interested in your customers' opinions about your sales associates and product quality, and in learning about their loyalty to your products. You plan to conduct a survey and use the results in an upcoming training workshop for your sales associates. You have obtained the e-mail addresses of customers who have opted in for product updates and reviews. You plan to design your own survey and want to get ideas by looking at examples of surveys and templates.

YOUR TASK. Search for free customer service survey templates, study the questions, and add the URL of the surveys you reviewed. Then design a customer service survey with a mix of seven or eight typical multiple-choice, scale, or open-ended questions.

10.10 Citations: Citing Secondary Resources Using MLA Format (Obj. 4)

E-mail

You will want to stay up-to-date on your career field by reading, saving current articles, and bookmarking valuable resources. Think about a current business topic related to your professional field that you would like to learn more about. This is your chance to learn more about, gather tips and strategies about, and follow current trends in your field of interest.

YOUR TASK. Look for three current (within the last two years) secondary research sources on a topic related to your field of study. In a memo or e-mail to your instructor, write a one-paragraph summary of each article or resource. Then list the citations for your three resources, using MLA standards. The citations should follow the format used on a works-cited page with citations in alphabetical order and using the hanging indent style.

10.11 Formal Business Report: Gathering Primary and Secondary Intercultural Data (Obj. 3)

Intercultural   Team   Web

U.S. businesses are expanding into foreign markets with manufacturing plants and branch offices. Many Americans, however, have little knowledge of or experience with people from other cultures. To prepare for participation in the global marketplace, you are to collect information for a report focused on an Asian, Latin American, European, or African country where English is not regularly spoken. Before selecting the country, though, consult your campus international student program for volunteers from other countries who are willing to be interviewed. Your instructor may make advance arrangements with international student volunteers.

YOUR TASK. In teams of three to five, collect information about your target country from electronic databases, the Web, and other sources. Then invite an international student from your target country to be interviewed by your group. As you conduct primary and secondary research, investigate the topics listed in Figure 10.26. Confirm what you learn in your secondary research by talking with your interviewee. When you complete your research, write a report for the CEO of your company (make up a name and company). Assume that your company plans to expand its operations abroad. Your report should advise the company's executives of the social customs, family life, societal attitudes, religious preferences and beliefs, education, and values of the target country. Remember that your company's interests are business oriented; do not dwell on tourist information. Compile your results and write the report.

Figure 10.26 Intercultural Interview Topics and Questions

Social Customs

- How do people react to strangers? Are they friendly? Reserved? Cautious? Suspicious?
- What is the typical greeting for friends? Family members and close friends? Business associates? Elderly people or relatives?
- What are appropriate topics of conversation in business settings? What topics should be avoided?
- What customs are associated with exchanging business cards?
- What are the hours of a typical work day?
- What are the attitudes toward personal space and touching?
- Is gift-giving appropriate when invited to someone's home? If so, what gifts are appropriate?
- What facial expressions or gestures are considered offensive? Is direct eye contact appropriate?
- What is the attitude toward punctuality in social situations? In business situations?
- What gestures indicate agreement? Disagreement? Frustration? Excitement?

Family Life

- What is a typical family unit? Do family units include extended family members?
- How do family life and family size differ in urban and rural settings?
- Do women and men have typical roles in families?
- Do women work outside of the home? In what occupations?
- Are children required by law to attend school? Do families value education?

Housing, Clothing, and Food

- How does housing differ in urban and rural areas? How does housing differ among various socioeconomic groups?
- What special occasions require traditional or ceremonial clothing?
- What types of clothing are considered inappropriate or in poor taste?
- What is appropriate business attire for men? For women?
- What are the typical eating times, and what foods are customary?
- What types of places, food, and drink are appropriate for business entertainment? Where is the seat of honor at a round table? At a rectangular table?

Class Structure

- Into what classes is society organized?
- Do racial, religious, or economic factors determine social status?
- Are there any minority groups? What is their social standing?

Political Patterns

- Are there any immediate threats or signs of political unrest in this country?
- How is political power manifested?
- What media channels are used for expressing political opinions?
- Is it appropriate to talk about politics in social situations?

Religious Preferences and Beliefs

- Are certain religious groups predominant?
- Do religious beliefs influence daily activities?
- Which places, objects, or animals are considered sacred?
- How do religious holidays affect business activities?

Economic Norms

- What are the country's principal exports and products?
- Are workers organized in unions?
- Are businesses owned by individuals, by large public corporations, or by the government?
- How is status shown in an organization? Private office? Floor level? Furnishings?
- Do business associates normally socialize before conducting business?

Value Systems

- Is competitiveness or cooperation more prized?
- Is politeness more important than honesty?
- To what extent is bribery accepted as a way of life?
- Do women own or manage businesses? If so, how are they treated?
- How do people perceive Americans? What behaviors exhibited by Americans are considered offensive?
- What was the hardest adjustment after coming to America?

10.12 Selecting Appropriate Graphics (Obj. 5)

Team

In teams identify which type of graphic (table, bar chart, line chart, pie chart, flowchart, infographic, illustration, or map) would best illustrate the following data:

a. Figures comparing the sales of three brands of smartphones over the past 12 months
b. Statistics on the rise of six popular social media platforms (Facebook, Google+, Twitter, YouTube, Instagram, Pinterest) in five of the largest cities in the world
c. National unemployment rate figures for the last 12 months
d. Location of significant earthquakes in the world over the last 30 days
e. Date, time, and place of each game scheduled in the World Cup

f. Recruitment process from the time a job is advertised until the time an offer is made

g. Portion of national budget that goes to defense, social security, safety net programs, interest on debt, and Medicare/Medicaid

10.13 Evaluating Graphics (Obj. 5)

Web

YOUR TASK. Select four graphics from newspapers or magazines in hard copy or online. Look in *The Wall Street Journal, USA Today, Bloomberg Businessweek, U.S. News & World Report, Fortune, Forbes,* or other business news publications. Add the title and the source of each graphic. In an e-mail or memo to your instructor, critique each graphic based on what you have learned in this chapter. Do you think the graphic could have been expressed more effectively in text? How effective are the labels and headings used in this graphic? How was color used to add clarity? If a legend is used, describe its placement and effectiveness. Is the appropriate graphic form used? What is your overall impression of the effectiveness of the graphic?

10.14 Creating a Bar Chart and Writing a Title (Obj. 5)

Web

YOUR TASK. Create a bar chart comparing the current number of Internet users (by millions) in the following eight countries: United States, India, Japan, Brazil, Indonesia, China, United Kingdom, and Russia. Find statistics within the last year and name the source of your information. Arrange the bars according to the country with the highest number of users to the lowest. Add a chart title and appropriate labels.

10.15 Infographics: Telling a Story and Expressing Ideas (Obj. 5)

Web   E-mail

Information graphics, or infographics, are wildly popular, especially in online environments. Infographics can use color, text, images, data, diagrams, time lines, and charts to express ideas or tell a compelling story. You have heard that even nondesigners can create infographics, and you want to use this tool for presentations, reports, and employee training. By looking at examples of well-designed infographics and learning which websites offer free tools and templates, you will be well on your way to becoming an infographic designer.

YOUR TASK. Search for and examine excellent infographics featured online. Find three infographics on topics of interest to you. The topics may or may not be related. In an e-mail or memo to your instructor, promote the idea of using infographics and list the URLs for the infographic examples you found. Briefly describe the main ideas of each. Add a comment on what aspects make each infographic so compelling. Then search for one website that offers free infographic designs and templates. In your e-mail or memo, briefly describe what tools are available on this site and add the website name and URL. Conclude your message with a brief paragraph stating the reasons you believe infographics have become so popular and widely used.

10.16 Formal Report: Analyzing "Congressional Watchdog" Reports (Obj. 6)

Web

The U.S. Government Accountability Office (GAO) is a nonpartisan agency that works for Congress and investigates how the federal government spends taxpayer dollars. For this reason the agency is often called the congressional watchdog. These archived reports are available as portable document format (PDF) files. You'll be examining two reports from the GAO website.

YOUR TASK. Visit the U.S. GAO website at **http://www.gao.gov** and click the link for Reports and Testimonies at the top of the page. Narrow the date to find reports issued within the last six months. Then browse by topic and select two reports on the topics of Employment or Health Care. (You may choose one report from each topic or both reports from one topic.) For each report, click the link above the title to open the PDF version. Write a one-page analysis of the report. Include the title, date, and number of pages in the report. Read the summary and write a brief paragraph describing the purpose of the report. Describe what sections are included in the report. Also describe what types of graphics were included to display information.

10.17 Formal Report: Comparing Before Buying (Objs. 2–6)

Web   Team

Study a consumer product that you or a business might consider buying. This might be a notebook or laptop, a smartphone, a digital camera, a widescreen TV, an espresso machine, a car, a combination print/scan/fax machine, a powerful office printer, or some other product.

YOUR TASK. Use at least four primary and four secondary sources to research your product. Your primary research will be in the form of interviews with individuals (owners, users, salespeople, technicians) in a position to comment on attributes of your product. Secondary research will be in the form of print or electronic sources, such as magazine articles, marketing websites with user reviews, and company websites. Use electronic databases and the Web to find appropriate articles. Your report should analyze and discuss at least three comparable models or versions of the target product. Decide what criteria you will use to compare the models, such as price, features, warranty, and service. Create at least one original graphic to display report data. Include the following components in the report: table of contents, executive summary, introduction (including background, purpose, scope of the report, and research methods), findings (organized by comparison criteria), summary of findings, conclusions, recommendations, and bibliography. Address the report to your instructor. You may work individually, in pairs, or in teams.

10.18 Report Topics for Proposals and Formal Reports (Objs. 1–6)

Team   Web

A list of nearly 100 Report Topics is available at the premium student site accessed at **www.cengagebrain.com**. Look under the tab Writing Resources. The topics are divided into the following categories: accounting, finance, personnel/human resources, marketing, information systems, management, and general business/education/campus issues. You can collect information for many of these reports by using electronic databases and the Web. Your instructor may assign them as individual or team projects. All involve critical thinking in organizing information, drawing conclusions, and making recommendations. The topics are appropriate for proposals and formal business reports.

YOUR TASK. As directed by your instructor, select a topic from the report list at **www.cengagebrain.com**.

GRAMMAR/MECHANICS CHECKUP—**10**

Apostrophes

Review Sections 2.20–2.22 in the Grammar/Mechanics Handbook. Then study each of the following statements. Underscore any inappropriate form. Write a correction in the space provided and record the number of the G/M principle(s) illustrated. If a sentence is correct, write C. When you finish, compare your responses with those at the back of the book. If your answers differ, study carefully the principles shown in parentheses.

years' _____ (2.20b)   EXAMPLE   In two <u>years</u> time, you could finish that degree.

_____ 1.   Did you know that Elizabeth Metz proposal was accepted?

_____ 2.   The company plans to double its earnings in three years time.

_____ 3.   All employees in the Human Resources Department must take their two weeks vacation before January 1.

_____ 4.   The attorneys agreed that Judge Millers comments were justified.

_____ 5.   Several employees records were accidentally removed from the files.

_____ 6.   The last witness testimony was the most convincing to the jury members.

_____ 7.   Lisas smoking led to health problems.

_____ 8.   I always get my moneys worth at my favorite restaurant.

_____ 9.   Three local companies went out of business last month.

_____ 10. In one months time we hope to have our new website up and running.

_____ 11. I need my boss signature on this expense claim.

_____ 12. Only one legal secretaries document was error-free.

_____ 13. Professor Sanchezes quizzes were always scheduled on Fridays.

_____ 14. My companys stock price rose dramatically last month.

_____ 15. In three months several businesses opening hours will change.

To fine-tune your grammar and mechanics skills, in every chapter you will be editing a message. This executive summary suffers from wordiness, proofreading, spelling, grammar, punctuation, and other writing faults that require correction. Study the guidelines in the Grammar/Mechanics Handbook as well as the lists of Confusing Words and Frequently Misspelled Words to sharpen your skills.

YOUR TASK. Edit the following message (a) by correcting errors in your textbook or on a photocopy using proofreading marks from Appendix A or (b) by downloading the message from **www.cengagebrain.com** and correcting at your computer. Your instructor may show you a possible solution.

EXECUTIVE SUMMARY

Problem

To remain successful the U.S. tuna industry must grow it's markets abroad. Particularly in regard to japan. Which is one of the worlds largest consumers of tuna. Tuna consumption is on the decline in the United States, however it is increasing in japan. The problem that is occurring for the American tuna industry is developing appropriate marketing strategies to boost it's current sales in Japanese markets. The fact is that even though japan produces much of its tuna domestically they still must rely on imported tuna to meet its consumers demands.

Summary of Findings

As shown herein, this report analyzes the Japanese market which at the current time consumes over eight hundred thousand tons of tuna per year. A single full grown bluefin tuna, the favorite species, can sell for $22,000. Much of the domestic consumption is supplied by imports which at this point in time total about 35% of sales. Our findings indicate that this trend will not only expand but also that Japans share of imports will continue to grow. The trend is alarming to Japans tuna industry leaders, because this important market, close to a $billion a year, is increasingly subject to the influence of foriegn imports. Declining catches by Japans own Tuna fleet as well as a sharp upward turn in food preference by affluent Japanese consumers, has contributed to this trend. In just two years time the demand for sashimi alone in Japan has increased in the amount of 15%.

The U.S. Tuna Industry are in the perfect position to meet this demand. Fishing techniques has been developed that maximize catch rates, while minimizing danger to the enviroment. Modern packaging procedures assure that tuna reaches Japan in the freshest possible condition. Let it be said that Japanese consumers have rated the quality of American tuna high. Which has only increased demand.

Recommendations

Upon the completion of our analisys, we are prepared to reccommend the following 5 marketing strategys for the U.S. Tuna industry.

1. Farm greater suppys of tuna to export.
2. Establish new fisheries around the World.
3. We should market our own value-added products.
4. Fresh tuna should be sold direct to the Tokyo Central wholesale market.
5. Direct sales should be made to Japanese Supermarket chains.

COMMUNICATION WORKSHOP

Evaluating the Credibility of Web Documents: Let the Reader Beware

Evaluating a website's credibility requires critical thinking and a good eye. Savvy Web users start the evaluation process by thinking about how they found the site in the first place. They may have accessed the site from the results page of a search engine or by following a link from a reputable site. Perhaps the site was recommended by a friend, which would add credibility. The processes for finding Web information may vary, but the reader alone is responsible for determining the validity, truthfulness, and integrity of that information. Because anyone with a computer and an Internet connection can publish on the Web, the reader must beware and wisely question all Web content.

Unlike the contents of journals, magazines, and newspapers found in research-oriented libraries, the content of most websites has not been reviewed by skilled editors. Some Web pages do not show authorship, credentials, or sponsoring organizations. The content cannot be verified. These sites have low credibility.

As a frequent Web user, you must learn to critically examine Web information for credibility. The following checklist of questions about authorship, publisher or sponsor, currency, content quality, and accuracy and organization will help you critically assess the validity of Web information.

Authorship

- Who authored this page or article?
- Are the author's credentials easily found? If not, check the author's credentials online.
- Is the author affiliated with a reputable organization?
- Is the author's contact information, such as an e-mail address, easily found?
- Are the About page and the Contact page easy to spot?

Publisher or Sponsor

- What organization publishes or sponsors this Web page? Is the publisher reputable?
- What domain is used in the URL? The domain name gives clues about who published the document (e.g., .com, .org, .edu, .gov, .net).
- Is the site published or sponsored in another country? Look for a two-letter code in the URL: .uk, .au, .br, .hu, .mx, .ca, .in.

Currency

- When was the Web page published or last updated? Readers expect this information at the bottom of the page.
- Is this a website that requires current, updated information (e.g., science, medicine, current events)?

- Are all links on this Web page current and working? Broken links are red flags.

Content Quality

- What is the purpose of the Web page? For example, does the page entertain, inform, persuade, sell, or express satire?
- Who is the intended audience of the page, based on its content, tone, and style?
- Do you see evidence of bias, and does the author acknowledge the bias?
- Does the site link to other reputable sites? Do those sites in turn link back to the site in question?
- Does the page contain distracting graphics or fill the screen with unwanted ads and pop-ups?

Accuracy and Organization

- Does the information appear to be well researched?
- If the site contains statistics and facts, are sources, dates, and/or citations provided?
- Is the information well organized with main points clearly presented?
- Is the site well designed and easy to navigate? Good design adds credibility.
- Does the page have broken links or graphics that don't load?
- Are the graphics appropriately placed and clearly labeled?
- Does the site have spelling, grammar, or usage errors? Careless errors are red flags.

CAREER APPLICATION. As interns in a news-gathering service, you have been asked to assess the quality of the following websites. Think about whether you would recommend these sites as trustworthy sources of information.

- Beef Nutrition (**http://www.beefnutrition.org**)
- Edmunds (**http://www.edmunds.com**)
- EarthSave (**http://www.earthsave.org**)
- The White House (**http://www.whitehouse.net**)
- The White House (**http://www.whitehouse.gov**)
- GulfLINK (**http://www.gulflink.osd.mil**)
- The Anaheim White House Restaurant (**http://www .anaheimwhitehouse.com**)
- National Anti-Vivisection Society (**http://www.navs.org**)
- PETA (**http://www.peta.org**)
- WebMD (**http://www.webmd.com**)

- Petrol Direct (**http://www.petroldirect.com**)
- Buy Dehydrated Water (**http://www.buydehydratedwater.com/ci.htm**)
- Smithsonian (**http://www.si.edu**)
- Hootsuite (**https://hootsuite.com**)
- Bureau of Sasquatch Affairs (**http://zapatopi.net/bsa**)
- Mint (**https://www.mint.com**)
- DHMO.org (**http://www.dhmo.org**)
- Lonely Planet (**http://www.lonelyplanet.com**)
- Drudge Report (**http://www.drudgereport.com**)
- American Cancer Society (**http://www.cancer.org**)
- The Onion (**http://www.theonion.com**)
- Pacific Northwest Tree Octopus (**http://zapatopi.net/treeoctopus**)

YOUR TASK. If you decide to use teams, divide the preceding list among team members. If you are working individually, select four of the sites. Analyze each site using the checklist of questions in each category. Then summarize your evaluation of each site in a memo or e-mail report addressed to your boss (your instructor). Your report may also become part of a team presentation or a class discussion. Add a comment about whether you would recommend this site for researchers of news articles. Be careful—even a hoax site can seem reputable and trustworthy at first glance. Be careful not to label sites as good or bad. Even biased sites may have large audiences and some merit.

ENDNOTES

1 Photo essay based on Markon, J., and Crites, A. (2014, February 9). Accenture, hired to help fix HealthCare.gov, has had a series of stumbles. *The Washington Post.* Retrieved from http://www.washingtonpost.com/politics/accenture-hired-to-fix-healthcaregov-has-troubled-past/2014/02/09/3d1a2dc4-8934-11e3-833c-33098f9e5267_story.html

2 City of Las Vegas. (2010, January 4). RFP for public private partnership parking initiative. Onvia DemandStar. Retrieved from http://www.lasvegasnevada.gov/Business/5990.htm?ID

3 Buck Institute for Research on Aging. (n.d.). Architecture. Retrieved from http://www.buckinstitute.org/architecture

4 Greenwood, G., & Greenwood, J. (2008). SBIR proposal writing basics: Resumes must be written well. Greenwood Consulting Group. Retrieved from http://www.g-jgreenwood.com/sbir_proposal_writing_basics91.htm

5 Cohen, J. S. (2009, December 28). Top 10 favorite foods preferred by college students. *Chicago Tribune.* Retrieved from http://www.inyork.com/ci_14080691?source=most_viewed

6 Giorgetti, D., & Sebastiani, F. (2003, December). Automating survey coding by multiclass text categories. *Journal of the American Society for Information Science and Technology, 54*(14), 1269. Retrieved from http://search.proquest.com

7 Goldsmith, B. (2002, June). The awesome power of asking the right questions. *OfficeSolutions,* 52; and Bracey, G. W. (2001, November). Research-question authority. *Phi Delta Kappan,* 191.

8 Berfield, S. (2009, August 17). Howard Schultz versus Howard Schultz. *BusinessWeek,* p. 31.

9 Writing Tutorial Services, Indiana University. (n.d.). *Plagiarism: What it is and how to recognize and avoid it.* Retrieved from http://www.indiana.edu/~wts/pamphlets/plagiarism.shtml

10 Photo essay based on Pemberton, K. (2013, October 22). Vancouver city staff to monitor how casinos adhere to health report recommendations. *The Vancouver Sun.* Retrieved from http://www.vancouversun.com/health/Vancouver+city+staff+monitor+casinos+adhere+health+report+recommendations/9069335/story.html

11 Saylor, M. (2012). *The mobile wave: How mobile intelligence will change everything.* New York: Vanguard Press, p. ix.

12 Berfield, S. (2009, August 17). Howard Schultz versus Howard Schultz. *BusinessWeek,* p. 31.

13 Ratner, H. M. (2012, March 1). 9 businesses that social media built. *Today's Chicago Woman.* Retrieved from http://www.tcwmag.com/9-businesses-social-media-built

14 Corporation for National and Community Service. (2013). What is service-learning? Retrieved from http://www.servicelearning.org/what-is-service-learning

ACKNOWLEDGMENTS

p. 304 Office Insider. Mary Piecewicz, Hewlett-Packard proposal manager, interview with Mary Ellen Guffey.

Business Presentations

12-1 Preparing Effective Business Presentations

Unlike motivational expert Anthony Robbins, activist Martin Luther King Jr., or the late Apple founder Steve Jobs, few of us will ever talk to an audience of millions—whether face-to-face or aided by technology. We won't be invited to give a TED Talk, motivate millions, or introduce a spectacular new product. At some point, however, all businesspeople have to inform others or sell an idea. Such informative and persuasive presentations are often conveyed in person and involve audiences of various sizes. If you are like most people, you have some apprehension when speaking in public. That's normal. Good speakers are made, not born. The good news is that you can conquer the fear of public speaking and hone your skills with instruction and practice.

12-1a Speaking Skills and Your Career

Many savvy future businesspeople fail to take advantage of opportunities in college to develop their speaking skills, even though such skills are often crucial for a successful career. As you have seen in Chapters 1 and 11, speaking skills rank very high on recruiters' wish lists. In a survey of employers, spoken communication took the top spot as the most desirable "soft skill" sought in job candidates. It even ranks above a strong work ethic, teamwork, analytical skills, and initiative.[1]

Speaking skills are useful at every career stage. You might, for example, have to make a sales pitch before customers, speak to a professional gathering, or describe

OBJECTIVES
After studying this chapter, you should be able to

12-1
Recognize various types of business presentations, and discuss two important first steps in preparing for any of these presentations.

12-2
Explain how to organize the introduction, body, and conclusion as well as how to build audience rapport in a presentation.

12-3
Understand visual aids and how to avoid ineffective PowerPoint practices.

12-4
Create an impressive, error-free multimedia presentation that shows a firm grasp of basic visual design principles.

12-5
Specify delivery techniques for use before, during, and after a presentation.

LEARNING OBJECTIVE 1

Recognize various types of business presentations, and discuss two important first steps in preparing for any of these presentations.

your company's expansion plans to your banker. This chapter prepares you to use speaking skills in making professional oral presentations, whether alone or as part of a team, whether face-to-face or virtually. Before we dive into the specifics of how to become an excellent presenter, the following section addresses the types of business presentations you may encounter in your career.

12-1b Understanding Presentation Types

A common part of a business professional's life is making presentations. Some presentations are informative, whereas others are persuasive. Some are face-to-face; others, virtual. Some are performed before big audiences, whereas others are given to smaller groups. Some presentations are elaborate; others are simple. Figure 12.1 shows a sampling of business presentations you may encounter in your career.

12-1c Knowing Your Purpose

Regardless of the type of presentation, you must prepare carefully to ensure that it is effective. The most important part of your preparation is deciding what you want to accomplish. Do you want to sell a health care program to a prospective client? Do you want to persuade management to increase the marketing budget? Whether your goal is to persuade or to inform, you must have a clear idea of where you are going. At the end of your presentation, what do you want your listeners to remember or do?

Sandra Castillo, a loan officer at First Fidelity Trust, faced such questions as she planned a talk for a class in small business management. (You can see the outline for her talk in Figure 12.4 on page 394.) Sandra's former business professor had asked her to return to campus and give his students advice about obtaining loans to start new businesses. Because Sandra knew so much about this topic, she found it difficult to extract a specific purpose statement for her presentation. After much thought she narrowed her purpose to this: *To inform potential entrepreneurs about three important factors that loan officers consider before granting start-up loans to launch small businesses.* Her entire presentation focused on ensuring that the students understood and remembered three principal ideas.

Figure 12.1 Types of Business Presentations

- Overview or summary of an issue, proposal, or problem
- Delivery of information, discussion of questions, collection of feedback

- Oral equivalent of business reports and proposals
- Informational or persuasive oral account, simple or elaborate

- Online, prerecorded audio clip delivered over the Web
- Opportunity to launch products, introduce and train employees, and sell products and services

- Collaboration facilitated by technology (telepresence or Web)
- Real-time meeting online with remote colleagues

- Web-based presentation, lecture, workshop, or seminar
- Digital transmission with or without video to train employees, interact with customers, and promote products

12-1d Knowing Your Audience

As in any type of communication, a second key element in preparation is analyzing your audience, anticipating its reactions, and adjusting to its needs if necessary. Audiences may fall into four categories, as summarized in Figure 12.2. By anticipating your audience, you have a better idea of how to organize your presentation. A friendly audience, for example, will respond to humor and personal experiences. A hostile audience demands a calm, controlled delivery style with objective data and expert opinion. Whatever type of audience you will face, remember to plan your presentation so that it focuses on audience benefits. People in your audience will want to know what's in it for them.

Other elements, such as the age, gender, education level, experience, and size of the audience, will affect your style and message. Analyze the following questions to determine your organizational pattern, delivery style, and supporting material:

- How will this topic appeal to this audience?
- How can I relate this information to my listeners' needs?
- How can I earn respect so that they accept my message?
- What would be most effective in making my point? Facts? Statistics? Personal experiences? Expert opinion? Humor? Cartoons? Graphic illustrations? Demonstrations? Case histories? Analogies?
- What measures must I take to ensure that this audience remembers my main points?

Figure 12.2 Succeeding With Four Audience Types

Audience Members	Organizational Pattern	Delivery Style	Supporting Material
Friendly			
They like you and your topic.	Use any pattern. Try something new. Involve the audience.	Be warm, pleasant, and open. Use lots of eye contact and smiles.	Include humor, personal examples, and experiences.
Neutral			
They are calm, rational; their minds are made up, but they think they are objective.	Present both sides of the issue. Use pro/con or problem/solution patterns. Save time for audience questions.	Be controlled. Do nothing showy. Use confident, small gestures.	Use facts, statistics, expert opinion, and comparison and contrast. Avoid humor, personal stories, and flashy visuals.
Uninterested			
They have short attention spans; they may be there against their will.	Be brief—no more than three points. Avoid topical and pro/con patterns that seem lengthy to the audience.	Be dynamic and entertaining. Move around. Use large gestures.	Use humor, cartoons, colorful visuals, powerful quotations, and startling statistics.

Avoid darkening the room, standing motionless, passing out handouts, using boring visuals, or expecting the audience to participate.

Audience Members	Organizational Pattern	Delivery Style	Supporting Material
Hostile			
They want to take charge or to ridicule the speaker; they may be defensive, emotional.	Organize using a noncontroversial pattern, such as a topical, chronological, or geographical strategy.	Be calm and controlled. Speak evenly and slowly.	Include objective data and expert opinion. Avoid anecdotes and humor.

Avoid a question-and-answer period, if possible; otherwise, use a moderator or accept only written questions.

LEARNING OBJECTIVE 2

Explain how to organize the introduction, body, and conclusion as well as how to build audience rapport in a presentation.

12-2 Organizing Content for Impact and Audience Rapport

After determining your purpose and analyzing the audience, you are ready to collect information and organize it logically. Good organization and intentional repetition are the two most powerful keys to audience comprehension and retention. In fact, many speech experts recommend the following admittedly repetitious, but effective, plan:

Step 1: Tell them what you are going to tell them.
Step 2: Tell them.
Step 3: Tell them what you have told them.

Although it is redundant, this strategy works well because most people retain information best when they hear it repeatedly. Let's examine how to construct the three parts of an effective presentation: introduction, body, and conclusion.

12-2a Capturing Attention in the Introduction

How many times have you heard a speaker begin with, *It's a pleasure to be here.* Or, *Today I'm going to talk about. . . .* Boring openings such as these get speakers off to a dull start. Avoid such banalities by striving to accomplish three goals in the introduction to your presentation:

- Capture listeners' attention and get them involved.
- Identify yourself and establish your credibility.
- Preview your main points.

If you are able to appeal to listeners and involve them in your presentation right from the start, you are more likely to hold their attention until the finish. Consider some of the techniques you used to open sales letters: a question, a startling fact, a joke, a story, or a quotation. Some speakers achieve involvement by opening with a question or command that requires audience members to raise their hands or stand up. Twelve techniques to gain and keep audience attention are presented in Figure 12.3.

To establish your credibility, you need to describe your position, knowledge, or experience—whatever qualifies you to speak. In addition, try to connect with your audience. Listeners respond particularly well to speakers who reveal something of themselves and identify with them. A consultant addressing office workers might reminisce about how she started as a temporary worker; a CEO might tell a funny story in which the joke is on him. Use humor if you can pull it off (not everyone can); self-effacing humor may work best for you.

After capturing attention and establishing your credibility, you will want to preview the main points of your topic, perhaps with a visual aid.

Take a look at Sandra Castillo's introduction, shown in Figure 12.4, to see how she integrated all the elements necessary for a good opening.

12-2b Organizing the Body of the Presentation

The most effective oral presentations focus on a few principal ideas. Therefore, the body of your short presentation (20 minutes or shorter) should include a limited number of main points—say, two to four. Develop each main point with adequate, but not excessive, explanation and details. Too many details can obscure the main

Figure 12.3 Gaining and Keeping Audience Attention

© iStockphoto.com/Izabela Habur

Experienced speakers know how to capture the attention of an audience and how to maintain that attention throughout a presentation. You can spruce up your presentations by trying these twelve proven techniques.

- **A promise.** Begin with a realistic promise that keeps the audience expectant (for example, *By the end of this presentation, you will know how you can increase your sales by 50 percent!*).

- **Drama.** Open by telling an emotionally moving story or by describing a serious problem that involves the audience. Throughout your talk include other dramatic elements, such as a long pause after a key statement. Change your vocal tone or pitch. Professionals use high-intensity emotions such as anger, joy, sadness, and excitement.

- **Eye contact.** As you begin, command attention by surveying the entire audience to take in all listeners. Give yourself two to five seconds to linger on individuals to avoid fleeting, unconvincing eye contact. Don't just sweep the room and the crowd.

- **Movement.** Leave the lectern area whenever possible. Walk around the conference table or down the aisles of the presentation room. Try to move toward your audience, especially at the beginning and end of your talk.

- **Questions.** Keep listeners active and involved with rhetorical questions. Ask for a show of hands to get each listener thinking. The response will also give you a quick gauge of audience attention.

- **Demonstrations.** Include a member of the audience in a demonstration (for example, *I'm going to show you exactly how to implement our four-step customer courtesy process, but I need a volunteer from the audience to help me*).

- **Samples/props.** If you are promoting a product, consider using items to toss out to the audience or to award as prizes to volunteer participants. You can also pass around product samples or promotional literature. Be careful, though, to maintain control.

- **Visuals.** Give your audience something to look at besides yourself. Use a variety of visual aids in a single session. Also consider writing the concerns expressed by your audience on a flipchart, a whiteboard, or a smart board as you go along.

- **Attire.** Enhance your credibility with your audience by dressing professionally for your presentation. Professional attire will help you look competent and qualified, making your audience more likely to listen and take you seriously.

- **Current events/statistics.** Mention a current event or statistic (the more startling, the better) that is relevant to your topic and to which the audience can relate.

- **A quote.** Quotations, especially those made by well-known individuals, can be powerful attention-getting devices. The quotation should be pertinent to your topic, short, and interesting.

- **Self-interest.** Review your entire presentation to ensure that it meets the critical *What's-in-it-for-me* audience test. People are most interested in things that benefit them.

message, so keep your presentation simple and logical. Remember, listeners have no pages to refer to should they become confused.

When Sandra Castillo began planning her presentation, she understood that listeners are not good at separating major and minor points. Therefore, instead of drowning her listeners in information, she sorted out a few main ideas. In the banking industry, loan officers generally ask the following three questions of each budding entrepreneur: (a) Are you ready to "hit the ground running" in starting your business? (b) Have you done your homework? and (c) Have you made realistic projections of potential sales, cash flow, and equity investment? These questions would become her main points, but Sandra wanted to streamline them further so that her audience would be sure to remember them. She encapsulated the questions

Figure 12.4 Outlining an Oral Presentation

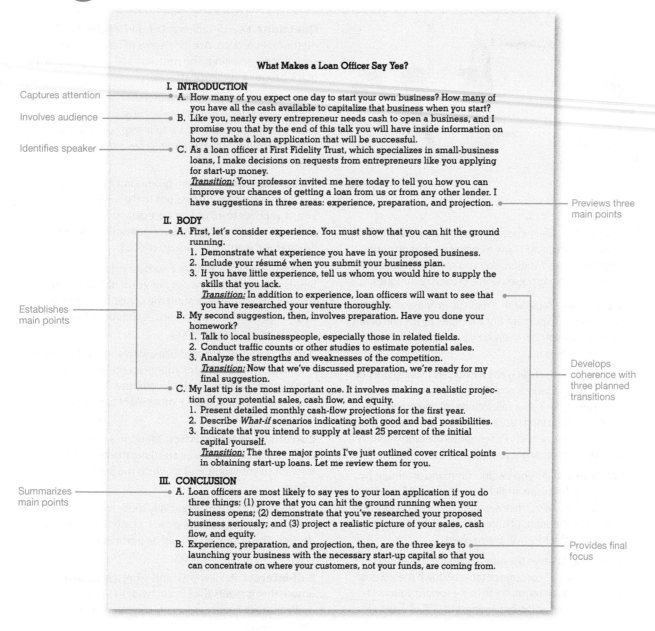

What Makes a Loan Officer Say Yes?

I. INTRODUCTION

Captures attention — A. How many of you expect one day to start your own business? How many of you have all the cash available to capitalize that business when you start?

Involves audience — B. Like you, nearly every entrepreneur needs cash to open a business, and I promise you that by the end of this talk you will have inside information on how to make a loan application that will be successful.

Identifies speaker — C. As a loan officer at First Fidelity Trust, which specializes in small-business loans, I make decisions on requests from entrepreneurs like you applying for start-up money.
Transition: Your professor invited me here today to tell you how you can improve your chances of getting a loan from us or from any other lender. I have suggestions in three areas: experience, preparation, and projection. — *Previews three main points*

II. BODY

A. First, let's consider experience. You must show that you can hit the ground running.
  1. Demonstrate what experience you have in your proposed business.
  2. Include your résumé when you submit your business plan.
  3. If you have little experience, tell us whom you would hire to supply the skills that you lack.
    Transition: In addition to experience, loan officers will want to see that you have researched your venture thoroughly.

Establishes main points — B. My second suggestion, then, involves preparation. Have you done your homework?
  1. Talk to local businesspeople, especially those in related fields.
  2. Conduct traffic counts or other studies to estimate potential sales.
  3. Analyze the strengths and weaknesses of the competition.
    Transition: Now that we've discussed preparation, we're ready for my final suggestion.

C. My last tip is the most important one. It involves making a realistic projection of your potential sales, cash flow, and equity. — *Develops coherence with three planned transitions*
  1. Present detailed monthly cash-flow projections for the first year.
  2. Describe *What-if* scenarios indicating both good and bad possibilities.
  3. Indicate that you intend to supply at least 25 percent of the initial capital yourself.
    Transition: The three major points I've just outlined cover critical points in obtaining start-up loans. Let me review them for you.

III. CONCLUSION

Summarizes main points — A. Loan officers are most likely to say yes to your loan application if you do three things: (1) prove that you can hit the ground running when your business opens; (2) demonstrate that you've researched your proposed business seriously; and (3) project a realistic picture of your sales, cash flow, and equity.

B. Experience, preparation, and projection, then, are the three keys to launching your business with the necessary start-up capital so that you can concentrate on where your customers, not your funds, are coming from. — *Provides final focus*

in three words: *experience, preparation*, and *projection*. As you can see in Figure 12.4, Sandra prepared a sentence outline showing these three main ideas. Each is supported by examples and explanations.

How to organize and sequence main ideas may not be immediately obvious when you begin working on a presentation. The following methods, which review and amplify those discussed in Chapter 10, provide many possible strategies and examples to help you organize a presentation:

- **Chronology:** A presentation describing the history of a problem, organized from the first sign of trouble to the present.

- **Geography/space:** A presentation about the changing diversity of the workforce, organized by regions in the country (East Coast, West Coast, and so forth).

- **Topic/function/conventional grouping:** A presentation discussing mishandled airline baggage, organized by names of airlines.
- **Comparison/contrast (pro/con):** A presentation comparing e-marketing with traditional direct mail.
- **Journalistic pattern (the six Ws):** A presentation describing how identity thieves can ruin your good name. Organized by *who, what, when, where, why*, and *how*.
- **Value/size:** A presentation describing fluctuations in housing costs, organized by prices of homes.
- **Importance:** A presentation describing five reasons a company should move its headquarters to a specific city, organized from the most important reason to the least important.
- **Problem/solution:** A presentation offering a solution to a problem of declining sales, such as reducing staff.
- **Simple/complex:** A presentation explaining the genetic modification of corn, organized from simple seed production to complex gene introduction.
- **Best case/worst case:** A presentation analyzing whether two companies should merge, organized by the best-case results (improved market share, profitability, employee morale) and the worst-case results (devalued stock, lost market share, employee malaise).

In the presentation outline shown in Figure 12.4, Sandra arranged the main points by importance, placing the most important point last, where it had maximum effect. When organizing any presentation, prepare a little more material than you think you will actually need. Savvy speakers always have something useful in reserve such as an extra handout, slide, or idea—just in case they finish early. At the same time, most speakers go about 25 percent over the time they spent practicing at home in front of the mirror. If your speaking time is limited, as it usually is in your classes, aim for less than the limit when rehearsing, so that you don't take time away from the next presenters.

12-2c Summarizing in the Conclusion

Nervous speakers often rush to wrap up their presentations because they can't wait to flee the stage. However, listeners will remember the conclusion more than any other part of a speech. That's why you should spend some time making it as effective as you can. Strive to achieve three goals:

- Summarize the main themes of the presentation.
- Leave the audience with a specific and memorable take-away.
- Include a statement that allows you to exit the podium gracefully.

A conclusion is like a punch line and must be memorable. Think of it as the high point of your presentation, a valuable kernel of information to take away. The valuable kernel of information, or take-away, should tie in with the opening or present a forward-looking idea. Avoid merely rehashing, in the same words, what you said before, but ensure that you will leave the audience with very specific information or benefits and a positive impression of you and your company. The take-away is the value of the presentation to the audience and the benefit audience members believe they have received. The tension that you built in the early parts of the talk now culminates in the close. Compare these poor and improved conclusions:

Poor conclusion: *Well, I guess that's about all I have to say. Thanks for your time.*
Improved: *In bringing my presentation to a close, I will restate my major purpose. . . .*
Improved: *In summary, my major purpose has been to. . . .*
Improved: *In conclusion, let me review my three major points. They are. . . .*

Notice how Sandra Castillo, in the conclusion shown in Figure 12.4, summarized her three main points and provided a final focus to listeners.

If you are making a recommendation, you might end as follows: *In conclusion, I recommend that we retain Matrixx Marketing to conduct a telemarketing campaign beginning September 1 at a cost of X dollars. To do so, I suggest that we (a) finance this campaign from our operations budget, (b) develop a persuasive message describing our new product, and (c) name Lisa Beck to oversee the project.*

In your conclusion you could use an anecdote, an inspiring quotation, or a statement that ties in the opener and offers a new insight. Whatever you choose, be sure to include a closing thought that indicates you are finished.

12-2d Establishing Audience Rapport

Good speakers are adept at building audience rapport. They form a bond with the audience; they entertain as well as inform. How do they do it? From observations of successful and unsuccessful speakers, we have learned that the good ones use a number of verbal and nonverbal techniques to connect with their audiences. Their helpful techniques include providing effective imagery, supplying verbal signposts, and using body language strategically.

Effective Imagery. You will lose your audience quickly if you fill your talk with abstractions, generalities, and dry facts. To enliven your presentation and enhance comprehension, try using some of the techniques presented in Figure 12.5. However, beware of exaggeration or distortion. Keep your imagery realistic and credible.

Verbal Signposts. Speakers must remember that listeners, unlike readers of a report, cannot control the rate of presentation or read through pages to review main points. As a result, listeners get lost easily. Knowledgeable speakers help the audience recognize the organization and main points in an oral message with verbal signposts. They keep listeners on track by including helpful previews, summaries, and transitions, such as these:

- Previewing
  The next segment of my talk presents three reasons for. . . .
  Let's now consider the causes of. . . .

- Summarizing
  Let me review with you the major problems I have just discussed.
  You see, then, that the most significant factors are. . . .

- Switching directions
  Thus far we have talked solely about . . . ; now let's move to. . . .
  I have argued that . . . and . . . , but an alternate view holds that. . . .

You can further improve any oral presentation by including appropriate transitional expressions such as *first, second, next, then, therefore, moreover, on the other hand, on the contrary,* and *in conclusion.* These transitional expressions build coherence, lend emphasis, and tell listeners where you are headed. Notice in Sandra Castillo's outline in Figure 12.4 the specific transitional elements designed to help listeners recognize each new principal point.

Nonverbal Messages. Although what you say is most important, the nonverbal messages you send can also have a powerful effect on how well your audience receives your message. How you look, how you move, and how you speak can make or break your presentation. The following suggestions focus on nonverbal tips to ensure that your verbal message resonates with your audience.

- **Look terrific!** Like it or not, you will be judged by your appearance. For everything but small in-house presentations, be sure to dress professionally. The rule of thumb is that you should dress at least as well as the best-dressed person in the audience.

Figure 12.5 Engaging the Audience With Effective Imagery

Metaphor — **Comparison between dissimilar things without the words *like* or *as***

- Our competitor's CEO is a snake when it comes to negotiating.
- My desk is a garbage dump.

Analogy — **Comparison of similar traits between dissimilar things**

- Product development is similar to conceiving, carrying, and delivering a baby.
- Downsizing is comparable to an overweight person's regimen of dieting and exercising.

Personalized Statistics — **Statistics that affect the audience**

- Look around you. Only three out of five graduates will find a job right after graduation.
- One typical meal at a fast food restaurant contains all the calories you need for an entire day.

Worst- or Best-Case Scenario — **The worst or best that could happen**

- If we don't back up now, a crash could wipe out all customer data.
- If we fix the system now, we can expand our customer files and also increase sales.

Personal Anecdote — **A personal story**

- Let me share a few personal blunders online and what I learned from my mistakes.
- I always worried about my pets while I was away. That's when I decided to start a pet hotel.

Simile — **Comparison that includes the words *like* or *as***

- Our critics used our report like a drunk uses a lamppost—for support rather than illumination.
- She's as happy as someone who just won the lottery.

- **Animate your body.** Be enthusiastic and let your body show it. Stand with good posture to show confidence. Emphasize ideas to enhance points about size, number, and direction. Use a variety of gestures, but don't plan them in advance.

- **Punctuate your words.** You can keep your audience interested by varying your tone, volume, pitch, and pace. Use pauses before and after important points. Allow the audience to take in your ideas.

- **Get out from behind the podium.** Avoid standing rigidly behind the podium. Movement makes you look natural and comfortable. You might pick a few places in the room to walk to. Even if you must stay close to your visual aids, make a point of leaving them occasionally so that the audience can see your whole body.

LEARNING OBJECTIVE 3

Understand visual aids and how to avoid ineffective PowerPoint practices.

- **Vary your facial expression.** Begin with a smile, but change your expressions to correspond with the thoughts you are voicing. You can shake your head to show disagreement, roll your eyes to show disdain, look heavenward for guidance, or wrinkle your brow to show concern or dismay.

Whenever possible, beginning presenters should have an experienced speaker watch them and give them tips as they rehearse. Your instructor is an important coach who can provide you with invaluable feedback. In the absence of helpers, record yourself and watch your nonverbal behavior on camera. Are you doing what it takes to build rapport?

12-3 Understanding Contemporary Visual Aids

Before you make a business presentation, consider this wise proverb: "Tell me, I forget. Show me, I remember. Involve me, I understand." Your goals as a speaker are to make listeners understand, remember, and act on your ideas. To get them interested and involved, include effective visual aids. Some experts say that we acquire as much as 85 percent of all our knowledge visually: "Professionals everywhere need to know about the incredible inefficiency of text-based information and the incredible effects of images," says developmental biologist John Medina.[2] Therefore, an oral presentation that incorporates visual aids is far more likely to be retained than one lacking visual enhancement.

Good visual aids serve many purposes. They emphasize and clarify main points, thus improving comprehension and retention. They increase audience interest, and they make the presenter appear more professional, better prepared, and more persuasive. Well-designed visual aids illustrate and emphasize your message more effectively than words alone; therefore, they may help shorten a meeting or achieve your goal faster. Good visuals also serve to jog the memory of a speaker, thus improving self-confidence, poise, and delivery.

12-3a Types of Visual Aids

Speakers have many forms of media at their fingertips to enhance their presentations. Figure 12.6 describes the pros and cons of several visual aids, both high-tech and low-tech, that can guide you in selecting the best one for any speaking occasion. Two of the most popular visuals for business presentations are multimedia slides and handouts. Zoom presentations, an alternative to multimedia slides, are growing in popularity.

Multimedia Slides. With today's excellent software programs—such as Microsoft PowerPoint, Apple Keynote, Apache OpenOffice Impress, Corel Presentations, and Adobe Presenter—you can create dynamic, colorful presentations with your desktop, laptop, tablet, or smartphone. The output from these programs is generally shown on a computer screen, a TV monitor, an LCD (liquid crystal display) panel, or a projection screen. With a little expertise and the right equipment, you can create multimedia presentations that include audio, videos, images, animation, and hyperlinks, as described in the next section on multimedia presentations. Digital slides can also be uploaded to a website or broadcast on the Web.

Handouts. You can enhance and complement your presentations by distributing pictures, outlines, brochures, articles, charts, summaries, or other supplements. Speakers who use multimedia presentation software often prepare a set of their slides along with notes to hand out to viewers. To avoid distractions and to keep control, you should announce and discuss handouts during the presentation but delay distributing them until after you finish.

Figure 12.6 Pros and Cons of Visual Aid Options

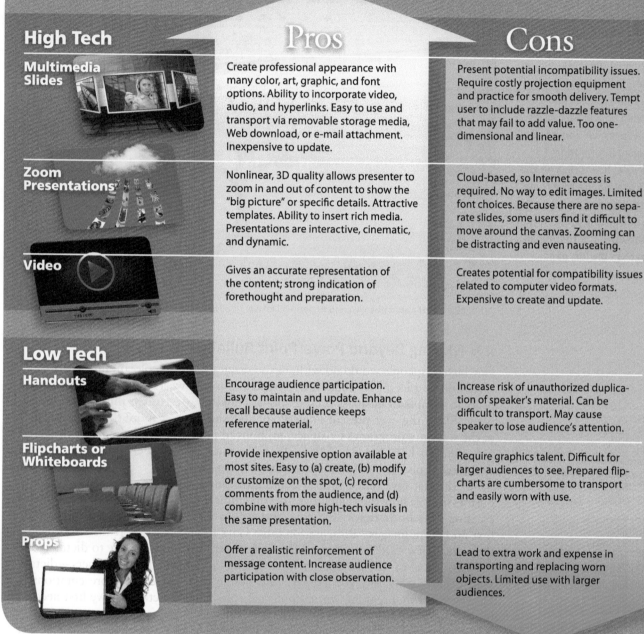

High Tech	Pros	Cons
Multimedia Slides	Create professional appearance with many color, art, graphic, and font options. Ability to incorporate video, audio, and hyperlinks. Easy to use and transport via removable storage media, Web download, or e-mail attachment. Inexpensive to update.	Present potential incompatibility issues. Require costly projection equipment and practice for smooth delivery. Tempt user to include razzle-dazzle features that may fail to add value. Too one-dimensional and linear.
Zoom Presentations	Nonlinear, 3D quality allows presenter to zoom in and out of content to show the "big picture" or specific details. Attractive templates. Ability to insert rich media. Presentations are interactive, cinematic, and dynamic.	Cloud-based, so Internet access is required. No way to edit images. Limited font choices. Because there are no separate slides, some users find it difficult to move around the canvas. Zooming can be distracting and even nauseating.
Video	Gives an accurate representation of the content; strong indication of forethought and preparation.	Creates potential for compatibility issues related to computer video formats. Expensive to create and update.
Low Tech		
Handouts	Encourage audience participation. Easy to maintain and update. Enhance recall because audience keeps reference material.	Increase risk of unauthorized duplication of speaker's material. Can be difficult to transport. May cause speaker to lose audience's attention.
Flipcharts or Whiteboards	Provide inexpensive option available at most sites. Easy to (a) create, (b) modify or customize on the spot, (c) record comments from the audience, and (d) combine with more high-tech visuals in the same presentation.	Require graphics talent. Difficult for larger audiences to see. Prepared flipcharts are cumbersome to transport and easily worn with use.
Props	Offer a realistic reinforcement of message content. Increase audience participation with close observation.	Lead to extra work and expense in transporting and replacing worn objects. Limited use with larger audiences.

Zoom Presentations. Many business presenters feel limited by multimedia slides, which tend to be linear. As a result, some communicators prefer more dynamic visual aids. Using software such as Prezi, which is a cloud-based presentation and storytelling tool, businesspeople can design 3D presentations. These 3D presentations allow the speaker to zoom out and in of images to help the audience better understand and remember content, details, and relationships.[3] Zoom presentations allow presenters to communicate their ideas in a more exciting, creative way. Audience members also seem to appreciate the cinematic, interactive quality of these presentations. Figure 12.7 shows what a typical Prezi canvas looks like during the design process.

Figure **12.7** Prezi Zoom Presentation

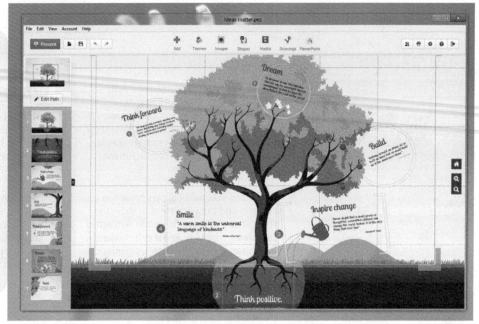

Source: http://prezi-a.akamaihd.net/presskit/Prezi%20Desktop/PreziDesktop_Windows.png

Prezi uses one canvas for a presentation rather than individual slides. Here is an example of the main canvas of a zoom presentation. Clicking on any section of this canvas will zoom in on detailed information. For example, if you click on the area around the tree roots, you will zoom in on a quote about thinking positively, as shown in the thumbnail images in the left pane.

12-3b Moving Beyond PowerPoint Bullets

Few businesspeople would do without the razzle-dazzle of colorful images to make their points. Electronic slideshows, created using PowerPoint in particular, have become a staple of business presentations. However, overuse or misuse may be the downside of the ever-present PowerPoint slideshow. Over more than two decades of the software program's existence, millions of poorly created and badly delivered presentations have tarnished PowerPoint's reputation as an effective communication tool. Tools are helpful only when used properly.

In the last few years, several communication consultants have tried to show businesspeople how they can move "beyond bullet points." The experts recommend creating slideshows that tell a story and send a powerful message with much less text and more images.[4] Presentation guru Garr Reynolds urges readers to unleash their creativity: "Do not rely on Microsoft or Apple or anyone else to dictate your choices. Most of all, do not let mere habit—and the habits of others—dictate your decisions on how you prepare and design and deliver your presentations."[5] However, before breaking with established rules and expectations, we first need to understand design basics.

Even much-touted alternatives to PowerPoint, such as Prezi and SlideRocket, require some knowledge of the sound design principles covered in the next section. Figure 12.8 shows some of the tools that SlideRocket provides to create a visually rich presentation. The goal is to abandon boring bulleted lists.

12-4 Preparing Engaging Multimedia Presentations

LEARNING OBJECTIVE 4
Create an impressive, error-free multimedia presentation that shows a firm grasp of basic visual design principles.

Some presenters prefer to create their visuals first and then develop the narrative around their visuals. Others prepare their content first and then create the visual component. The risk associated with the first approach is that you may be tempted to spend too much time making your visuals look good and not enough time

Figure **12.8** SlideRocket Presentation

SlideRocket is a cloud-based presentation software. Like PowerPoint, it allows users to create slides, but it takes the emphasis off bullet points. Instead, SlideRocket offers numerous tools to help users create visually rich slides: stock photos, flash animation, 2D and 3D transitional effects, tables, and charts.

Source: http://www.sliderocket.com/product/

preparing your content. Remember that great-looking slides never compensate for thin content.

The following sections explain how to adjust your visuals to the situation and your audience. You will also receive how-to instructions for creating engaging and visually appealing PowerPoint, SlideRocket, and Prezi presentations.

12-4a Analyzing the Situation and Purpose

Making the best design choices for your presentation depends greatly on your analysis of the situation and the purpose of your slideshow. Will your slides be used during a live presentation? Will they be part of a self-running presentation such as in a store kiosk? Will they be saved on a server so that users can watch the presentation online at their convenience? Will they be sent as a PowerPoint show or a PDF slide deck to a client instead of a hard-copy report? Are you converting your presentation for viewing on smartphones or tablets?

If you are e-mailing the presentation or posting it online as a self-contained file, or slide deck, it should feature more text than one that you would deliver orally. If, on the other hand, you are creating slides for a live presentation, you will likely rely more on images than on text.

12-4b Adjusting Slide Design to Your Audience

Think about how you can design your presentation to get the most positive response from your audience. Audiences respond, for example, to the colors, images, and special effects you use. Primary ideas are generally best conveyed with bold colors such as blue, green, and purple. Because the messages that colors convey can vary from culture to culture, presenters must choose colors and other design elements carefully.

The Meaning of Color. In the United States, blue is the color of credibility, tranquility, conservatism, and trust. Therefore, it is the background color of choice for many business presentations and social media sites. Green relates to interaction, growth, money, and stability. It can work well as a background or an accent color. Purple can also work as a background or accent color. It conveys spirituality, royalty, dreams, and humor.[6] As for text, adjust the color in such a way that it provides high contrast so it is readable. White or yellow, for example, usually works well on dark backgrounds.

Adapt the slide colors based on where you will give the presentation. Use light text on a dark background for presentations in darkened rooms. Use dark text on

a light background for presentations in lighted rooms. Avoid using a dark font on a dark background, such as red text on a dark blue background. In the same way, avoid using a light font on a light background, such as white text on a pale blue background.

The Power of Images. Adapt the amount of text on your slide to how your audience will use the slides. As a general guideline, most graphic designers encourage the use of *the 6-x-6 rule*: "Six bullets per screen, max; six words per bullet, max."[7] You may find, however, that breaking this rule is sometimes necessary, particularly when your users will be viewing the presentation on their own with no speaker assistance. For most purposes, though, strive to break free from bulleted lists whenever possible and minimize the use of text.

When using presentation software such as PowerPoint, try to avoid long, boring bulleted lists. You can alter layouts by repositioning, resizing, or changing the fonts for the placeholders in which your title, bulleted list, organization chart, video clip, photograph, or other elements appear. Figure 12.9 shows how to make your slides visually more appealing and memorable even with relatively small changes.

Notice that the bulleted items on the Before Revision slide in Figure 12.9 are not parallel. The wording looks as if the author had been brainstorming or freewriting a first draft. The bullets on the After Revision slide are very short and well within the 6-x-6 rule, although they are complete sentences. The illustrations in the revised slide add interest and highlight the message. You may use stock photos that you can download from the Web for personal or school use without penalty, or consider taking your own digital pictures.

You can also use other PowerPoint features, such as SmartArt, to add variety and pizzazz to your slides. Converting pure text and bullet points to graphics, charts, and other images will keep your audiences interested and help them retain the information you are presenting.

The Impact of Special Effects. Just as you anticipate audience members' reactions to color and images, you can usually anticipate their reactions to special effects. Using animation and sound effects—flying objects, swirling text, clashing cymbals, and the like—only because they are available is not a good idea. Special effects distract your audience, drawing attention away from your main points. Add

Figure **12.9** Revising and Enhancing Slides for Greater Impact

The slide on the left contains bullet points that are not parallel and that overlap in meaning. The second and sixth bullet points say the same thing. Moreover, some bullet points are too long. After revision, the slide on the right has a more convincing title illustrating the "you" view. The bullet points are shorter, and each begins with a verb for parallelism and an emphasis on action. The illustrations add interest.

animation features only if doing so helps convey your message or adds interest to the content. When your audience members leave, they should be commenting on the ideas you conveyed—not on the wild swivels and sound effects. The zooming effect of Prezi presentations can add value to your presentation as long as it helps your audience understand connections and remember content. The motion should not make your listeners dizzy.

12-4c Building Your Business Presentation

After considering design principles and their effects, you are ready to start putting together your presentation. In this section you will learn how to organize and compose your presentation, which templates to choose, and how to edit, proofread, and evaluate your work.

Organizing Your Presentation. When you prepare your presentation, translate the major headings in your outline into titles for slides. Then build bullet points using short phrases. In Chapter 4 you learned to improve readability by using graphic highlighting techniques, including bullets, numbers, and headings. In preparing a PowerPoint, SlideRocket, or Prezi presentation, you will use those same techniques.

The slides (or canvas) you create to accompany your spoken ideas can be organized with visual elements that will help your audience understand and remember what you want to communicate. Let's say, for example, that you have three points in your presentation. You can create a blueprint slide that captures the three points in a visually appealing way, and then you can use that slide several times throughout your presentation. Near the beginning, the blueprint slide provides an overview of your points. Later, it provides transitions as you move from point to point. For transitions, you can direct your audience's attention by highlighting the next point you will be talking about. Finally, the blueprint slide can be used near the end to provide a review of your key points.

Composing Your Presentation. During the composition stage, many users fall into the trap of excessive formatting and programming. They fritter away precious time fine-tuning their slides or canvas and don't spend enough time on what they are going to say and how they will say it. To avoid this trap, set a limit for how much time you will spend making your slides or canvas visually appealing. Your time limit will be based on how many "bells and whistles" (a) your audience expects and (b) your content requires to make it understandable. Remember that not every point nor every thought requires a visual. In fact, it's smart to switch off the presentation occasionally and direct the focus to yourself. Darkening the screen while you discuss a point, tell a story, give an example, or involve the audience will add variety to your presentation.

Create a slide or canvas only if it accomplishes at least one of the following purposes:

- Generates interest in what you are saying and helps the audience follow your ideas
- Highlights points you want your audience to remember
- Introduces or reviews your key points
- Provides a transition from one major point to the next
- Illustrates and simplifies complex ideas

Consider perusing the Help articles built into your presentation software or purchasing one of many inexpensive guides to electronic slide presentations. Your presentations will be more appealing and you will save time if you know, for example, how to design with master slides and how to create your own templates.

Working With Templates. All presentation programs require you to (a) select or create a template that will serve as the background for your presentation and (b) make each slide by selecting a layout that best conveys your message. Novice and even advanced users often choose existing templates because they are designed by

sjenner13/iStock/Thinkstock

professionals who know how to combine harmonious colors, borders, bullet styles, and fonts for pleasing visual effects. If you prefer, you can alter existing templates so they better suit your needs. Adding a corporate logo, adjusting the color scheme to better match the colors used on your organization's website, or selecting a different font are just some of the ways you can customize existing templates. One big advantage of templates is that they get you started quickly.

Be careful, though, of what one expert has labeled "visual clichés."[8] Overused templates and clip art that come preinstalled with PowerPoint, SlideRocket, and Prezi can weary viewers who have seen them repeatedly in presentations. Instead of using a standard template, search for *PowerPoint template*, *SlideRocket template*, or *Prezi template* in your favorite search tool. You will see hundreds of templates available as free downloads. Unless your employer requires that presentations all have the same look, your audience will appreciate fresh templates that complement the purpose of your presentation and provide visual variety.

Revising and Proofreading. Use the PowerPoint slide sorter view to rearrange, insert, and delete slides during the revision process. You can also use the Prezi editor to make any necessary changes to your canvas. This is the time to focus on making your presentation as clear and concise as possible. If you are listing items, be sure they all use parallel grammatical form. Figure 12.10 shows how to revise a PowerPoint slide to improve it for conciseness, parallelism, and other features. Study the design tips described in the first slide and determine which suggestions their author did not follow. Then compare it with the revised slide.

As you are revising, check carefully to find spelling, grammar, punctuation, and other errors. Use the PowerPoint, SlideRocket, or Prezi spell-check feature, but don't rely on it solely. Careful proofing, preferably from a printed copy of the slideshow, is a must. Nothing is as embarrassing as projecting errors on a huge screen in front of an audience. Also, check for consistency in how you capitalize and punctuate points throughout the presentation.

Evaluating Your Presentation. Finally, critically evaluate your slideshow. Is your message presented in a visually appealing way? Have you tested your slides on the equipment and in the room you will be using during your presentation? Do the

Figure **12.10** Designing More Effective Slides

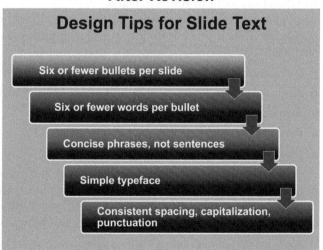

The slide on the left uses a difficult-to-read font style. In addition, the slide includes too many words per bullet and violates most of the slide-making rules it covers. After revision, the slide on the right provides a pleasing color combination, uses short bullet points in a readable font style, and creates an attractive list using PowerPoint SmartArt features.

Figure PowerPoint Slides That Illustrate Multimedia Presentations

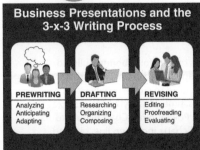

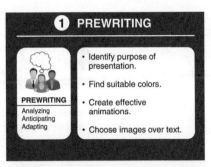

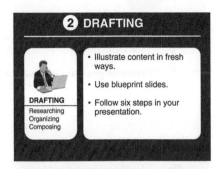

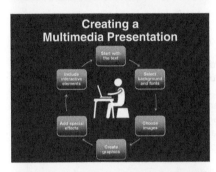

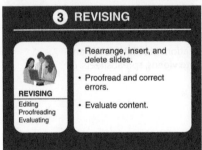

© 2016 Cengage Learning*; © Iadam/Fotolia; © denis_pc/Fotolia; © Jeremy/Fotolia; © Andrey/Fotolia; © kyoko/Fotolia

Source: Microsoft; © HaywireMedia/Fotolia;

colors you selected work in this new setting? Are the font styles and sizes readable from the back of the room? Figure 12.11 shows examples of PowerPoint slides that incorporate what you have learned in this discussion.

The dark purple background and the matching hues in the slideshow shown in Figure 12.11 are standard choices for many business presentations. With an unobtrusive dark background, white fonts are a good option for maximum contrast and, hence, readability. The creator of the presentation varied the slide design to break the monotony of bulleted or numbered lists. Images and animated diagrams add interest and zing to the slides.

Some presenters allow their PowerPoint slides, SlideRocket slides, or Prezi canvases to steal their thunder. One expert urges speakers to "use their PowerPresence in preference to their PowerPoint."[9] Although multimedia presentations supply terrific sizzle, they cannot replace the steak. In developing a presentation, don't expect your slides to carry the show. You can avoid being upstaged by not relying totally on your slides or canvas. Remember that you are the main attraction!

12-4d Seven Steps to Making a Powerful Multimedia Presentation

We have now discussed many suggestions for making effective PowerPoint, SlideRocket, and Prezi presentations, but you may still be wondering how to put it all together. Figure 12.12 presents a step-by-step process for creating a powerful multimedia presentation.

Figure **12.12** Seven Steps to a Powerful Multimedia Presentation

1 Start with the text.

What do you want your audience to believe, do, or remember? Organize your ideas into an outline with major and minor points.

2 Select background and fonts.

Choose a template or create your own. Focus on consistent font styles, sizes, colors, and backgrounds. Try to use no more than two font styles in your presentation. The point size should be between 24 and 36, and title fonts should be larger than text font.

3 Choose images that help communicate your message.

Use relevant clip art, infographics, photographs, maps, or drawings to illustrate ideas. Microsoft Office Online is accessed in PowerPoint and contains thousands of clip art images and photographs, most of which are in the public domain and require no copyright permissions. Before using images from other sources, determine whether permission from the copyright holder is required.

4 Create graphics.

Use software tools to transform boring bulleted items into appealing graphics and charts. PowerPoint's SmartArt feature can be used to create organization charts, cycles and radials, time lines, pyramids, matrixes, and Venn diagrams. Use PowerPoint's Chart feature to develop various types of charts including line, pie, and bar charts. But don't overdo the graphics!

5 Add special effects.

To keep the audience focused, use animation and transition features to control when objects or text appear. With motion paths, 3D, and other animation options, you can move objects to various positions on the slide and zoom in and out of images and text on your canvas; or to minimize clutter, you can dim or remove them once they have served their purpose.

6 Create hyperlinks.

Make your presentation more interactive and intriguing by connecting to videos, spreadsheets, or websites.

7 Move your presentation online.

Make your presentation available by posting it to the Internet or an organization's intranet. Even if you are giving a face-to-face presentation, attendees appreciate these electronic handouts. The most complex option for moving your multimedia presentation to the Web involves a Web conference or broadcast. You can convert your presentations to PDF documents or send them via e-mail as files that open directly in PowerPoint or Prezi. SlideRocket presentations can be embedded in a website or blog to be viewed by anyone who visits the site.

12-5 Polishing Your Delivery and Following Up

Once you have organized your presentation and prepared visuals, you are ready to practice delivering it. You will feel more confident and appear more professional if you know more about delivery methods and techniques to use before, during, and after your presentation.

12-5a Choosing a Delivery Method

Inexperienced speakers often hold on to myths about public speaking. They may believe that they must memorize an entire presentation or read from a manuscript to be successful. Let's debunk the myths and focus on effective delivery techniques.

Avoid Memorizing Your Presentation. Unless you are an experienced performer, you will sound robotic and unnatural if you try to recite your talk by heart. What's more, forgetting your place can be disastrous! That's why we don't recommend memorizing an entire oral presentation. However, memorizing significant parts—the introduction, the conclusion, and perhaps a meaningful quotation—can make your presentation dramatic and impressive.

Don't Read From Your Notes. Reading your business presentation to an audience from notes or a manuscript is boring, and listeners will quickly lose interest. Because reading suggests that you don't know your topic well, the audience loses confidence in your expertise. Reading also prevents you from maintaining eye contact. You can't see audience reactions; consequently, you can't benefit from feedback.

Deliver Your Presentation Extemporaneously. The best plan for delivering convincing business presentations, by far, is to speak extemporaneously, especially when you are displaying a multimedia presentation, such as a PowerPoint slideshow, SlideRocket slideshow, or Prezi canvas. Extemporaneous delivery means speaking freely, generally without notes, after preparing and rehearsing. This includes commenting on the multimedia visuals you have prepared. Reading notes or a manuscript in addition to a PowerPoint slideshow, SlideRocket slides, or a Prezi canvas will damage your credibility.

Know When Notes Are Appropriate. If you give a talk without multimedia technology, you may use note cards or an outline containing key sentences and major ideas, but beware of reading from a script. By preparing and then practicing with your notes, you can use them while also talking to your audience in a conversational manner. Your notes should be neither entire paragraphs nor single words. Instead, they should contain a complete sentence or two to introduce each major idea. Below the topic sentence(s), outline subpoints and illustrations. Note cards will keep you on track and prompt your memory, but only if you have rehearsed the presentation thoroughly.

Workplace in Focus

Many people fear public speaking. And while tips for overcoming performance anxiety often suggest calming down before a presentation, one Harvard researcher says that the cure for stage fright is not relaxing oneself, but recasting anxiety as excitement—and embracing it. According to a recent study by Alison Wood Brooks of Harvard Business School, individuals who convinced themselves that their nervousness was "excitement" prior to giving a speech performed better than those who attempted to relax. Brooks argues that speakers can recast anxiety as excitement simply through active self-talk, such as saying aloud "I am excited" or "get excited." What other tips can speakers use to help overcome stage fright EN?[11]

© iStockphoto.com/GlobalStock

12-5b Before Your Presentation

Speaking in front of a group will be less daunting if you prepare adequately and rehearse sufficiently. Being prepared and confident so you can interact with the audience, and being familiar with the equipment to limit surprises, will add to your peace of mind. Review the tips in the following sections for a smooth start.

Prepare Thoroughly. One of the most effective strategies for reducing stage fright is knowing your subject thoroughly. Research your topic diligently and prepare a careful sentence outline. One expert advises presenters to complete their PowerPoint slides, SlideRocket slides, or Prezi canvases a week before the actual talk and rehearse several times each day before the presentation.[10] Those who try to "wing it" usually suffer the worst butterflies—and give the worst presentations. Figure 12.13 offers tips for combating the fear of public speaking.

Rehearse Repeatedly. When you rehearse, practice your entire presentation. In PowerPoint you may print out speaker's notes, an outline, or a handout featuring miniature slides, which are excellent for practice. If you don't use an electronic slideshow, place your outline sentences on separate note cards. You may also wish to include transitional sentences to help you move to the next topic as you practice. Rehearse alone or before friends and family. Also consider making an audio or video recording of your rehearsals so you can evaluate your effectiveness.

Figure **12.13** Conquering Stage Fright

© Maridav/Shutterstock.com

Ever get nervous before making a presentation? Everyone does! And it's not all in your head, either. When you face something threatening or challenging, your body reacts in what psychologists call the fight-or-flight response. This physical reflex provides your body with increased energy to deal with threatening situations. It also creates those sensations—dry mouth, sweaty hands, increased heartbeat, and stomach butterflies—that we associate with stage fright. The fight-or-flight response arouses your body for action—in this case, making a presentation.

Because everyone feels some form of apprehension before speaking, it's impossible to eliminate the physiological symptoms altogether. However, you can reduce their effects with the following techniques:

- **Breathe deeply.** Use deep breathing to ease your fight-or-flight symptoms. Inhale to a count of ten, hold this breath to a count of ten, and exhale to a count of ten. Concentrate on your counting and your breathing; both activities reduce your stress.

- **Convert your fear.** Don't view your sweaty palms and dry mouth as evidence of fear. Interpret them as symptoms of exuberance, excitement, and enthusiasm to share your ideas.

- **Know your topic and come prepared.** Feel confident about your topic. Select a topic that you know well and that is relevant to your audience. Prepare thoroughly and practice extensively.

- **Use positive self-talk.** Remind yourself that you know your topic and are prepared. Tell yourself that the audience is on your side—because it is! Moreover, most speakers appear to be more confident than they feel. Make this apparent confidence work for you.

- **Take a sip of water.** Drink some water to alleviate your dry mouth and constricted voice box, especially if you're talking for more than 15 minutes.

- **Shift the spotlight to your visuals.** At least some of the time the audience will be focusing on your slides, transparencies, handouts, or whatever you have prepared—and not totally on you.

- **Ignore any stumbles.** If you make a mistake, ignore the stumble and keep going. Don't apologize or confess your nervousness. The audience will forget any mistakes quickly.

- **Feel proud when you finish.** You will be surprised at how good you feel when you finish. Take pride in what you have accomplished, and your audience will reward you with applause and congratulations. Your body, of course, will call off the fight-or-flight response and return to normal!

Time Yourself. Most audiences tend to get restless during longer talks. Therefore, try to complete your presentation in 20 minutes or less. If you have a time limit, don't go over it. Set a simple kitchen timer during your rehearsal to keep track of time. Better yet, use the PowerPoint function Rehearse Timings in the Slide Show tab to measure the length of your talk as you practice. Other presentation software packages offer similar features.

Dress Professionally. Dressing professionally for a presentation will make you look more credible to your audience. You will also feel more confident. If you are not used to professional attire, practice wearing it so you appear comfortable during your presentation.

Request a Lectern. Every beginning speaker needs the security of a high desk or lectern from which to deliver a presentation. It serves as a note holder and a convenient place to rest wandering hands and arms. Don't, however, lean on it. Eventually, you will want to interact with the audience without any physical barriers.

Check the Room. If you are using a computer, a projector, or sound equipment, be certain they are operational. Allow plenty of time to set up and test your equipment. Before you start, check the lighting, the electrical outlets, and the position of the viewing screen. Confirm that the places you plan to stand are not in the line of the projected image. Audience members don't appreciate having part of the slide displayed on your body. Ensure that the seating arrangement is appropriate to your needs. Make sure that all video or Web links are working and that you know how to operate all features the first time you try.

Greet Members of the Audience. Try to make contact with a few members of the audience when you enter the room, while you are waiting to be introduced, or when you walk to the podium. Your body language should convey friendliness, confidence, and enjoyment.

Practice Stress Reduction. If you feel tension and fear while you are waiting to speak, use stress-reduction techniques, such as deep breathing. Additional techniques to help you conquer stage fright are presented in Figure 12.13.

No matter how much time you put into preshow setup and testing, you still have no guarantee that all will go smoothly. Therefore, always bring backups of your presentation. Overhead transparencies and handouts of your presentation provide good substitutes. Transferring your presentation to a CD or a USB flash drive that could run from any available computer might prove useful as well. Likewise, copying your file to the cloud (e.g., Dropbox or Google Drive) or sending it to yourself as an e-mail attachment can be beneficial.

12-5c During Your Presentation

To stay in control during your talk, to build credibility, and to engage your audience, follow these time-tested guidelines for effective speaking:

Start With a Pause and Present Your First Sentence From Memory. When you first approach the audience, take a moment to make yourself comfortable. Establish your control of the situation. By memorizing your opening, you can immediately develop rapport with the audience through eye contact. You will also sound confident and knowledgeable.

Maintain Eye Contact. If the size of the audience overwhelms you, pick out two individuals on the right and two on the left. Talk directly to these people. Don't ignore listeners in the back of the room. Even when presenting to a large audience, try to make genuine, not fleeting eye contact with as many people as possible during your presentation.

Control Your Voice and Vocabulary. This means speaking in moderated tones but loudly enough to be heard. Eliminate verbal static, such as *ah, er, like, you know,* and *um.* Silence is preferable to meaningless fillers when you are thinking of your next idea.

Show Enthusiasm. If you are not excited about your topic, how can you expect your audience to be? Show passion for your topic through your tone, facial expressions, and gestures. Adding variety to your voice also helps to keep your audience alert and interested.

Skip the Apologies. Avoid weak openings, such as *I know you have heard this before, but we need to review it anyway.* Or: *I had trouble with my computer and the slides, so bear with me.* Unless the issue is blatant, such as not being able to load the presentation or make the projector work, apologies are counterproductive. Focus on your presentation.

Slow Down and Know When to Pause. Many novice speakers talk too rapidly, displaying their nervousness and making it very difficult for audience members to understand their ideas. Put the brakes on and listen to what you are saying. Pauses give the audience time to absorb an important point. Silence can be effective especially when you are transitioning from one point to another. Paraphrase and elaborate on what the listeners have seen. Don't read verbatim from the slides.

Move Naturally. If you have a lectern, don't hide behind it. Move about casually and naturally. Using a remote clicker to advance slides will give you the freedom to move about. Avoid fidgeting with your clothing, hair, or items in your pockets. Do not roll up your sleeves or put your hands in your pockets. Learn to use your body to express a point.

Use Visual Aids Effectively. You should discuss and interpret each visual aid for the audience. Move aside as you describe it so people can see it fully. Use a laser pointer if necessary, but steady your hand if it is shaking. Don't leave your slides on-screen when you finish discussing them; if you are not ready to continue, dim the slideshow. In Slide Show view in PowerPoint, press *B* on the keyboard to turn on or off the screen image by blackening it. Pressing *W* will turn the screen white. In Prezi, remember to zoom back out when necessary.

Avoid Digressions. Stick to your outline and notes. Don't suddenly include clever little anecdotes or digressions that occur to you on the spot. If it is not part of your rehearsed material, leave it out so you can finish on time.

Summarize Your Main Points and Drive Home Your Message. Conclude your presentation by reiterating your main points or by emphasizing what you want the audience to think or do. Once you have announced your conclusion, proceed to it directly.

12-5d After Your Presentation

As you are concluding you presentation, handle questions and answers competently and provide handouts, if appropriate. Try the following techniques:

Distribute Handouts. If you prepared handouts with data the audience will not need during the presentation, pass them out when you finish to prevent any distractions during your talk.

Encourage Questions but Keep Control. If the situation permits a question-and-answer period, announce it at the beginning of your presentation. Then, when you finish, ask for questions. Set a time limit for questions and answers. If you don't know the answer to a question, don't make one up or panic. Instead, offer to find the answer within a day or two. If you make such a promise to your audience, be sure to follow through. As you're answering questions, don't allow one individual to dominate the conversation. Keep the entire audience involved.

Repeat Questions. Although you may have heard the question, some audience members may not have. Begin each answer by repeating the question. This also gives you thinking time. Then, direct your answer to the entire audience.

Reinforce Your Main Points. You can use your answers to restate your primary ideas (*I'm glad you brought that up because it gives me a chance to elaborate on . . .*). In answering questions, avoid becoming defensive or debating the questioner.

Avoid *Yes, but* Answers. The word *but* immediately cancels any preceding message. Try replacing it with *and*. For example, *Yes, X has been tried. And Y works even better because. . . .*

End With a Summary and Appreciation. To signal the end of the session before you take the last question, say something like *We have time for just one more question.* As you answer the last question, try to work it into a summary of your main points. Then, express appreciation to the audience for the opportunity to present.

. . . .

SUMMARY OF LEARNING OBJECTIVES

12-1 Recognize various types of business presentations, and discuss two important first steps in preparing for any of these presentations.
- Excellent presentation skills are sought by employers and will benefit you at any career stage.
- Presentation types include briefings, reports, podcasts, and webinars; they can be informative or persuasive, face-to-face or virtual, and complex or simple.
- Savvy speakers know what they want to accomplish and are able to adjust to friendly, neutral, uninterested, as well as hostile audiences.

12-2 Explain how to organize the introduction, body, and conclusion as well as how to build audience rapport in a presentation.
- In the opening, capture the audience's attention, introduce yourself and establish your credibility, and preview your talk.
- Organize the body using chronology, space, function, comparison/contrast, a journalistic pattern, value/size, importance, problem/solution, simple/complex, or best case/worst case.
- In the conclusion, summarize the main topics of your talk, leave the audience with a memorable take-away, and end with a statement that provides a graceful exit.
- Build rapport by using effective imagery, verbal signposts, and positive nonverbal messages.

12-3 Understand visual aids and how to avoid ineffective PowerPoint practices.
- Your audience is more likely to retain your talk if you use well-prepared visual aids.
- Good visuals emphasize and clarify main points, increase audience interest, prove you are professional, illustrate your message better than words alone, and serve to jog your memory.
- Common types of visual aids are multimedia slides, zoom presentations, videos, handouts, flipcharts and whiteboards, as well as props.
- In good hands PowerPoint is helpful, but you should focus on using more images and less text.

12-4 Create an impressive, error-free multimedia presentation that shows a firm grasp of basic visual design principles.
- The purpose and the audience determine the slide design, which includes color, images, and special effects.
- Building a presentation involves organizing and composing slide content, avoiding overused templates, and revising, proofreading, and evaluating the final product.
- The seven steps to creating impressive multimedia slides are as follows: start with the text, select a template, choose images, create graphics, add special effects, create hyperlinks, and post online.

12-5 Specify delivery techniques for use before, during, and after a presentation.

- When delivering a business presentation, don't memorize your talk or read from notes; rather, speak extemporaneously and use notes only when you're not using presentation software.
- Before your presentation prepare and rehearse, time yourself, dress professionally, request a lectern, check the room, greet members of the audience, and practice stress reduction.
- During the presentation deliver your first sentence from memory, maintain eye contact, control your voice, show enthusiasm, slow down, move naturally, use visual aids skillfully, and stay on topic.
- After the presentation distribute handouts, encourage and repeat questions, reinforce your main points, avoid *Yes, but* answers, and end with a summary and appreciation.

CHAPTER REVIEW

1. List and describe five types of presentations a business professional might make. (Obj. 1)

2. The age, gender, education level, experience, and size of the audience will affect your presentation style and message. List at least five questions you should answer to determine your organizational pattern, delivery style, and supporting material. (Obj. 1)

3. Which effective three-step organizational plan do many speech experts recommend, and why does it work well for oral presentations despite its redundancy? (Obj. 2)

4. What three goals should you accomplish in the introduction to your presentation? (Obj. 2)

5. Name at least eight techniques that can help you gain and keep audience attention. (Obj. 2)

6. List high-tech and low-tech visual aids that you can use when speaking to an audience. Which two are the most popular? (Obj. 3)

7. What is the 6-x-6 rule, and what might prompt a presentation slide creator to break it? (Obj. 4)

8. What questions might help you critically evaluate a slideshow? (Obj. 4)

9. Which delivery method is best for persuasive business presentations? Explain why. (Obj. 5)

10. How can speakers overcome stage fright? Name at least six helpful techniques. (Obj. 5)

CRITICAL THINKING

11. Most people never address large audiences and live in fear of public speaking. Why then should you hone your presentation skills? (Obj. 1)

12. Communication expert Dianna Booher claims that enthusiasm is infectious and "boredom is contagious."[12] What does this mean for you as a presenter? How can you avoid being a boring speaker? (Objs. 2, 4, and 5)

13. Why do many communication consultants encourage businesspeople to move beyond bullet points? What do they recommend instead and why? (Obj. 3)

14. How can you prevent multimedia presentation software from stealing your thunder? (Obj. 4)

15. U.S. senator from New Jersey, Cory A. Booker, himself a popular and gifted orator, related his father's philosophy on public speaking as follows: "My dad worked for IBM. He said, 'Look, I can't sell products I don't believe in. People will see right through me. But if I'm passionate and have a deep conviction about what I'm doing, I'm the greatest salesman there is.'"[13] What qualities is Senator Booker describing, and why are they important in business? (Objs. 2, 5)

ACTIVITIES AND CASES

12.1 Learning From the Best: Analyzing a Famous Speech (Objs. 1–5)

< Web >

YOUR TASK. Search online for a speech by a significant businessperson or well-known political figure. Consider watching the following iconic political speeches, thought to be among the best in the 20th century: Martin Luther King Jr.'s "I Have a Dream" speech, President Kennedy's inaugural address, and Franklin Delano Roosevelt's Pearl Harbor address.[14] If you prefer business tycoons dispensing advice, search for the best-known commencement speeches; for example, Steve Jobs' "Stay Hungry, Stay Foolish" Stanford address, Salman Khan's "Live Your Life Like It's Your Second Chance" speech, or Sheryl Sandberg's "Rocketship" commencement speech at Harvard. Transcripts of these and other well-known speeches are also available online.[15] Write a memo report or give a short presentation to your class critiquing the speech in terms of the following:

a. Effectiveness of the introduction, body, and conclusion

b. Evidence of effective overall organization

c. Use of verbal signposts to create coherence

d. Emphasis of two to four main points

e. Effectiveness of supporting facts (use of examples, statistics, quotations, and so forth)

f. Focus on audience benefits

g. Enthusiasm for the topic

h. Body language and personal mannerisms

12.2 Sizing Up Your Audience (Objs. 2, 4)

YOUR TASK. Select a recent issue of *Fortune, The Wall Street Journal, Fast Company, Bloomberg Businessweek, The Economist*, or another business periodical approved by your instructor. Based on an analysis of your classmates, select an article that will appeal to them and that you can relate to their needs. Submit to your instructor a one-page summary that includes the following: (a) the author, article title, source, issue date, and page reference; (b) a one-paragraph article summary; (c) a description of why you believe the article will appeal to your classmates; and (d) a summary of how you can relate the article to their needs.

12.3 Hiring a Famous Motivational Speaker (Objs. 1, 2, 4, and 5)

< Communication Technology > < Social Media > < Team > < Web >

Have you ever wondered why famous business types, politicians, athletes, and other celebrities can command high speaking fees? How much are they really making per appearance, and what factors may justify their sometimes exorbitant fees? You may also wonder how a motivational speaker or corporate trainer might benefit you and your class or your campus community. Searching for and selecting an expert is easy online with several commercial speaker bureaus vying for clients. All bureaus provide detailed speaker bios, areas of expertise, and fees. One even features video previews of its clients.

The three preeminent agencies for booking talent are Speakerpedia, BigSpeak Speakers Bureau, and Brooks International. Speakerpedia represents the likes of economist Nouriel Roubini, Donald Trump, Jack Welch, Richard Branson, and Suze Orman. BigSpeak standouts are Deepak Chopra, Dr. Susan Love, and distance swimmer Diana Nyad. Brooks International features financier and philanthropist Mike Milken and TV commentator and personal finance expert Terry Savage, among others. Imagine that you have a budget of up to $100,000 to hire a well-known public speaker.

YOUR TASK. In teams or individually, select a business-related category of speaker by visiting one of the speaker bureaus online. For example, choose several prominent personal finance gurus (Orman, Savage, and others) or successful entrepreneurs and venture capitalists (Branson, Trump, Jack Welch, and so forth). Other categories are motivational speakers, philanthropists, and famous economists. Study their bios for clues to their expertise and accomplishments. Comparing at least three, come up with a set of qualities that apparently make these people sought-after speakers. Consider how those qualities could enlighten you and your peers. To enrich your experience and enhance your knowledge, watch videos of your chosen speakers on YouTube or TED, if available. Check talent agencies, personal websites, and Facebook for further information. Write a memo report about your speaker group, or present your findings orally, with or without PowerPoint. If your instructor directs, recommend your favorite speaker and give reasons for your decision.

12.4 Follow Your Favorite Business Personality on Twitter (Objs. 1–5)

< Social Media > < Web > < Communication Technology >

YOUR TASK. On Twitter, in the Search window on top of the page, enter the name of the businessperson whose tweets you wish to follow. Donald Trump, Jack Welch, Richard Branson, Suze Orman, Guy Kawasaki, and other well-known businesspeople are avid Twitter users. Over the course of a few days, read the tweets of your favorite expert. After a while, you should be able to discern certain trends and areas of interest. Note whether and how your subject responds to queries from followers. What are his or her favorite topics? Report your findings to the class, verbally with notes or using PowerPoint. If you find particularly intriguing tweets and links, share them with the class.

12.5 Taming Stage Fright (Obj. 5)

> Team

What scares you the most about making a presentation in front of your class? Being tongue-tied? Fearing all eyes on you? Messing up? Forgetting your ideas and looking silly?

YOUR TASK. Discuss the previous questions as a class. Then, in groups of three or four, talk about ways to overcome these fears. Your instructor may ask you to write a memo (individual or collective) summarizing your suggestions, or you may break out of your small groups and report your best ideas to the entire class.

12.6 How Much Speaking Can You Expect in Your Field? (Obj. 1)

YOUR TASK. Interview one or two individuals in your professional field. How is oral communication important in this profession? Does the need for oral skills change as one advances? What suggestions can these people make to newcomers to the field for developing proficient oral communication skills? Discuss your findings with your class.

12.7 Creating an Outline for an Oral Presentation (Obj. 2)

One of the hardest parts of preparing an oral presentation is developing the outline.

YOUR TASK. Select an oral presentation topic from the list in Activity 12.14, or suggest an original topic. Prepare an outline for your presentation using the following format:

Title
Purpose

I. INTRODUCTION

State your name   A.
Gain attention and involve the audience   B.
Establish credibility   C.
Preview main points   D.
Transition

II. BODY

Main point   A.
Illustrate, clarify, contrast   1.
    2.
    3.

Transition
Main point   B.
Illustrate, clarify, contrast   1.
    2.
    3.

Transition
Main point   C.
Illustrate, clarify, contrast   1.
    2.
    3.

Transition

III. CONCLUSION

Summarize main points   A.
Provide final focus or take-away   B.
Encourage questions   C.

12.8 Learning From "Life After Death by PowerPoint" (Objs. 1–5)

Social Media ⟩ ⟨ Web ⟩

YOUR TASK. Watch Don McMillan's now famous YouTube classic "Life After Death by PowerPoint 2012." Which specific PowerPoint ills is McMillan satirizing? Write a brief summary of the short clip for discussion in class. With your peers, discuss whether the bad habits the YouTube video parodies correspond with design principles introduced in this chapter.

12.9 Observing and Outlining a TED Talk (Objs. 1–5)

⟨ E-mail ⟩ ⟨ Social Media ⟩ ⟨ Web ⟩

To learn from the presentation skills of the best speakers today, visit the TED channel on YouTube or the TED website. Watch one or more of the 1,600 TED Talks (motto: *Ideas worth spreading*) available online. Standing at over one billion views worldwide, the presentations cover topics from the fields of technology, entertainment, and design (TED).

YOUR TASK. If your instructor directs, select and watch one of the TED Talks and outline it. You may also be asked to focus on the selected speaker's presentation techniques based on the guidelines you have studied in this chapter. Jot down your observations either as notes for a classroom discussion or to serve as a basis for an informative memo or e-mail. If directed by your instructor, compose a concise yet informative tweet directing Twitter users to your chosen TED Talk and commenting on it.

12.10 Talking About Your Job (Objs. 1–5)

⟨ Communication Technology ⟩

What if you had to create a presentation for your classmates and instructor, or perhaps a potential recruiter, that describes the multiple tasks you perform at work? Could you do it in a five-minute multimedia presentation?

Your instructors, for example, may wear many hats. Most academics (a) teach; (b) conduct research to publish; and (c) provide service to the department, college, university, and community. Can you see how those aspects of their profession lend themselves to an outline of primary slides (teaching, publishing, service) and second-level slides (instructing undergraduate and graduate classes, presenting workshops, and giving lectures under the *teaching* label)?

YOUR TASK. Now it's your turn to introduce the duties you perform (or performed) in a current or a past job, volunteer activity, or internship in a brief, simple, yet well-designed PowerPoint presentation. Your goal is to inform your audience of your job duties in a three- to five-minute talk. Use animation features and graphics where appropriate. Your instructor may show you a completed example of this project.

12.11 Calling All Angel Investors (Objs. 1–5)

⟨ Communication Technology ⟩

Venture capitalist and angel investor Guy Kawasaki believes that persuasive PowerPoint presentations should be no more than 10 slides long, last 20 minutes at most, and contain 30-point fonts or bigger (the 10/20/30 rule). Kawasaki is convinced that presentations deviating from this rule will fall short of their purpose, which is typically to reach some type of agreement.

Could you interest an investor such as Guy Kawasaki in your business idea? The venture capitalist believes that if you must use more than 10 slides to explain your business, you probably don't have one. Furthermore, Kawasaki claims that the 10 topics a venture capitalist cares about are the following:

1. Problem
2. Your solution
3. Business model
4. Underlying magic/technology
5. Marketing and sales

6. Competition
7. Team
8. Projections and milestones
9. Status and time line
10. Summary and call to action

YOUR TASK. Dust off that start-up fantasy you may have, and get to work. Prepare a slideshow that would satisfy Kawasaki's 10/20/30 rule: In 10 slides and a presentation of no more than 20 minutes, address the 10 topics that venture capitalists care about. Make sure that the fonts on your slides are at least 30 points in size.

12.12 Perfecting the Art of the Elevator Pitch (Objs 1, 2)

"Can you pass the elevator test?" asks presentation whiz Garr Reynolds in a new twist on the familiar scenario.[16] He suggests that this technique will help you sharpen your core message. In this exercise you need to pitch your idea in a few brief moments instead of the 20 minutes you had been granted with your vice president of product marketing. You arrive at her door for your appointment as she is leaving, coat and briefcase in hand. Something has come up. This meeting is a huge opportunity for you if you want to get the OK from the executive team. Could you sell your idea during the elevator ride and the walk to the parking lot? Reynolds asks. Although this scenario may never happen, you will possibly be asked to shorten a presentation, say, from an hour to 30 minutes or from 20 minutes to 5 minutes. Could you make your message tighter and clearer on the fly?

YOUR TASK. Take a business idea you may have, a familiar business topic you care about, or a promotion or raise you wish to request in a time of tight budgets. Create an impromptu two- to five-minute speech making a good case for your core message. Even though you won't have much time to think about the details of your speech, you should be sufficiently familiar with the topic to boil it down and yet be persuasive.

12.13 Understanding *Fortune* Lists (Objs. 1, 2)

> Web

YOUR TASK. Using a research database, perform a search to learn how *Fortune* magazine determines which companies make its annual lists. Research the following lists. Then organize and present a five- to ten-minute informative talk to your class.

a. Fortune 500
b. Global 500
c. 100 Best Companies to Work For
d. America's Most Admired Companies

12.14 Something to Talk About: Topics for an Oral Presentation (Objs. 1–5)

> Communication Technology   Web

YOUR TASK. Select a report topic from the following suggestions or from the expanded list of Report Topics at **www.cengagebrain .com**. Prepare a five- to ten-minute oral presentation. Consider yourself an expert who has been called in to explain some aspect of the topic before a group of interested people. Because your time is limited, prepare a concise yet forceful presentation with effective visual aids.

a. What kind of incentives could your company offer to motivate employees to make healthier food choices and to exercise more?
b. How can businesses benefit from Facebook and Twitter? Cite specific examples in your chosen field.
c. Which is financially more beneficial to a business, leasing or buying copiers?
d. Tablet computers are eroding the market share previously held by laptops and netbooks. Which brands are businesses embracing and why? Which features are must-haves?
e. What kind of marketing works with students on college campuses? Word of mouth? Internet advertising? Free samples? How do students prefer to get information about goods and services?
f. How can consumers protect themselves from becoming victims of identity theft?
g. How can companies and nonprofits protect themselves from hackers?
h. How could an intercultural training program be initiated in your school?
i. Companies usually do not admit shortcomings. However, some admit previous failures and use them to strategic advantage. For example, Microsoft acknowledged the shortcomings of Windows 8, its redesigned operating system that users find confusing and annoying. Find three or more examples of companies admitting weaknesses, and draw conclusions from their strategies. Would you recommend this as a sound marketing ploy?
j. How can students and other citizens contribute to conserving gasoline and other fossil fuels to save money and help slow global climate change?
k. What is the career outlook in a field of your choice? Consider job growth, compensation, and benefits. What kind of academic or other experience is typically required in your field?
l. Find a recent "disruptive" (i.e., game-changing or groundbreaking) start-up and study its business model. What need does it fill? Is it about to change its industry significantly? What are its prospects? (For example, check out Uber, Airbnb, or Coursera.)
m. What is telecommuting, and for what kinds of workers is it an appropriate work alternative?
n. What options (think aid, grants, and scholarships) do students have to finance their college tuition and fees as costs continue to rise?
o. What is the economic outlook for a given product, such as hybrid cars, laptop computers, digital cameras, fitness equipment, or a product of your choice?
p. What is Bitcoin and why are banks and law enforcement authorities concerned?
q. What franchise would offer the best investment opportunity for an entrepreneur in your area?
r. How should a job candidate prepare for a video interview via Skype or FaceTime?
s. What should a guide to proper cell phone use include?
t. Are internships worth the effort?

u. Why should a company have a written e-mail and social media policy?

v. Where should your organization hold its next convention?

w. What is the outlook for real estate (commercial or residential) investment in your area?

x. What do personal assistants for celebrities do, and how does one become a personal assistant? (Investigate the Association of Celebrity Personal Assistants.)

y. What kinds of gifts are appropriate for businesses to give clients and customers during the holiday season?

z. What rip-offs are on the Federal Trade Commission's List of Top 10 Consumer Scams, and how can consumers avoid falling for them?

12.15 Impromptu or Extemporaneous Talk: Becoming a Professional Speaker (Objs. 1–5)

Communication Technology | **Social Media** | **Web**

Professional speakers come in two flavors. On the one hand, celebrities such as famous athletes, businesspeople, and politicians command astronomical fees. On the other hand, ordinary people who have built a following by marketing themselves well and providing useful content also ply the speaking circuit, but they do so at more moderate rates, ranging between $4,500 and $7,500 per speech. One expert estimates that 95 percent of professional speakers make less than $10,000 per speaking engagement, still a hefty sum.

Professional speaker Chris Widener[17] offers the following insights to aspiring speakers:

Skip the speakers bureaus. Before the Internet, speakers bureaus were helpful intermediaries with strong corporate ties. Today, newcomers can bypass them and go into business without them.

Develop multiple sources of revenue. Collecting speaking fees is one thing; selling one's CDs, DVDs, e-books, and print books is another. Widener sells up to $140,000 in products after a talk.

Create free valuable content. Widener wrote 450 articles on success and business that became his signature. After building a list of 100,000 people, he self-published his books.

Develop a social media presence. Between Facebook and Twitter, Widener has almost 900,000 followers. He self-markets his content but also pays for Facebook marketing and ads.

Consider your fee your résumé. The honorarium should match the speaker's accomplishments. Widener raises his fee as his reputation grows, after TV appearances, after publishing a new book, and after speaking at prestigious events.

Think creatively to find the money. Widener gets around associations' or companies' limited speakers budgets by, for example, targeting their "education budgets." Also, he encourages organizations to seek funding from several corporate sponsors to share the cost of paying him.

What other strategies might work to help you develop a following and be a sought-after speaker?

YOUR TASK. Use this activity to give a brief impromptu speech. Without much preparation, objectively paraphrase and summarize the information to convey to your listeners what it takes to become a successful professional speaker. Include all relevant details and organize your summary well. Alternatively, conduct additional research to learn how one might become a professional speaker. Use search terms such as *speakers bureau* and *Toastmasters*. Once you have assembled enough additional information, create a multimedia slideshow using presentation software or give a concise extemporaneous briefing. Be sure to outline your talk and to rehearse.

12.16 Reporting About a Relevant Business Topic in the Media (Objs. 1–3)

Social Media | **Web**

YOUR TASK. Find an intriguing business article, and verbally present it to the class with or without notes. Summarize the article and explain why you have chosen it and why you believe it's valuable. Another option is to select a short business-related video clip. First introduce the video and summarize it. Time permitting, show the video in class. Visit any business website—for example, *The Wall Street Journal*, *Forbes*, or *Bloomberg Businessweek*. If your instructor directs, compose a tweet recommending or commenting on your article or video clip. Of the available 140 characters, leave at least 10 for retweeting.

12.17 Persuasive Presentation: Become an Ambassador for a Cause Close to Your Heart (Objs. 1–5)

Communication Technology | **Social Media** | **Web**

Do you care deeply about a particular nonprofit organization or cause? Perhaps you have donated to a cancer charity or volunteered for a local faith-based nonprofit. The Red Cross, Greenpeace, and the World Wildlife Fund (WWF) may be household names, but thousands of lesser-known nonprofit organizations are also trying to make the world a better place.

Professional fund-raiser and nonprofit service expert Sarah W Mackey encourages volunteers-to-be to become ambassadors for their favorite organizations. Much like brand ambassadors, advocates for nonprofits should wear the nonprofit's logo, invite friends, tell their families, raise money, volunteer, and spread the word on social media, Mackey says.[18] Some nonprofits—for example, the California-based environmental group Heal the Bay—are proactive. They offer speaker training to volunteers eager to reach out to their communities and raise awareness.[19] Ambassadors do good, become professional speakers, and acquire valuable skills to put on their résumés, a win-win-win!

YOUR TASK. Select your favorite charity. If you need help, find your charity or cause by visiting GuideStar, a nongovernmental watch-dog that monitors nonprofits, or simply google *list of nonprofits*. Learn as much as you can from your organization's website and from articles written about it. Also, vet your charity by checking it out on GuideStar. Then assemble your information into a logical outline, and create a persuasive oral presentation using presentation software. Your goal is not only to introduce the charity but also to inspire your peers to seek more information and to volunteer. Tip: Focus on the benefits, direct and indirect, of volunteering for this charity. Finally, if your instructor asks, practice writing tweets advocating for your organization and calling the public to action.

12.18 What Is My Credit Score and What Does It Mean? (Objs. 1–5)

> Web

The program chair for the campus business club has asked you to present a talk to the group about consumer credit. He saw a newspaper article saying that only 10 percent of Americans know their credit scores. Many consumers, including students, have dangerous misconceptions about their scores. Not knowing your score could result in a denial of credit as well as difficulty obtaining needed services and even a job.

YOUR TASK. Using research databases and the Web, learn more about credit scores and typical misconceptions. For example, is a higher or lower credit score better? Can you improve your credit score by marrying well? If you earn more money, will you improve your score? If you have a low score, can you raise it? Can you raise your score by maxing out all of your credit cards? (One survey reported that 28 percent of consumers believed the latter statement was true!) Prepare an oral presentation with or without a multimedia slideshow appropriate for a student audience. Conclude with appropriate recommendations.

12.19 Creating a Multimedia Presentation (No additional research required) (Objs. 1–5)

You are a consultant and have been hired to improve the effectiveness of corporate trainers. These trainers frequently make presentations to employees on topics such as conflict management, teamwork, time management, problem solving, performance appraisals, and employment interviewing. Your goal is to teach these trainers how to make better presentations.

YOUR TASK. Create six visually appealing slides based on the following content, which will be spoken during your presentation titled Effective Employee Training. The comments shown here are only a portion of a longer presentation.

Trainers have two options when they make presentations. The first option is one-way communication in which the trainer basically dumps the information on the audience and leaves. The second option is a two-way approach that involves the audience. The benefits of the two-way approach are that it helps the trainer connect with the audience and reinforce key points, it increases audience retention rates, and it changes the pace and adds variety to the presentation. The two-way approach also encourages audience members to get to know each other. Because today's employees demand more than just a "talking head," trainers must engage their audiences by involving them in a dialogue.

If you decide to interact with your audience, you need to choose an approach that suits your delivery style. Also, think about which options your audience would be likely to respond to most positively. Let's consider some interactivity approaches now. Realize, though, that these ideas are presented to help you get your creative juices flowing. After reading the list, think about situations in which these options might be effective. You could also brainstorm to come up with creative ideas to add to this list.

- Ask employees to guess at statistics before revealing them.
- Ask an employee to share examples or experiences.
- Ask a volunteer to help you demonstrate something.
- Ask the audience to complete a questionnaire or worksheet.
- Ask the audience to brainstorm or list things as fast as possible.
- Ask a variety of question types to achieve different purposes.
- Invite the audience to work through a process or examine an object.
- Survey the audience.
- Pause to let the audience members read something to themselves.
- Divide the audience into small groups to discuss an issue.

Capitalization

Review Sections 3.01–3.16 in the Grammar/Mechanics Handbook. Then study each of the following statements. Draw three underlines below any letter that should be capitalized. Draw a slash (/) through any capital letter that you wish to change to lowercase. Indicate in the space provided the number of changes you made in each sentence, and record the number of the G/M principle(s) illustrated. If you made no changes, write *0*. When you finish, compare your responses with those provided at the back of the book. If your responses differ, study carefully the principles in parentheses.

<u>5</u>   (3.01, 3.06a)   **EXAMPLE** Once the Management Team and the Union members finally agreed, mayor Johnson signed the Agreement.

1. All united passengers must exit the Plane at gate 16 when they reach the key west international airport.

2. Personal tax rates for japanese citizens are low by International standards; rates for japanese corporations are high, according to Iwao Nakatani, an Economics Professor at Osaka university.

3. Stephanie, an aspiring Entrepreneur, hopes to open her own Consulting Firm one day.

4. Randy plans to take courses in Psychology, Math, History, and english next semester.

5. Did you see *The new york times* article titled "Reebok to pay $25 million for toning shoe claims"?

6. I purchased the dell inspiron 2200, but you may purchase any Tablet Computer you choose.

7. According to a Federal Government report, any regulation of State and County banking must receive local approval.

8. The vice president of the united states said, "we continue to look for Foreign investment opportunities."

9. The Comptroller of Zarconi Industries reported to the President and the Board of Directors that the securities and exchange commission was beginning an investigation of their Company.

10. My Father, who lives near death valley, says that the Moon and Stars are especially brilliant on a cold, clear night.

11. Our Marketing Director met with Karin Bloedorn, Advertising Manager, to plan an Ad Campaign for our newly redesigned Smartphone.

12. In the Spring our Admissions Director plans to travel to venezuela, colombia, and ecuador to recruit new Students.

13. To reach Belle Isle park, which is located on an Island in the Detroit river, tourists pass over the Douglas MacArthur bridge.

14. On page 8 of the report, you'll find a list of all employees in our accounting department with Master's degrees.

15. Please consult figure 3.2 in chapter 5 for U.S. census bureau figures regarding non-english-speaking residents.

EDITING CHALLENGE—**12**

To fine-tune your grammar and mechanics skills, in every chapter you will be editing a message. The following outline of a presentation written by your office manager has problems with capitalization, grammar, punctuation, spelling, proofreading, number expression, and other writing techniques you have studied. Study the guidelines in the Grammar/Mechanics Handbook as well as the lists of Confusing Words and Frequently Misspelled Words to sharpen your skills.

YOUR TASK. Edit the following message (a) by correcting errors in your textbook or on a photocopy using proofreading marks from Appendix A or (b) by downloading the message from **www.cengagebrain.com** and correcting at your computer. Your instructor may show you a possible solution.

Developing an Office Recycling Plan

I. Introduction

Paper makes up about 40 percent of the solid waste stream in our City. By recycling our office paper we can help the Environment and save trees. Every ton of paper made from recycled fiber saves about 17 trees. It also saves about 25 gallons of Water, and reduces air pollution by an estimated 60 pounds. Here in our office we use a lot of white Paper. When Paper is recycled it goes into such products as tissue, paperboard, stationary, magazines, new office paper and other paper products. In interviewing 3 experts including Dr Walter Yang at the university of west virginia I learned how we can develop our own office recycling plan that could be implemented within 60 days.

II. Body

Companies can easily integrate Paper recycling into their normal business operations. One of the first steps is placing Recycling Bins next to employees desks. In addition the most successful programs conduct Seminars to educate employee. They also hire an Office Recycling Coordinator to facilitate the program. Some examples include the following:

- Bank of america initiated a program that grew from recycling 1,400 tons per year of computer and white paper to nearly fifteen thousand tons within 20 years. This Program saved nearly 500 thousand dollars in trash hauling fees.

- Hewlett Packard was able to divert 91 million pounds of Solid Waste, including 43 million pounds of Paper. H-P vice president william morris said that it saved more than 367,000 trees!

Our Vice President agrees with me that setting up a Office Recycling Program doesn't happen over night. It usually involves finding motivated employees, and educating the Office Staff. It may also require a Capitol investment in recycling bins.

A successful paper recycling plan will work best if we keep it very, very simple. First however we will need top Managements support. We must also provide sufficient instructions on what to put in, and what to keep out. We will need surveys, interviews and inspections to see how the Plan is working. Because the recycling bins and trash cans must be clean and items sorted properly we will need monitors checking to be sure every one is following instrutions.

III. Conclusion

Paper recycling is relatively easy to do, we just need to make a committment. We could start with 5 of our 15 offices to work out the best procedures. If you all agree I will meet with the CEO within 1 week. If Management supports the idea our goal should be to start a Program within 2 months. Our Companies disposal costs can decrease dramatically and we can help the Environment as well. Let's do it!

COMMUNICATION WORKSHOP

Effective and Professional Team Presentations

If you have been part of a team that created an oral presentation together, you know that the process can be frustrating. Sometimes team members don't carry their weight or produce poor-quality work. Very often members struggle to resolve conflict. On the other hand, team projects can be harmonious and productive when members establish ground rules and follow these steps:

- **Prepare to work together.** First, you should (a) compare schedules of team members in order to set up the best meetings times, (b) plan regular face-to-face and virtual meetings, and (c) discuss how you will deal with team members who are not contributing to the project or submitting shoddy work.

- **Plan the presentation.** Your team will need to agree on (a) the specific purpose of the presentation, (b) your audience, (c) the length of the presentation, (d) the types of visuals to include, and (e) the basic structure and content of the presentation.

- **Assign duties.** Once you decide what your presentation will cover, give each team member a written assignment that details his or her responsibilities, such as researching content, producing visuals, developing handouts, building transitions between segments, and showing up for team meetings and rehearsals.

- **Collect information.** To gather or generate information, teams can brainstorm together, conduct interviews, or search the Web. The team should set deadlines for collecting information and should discuss how to ensure the accuracy and currency of the information collected. Team members should exchange periodic progress reports on how their research is coming along.

- **Organize and develop the presentation.** Once your team has completed the research, start working on the presentation. Determine the organization of the presentation, compose a draft in writing, and prepare presentation slides and other visual aids. The team should meet often in person or online to discuss the presentation and to decide which members are responsible for delivering what parts of the presentation. Each member should build a transition to the next member's topic and strive for logical connections between segments.

- **Edit, rehearse, and evaluate.** Before you deliver the presentation, rehearse several times as a team. Make sure transitions from speaker to speaker are smooth. For example, a speaker might say, *Now that I have explained how to prepare for the meeting, Ashley is going to discuss how to get the meeting started.* Decide who will be responsible for advancing slides during the presentation (either on the computer or using a remote). Practice fielding questions if you plan to have a question-and-answer session. Decide how you are going to dress to look professional and competent. Run a spell-checker and proofread your presentation slides to ensure that the design, format, and vocabulary are consistent.

- **Deliver the presentation.** Show up on time for your presentation and wear appropriate attire. Deliver your part of the presentation professionally and enthusiastically. Remember that your audience is judging the team on its performance, not the individuals. Do what you can to make your team shine!

CAREER APPLICATION. Your boss named you to a team that is to produce an organizational social media communication strategy for your company. You know this assignment will end with an oral presentation to management. Your first reaction is dismay. You have been on teams before in the classroom, and you know how frustrating they can be. However, you want to give your best, and you resolve to contribute positively to this team effort.

YOUR TASK. In small groups or with the entire class, discuss effective collaboration. How can members contribute positively to teams? How should teams deal with members who aren't contributing or who have negative attitudes? What should team members do to ensure that the final presentation is professional and well coordinated? How can the team use technology to improve collaboration? If your instructor directs, summarize your findings in writing or in a brief presentation.

ENDNOTES

1. Korn, M. (2010, December 3). Wanted: Good speaking skills. *The Wall Street Journal*. Retrieved from Hire Education blog at http://blogs.wsj.com /hire-education/2010/12/03/wanted-good-speaking-skills
2. Dr. John J. Medina quoted in Reynolds, G. (2010). *Presentation Zen design*. Berkeley, CA: New Riders, p. 97.
3. The Basics. (2012). Retrieved from http://prezi.com/the-basics
4. Atkinson, C. (2008). *Beyond bullet points* (2nd ed.). Redmond, WA: Microsoft Press.
5. Reynolds, G. (2008). *Presentation Zen*. Berkeley, CA: New Riders, p. 220. See also Reynolds, G. (2010). *Presentation Zen design*. Berkeley, CA: New Riders.
6. Booher, D. (2003). *Speak with confidence: Powerful presentations that inform, inspire, and persuade*. New York: McGraw-Hill Professional, p. 126. See also http://www.indezine.com/ideas/prescolors.html
7. Bates, S. (2005). *Speak like a CEO: Secrets for commanding attention and getting results*. New York: McGraw-Hill Professional, p. 113.
8. Sommerville, J. (n. d.). The seven deadly sins of PowerPoint Presentations. About.com: Entrepreneurs. Retrieved from http://entrepreneurs.about .com/cs/marketing/a/7sinsofppt.htm
9. Ellwood, J. (2004, August 4). Less PowerPoint, more powerful points. *The Times* (London), p. 6.
10. Graves, P. R., & Kupsh, J. (2011, January 21). Presentation design and delivery. Bloomington, IN: Xlibris, p. 10.
11. Photo essay based on Berry, S. (2014, February 3). Suffer stage fright? Why you should get excited. *The Sydney Morning Herald*. Retrieved from http://www.smh.com.au/lifestyle/life/suffer-stage-fright-why-you-should-get-excited-20140203-31ww4.html
12. Booher, D. (2011). Speak with confidence. AudioInk.
13. Booker, C. (2013, April 11). How to get people to listen. *Bloomberg Businessweek*. Retrieved from http://www.businessweek.com /articles/2013-04-11/how-to-get-people-to-listen-by-newark-mayor-cory-booker
14. Search YouTube or search the top 100 speeches at American Rhetoric: http://www.americanrhetoric.com/top100speechesall.html
15. Nisen, M., & Guey, L. (2013, May 15). 23 of the best pieces of advice ever given to graduates. Business Insider. Retrieved from http://www .businessinsider.com/best-commencement-speeches-of-all-time-2013-5
16. Reynolds, G. (2008). *Presentation Zen*. Berkeley, CA: New Riders, pp. 64ff.
17. Clark, D. (2013, June 10). How to become a successful professional speaker. *Forbes*. Retrieved from http://www.forbes.com/sites /dorieclark/2013/06/10/how-to-become-a-successful-professional-speaker
18. Mackey, S. W. (2012, November 4). Step up: Be an ambassador. Retrieved from http://sarahwmackey.com/2012/11/04/step-up-be-an-ambassador
19. Volunteer. (n.d.). Heal the Bay. Retrieved from http://www.healthebay.org /volunteer

ACKNOWLEDGMENTS

p. 390 Office Insider based on Dlugan, A. (2008, April 10). 10 ways your presentation skills generate career promotions. Six Minutes. Retrieved from http:// sixminutes.dlugan.com/2008/04/10/career-promotions-presentation-skills

p. 392 Office Insider based on Booher, D. (2003). On speaking. Quotes by Dianna Booher. Booher Consultants. Retrieved from http://www.booher.com/ quotes.html#speaking

p. 396 Office Insider based on Dugdale, S. (n.d.). Building rapport—building harmony. Write-out-loud.com. Retrieved from http://www.write-out-loud.com/ building-rapport.html

p. 398 Office Insider based on Howder, R. (n.d.). About Prezi. Retrieved from http://prezi.com/about

p. 402 Office Insider based on Paradi, D. (2004). PowerPoint sucks! No it doesn't!! Think Outside The Slide. Retrieved from http://www.bearriverbands.org/ tech/paradi.pdf

p. 403 Office Insider based on Kupsh, J. (2010, November 4). 15 guidelines to effective presentations. Training. Retrieved from http://www.trainingmag.com/ article/15-guidelines-effective-presentations

p. 410 Office Insider based on Booher, D. (2003). On speaking. Quotes by Dianna Booher. Booher Consultants. Retrieved from http://www.booher.com/ quotes.html#speaking

CHAPTER

6

The Job Search and Résumés in the Digital Age

© Lisa S./Shutterstock.com

13-1 Job Searching in the Digital Age

There's no doubt about it. The job market has become increasingly complex and not just because of the economy, offshoring, outsourcing, and globalization. In this digital age, the Internet has fundamentally changed the way we search for jobs. Job boards, search engines, and social networks have all become indispensable tools in hunting for a job. Surprisingly, however, even in this digital age, personal networking and referrals continue to be the primary route to hiring.[1]

This chapter presents cutting-edge digital and personal networking strategies to help you land a job. You may be depressed about searching for a job because of the uncertain economy and highly competitive job market. However, you have a lot going for you. As a college student, think about your recent training, current skills, and enthusiasm. Remember, too, that you are less expensive to hire than older, experienced candidates. In addition, you have this book with the latest research, invaluable advice, and perfect model documents to guide you in your job search. Think positively! The more you understand the changing job market, the better equipped you will be to enter it wisely.

13-1a Understanding the Changing Job Market

Today, the major emphasis of the job search has changed. In years past the emphasis was on what the applicant wanted. Today it's on what the employer wants.[2] Employers are most interested in how a candidate will add value to their organizations. That's

172

Beyond your interests and goals, take a good look at your qualifications. Remember that today's job market is not so much about what you want, but what the employer wants. What assets do you have to offer? Your responses to the following questions will refine your thinking as well as prepare a foundation for your resume. Always keep in mind, though, that employers seek more than empty assurances; they will want proof of your qualifications.

- ... you familiar with, what job experience, in your roles, and what verbal skills can you offer?
- Do you communicate well in speech and in writing? How can you verify these talents?
- What other skills have you acquired in school, on the job, or through activities? How can you demonstrate these skills?
- Do you work well with people? Do you enjoy teamwork? What proof can you offer? Consider extracurricular activities, clubs, class projects, and jobs.
- Are you a leader, self-starter, or manager? What evidence can you offer? What leadership roles have you held?
- Do you speak, write, or understand another language?
- Do you learn quickly? Are you creative? How can you demonstrate these characteristics?
- What online qualifications can you offer that make you stand out among candidates?

9-1d Exploring Career Opportunities

The job picture in the United States is extraordinarily dynamic and flexible. On average, workers between ages eighteen and thirty-eight in the United States will have ten different employers over the course of their careers. The median job tenure of wage earners and salaried workers is 4.6 years with a single employer. Although you may be frequently changing jobs in the future, you'll still need to train for a specific career now. In exploring job opportunities, you will make the best decisions when you can match your interests and qualifications with the requirements and rewards of specific careers. Where can you find the best career data? Here are some suggestions.

- Visit your campus career center. Most campus career centers have libraries, inventories, career-related software programs, and employment or internship databases that allow you to explore such fields as accounting, finance, information systems, hotel management, and so forth. Some have well-trained job counselors who can tailor their resources to your needs. They may also offer career exploration workshops, job skills seminars, career days with visiting companies, assistance with resume preparation, and mock interviews.
- Search the Web. Many job-search sites—such as Monster, CareerBuilder, and College Grad—offer career-planning information and resources. You will learn about some of the best career sites in this next section.
- Use your library. Print and online resources in your library are especially helpful. Consult O*NET Occupational Information Network, Dictionary of Occupational Titles, Occupational Outlook Handbook, and Jobs Rated Almanac for information about job requirements, qualifications, salaries, and employment trends.
- Take a summer job, internship, or part-time position in your field. Nothing is better than trying out a career by actually working in it or in a related area. Many companies offer internships and temporary or part-time jobs.

13-1c Assessing Your Qualifications

Beyond your interests and goals, take a good look at your qualifications. Remember that today's job market is not so much about what you want, but what the employer wants. What assets do you have to offer? Your responses to the following questions will target your thinking as well as prepare a foundation for your résumé. Always keep in mind, though, that employers seek more than empty assurances; they will want proof of your qualifications.

- What technology skills can you present? What specific software programs are you familiar with, what Web experience do you have, and what social media skills can you offer?
- Do you communicate well in speech and in writing? How can you verify these talents?
- What other skills have you acquired in school, on the job, or through activities? How can you demonstrate these skills?
- Do you work well with people? Do you enjoy teamwork? What proof can you offer? Consider extracurricular activities, clubs, class projects, and jobs.
- Are you a leader, self-starter, or manager? What evidence can you offer? What leadership roles have you held?
- Do you speak, write, or understand another language?
- Do you learn quickly? Are you creative? How can you demonstrate these characteristics?
- What unique qualifications can you offer that make you stand out among candidates?

13-1d Exploring Career Opportunities

The job picture in the United States is extraordinarily dynamic and flexible. On average, workers between ages eighteen and thirty-eight in the United States will have ten different employers over the course of their careers. The median job tenure of wage earners and salaried workers is 4.4 years with a single employer.[3] Although you may be frequently changing jobs in the future (especially before you reach age forty), you still need to train for a specific career now. In exploring job opportunities, you will make the best decisions when you can match your interests and qualifications with the requirements and rewards of specific careers. Where can you find the best career data? Here are some suggestions:

- **Visit your campus career center.** Most campus career centers have literature, inventories, career-related software programs, and employment or internship databases that allow you to explore such fields as accounting, finance, office technology, information systems, hotel management, and so forth. Some have well-trained job counselors who can tailor their resources to your needs. They may also offer career exploration workshops, job skills seminars, career days with visiting companies, assistance with résumé preparation, and mock interviews.
- **Search the Web.** Many job-search sites—such as Monster, CareerBuilder, and CollegeGrad—offer career-planning information and resources. You will learn about some of the best career sites in the next section.
- **Use your library.** Print and online resources in your library are especially helpful. Consult *O*NET Occupational Information Network, Dictionary of Occupational Titles, Occupational Outlook Handbook*, and *Jobs Rated Almanac* for information about job requirements, qualifications, salaries, and employment trends.
- **Take a summer job, internship, or part-time position in your field.** Nothing is better than trying out a career by actually working in it or in a related area. Many companies offer internships and temporary or part-time jobs

to begin training college students and to develop relationships with them. Unsurprisingly, lots of those internships turn into full-time positions. One recent study revealed that 60 percent of students who completed paid internships were offered full-time jobs.[4]

- **Interview someone in your chosen field.** People are usually flattered when asked to describe their careers. Inquire about needed skills, required courses, financial and other rewards, benefits, working conditions, future trends, and entry requirements.

- **Volunteer with a nonprofit organization.** Many colleges and universities encourage service learning. In volunteering their services, students gain valuable experience, and nonprofits appreciate the expertise and fresh ideas that students bring.

- **Monitor the classified ads.** Early in your college career, begin monitoring want ads and the websites of companies in your career area. Check job availability, qualifications sought, duties, and salary ranges. Don't wait until you are about to graduate to see how the job market looks.

- **Join professional organizations in your field.** Frequently, professional organizations offer student memberships at reduced rates. Such memberships can provide inside information on issues, career news, and jobs. Student business clubs and organization such as Phi Beta Lambda can also provide leadership development trainings, career tips, and networking opportunities.

13-2 Developing a Job-Search Strategy Focused on the Open Job Market

LEARNING OBJECTIVE 2
Develop savvy search strategies by recognizing job sources and using digital tools to explore the open job market.

Once you have analyzed what you want in a job and what you have to offer, you are ready to focus on a job-search strategy. You're probably most interested in the sources of today's jobs. Figure 13.2 shows the job source trends revealed by a Right Management survey of between 46,000 and 55,000 job seekers over a period of six years. Surprisingly, despite the explosion of digital job sources, person-to-person networking remains the No. 1 tool for finding a position. The job search, however, is changing, as the figure shows. The line between online and traditional networking blurs as technology plays an increasingly significant role. Carly McVey, Right Management executive, says, "Online social networking may not always be separate from traditional networking since one so often leads to the other. A job seeker uses the Internet to track down former associates or acquaintances and then reaches out to them in person."[5]

Both networking and online searching are essential tools in locating jobs, but where are those jobs? The *open job market* consists of jobs that are advertised or listed. The *hidden job market* consists of jobs that are never advertised or listed. Some analysts and authors claim that between 50 and 80 percent of all jobs are filled before they even make it to online job boards or advertisements.[6] Those openings are in the hidden job market, which we will explore shortly. First, let's start where most job seekers start—in the open job market.

13-2a Searching the Open Job Market

The open job market consists of positions that are advertised or listed publicly. Most job seekers start searching the open job market by using the Internet. Searching online is a common, but not always fruitful, approach. Both recruiters and job seekers complain about online job boards. Corporate recruiters say that the big job boards bring a flood of candidates, many of whom are not suited for the listed jobs. Job candidates grumble that listings are frequently outdated and fail to produce

Figure **13.2** Trends in Sources of New Jobs

	2008	2010	2013
Networking (person-to-person contacts)	41%	47%	50%
Internet job boards (such as Monster, CollegeGrad, and company websites)	19%	24%	22%
Agencies (search firms placing candidates for a fee)	12%	10%	19%
Direct approach (cold calling)	9%	8%	8%
Newspapers/periodicals (classified ads)	7%	2%	1%
Other (combination of above, direct referral, and luck)	12%	9%	0%

Source: Based on a Right Management (ManpowerGroup) Survey of 46,000–55,000 job seekers

© Yuriy Rudyy/Shutterstock.com

leads. Some career advisors call these sites black holes, into which résumés vanish without a trace. Almost as worrisome is the fear that an applicant's identity may be stolen through information posted at big boards.

Although the Internet may seem like a giant swamp where résumés disappear into oblivion, many job counselors encourage job seekers to spend a few minutes each day tracking online openings in their fields and locales. Moreover, job boards provide valuable job-search information such as résumé, interviewing, and salary tips. Job boards also serve as a jumping-off point in most searches. They inform candidates about the kinds of jobs that are available and the skill sets required.

However, job searching online can also be a huge time waster. Probably the most important tip you can apply is staying focused. In the hyperlinked utopia of endlessly fascinating sites, it's too easy to mindlessly follow link after link. Staying focused on a specific goal is critical. When you focus on the open job market, you will probably be checking advertised jobs on the big boards, company career sites, niche sites, LinkedIn, and other social networking sites.

Exploring the Big Boards. As Figure 13.2 indicates, the number of jobs found through all job boards is increasing; therefore, it makes sense to check them out. However, with tens of thousands of job boards and employment websites deluging the Internet, it's hard to know where to start. We suggest a few general sites as well as sites for college grads.

- **CareerBuilder** claims to be the largest online career site with more than 1 million jobs and 49 million résumés.

- **Monster** offers access to information on millions of jobs worldwide. It uses a search technology called 6Sense to match applicants with the best job opportunities. Many consider Monster to be the Web's premier job site.

- **CollegeGrad** describes itself as the "number one entry-level job site" for students and graduates. Applicants can search for entry-level jobs, internships, summer jobs, and jobs requiring one or more years of work experience.
- **Indeed** aggregates job listings from thousands of websites including company career pages, job boards, newspaper advertisements, associations, and blogs.

Exploring Company Websites. Probably the best way to find a job online is at a company's own website. Many companies now post job openings only at their own sites to avoid being inundated by the volume of applicants responding to postings at online job boards. A company's website is the first place to go if you have a specific employer in mind. You might find vision and mission statements, a history of the organization, and names of key hiring managers. Possibly you will see a listing for a position that doesn't fit your qualifications. Even though you're not right for this job, you have discovered that the company is hiring. Don't be afraid to send a résumé and cover message expressing your desire to be considered for future jobs. Rather than seeking individual company sites, you might prefer to visit aggregator LinkUp. It shows constantly updated job listings from small, midsized, and large companies.

Checking Niche Sites. If you seek a job in a specialized field, look for a niche site, such as Dice for technology jobs, Advance Healthcare Network for jobs in the medical field, and Accountemps for temporary accounting positions. Niche websites also exist for job seekers with special backgrounds or needs, such as GettingHired for disabled workers and Workforce50 for older workers. If you are looking for a short-term job, check out CoolWorks, which specializes in seasonal employment. Are you interested in living or working abroad? iHipo, the "high potential network," assists students and graduates in finding international internships, jobs, and graduate programs at businesses around the world. If you yearn for a government job, try USA Student Jobs, a website for students and recent graduates interested in federal service.

Using LinkedIn and Social Networking Sites. LinkedIn continues to dominate the world of job searching and recruiting. In a recent poll of 1,843 staffing professionals, 97 percent said they used LinkedIn as a recruiting tool.[7] At LinkedIn, job seekers can search for job openings directly, and they can also follow companies for the latest news and current job openings. (You will learn more about using LinkedIn when we discuss networking.) Beyond LinkedIn, other social networking sites such as Facebook and Twitter also advertise job openings and recruit potential employees. Because organizations may post open jobs to their Facebook or Twitter pages prior to advertising them elsewhere, you might gain a head start on submitting an application by following them on these sites.

When posting job-search information online, it's natural to want to put your best foot forward and openly share information that will get you a job. The challenge is striking a balance between supplying enough information and protecting your privacy. To avoid some of the risks involved, see Figure 13.3.

Checking Newspapers. Jobs in the open market may also be listed in local newspapers. Don't overlook this possibility, especially for local jobs. However, you don't have to buy a paper to see the listings. Most newspapers list their classified ads online.

13-3 Pursuing the Hidden Job Market With Networking

LEARNING OBJECTIVE **3**

Expand your job-search strategies by using both traditional and digital tools in pursuing the hidden job market.

Not all available positions are announced or advertised in the open job market. As mentioned earlier, between 50 and 80 percent of jobs may be in the hidden job market.[8] Companies prefer not to openly advertise for a number of reasons. They don't welcome the deluge of unqualified candidates. What's more, companies

Figure 13.3 Protecting Yourself When Posting at Online Job Boards

- **Use reputable, well-known sites** and never pay to post your résumé.

- **Don't divulge personal data** such as your date of birth, social security number, or home address. Use your city and state or region in place of your home address.

- **Set up a separate e-mail account** with a professional-sounding e-mail address for your job search.

- **Post privately** if possible. Doing so means that you can control who has access to your e-mail address and other information.

- **Keep careful records** of every site on which you posted. At the end of your job search, remove all posted résumés.

- **Don't include your references** or reveal their contact information without permission.

- **Don't respond to "blind" job postings** (those without company names or addresses). Unfortunately, scammers use online job boards to post fake job ads to gather your personal information.

dislike hiring unknown quantities. Career coach Donald Asher, author of *Cracking the Hidden Job Market*, sets this scene: Imagine you are a hiring manager facing hundreds of résumés on your desk and a coworker walks in with the résumé of someone she vouches for. Which résumé do you think hits the top of the stack?[9] Companies prefer known quantities.

The most successful job candidates seek to transform themselves from unknown into known quantities through networking. More jobs today are found through referrals and person-to-person contacts than through any other method. That's because people trust what they know. Therefore, your goal is to become known to a large network of people, and this means going beyond close friends.

Building a Personal Network. Because most candidates find jobs today through networking, be prepared to work diligently to build your personal networks. This effort involves meeting people and talking to them about your field or industry so that you can gain information and locate possible job vacancies. Not only are many jobs never advertised, but some positions aren't even contemplated until the right person appears. One recent college grad underwent three interviews for a position, but the company hired someone else. After being turned down, the grad explained why he thought he was perfect for this company but perhaps in a different role. Apparently, the hiring manager agreed and decided to create a new job (in social media) because of the skills, personality, and perseverance of this determined young grad. Networking pays off, but it requires dedication. Here are three steps that will help you establish your own network:

Step 1. Develop a contact list. Make a list of anyone who would be willing to talk with you about finding a job. Figure 13.4 suggests possibilities. Even if you haven't talked with people in years, reach out to them in person or online. Consider asking your campus career center for alumni willing to talk with students. Also dig into your social networking circles, which we will discuss shortly.

Figure 13.4 Whom to Contact in Networking

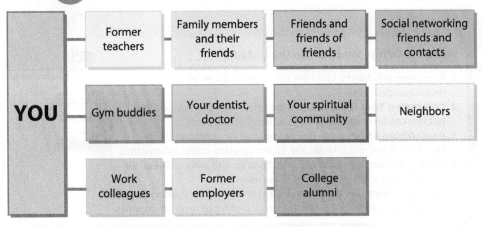

Step 2. Make contacts in person and online. Call the people on your list or connect online. To set up a meeting in person, say, *Hi,_____. I'm looking for a job and I wonder if you could help me out. When could I come over to talk about it?* During your visit be friendly, well organized, polite, and interested in what your contact has to say. Provide a copy of your résumé, and try to keep the conversation centered on your job search. Your goal is to get two or more referrals. In pinpointing your request, ask, *Do you know of anyone who might have an opening for a person with my skills?* If the person does not, ask, *Do you know of anyone else who might know of someone who would?*

Step 3. Follow up on your referrals. Call or contact the people on your list. You might say something like, *Hello. I'm Stacy Rivera, a friend of Jason Tilden. He suggested that I ask you for help. I'm looking for a position as a marketing trainee, and he thought you might be willing to spare a few minutes and steer me in the right direction.* Don't ask for a job. During your referral interview, ask how the individual got started in this line of work, what he or she likes best (or least) about the work, what career paths exist in the field, and what problems must be overcome by a newcomer. Most important, ask how a person with your background and skills might get started in the field. Send an informal thank-you note to anyone who helps you in your job search, and stay in touch with the most promising people. Ask whether you could stay in contact every three weeks or so during your job search.

Using Social Media to Network. As digital technology continues to change our lives, job candidates have a powerful new tool at their disposal: social media networks. These networks not only keep you in touch with friends but also function beautifully in a job search. If you just send out your résumé blindly, chances are good that not much will happen. However, if you have a referral, your chances of getting a job multiply. Today's expansion of online networks results in an additional path to developing coveted referrals. Job seekers today are increasingly expanding their networking strategies to include social media sites such as LinkedIn, Facebook, and Twitter.

Making the Most of LinkedIn to Search for a Job. If you are looking for a job, LinkedIn is the No. 1 social media site for you to use. Although some young people have the impression that LinkedIn is for old fogies, that perception is changing as more and more college students and grads sign up. LinkedIn is where you can let recruiters know of your talents and where you begin your professional networking, as illustrated in Figure 13.5. For hiring managers to find your LinkedIn profile, however, you may need to customize your URL (uniform resource locator), which is the address of your page. To drive your name to the top of a Google search,

Figure 13.5 Harnessing the Power of LinkedIn

Five Ways College Students Can Use LinkedIn

1. **Receiving Job Alerts.** LinkedIn sends notifications of recommended jobs.
2. **Leveraging Your Network.** You may start with two connections but you can leverage those connections to thousands.
3. **Researching a Company.** Before applying to a company, you can check it out on LinkedIn and locate valuable inside information.
4. **Getting Recommendations.** LinkedIn takes the awkwardness out of asking for recommendations. It's so easy!
5. **Helping Companies Find You.** Many companies are looking for skilled college grads, and a strong profile on LinkedIn can result in inquiries.

© iStockphoto.com/huronphoto

Workplace in Focus

©Valua Vitaly/Shutterstock.com

Choosing the right words to describe yourself is important when setting up a career profile on social media. Each year LinkedIn publishes a list of the most popular self-descriptive words found in members' profiles. In 2013, the word that LinkedIn members used most frequently to represent themselves in the marketplace was "responsible." Other top keywords included "strategic," "creative," and "effective." Members use these buzzwords most frequently because they match the qualities that employers say they value in job candidates. What words would you use to describe yourself to a prospective employer?[12]

advises career coach Susan Adams, scroll down to the LinkedIn "public profile" on your profile page, and edit the URL. Try your first and last name and then your last name and first name, and then add a middle initial, if necessary. Test a variety of combinations with punctuation and spacing until the combination leads directly to your profile.[10]

In writing your LinkedIn career summary, use keywords and phrases that might appear in job descriptions. Include quantifiable achievements and specifics that reveal your skills. You can borrow most of this from your résumé. In the Work Experience and Education fields, include all of your experience, not just your current position. For the Recommendations section, encourage instructors and employers to recommend you. Having more recommendations in your profile makes you look more credible, trustworthy, and reliable. Career coach Adams even encourages job seekers to offer to write the draft for the recommender; in the world of LinkedIn, she says, this is acceptable.[11]

One of the best ways to use LinkedIn is to search for a company in which you are interested. Try to find company employees who are connected to other people you know. Then use that contact as a referral when you apply. You can also send an e-mail to everyone in your LinkedIn network asking for help or for people they could put you in touch with. Don't be afraid to ask an online contact for advice on getting started in a career and for suggestions to help a newcomer break into that career. Another excellent way to use a contact is to have that person look at your résumé and help you tweak it. Like Facebook, LinkedIn has status updates, and it's a good idea to update yours regularly so that your connections know what is happening in your career search.

Enlisting Other Social Networks in Job Hunting. In addition to LinkedIn, job seekers can join Facebook, Twitter, and Google+ to find job opportunities, market themselves to companies, showcase their skills, highlight their experience, and possibly land that dream job. However, some career experts believe that social media sites such as Facebook do not mix well with business.[13] If you decide to use Facebook for professional networking, examine your profile and decide what you want prospective employers to see—or not see. Create a simple profile with minimal graphics, widgets, and photos. Post only content relevant to your job search or career, and choose your friends wisely.[14]

Employers often use these social media sites to check the online presence of a candidate. In fact, one report claimed that 91 percent of recruiters check Facebook, Twitter, and LinkedIn to filter out applicants.[15] Make sure your social networking accounts represent you professionally. You can make it easy for your potential employer to learn more about you by including an informative bio in your Twitter or Facebook profile that has a link to your LinkedIn profile. You can also make yourself more discoverable by posting thoughtful blog posts and tweets on topics related to your career goal.

13-3a Building Your Personal Brand

A large part of your job-search strategy involves building a brand for yourself. You may be thinking, *Who me? A brand?* Yes, absolutely! Even college grads should seriously consider branding because finding a job today is tough. Before you get into the thick of the job hunt, focus on developing your brand so that you know what you want to emphasize.

Personal branding involves deciding what makes you special and desirable in the job market. What is your unique selling point? What special skill set makes you stand out among all job applicants? What would your instructors or employers say is your greatest strength? Think about your intended audience. What are you promoting about yourself?

Try to come up with a tagline that describes what you do and who you are. Ask yourself questions such as these: Do you follow through with every promise? Are you a fast learner? Hardworking? What can you take credit for? It's OK to shed a little modesty and strut your stuff. However, do keep your tagline simple, short, and truthful so that it's easy to remember. See Figure 13.6 for some sample taglines appropriate for new grads.

Once you have a tagline, prepare a professional-looking business card with your name and tagline. Include an easy-to-remember e-mail address such as *firstname .lastname@domain.com*.

Now that you have your tagline and business card, work on an elevator speech. This is a pitch that you can give in 30 seconds or less describing who you are and what you can offer. Tweak your speech for your audience, and practice until you can say it naturally. Here's an example:[16]

Possible Elevator Speech for New Grad

Hi, my name is _____. I will be graduating from _____ with a degree in _____. I'm looking to _____. I recently _____. May I take you out for coffee sometime to get your advice?

13-4 Creating a Customized Résumé

LEARNING OBJECTIVE 4

Organize your qualifications and information into effective résumé segments to create a winning, customized résumé.

In today's challenging and digital job market, the focus is not so much on what you want but on what the employer needs. That's why you will want to prepare a tailored résumé for every position you seek. The competition is so stiff today that

Figure **13.6** Branding YOU

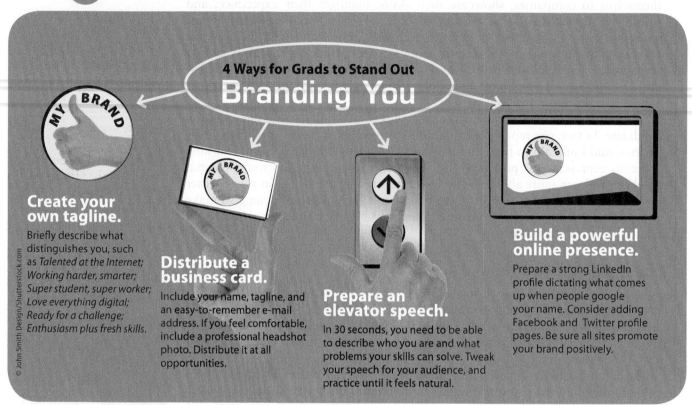

4 Ways for Grads to Stand Out
Branding You

© John Smith Design/Shutterstock.com

Create your own tagline.

Briefly describe what distinguishes you, such as *Talented at the Internet; Working harder, smarter; Super student, super worker; Love everything digital; Ready for a challenge; Enthusiasm plus fresh skills.*

Distribute a business card.

Include your name, tagline, and an easy-to-remember e-mail address. If you feel comfortable, include a professional headshot photo. Distribute it at all opportunities.

Prepare an elevator speech.

In 30 seconds, you need to be able to describe who you are and what problems your skills can solve. Tweak your speech for your audience, and practice until it feels natural.

Build a powerful online presence.

Prepare a strong LinkedIn profile dictating what comes up when people google your name. Consider adding Facebook and Twitter profile pages. Be sure all sites promote your brand positively.

you cannot get by with a generic, all-purpose résumé. Although you can start with a basic résumé, you should customize it to fit each company and position if you want it to stand out from the crowd.

The Web has made it so easy to apply for jobs that recruiters are swamped with applications. As a job seeker, you have about five seconds to catch the recruiter's eye—if your résumé is even read by a person. It may very well first encounter an *applicant tracking system* (ATS). This software helps businesses automatically post openings, screen résumés, rank candidates, and generate interview requests. These automated systems make writing your résumé doubly challenging. Although your goal is to satisfy a recruiter or hiring manager, that person may never see your résumé unless it is selected by the ATS. You will learn more about applicant tracking systems shortly.

You may not be in the job market at this moment, but preparing a résumé now has advantages. Having a current résumé makes you look well organized and professional should an unexpected employment opportunity arise. Moreover, preparing a résumé early may reveal weaknesses and give you time to address them. If you have accepted a position, it's still a good idea to keep your résumé up-to-date. You never know when an opportunity might come along!

13-4a Choosing a Résumé Style

Résumés usually fall into two categories: chronological and functional. This section presents basic information as well as insider tips on how to choose an appropriate résumé style, determine its length, arrange its parts, and increase its chances of being selected by an applicant tracking system. You will also learn about adding a summary of qualifications, which busy recruiters welcome. Models of the résumé styles discussed in the following sections are shown in our comprehensive Résumé Gallery beginning on page 443.

Chronological. The most popular résumé format is the chronological format, shown in Figures 13.9 through 13.11 in our Résumé Gallery. The chronological résumé lists work history job by job but in reverse order, starting with the most recent position. Recruiters favor the chronological format because they are familiar with it and because it quickly reveals a candidate's education and experience. The chronological style works well for candidates who have experience in their field of employment and for those who show steady career growth, but it is less appropriate for people who have changed jobs frequently or who have gaps in their employment records. For college students and others who lack extensive experience, the functional résumé format may be preferable.

Functional. The functional résumé, shown in Figure 13.12 on page 446, focuses on a candidate's skills rather than on past employment. Like a chronological résumé, a functional résumé begins with the candidate's name, contact information, job objective, and education. Instead of listing jobs, though, the functional résumé groups skills and accomplishments in special categories, such as Supervisory and Management Skills or Retailing and Marketing Experience. This résumé style highlights accomplishments and can de-emphasize a negative employment history.

People who have changed jobs frequently, who have gaps in their employment records, or who are entering an entirely different field may prefer the functional résumé. Recent graduates with little or no related employment experience often find the functional résumé useful. Older job seekers who want to downplay a long job history and job hunters who are afraid of appearing overqualified may also prefer the functional format. Be aware, though, that online job boards may insist on the chronological format. In addition, some recruiters are suspicious of functional résumés, thinking the candidate is hiding something.

13-4b Deciding on Length

Experts disagree on how long a résumé should be. Conventional wisdom has always held that recruiters prefer one-page résumés. However, recruiters who are serious about candidates often prefer the kind of details that can be provided in a two-page or longer résumé. The best advice is to make your résumé as long as needed to present your skills to recruiters and hiring managers. Individuals with more experience will naturally have longer résumés. Those with fewer than ten years of experience, those making a major career change, and those who have had only one or two employers will likely have one-page résumés. Those with ten years or more of related experience may have two-page résumés. Finally, some senior-level managers and executives with a lengthy history of major accomplishments might have résumés that are three pages or longer.[17]

13-4c Organizing Your Information Into Effective Résumé Categories

Although résumés have standard categories, their arrangement and content should be strategically planned. A customized résumé emphasizes skills and achievements aimed at a particular job or company. It shows a candidate's most important qualifications first, and it de-emphasizes weaknesses. In organizing your qualifications and information, try to create as few headings as possible; more than six looks cluttered. No two résumés are ever exactly alike, but most writers consider including all or some of these categories: Main Heading, Career Objective, Summary of Qualifications, Education, Experience, Capabilities and Skills, Awards and Activities, Personal Information, and References.

Main Heading. Your résumé, whether chronological or functional, should start with an uncluttered and simple main heading. The first line should always be your name; add your middle initial for an even more professional look.

Format your name so that it stands out on the page. Following your name, list your contact information, including your address, phone number, and e-mail address. More recently, some candidates are omitting their street and city addresses as they consider such information unnecessary. Your telephone should be one where you can receive messages. The outgoing message at this number should be in your voice, it should state your full name, and it should be concise and professional. If you include your cell phone number and are expecting an important call from a recruiter, pick up only when you are in a quiet environment and can concentrate.

For your e-mail address, be sure it sounds professional instead of something like *toosexy4you@gmail.com* or *sixpackguy@yahoo.com*. Also be sure that you are using a personal e-mail address. Putting your work e-mail address on your résumé announces to prospective employers that you are using your current employer's resources to look for another job. If you have a website where an e-portfolio or samples of your work can be viewed, include the address in the main heading.

If you have an online presence, think about adding a *Quick Response* (QR) code to your résumé. This is a barcode that can be scanned by a smartphone, linking recruiters to your online portfolio or your LinkedIn profile page.

Career Objective. Opinion is divided about the effectiveness of including a career objective on a résumé. Recruiters think such statements indicate that a candidate has made a commitment to a career and is sure about what he or she wants to do. Yet, some career coaches today say objectives "feel outdated" and too often are all about what the candidate wants instead of what the employer wants.[18]

One job-trends researcher, Professor Charlyse Smith Diaz, contends that an objective should be included "only if it can be used persuasively to show how an applicant might fit with a company." She suggests three questions that might help a candidate decide whether to include an objective: "(1) Can you use a definitive, memorable descriptor? (2) Do you hold a required prerequisite or qualification for the position? (3) Are you seasoned in a specific profession?"[19] If you can answer yes to any of those questions, then include a career objective.

A well-written objective—customized for the job opening—makes sense, especially for new grads with fresh training and relevant skills. The objective can include strategic keywords for applicant tracking systems. If you decide to include an objective, focus on what you can contribute to the organization, not on what the organization can do for you.

Poor:	To obtain a position with a well-established organization that will lead to a lasting relationship in the field of marketing. (Sounds vague and self-serving.)
Improved:	To obtain a marketing position in which I use my recent training in writing and computer skills to increase customer contacts and expand brand penetration using social media. (Names specific skills and includes many nouns that might snag an applicant tracking system.)

Avoid the phrase *entry-level* in your objective, because it emphasizes lack of experience. If you omit a career objective, be sure to discuss your career goals in your cover message.

Optional Summary of Qualifications. "The biggest change in résumés over the last decade has been a switch from an objective to a summary at the top," says career expert Wendy Enelow.[20] Recruiters are busy, and smart job seekers add a summary of qualifications to their résumés to save the time of recruiters and hiring managers. Once a job is advertised, a hiring manager may get hundreds or even thousands of résumés in response. A summary at the top of your résumé makes it easier to read and ensures that your most impressive qualifications are not overlooked by a recruiter who is skimming résumés quickly. In addition, because résumés today may be viewed on tablets and smartphones, make sure that the first third spotlights your most compelling qualifications.

A summary of qualifications (also called a *career profile*, a *job summary*, or *professional highlights*) should include three to eight bulleted statements that prove that you are the ideal candidate for the position. When formulating these statements, consider your experience in the field, your education, your unique skills, awards you have won, certifications you hold, and any other accomplishments that you want to highlight. Strive to quantify your achievements wherever possible. Target the most important qualifications an employer will be looking for in the person hired for this position. Focus on nouns that might be selected as keywords by an applicant tracking system. Examples appear in Figures 13.9 and 13.11.

Education. The next component in a chronological résumé is your education—if it is more noteworthy than your work experience. In this section you should include the name and location of schools, dates of attendance, major fields of study, and degrees received. By the way, once you have attended college, you don't need to list high school information on your résumé.

Your grade point average and/or class ranking may be important to prospective employers. One way to enhance your GPA is to calculate it in your major courses only (for example, *3.6/4.0 in major*). It is not unethical so long as you clearly show that your GPA is in the major only. Looking to improve their hiring chances, some college grads are now offering an unusual credential: their scores on the Graduate Record Examination. Large companies and those specializing in computer software and financial services reportedly were most interested in applicants' GRE scores.[21]

Under Education you might be tempted to list all the courses you took, but such a list makes for dull reading and consumes valuable space. Refer to courses only if you can relate them to the position sought. When relevant, include certificates earned, seminars attended, workshops completed, scholarships awarded, and honors earned. If your education is incomplete, include such statements as *BS degree expected 6/18* or *80 units completed in 120-unit program*. Title this section Education, Academic Preparation, or Professional Training. If you are preparing a functional résumé, you will probably put the Education section below your skills summary, as Cooper Jackson has done in Figure 13.12.

Work Experience or Employment History. When your work experience is significant and relevant to the position sought, this information should appear before your education. List your most recent employment first and work backward, including only those jobs that you think will help you win the targeted position. A job application form may demand a full employment history, but your résumé may be selective. Be aware, though, that time gaps in your employment history will probably be questioned in the interview. For each position show the following:

- Employer's name, city, and state
- Dates of employment (month and year)
- Most important job title
- Significant duties, activities, accomplishments, and promotions

Your employment achievements and job duties will be easier to read if you place them in bulleted lists. Rather than list every single thing you have done, customize your information so that it relates to the target job. Your bullet points should be concise but not complete sentences, and they usually do not include personal pronouns (*I, me, my*). Strive to be specific:

Poor:	Worked with customers
Improved:	Developed customer service skills by successfully interacting with 40+ customers daily

Whenever possible, quantify your achievements:

Poor:	Did equipment study and report
Improved:	Conducted research and wrote final study analyzing equipment needs of 100 small businesses in Houston
Poor:	Was successful in sales
Improved:	Personally generated orders for sales of $90,000 annually

In addition to technical skills, employers seek individuals with communication, management, and interpersonal capabilities. This means you will want to select work experiences and achievements that illustrate your initiative, dependability, responsibility, resourcefulness, flexibility, and leadership. Employers also want people who can work in teams.

Poor:	Worked effectively in teams
Improved:	Collaborated with five-member interdepartmental team in developing ten-page handbook for temporary workers
Poor:	Joined in team effort on campus
Improved:	Headed 16-member student government team that conducted most successful voter registration in campus history

Statements describing your work experience should include many nouns relevant to the job you seek. These nouns may match keywords sought by the applicant tracking system. To appeal to human readers, your statements should also include action verbs, such as those in Figure 13.7. Starting each of your bullet points with an action verb helps ensure that your bulleted lists are parallel.

Capabilities and Skills. Recruiters want to know specifically what you can do for their companies. Therefore, list your special skills. In this section be sure to include many nouns that relate to the targeted position. Include your ability to use

Figure **13.7** Action Verbs for a Powerful Résumé

Communication Skills	Teamwork, Supervision Skills	Management, Leadership Skills	Research Skills	Clerical, Detail Skills	Creative Skills
clarified	advised	analyzed	assessed	activated	acted
collaborated	coordinated	authorized	collected	approved	conceptualized
explained	demonstrated	coordinated	critiqued	classified	designed
interpreted	developed	directed	diagnosed	edited	fashioned
integrated	evaluated	headed	formulated	generated	founded
persuaded	expedited	implemented	gathered	maintained	illustrated
promoted	facilitated	improved	interpreted	monitored	integrated
resolved	guided	increased	investigated	proofread	invented
summarized	motivated	organized	reviewed	recorded	originated
translated	set goals	scheduled	studied	streamlined	revitalized
wrote	trained	strengthened	systematized	updated	shaped

the Web, software programs, social media, office equipment, and communication technology tools. Use expressions such as *proficient in, competent in, experienced in*, and *ability to* as illustrated in the following:

Poor:	Have payroll experience
Improved:	Proficient in preparing federal, state, and local payroll tax returns as well as franchise and personal property tax returns
Poor:	Trained in computer graphics
Improved:	Certified in graphic design including infographics through an intensive 350-hour classroom program
Poor:	Have writing skills
Improved:	Competent in writing, editing, and proofreading reports, tables, letters, memos, e-mails, manuscripts, and business forms

You will also want to highlight exceptional aptitudes, such as working well under stress, learning computer programs quickly, and interacting with customers. If possible, provide details and evidence that back up your assertions. Include examples of your writing, speaking, management, organizational, interpersonal, and presentation skills—particularly those talents that are relevant to your targeted job. For recent graduates, this section can be used to give recruiters evidence of your potential and to highlight successful college projects.

Awards, Honors, and Activities. If you have three or more awards or honors, highlight them by listing them under a separate heading. If not, put them in the Education or Work Experience section if appropriate. Include awards, scholarships (financial and other), fellowships, dean's list, honors, recognition, commendations, and certificates. Be sure to identify items clearly. Your reader may be unfamiliar, for example, with Greek organizations, honoraries, and awards; tell what they mean.

Poor:	Recipient of Star award
Improved:	Recipient of Star award given by Pepperdine University to outstanding graduates who combine academic excellence and extracurricular activities

It's also appropriate to include school, community, volunteer, and professional activities. Employers are interested in evidence that you are a well-rounded person. This section provides an opportunity to demonstrate leadership and interpersonal skills. Strive to use action statements.

Poor:	Treasurer of business club
Improved:	Collected dues, kept financial records, and paid bills while serving as treasurer of 35-member business management club

Personal Data. Résumés in the United States omit personal data, such as birth date, marital status, height, weight, national origin, health, disabilities, and religious affiliation. Such information doesn't relate to genuine occupational qualifications, and recruiters are legally barred from asking for such information. Some job seekers do, however, include hobbies or interests (such as skiing or photography) that might grab the recruiter's attention or serve as conversation starters. For example, let's say you learn that your hiring manager enjoys distance running. If you have run a marathon, you may want to mention it. Many executives practice tennis or golf, two sports highly suitable for networking. You could also indicate your willingness to travel or to relocate since many companies will be interested.

References. Listing references directly on a résumé takes up valuable space. Moreover, references are not normally instrumental in securing an interview—few companies check them before the interview. Instead, recruiters prefer that you bring to the interview a list of individuals willing to discuss your qualifications. Therefore, you should prepare a separate list, such as that in Figure 13.8, when you begin your job search. Consider three to five individuals, such as instructors, your current employer or previous employers, colleagues or subordinates, and other professional contacts. Ask whether they would be willing to answer inquiries regarding your qualifications for employment. Be sure, however, to provide them with an opportunity to refuse. No reference is better than a negative one. Better yet, to avoid rejection and embarrassment, ask only those contacts who you are confident will give you a glowing endorsement.

Do not include personal or character references, such as friends, family, or neighbors, because recruiters rarely consult them. Companies are more interested in the opinions of objective individuals who know how you perform professionally and academically. One final note: most recruiters see little reason for including the statement *References furnished upon request*. It is unnecessary and takes up precious space.

13-4d Online Résumé Reading Patterns

With increasing numbers of résumés being read online, it's wise for job applicants to know what researchers have found about how people read online text. Eye-tracking research revealed that people read text-based pages online in an F-shaped pattern.[22] That is, they read horizontally from the top of the page, concentrating on the top third and then focusing on the left side as they read downward. This roughly corresponds to the shape of a capital F. Smart applicants will arrange the most important information in the top section of the résumé. Additional significant information should appear at the beginning of each group down the left side.

Figure **13.8** Sample Reference List

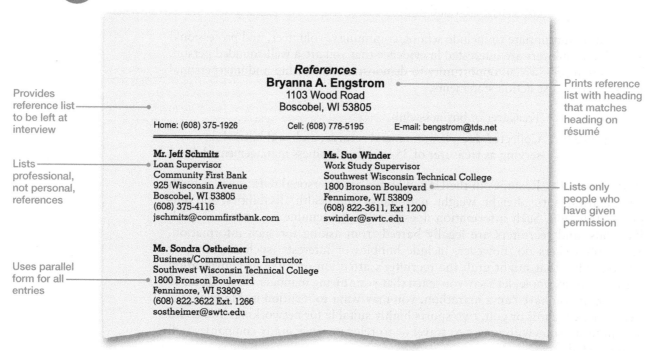

Résumé Gallery

Figure 13.9 Chronological Résumé: Recent College Graduate With Related Experience

Bryanna Engstrom used a chronological résumé to highlight her work experience, most of which is related directly to the position she seeks. Although she is a recent graduate, she has accumulated experience in two part-time jobs and one full-time job. She included a summary of qualifications to highlight her skills, experience, and interpersonal traits aimed at a specific position.

Notice that Bryanna designed her résumé in two columns with the major categories listed in the left column. In the right column she included bulleted items for each of the four categories. Conciseness and parallelism are important in writing an effective résumé. In the *Experience* category, she started each item with an active verb, which improved readability and parallel form.

Bryanna A. Engstrom
1103 Wood Road
Boscobel, WI 53805

Home: (608) 375-1926   Cell: (608) 778-5195   E-mail: bengstrom@tds.net

Omits objective to keep all options open

SUMMARY OF QUALIFICATIONS

- Over three years' experience in administrative positions, working with business documents and interacting with customers
- Ability to keyboard (68 wpm) and use ten-key calculator (150 kpm)
- Proficient with Microsoft Word, Excel, Access, PowerPoint, SharePoint, and Publisher (passed MOS certification exam)

Focuses on skills and aptitudes that employers seek

- Competent in Web research, written and oral communication, records management, desktop publishing, and proofreading and editing business documents
- Trained in QuickBooks, Flash, Photoshop, Dreamweaver

EXPERIENCE

Administrative Assistant, Work Study
Southwest Wisconsin Technical College, Fennimore, Wisconsin
August 2013–present

Uses present-tense verb for current job

- Create letters, memos, reports, and forms in Microsoft Word
- Develop customized reports and labels using Microsoft Access
- Maintain departmental Microsoft Excel budget

Loan Support Specialist
Community First Bank, Boscobel, Wisconsin, May 2012– September 2013

- Prepared loan documents for consumer, residential, mortgage, agricultural, and commercial loans
- Ensured compliance with federal, state, and bank regulations
- Originated correspondence (oral and written) with customers and insurance agencies

Arranges employment by job title for easy recognition

- Ordered and interpreted appraisals, titles, and credit reports

Customer Sales Representative
Lands' End, Dodgeville, Wisconsin, Winter seasons 2012–2013

- Developed customer-service skills by serving 40+ online customers a day
- Resolved customer problems
- Entered catalog orders into computer system

EDUCATION

Southwest Wisconsin Technical College, Fennimore, Wisconsin
Major: Administrative Assistant with Help Desk certificate
AA degree expected May 2015. GPA in major: 3.8 (4.0 = A)

ACTIVITIES AND AWARDS

Combines activities and awards to show extracurricular involvement

- Placed first in state BPA Administrative Assistant competition
- Served as SWTC Student Senate Representative
- Nominated for SWTC Ambassador Award (recognizes outstanding students for excellence in and out of classroom)

Hung-Wei Chun used Microsoft Word to design a traditional chronological print-based résumé that he plans to give to recruiters at the campus job fair or during interviews. Notice that he formatted his résumé in two columns. An easy way to do this is to use the Word table feature and remove the borders so that no lines show.

Although Hung-Wei has work experience unrelated to his future employment, his résumé looks impressive because he has transferable skills. His internship is related to his future career, and his language skills and study abroad experience will help him score points in competition with other applicants. Hung-Wei's volunteer experience is also attractive because it shows him to be a well-rounded, compassionate individual. Because his experience in his future field is limited, he omitted a summary of qualifications.

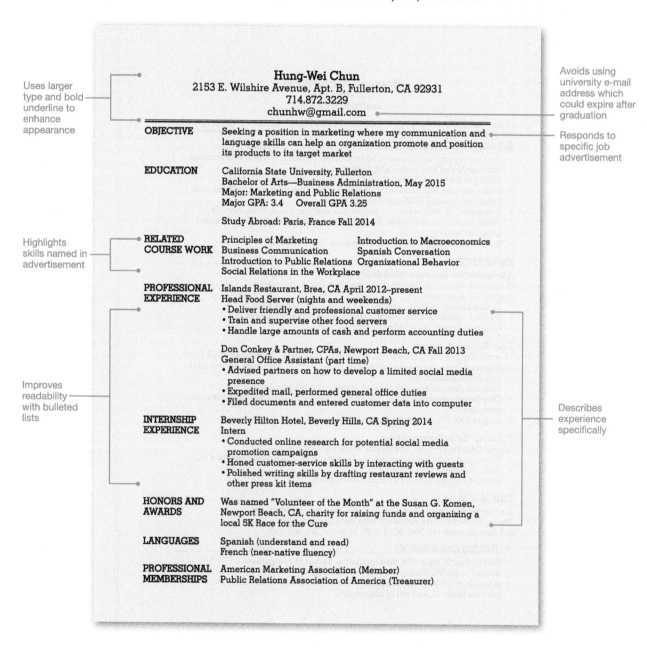

Uses larger type and bold underline to enhance appearance

Avoids using university e-mail address which could expire after graduation

Hung-Wei Chun
2153 E. Wilshire Avenue, Apt. B, Fullerton, CA 92931
714.872.3229
chunhw@gmail.com

OBJECTIVE Seeking a position in marketing where my communication and language skills can help an organization promote and position its products to its target market

Responds to specific job advertisement

EDUCATION California State University, Fullerton
Bachelor of Arts—Business Administration, May 2015
Major: Marketing and Public Relations
Major GPA: 3.4   Overall GPA 3.25

Study Abroad: Paris, France Fall 2014

Highlights skills named in advertisement

RELATED COURSE WORK
Principles of Marketing   Introduction to Macroeconomics
Business Communication   Spanish Conversation
Introduction to Public Relations Organizational Behavior
Social Relations in the Workplace

PROFESSIONAL EXPERIENCE
Islands Restaurant, Brea, CA April 2012–present
Head Food Server (nights and weekends)
• Deliver friendly and professional customer service
• Train and supervise other food servers
• Handle large amounts of cash and perform accounting duties

Don Conkey & Partner, CPAs, Newport Beach, CA Fall 2013
General Office Assistant (part time)
• Advised partners on how to develop a limited social media presence
• Expedited mail, performed general office duties
• Filed documents and entered customer data into computer

Improves readability with bulleted lists

INTERNSHIP EXPERIENCE
Beverly Hilton Hotel, Beverly Hills, CA Spring 2014
Intern
• Conducted online research for potential social media promotion campaigns
• Honed customer-service skills by interacting with guests
• Polished writing skills by drafting restaurant reviews and other press kit items

Describes experience specifically

HONORS AND AWARDS
Was named "Volunteer of the Month" at the Susan G. Komen, Newport Beach, CA, charity for raising funds and organizing a local 5K Race for the Cure

LANGUAGES
Spanish (understand and read)
French (near-native fluency)

PROFESSIONAL MEMBERSHIPS
American Marketing Association (Member)
Public Relations Association of America (Treasurer)

Figure 13.11 Chronological Résumé: University Graduate With Substantial Experience

Because Rachel has many years of experience and seeks executive-level employment, she highlighted her experience by placing it before her education. Her summary of qualifications highlighted her most impressive experience and skills. This chronological two-page résumé shows the steady progression of her career to executive positions, a movement that impresses and reassures recruiters.

RACHEL M. CHOWDHRY

374 Cabot Drive
Thousand Oaks, CA 91359

E-Mail: rchowdhry@west.net
(805) 490-3310

OBJECTIVE Senior Financial Management Position

SUMMARY OF QUALIFICATIONS
- Over 12 years' comprehensive experience in accounting industry, including over 8 years as a controller
- Certified Public Accountant (CPA)
- Demonstrated ability to handle all accounting functions for large, midsized, and small firms
- Ability to isolate problems, reduce expenses, and improve the bottom line, resulting in substantial cost savings
- Proven talent for interacting professionally with individuals at all levels, as demonstrated by performance review comments
- Experienced in P&L, audits, taxation, internal control, inventory, management, A/P, A/R, and cash management

Lists most impressive credentials

PROFESSIONAL HISTORY AND ACHIEVEMENTS
11/12 to present CONTROLLER
United Plastics, Inc., Newbury Park, California (extruder of polyethylene film for plastic aprons and gloves)
- Direct all facets of accounting and cash management for 160-employee, $3 billion business
- Supervise inventory and production operations for tax compliance
- Talked owner into reducing sales prices, resulting in doubling first quarter 2014 sales
- Created cost accounting by product and pricing based on gross margin
- Increased line of credit with 12 major suppliers

Explains nature of employer's business because it is not immediately recognizable

Uses action verbs but includes many good nouns for possible computer scanning

1/10 to 10/12 CONTROLLER
Burgess Inc., Freeport, Illinois (major manufacturer of flashlight and lantern batteries)
- Managed all accounting, cash, payroll, credit, and collection operations for 175-employee business
- Implemented a new system for cost accounting, inventory control, and accounts payable, resulting in a $100,000 annual savings
- Reduced staff from 11 persons to 5 with no loss in productivity
- Successfully reduced inventory levels from $1.1 million to $600,000

Emphasizes steady employment history by listing dates FIRST

Describes and quantifies specific achievements

8/08 to 11/09 TREASURER/CONTROLLER
The Builders of Winter, Winter, Wisconsin (manufacturer of modular housing)
- Supervised accounts receivable/payable, cash management, payroll, insurance
- Directed monthly and year-end closings, banking relations, and product costing
- Refinanced company with long-term loan, ensuring stability

Rachel M. Chowdhry   Page 2

4/04 to 6/08 SUPERVISOR OF GENERAL ACCOUNTING
Levin National Batteries, St. Paul, Minnesota (local manufacturer of flashlight batteries)
- Completed monthly and year-end closing of ledgers for $2 million business
- Audited freight bills, acted as interdepartmental liaison, prepared financial reports

ADDITIONAL INFORMATION
Education: BBA degree, University of Minnesota, major: Accounting, 2003
Certification: Certified Public Accountant (CPA), 2005
Personal: Will travel and/or relocate

De-emphasizes education because work history is more important for mature candidates

Recent graduate Cooper Jackson chose this functional format to de-emphasize his meager work experience and emphasize his potential in sales and marketing. This version of his résumé is more generic than one targeted for a specific position. Nevertheless, it emphasizes his strong points with specific achievements and includes an employment section to satisfy recruiters. The functional format presents ability-focused topics. It illustrates what the job seeker can do for the employer instead of narrating a history of previous jobs. Although recruiters prefer chronological résumés, the functional format is a good choice for new graduates, career changers, and those with employment gaps.

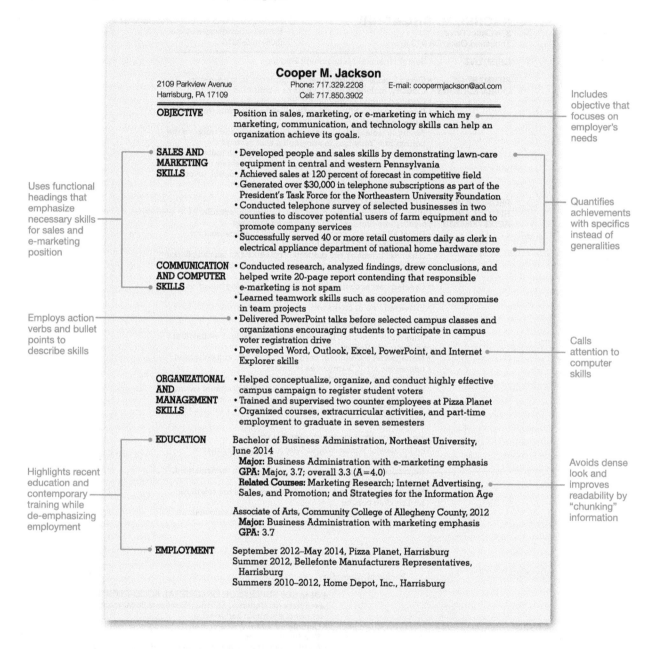

13-4e Polishing Your Résumé and Keeping It Honest

As you continue to work on your résumé, look for ways to improve it. For example, consider consolidating headings. By condensing your information into as few headings as possible, you will produce a clean, professional-looking document. Study other résumés for valuable formatting ideas. Ask yourself what graphic highlighting

Figure 13.13 Chronological Résumé: Student Seeking Internship

Although Haley has had one internship, she is seeking another as she is about to graduate. To aid her search, she prepared a chronological résumé that emphasizes her education and related coursework. She elected to omit her home address because she prefers that all communication take place digitally or by telephone. Her career objective states exactly the internship position she seeks.

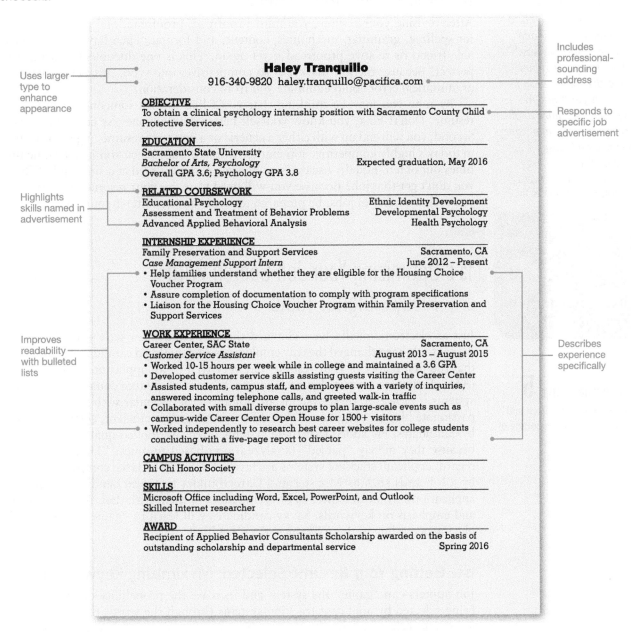

Uses larger type to enhance appearance

Highlights skills named in advertisement

Improves readability with bulleted lists

Includes professional-sounding address

Responds to specific job advertisement

Describes experience specifically

Haley Tranquillo
916-340-9820 haley.tranquillo@pacifica.com

OBJECTIVE
To obtain a clinical psychology internship position with Sacramento County Child Protective Services.

EDUCATION
Sacramento State University
Bachelor of Arts, Psychology   Expected graduation, May 2016
Overall GPA 3.6; Psychology GPA 3.8

RELATED COURSEWORK
Educational Psychology   Ethnic Identity Development
Assessment and Treatment of Behavior Problems   Developmental Psychology
Advanced Applied Behavioral Analysis   Health Psychology

INTERNSHIP EXPERIENCE
Family Preservation and Support Services   Sacramento, CA
Case Management Support Intern   June 2012 – Present
• Help families understand whether they are eligible for the Housing Choice Voucher Program
• Assure completion of documentation to comply with program specifications
• Liaison for the Housing Choice Voucher Program within Family Preservation and Support Services

WORK EXPERIENCE
Career Center, SAC State   Sacramento, CA
Customer Service Assistant   August 2013 – August 2015
• Worked 10-15 hours per week while in college and maintained a 3.6 GPA
• Developed customer service skills assisting guests visiting the Career Center
• Assisted students, campus staff, and employees with a variety of inquiries, answered incoming telephone calls, and greeted walk-in traffic
• Collaborated with small diverse groups to plan large-scale events such as campus-wide Career Center Open House for 1500+ visitors
• Worked independently to research best career websites for college students concluding with a five-page report to director

CAMPUS ACTIVITIES
Phi Chi Honor Society

SKILLS
Microsoft Office including Word, Excel, PowerPoint, and Outlook
Skilled Internet researcher

AWARD
Recipient of Applied Behavior Consultants Scholarship awarded on the basis of outstanding scholarship and departmental service   Spring 2016

techniques you can use to improve readability: capitalization, underlining, indenting, and bulleting. Experiment with headings and styles to achieve a pleasing, easy-to-read message. Moreover, look for ways to eliminate wordiness. For example, instead of *Supervised two employees who worked at the counter*, try *Supervised two counter employees*. Review Chapter 4 for more tips on writing concisely.

A résumé is expected to showcase a candidate's strengths and minimize weaknesses. For this reason, recruiters expect a certain degree of self-promotion. Some

LEARNING OBJECTIVE 5

Optimize your job search and résumé by taking advantage of today's digital tools.

résumé writers, however, step over the line that separates honest self-marketing from deceptive half-truths and flat-out lies. Distorting facts on a résumé is unethical; lying may be illegal. Most important, either practice can destroy a career. In the Communication Workshop at the end of this chapter, learn more about how to keep your résumé honest and the consequences of fudging the facts.

13-4f Proofreading Your Résumé

After revising your résumé, you must proofread, proofread, and proofread again for spelling, grammar, mechanics, content, and format. Then have a knowledgeable friend or relative proofread it yet again. This is one document that must be perfect. Because the job market is so competitive, one typo, misspelled word, or grammatical error could eliminate you from consideration.

By now you may be thinking that you'd like to hire someone to write your résumé. Don't! First, you know yourself better than anyone else could know you. Second, you will end up with either a generic or a one-time résumé. A generic résumé in today's highly competitive job market will lose out to a customized résumé nine times out of ten. Equally useless is a one-time résumé aimed at a single job. What if you don't get that job? Because you will need to revise your résumé many times as you seek a variety of jobs, be prepared to write (and rewrite) it yourself.

13-5 Optimizing Your Job Search With Today's Digital Tools

Just as electronic media have changed the way candidates seek jobs, these same digital tools have changed the way employers select qualified candidates. This means that the first reader of your résumé may very well be an applicant tracking system (ATS). Estimates suggest that as many as 90 percent of large companies use these systems.[23] However, these systems are not altogether popular with applicants. One passionate blogger complained that ATSs were highly inefficient, costly, and hated by candidates. He added that these systems often overlooked qualified candidates because they merely "parsed" (analyzed) text-based résumés.[24] Despite their low regard, applicant tracking systems are favored not only by large companies but also by job boards such as Monster and CareerBuilder to screen candidates and filter applications. You can expect to be seeing more of them with their restrictive forms and emphasis on keywords. Savvy candidates will learn to "game" the system by playing according to the ATS rules. Keep reading!

13-5a Getting Your Résumé Selected: Maximizing Keyword Hits

Job hunters can "game" the system and increase the probability of their résumés being selected by applicant tracking systems through the words they choose. The following techniques, in addition to those cited earlier, can boost the chance of having an ATS select your résumé:

- **Include specific keywords or keyword phrases.** Study carefully any advertisements and job descriptions for the position you want. Describe your experience, education, and qualifications in terms associated with the job advertisement or job description for this position.

- **Focus on nouns.** Although action verbs will make your résumé appeal to a recruiter, the applicant tracking system will often be looking for nouns in three categories: (a) a job title, position, or role (e.g., *accountant, Web developer, team leader*); (b) a technical skill or specialization (e.g., *Javascript, e-newsletter* *editor*); and (c) a certification, a tool used, or specific experience (e.g., *Certified Financial Analyst, experience with WordPress*).[25]

- **Use variations of the job title.** Tracking systems may seek a slightly different job title from what you list. To be safe, include variations and abbreviations (e.g., *occupational therapist, certified occupational therapist*, or *COTA*). If you don't have experience in your targeted area, use the job title you seek in your objective.

- **Concentrate on the Skills section.** A majority of keywords sought by employees relate to specialized or technical skill requirements. Therefore, be sure the Skills section of your résumé is loaded with nouns that describe your skills and qualifications. See page 440 for more suggestions on skills categories.

- **Skip a keyword summary.** Avoid grouping nouns in a keyword summary because recruiters may perceive them to be manipulative.[26]

13-5b Showcasing Your Qualifications in a Career E-Portfolio

With the workplace becoming increasingly digital, you have yet another way to display your qualifications to prospective employers—the career e-portfolio. This is a collection of digital files that can be navigated with the help of menus and hyperlinks much like a personal website.

What Goes in a Career E-Portfolio? An e-portfolio provides viewers with a snapshot of your talents, accomplishments, and technical skills. It may include a copy of your résumé, reference letters, commendations for special achievements, awards, certificates, work samples, a complete list of your courses, thank-you letters, and other items that tout your accomplishments. An e-portfolio could also offer links to digital copies of your artwork, film projects, videos, blueprints, documents, photographs, multimedia files, and blog entries that might otherwise be difficult to share with potential employers.

Because e-portfolios offer a variety of resources in one place, they have many advantages, as seen in Figure 13.14. When they are posted on websites, they can be

Figure **13.14** Making a Career E-Portfolio

Why create a career e-portfolio?
- Demonstrate your technology skills.
- Support and extend your résumé.
- Present yourself in a lively format.
- Make data instantly accessible.
- Target a specific job.

What goes in it?
- Relevant course work
- Updated résumé, cover message
- Real work examples
- Recommendations
- Images, links, or whatever showcases your skills

How to make and publish it?
- Use a portfolio or blog template.
- Design your own website.
- Host at a university or private site.
- Publish its URL in your résumé and elsewhere.

viewed at an employer's convenience. Let's say you are talking on the phone with an employer in another city who wants to see a copy of your résumé. You can simply refer the employer to the website where your résumé resides. E-portfolios can also be seen by many individuals in an organization without circulating a paper copy. However, the main reason for preparing an e-portfolio is that it shows off your talents and qualifications more thoroughly than a print résumé does.

Some recruiters may be skeptical about e-portfolios because they fear that such presentations will take more time to view than paper-based résumés do. As a result, nontraditional job applications may end up at the bottom of the pile or be ignored. That's why some applicants submit a print résumé in addition to an e-portfolio.

How Are E-Portfolios Accessed? E-portfolios are generally accessed at websites, where they are available around the clock to employers. If the websites are not password protected, however, you should remove personal information. Some colleges and universities make website space available for student e-portfolios. In addition, institutions may provide instruction and resources for scanning photos, digitizing images, and preparing graphics. E-portfolios may also be burned onto CDs and DVDs to be mailed to prospective employers.

To learn more about making a career e-portfolio, take a look at a tutorial written by a recent university graduate who tells exactly how he did it. This tutorial is available at the student website for this book: **www.cengagebrain.com**.

13-5c Expanding Your Employment Chances With a Video Résumé

Still another way to expand your employment possibilities is with a video résumé. Video résumés enable job candidates to present their experience, qualifications, and interests in video form. This format has many benefits. It allows candidates to demonstrate their public speaking, interpersonal, and technical skills more impressively than they can in traditional print résumés. Both employers and applicants can save recruitment and travel costs by using video résumés. Instead of flying distant candidates to interviews, organizations can see them digitally.

Video résumés are becoming more prevalent with the emergence of YouTube, inexpensive webcams, and widespread broadband. With simple edits on a computer, you can customize a video message to a specific employer and tailor your résumé for a particular job opening. In making a video résumé, dress professionally in business attire, just as you would for an in-person interview. Keep your video to three minutes or less. Explain why you would be a good employee and what you can do for the company that hires you.

Before committing time and energy to a video résumé, decide whether it is appropriate for your career field. Such presentations make sense for online, media, social, and creative professions. Traditional organizations, however, may be less impressed. Done well, a video résumé might give you an edge. Done poorly, however, it could bounce you from contention.

13-5d Wowing Them With an Infographic Résumé

A hot trend among creative types is the infographic résumé. It uses colorful charts, graphics, and time lines to illustrate a candidate's work history and experience. No one could deny that an infographic résumé really stands out. "Anyone looking at it," effuses blogger Randy Krum, "is 650% more likely to remember it days later."[27] Those preparing infographic résumés are often in the field of graphic design or journalism. James Coleman, a graduating senior from the University of Missouri, created an infographic résumé that secured a job. Shown in Figure 13.15, James's résumé uses a time line to track his experience and education. Colorful bubbles indicate his digital skills.

Figure 13.15 Infographics: A Novel Way to Show Education, Experience, and Skills

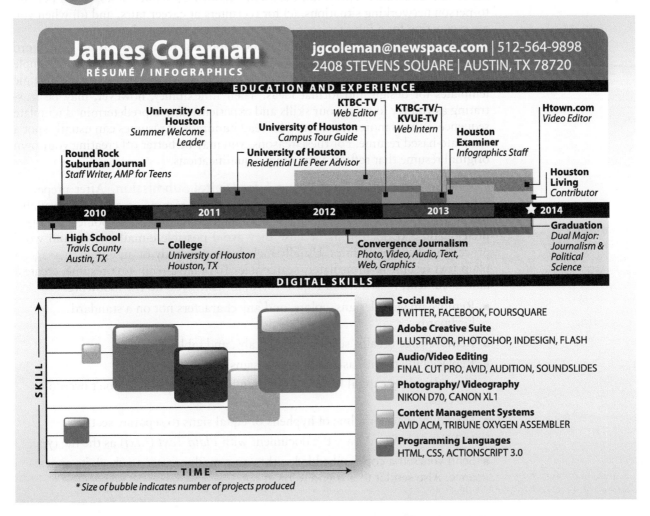

Most of us, however, are not talented enough to create professional-looking infographics. To the rescue are many companies that now offer infographic apps. Vizualize.me turns a user's LinkedIn profile information into a beautiful Web-based infographic. Re.vu also pulls in LinkedIn data to produce a stylish Web-based infographic. Brazen Careerist offers a Facebook application that generates an infographic résumé from a user's Facebook, Twitter, and LinkedIn information.

Will a dazzling infographic get you a job? Among hiring managers, the consensus is that infographic résumés help candidates set themselves apart, but such visual displays may not be appropriate for every kind of job.[28] In more traditional fields such as accounting and financial services, hiring managers want to see a standard print-based résumé. One hiring manager pointed out that traditional résumés evolved this way for a reason: they make comparison, evaluation, and selection easier for employers.[29]

13-5e How Many Résumés and What Format?

At this point you may be wondering how many résumés you should make, and what format they should follow. The good news is that you need only one basic résumé that you can customize for various job prospects and formats.

Preparing a Basic Print-Based Résumé. The one basic résumé you should prepare is a print-based traditional résumé. It should be attractively formatted to maximize readability. This résumé is useful (a) during job interviews, (b) for person-to-person networking situations, (c) for recruiters at career fairs, and (d) when you are competing for a job that does not require an electronic submission.

You can create a basic, yet professional-looking résumé by using your word processing program. The Résumé Gallery in this chapter provides ideas for simple layouts that are easily duplicated and adapted. You can also examine résumé templates for design and format ideas. Their inflexibility, however, may be frustrating as you try to force your skills and experience into a predetermined template sequence. What's more, recruiters who read hundreds of résumés can usually spot a template-based résumé. For these reasons, you may be better off creating your own original résumé that reflects your unique qualifications.

Converting to a Plain-Text Résumé for Digital Submission. After preparing a basic résumé, you can convert it to a plain-text résumé so that it is available for e-mailing or pasting into online résumé submission forms. Some employers prefer plain-text documents because they avoid possible e-mail viruses and word processing incompatibilities. Usually included in the body of an e-mail message, a plain-text résumé is immediately searchable. To make a plain-text résumé, create a new document, illustrated in Figure 13.16, in which you do the following:

- Remove images, designs, colors, and any characters not on a standard keyboard.
- Remove page breaks, section breaks, tabs, and tables.
- Replace bullets with asterisks or plus signs.
- Consider using capital letters rather than boldface type—but don't overdo the caps.
- Use white space or a line of hyphens or equal signs to separate sections.
- In Microsoft Word, save the document with *Plain Text* (**.txt*) as the file type.
- Send yourself a copy embedded within an e-mail message to check its appearance. Also send it to a friend to try it out.

13-5f Submitting Your Résumé

The format you choose for submitting your résumé depends on what is required. If you are responding to a job advertisement, be certain to read the listing carefully to learn how the employer wants you to submit your résumé. Not following the prospective employer's instructions can eliminate you from consideration before your résumé is even reviewed. If you have any doubt about what format is desired, send an e-mail inquiry to a company representative, or call and ask. Most organizations request one of the following submission formats:

- **Word document.** Some organizations ask candidates to send their résumés and cover messages by surface mail. Others request that résumés be submitted as Word documents attached to e-mail messages, despite the fear of viruses.
- **Plain-text document.** As discussed earlier, many employers expect applicants to submit résumés and cover letters as plain-text documents. This format is also widely used for posting to an online job board or for sending by e-mail. Plain-text résumés may be embedded within or attached to e-mail messages.
- **PDF document.** For safety reasons some employers prefer PDF (portable document format) files. A PDF résumé looks exactly like the original and cannot be altered. Most computers have Adobe Acrobat Reader installed for easy reading of PDF files. Converting your résumé to a PDF file can be easily done by saving it as a PDF file, which preserves all formatting.

Figure 13.16 Portion of Plain-Text Résumé

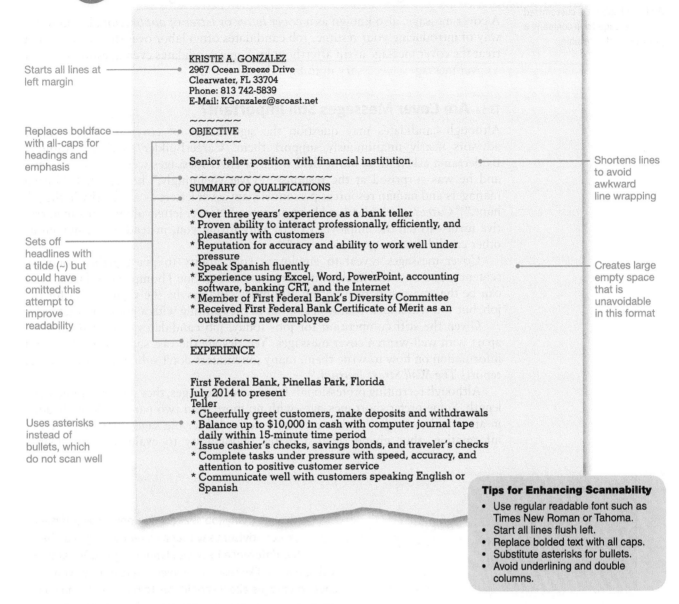

Starts all lines at left margin

Replaces boldface with all-caps for headings and emphasis

Sets off headlines with a tilde (~) but could have omitted this attempt to improve readability

Uses asterisks instead of bullets, which do not scan well

Shortens lines to avoid awkward line wrapping

Creates large empty space that is unavoidable in this format

```
KRISTIE A. GONZALEZ
2967 Ocean Breeze Drive
Clearwater, FL 33704
Phone: 813 742-5839
E-Mail: KGonzalez@scoast.net

~~~~~~
OBJECTIVE
~~~~~~

Senior teller position with financial institution.

~~~~~~~~~~~~~~~~~
SUMMARY OF QUALIFICATIONS
~~~~~~~~~~~~~~~~~

* Over three years' experience as a bank teller
* Proven ability to interact professionally, efficiently, and
  pleasantly with customers
* Reputation for accuracy and ability to work well under
  pressure
* Speak Spanish fluently
* Experience using Excel, Word, PowerPoint, accounting
  software, banking CRT, and the Internet
* Member of First Federal Bank's Diversity Committee
* Received First Federal Bank Certificate of Merit as an
  outstanding new employee

~~~~~~~~
EXPERIENCE
~~~~~~~~

First Federal Bank, Pinellas Park, Florida
July 2014 to present
Teller
* Cheerfully greet customers, make deposits and withdrawals
* Balance up to $10,000 in cash with computer journal tape
  daily within 15-minute time period
* Issue cashier's checks, savings bonds, and traveler's checks
* Complete tasks under pressure with speed, accuracy, and
  attention to positive customer service
* Communicate well with customers speaking English or
  Spanish
```

Tips for Enhancing Scannability

- Use regular readable font such as Times New Roman or Tahoma.
- Start all lines flush left.
- Replace bolded text with all caps.
- Substitute asterisks for bullets.
- Avoid underlining and double columns.

- **Company database.** Larger organizations may prefer that you complete an online form with your résumé information. This enables them to plug your data into their formats for rapid searching. You might be able to cut and paste the information from your résumé into the form.

- **Fax.** Although fading in office use, fax transmission might be requested. Sending your résumé via fax gets your information to an employer safely and quickly. However, because print quality is often poor, use the fax method only if requested or if a submission deadline is upon you. Then, follow up with your polished printed résumé.

Because your résumé is probably the most important message you will ever write, you will revise it many times. With so much information in concentrated form and with so much riding on its outcome, your résumé demands careful polishing, proofreading, and critiquing.

LEARNING OBJECTIVE 6

Draft and submit a customized cover message to accompany a print or digital résumé.

13-6 Creating Customized Cover Messages

A cover message, also known as a *cover letter* or *letter of application*, is a graceful way of introducing your résumé. Job candidates often labor over their résumés but treat the cover message as an afterthought. Some candidates even question whether a cover message is necessary in today's digital world.

13-6a Are Cover Messages Still Important?

Although candidates may question the significance of cover messages, career advisors nearly unanimously support them. CareerBuilder specialist Anthony Balderrama asked those in the field whether cover messages were a waste of time, and he was surprised at the response. "Overwhelmingly," he reported, "hiring managers and human resources personnel view cover letters as a necessity in the job hunt."[30] Career coach Heather Huhman agrees: "Cover letters allow you—in narrative form—to tell the employer exactly why hiring you, instead of the numerous other candidates, is a good decision."[31]

Cover messages reveal to employers your ability to put together complete sentences and to sound intelligent. Corporate trainer Sue Thompson declares, "You can be the smartest person within 100 miles, and maybe the right person for the job, but you will knock yourself right out of the running with a poor cover letter."[32]

Given the stiff competition for jobs today, job candidates can set themselves apart with well-written cover messages. Yet, despite the vast support for them and information on how to write them, many job hunters don't submit cover messages, reports *The Wall Street Journal*.[33]

Although recruiting professionals favor cover messages, they disagree about their length. Some prefer short messages with no more than two paragraphs embedded in an e-mail message.[34] Other recruiters desire longer messages that supply more information, thus giving them a better opportunity to evaluate a candidate's

Workplace in Focus

Courtesy of LinkedIn

Although many job seekers downplay cover letters, career advisors say that a cover message can be the difference between landing a job offer and losing one. Unlike résumés, which are factoid-driven, cover messages allow candidates to make a human connection and express creatively why they are right for the job. In one recent employment scenario, in which a Seattle woman earned a job with self-improvement firm Mindbloom, the applicant's letter opened, "Dear Mindbloomers: Please find my résumé for review in regards to no employment opportunities you have available at the moment." The woman proceeded to make a case for why the company should hire her as the "Director of Happiness," even though no such position existed. What tips can help job candidates write effective cover messages?[35]

qualifications and writing skills. These recruiters argue that hiring and training new employees is expensive and time consuming; therefore, they welcome extra data to guide them in making the best choice the first time. Follow your judgment in writing a brief or a longer cover message. If you feel, for example, that you need space to explain in more detail what you can do for a prospective employer, do so.

Regardless of its length, a cover message should have three primary parts: (a) an opening that captures attention, introduces the message, and identifies the position; (b) a body that sells the candidate and focuses on the employer's needs; and (c) a closing that requests an interview and motivates action. When putting your cover message together, remember that the biggest mistake job seekers make when writing cover messages is being too generic. You should, therefore, write a personalized, customized cover message for every position that interests you.

13-6b Gaining Attention in the Opening

Your cover message will be more appealing—and more likely to be read—if it begins by addressing the reader by name. Rather than sending your letter to the *Hiring Manager* or *Human Resources Department*, try to identify the name of the appropriate individual. Kelly Renz, vice president for a recruiting outsourcing firm, says that savvy job seekers "take control of their application's destiny." She suggests looking on the company's website, doing an Internet search for a name, or calling the human resources department and asking the receptionist the name of the person in charge of hiring. Ms. Renz also suggests using LinkedIn to find someone working in the same department as the position in the posted job. This person may know the name of the hiring manager.[36] If you still cannot find the name of any person to address, you might replace the salutation of your letter with a descriptive subject line such as *Application for Marketing Specialist Position*.

How you open your cover message depends largely on whether the application is solicited or unsolicited. If an employment position has been announced and applicants are being solicited, you can use a direct approach. If you do not know whether a position is open and you are prospecting for a job, use an indirect approach. Whether direct or indirect, the opening should attract the attention of the reader. Strive for openings that are more imaginative than *Please consider this letter an application for the position of . . .* or *I would like to apply for. . . .*

Openings for Solicited Jobs. When applying for a job that has been announced, consider some of the following techniques to open your cover message:

- **Refer to the name of an employee in the company.** Remember that employers always hope to hire known quantities rather than complete strangers.

    Brendan Borello, a member of your Customer Service Department, told me that Alliance Resources is seeking an experienced customer service representative. The enclosed summary of my qualifications demonstrates my preparation for this position.

    At the suggestion of Heather Bolger, in your Legal Services Department, I submit my qualifications for the position of staffing coordinator.

    Montana Morano, placement director at Southwest University, told me that Dynamic Industries has an opening for a technical writer with knowledge of Web design and graphics.

- **Refer to the source of your information precisely.** If you are answering an advertisement, include the exact position advertised and the name and date of the publication. If you are responding to a position listed on an online job board, include the website name and the date the position was posted.

    From your company's website, I learned about your need for a sales representative for the Ohio, Indiana, and Illinois regions. I am very interested

sjenner13/iStock/Thinkstock

in this position and am confident that my education and experience are appropriate for the opening.

My talent for interacting with people, coupled with more than five years of customer service experience, make me an ideal candidate for the director of customer relations position you advertised on the CareerJournal website on August 3.

- **Refer to the job title, and describe how your qualifications fit the requirements.** Hiring managers are looking for a match between an applicant's credentials and the job needs.

Ceradyne Company's marketing assistant opening is an excellent match with my qualifications. As a recent graduate of Western University with a major in marketing, I offer solid academic credentials as well as industry experience gained from an internship at Flotek Industries.

Will an honors graduate with a degree in recreation and two years of part-time experience organizing social activities for a convalescent hospital qualify for your position of activity director?

Because of my specialized training in finance and accounting at Michigan State University, I am confident that I have the qualifications you described in your advertisement for a staff accountant trainee.

Openings for Unsolicited Jobs. If you are unsure whether a position actually exists, you might use a more persuasive opening. Because your goal is to convince this person to read on, try one of the following techniques:

- **Demonstrate an interest in and knowledge of the reader's business.** Show the hiring manager that you have done your research and that this organization is more than a mere name to you.

Because Signa HealthNet, Inc., is organizing a new information management team for its recently established group insurance division, could you use the services of a well-trained information systems graduate who seeks to become a professional systems analyst?

I read with great interest the article in Forbes announcing the upcoming launch of US Bank. Congratulations on this new venture and its notable $50 million in loans precharter! The possibility of helping your bank grow is exciting, and I would like to explore a potential employment match that I am confident will be mutually beneficial.

- **Show how your special talents and background will benefit the company.** Human resources managers need to be convinced that you can do something for them.

Could your rapidly expanding publications division use the services of an editorial assistant who offers exceptional language skills, an honors degree from the University of Mississippi, and two years' experience in producing a campus literary publication?

In applying for an advertised job, Shenice Williams wrote the solicited cover letter shown in Figure 13.17. Notice that her opening identifies the position advertised on the company's website so that the reader knows exactly what advertisement Shenice means. Using features on her word processing program, Shenice designed her own letterhead that uses her name and looks like professionally printed letterhead paper.

More challenging are unsolicited cover messages, such as the letter of Donald Vinton shown in Figure 13.18. Because he hopes to discover or create a job, his opening must grab the reader's attention immediately. To do that, he capitalizes

Figure 13.17 Solicited Cover Letter

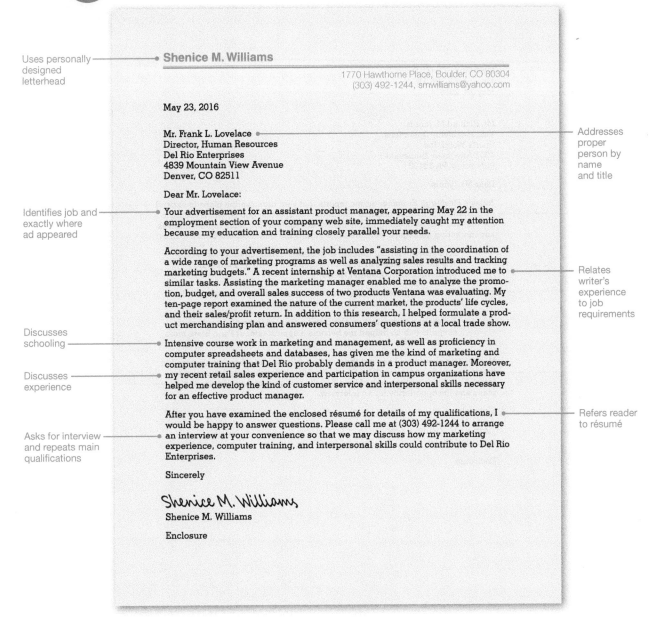

Uses personally designed letterhead → **Shenice M. Williams**

1770 Hawthorne Place, Boulder, CO 80304
(303) 492-1244, smwilliams@yahoo.com

May 23, 2016

Addresses proper person by name and title → Mr. Frank L. Lovelace
Director, Human Resources
Del Rio Enterprises
4839 Mountain View Avenue
Denver, CO 82511

Dear Mr. Lovelace:

Identifies job and exactly where ad appeared → Your advertisement for an assistant product manager, appearing May 22 in the employment section of your company web site, immediately caught my attention because my education and training closely parallel your needs.

Relates writer's experience to job requirements → According to your advertisement, the job includes "assisting in the coordination of a wide range of marketing programs as well as analyzing sales results and tracking marketing budgets." A recent internship at Ventana Corporation introduced me to similar tasks. Assisting the marketing manager enabled me to analyze the promotion, budget, and overall sales success of two products Ventana was evaluating. My ten-page report examined the nature of the current market, the products' life cycles, and their sales/profit return. In addition to this research, I helped formulate a product merchandising plan and answered consumers' questions at a local trade show.

Discusses schooling → Intensive course work in marketing and management, as well as proficiency in computer spreadsheets and databases, has given me the kind of marketing and computer training that Del Rio probably demands in a product manager. Moreover,
Discusses experience → my recent retail sales experience and participation in campus organizations have helped me develop the kind of customer service and interpersonal skills necessary for an effective product manager.

Refers reader to résumé → After you have examined the enclosed résumé for details of my qualifications, I would be happy to answer questions. Please call me at (303) 492-1244 to arrange
Asks for interview and repeats main qualifications → an interview at your convenience so that we may discuss how my marketing experience, computer training, and interpersonal skills could contribute to Del Rio Enterprises.

Sincerely

Shenice M. Williams

Shenice M. Williams

Enclosure

---

on company information appearing in an online article. Donald purposely kept his cover letter short and to the point because he anticipated that a busy executive would be unwilling to read a long, detailed letter. Donald's unsolicited letter "prospects" for a job. Some job candidates feel that such letters may be even more productive than efforts to secure advertised jobs, because prospecting candidates face less competition and show initiative. Notice that Donald's letter uses a personal business letter format with his return address above the date.

13-6c Promoting Your Strengths in the Message Body

Once you have captured the attention of the reader and identified your purpose in the letter opening, you should use the body of the letter to plug your qualifications for this position. If you are responding to an advertisement, you will want to

Figure 13.18 Unsolicited Cover Letter

Uses personal business style with return address above date

2250 Turtle Creek Drive
Monroeville, PA 15146
May 29, 2016

Mr. Richard M. Jannis
Vice President, Operations
Sports World, Inc.
4907 Allegheny Boulevard
Pittsburgh, PA 16103

Dear Mr. Jannis:

Today's *Pittsburgh Examiner* online reports that your organization plans to expand its operations to include national distribution of sporting goods, and it occurs to me that you will be needing highly motivated, self-starting sales representatives and marketing managers. Here are three significant qualifications I have to offer:

- Four years of formal training in business administration, including specialized courses in sales management, retailing, marketing promotion, and consumer behavior

- Practical experience in demonstrating and selling consumer products, as well as successful experience in telemarketing

- Excellent communication skills and a strong interest in most areas of sports (which helped me become a sportscaster at Penn State radio station WGNF)

May we talk about how I can put these qualifications, and others summarized in the enclosed résumé, to work for Sports World as it develops its national sales force? I'll call during the week of June 5 to discuss your company's expansion plans and the opportunity for an interview.

Sincerely yours,

Donald W. Vinton

Donald W. Vinton

Enclosure

Annotations (margin notes):
- Shows resourcefulness and knowledge of company
- Uses bulleted list to make letter easier to read
- Refers to enclosed résumé
- Keeps letter brief to retain reader's attention
- Takes initiative for follow-up

explain how your preparation and experience fulfill the stated requirements. If you are prospecting for a job, you may not know the exact requirements. Your employment research and knowledge of your field, however, should give you a reasonably good idea of what is expected for the position you seek.

It is also important to stress reader benefits. In other words, you should describe your strong points in relation to the needs of the employer. Hiring officers want you to tell them what you can do for their organizations. This is more important than telling what courses you took in college or what duties you performed in your previous jobs.

Poor: I have completed courses in business communication, report writing, and technical writing,

| Improved: | Courses in business communication, report writing, and technical writing have helped me develop the research and writing skills required of your technical writers. |

Choose your strongest qualifications and show how they fit the targeted job. Remember that students with little experience are better off spotlighting their education and its practical applications:

| Poor: | I have taken classes that prepare me to be an administrative assistant. |
| Improved: | Composing e-mail messages, business letters, memos, and reports in my business communication and office technology courses helped me develop the writing, language, proofreading, and computer skills mentioned in your ad for an administrative assistant. |

In the body of your letter, you may choose to discuss relevant personal traits. Employers are looking for candidates who, among other things, are team players, take responsibility, show initiative, and learn easily. Don't just list several personal traits, though; instead, include documentation that proves you possess these traits. Notice how the following paragraph uses action verbs to paint a picture of a promising candidate:

In addition to developing technical and academic skills at Florida Central University, I have gained interpersonal, leadership, and organizational skills. As vice president of the business students' organization, Gamma Alpha, I helped organize and supervise two successful fund-raising events. These activities involved conceptualizing the tasks, motivating others to help, scheduling work sessions, and coordinating the efforts of 35 diverse students. I enjoyed my success with these activities and look forward to applying my experience in your management trainee program.

Finally, in this section or the next, refer the reader to your résumé. Do so directly or as part of another statement.

| Direct reference to résumé: | Please refer to the attached résumé for additional information regarding my education, experience, and skills. |
| Part of another statement: | As you will notice from my enclosed résumé, I will graduate in June with a bachelor's degree in business administration. |

13-6d Motivating Action in the Closing

After presenting your case, you should conclude by asking confidently for an interview. Don't ask for the job. To do so would be presumptuous and naïve. In requesting an interview, you might suggest reader benefits or review your strongest points. Sound sincere and appreciative. Remember to make it easy for the reader to agree by supplying your telephone number and the best times to call you. In addition, keep in mind that some hiring officers prefer that you take the initiative to call them. Avoid expressions such as *I hope*, which weaken your closing. Here are possible endings:

| Poor: | I hope to hear from you soon. |
| Improved: | This brief description of my qualifications and the additional information on my résumé demonstrate my readiness to put my accounting skills to work for McLellan and Associates. |

	Please call me at (405) 488-2291 before 10 a.m. or after 3 p.m. to arrange an interview.
Poor:	I look forward to a call from you.
Improved:	To add to your staff an industrious, well-trained administrative assistant with proven Internet and communication skills, call me at (350) 492-1433 to arrange an interview. I look forward to meeting with you to discuss further my qualifications.
Poor:	Thanks for looking over my qualifications.
Improved:	I look forward to the opportunity to discuss my qualifications for the financial analyst position more fully in an interview. I can be reached at (213) 458-4030.

13-6e Sending Your Résumé and Cover Message

Many applicants using technology make the mistake of not including cover messages with their résumés submitted by e-mail or fax. A résumé that arrives without a cover message makes the receiver wonder what it is and why it was sent. Some candidates either skip the cover message or think they can get by with a one-line cover such as this: *Please see attached résumé, and thanks for your consideration.*

How you submit your résumé depends on the employer's instructions, which usually involve one of the following methods:

- Submit both your cover message and résumé in an e-mail message. Convert both to plain text.

- Send your cover message in an e-mail and attach your résumé (plain text, Word document, or PDF).

- Send a short e-mail message with both your cover message and résumé attached.

- Send your cover message and résumé as printed Word documents by U.S. mail.

If you are serious about landing the job, take the time to prepare a professional cover message. What if you are e-mailing your résumé? Just use the same cover message you would send by surface mail, but shorten it a bit. As illustrated in Figure 13.19, an inside address is unnecessary for an e-mail recipient. Also, move your return address from the top of the letter to just below your name. Include your e-mail address and phone number. Remove tabs, bullets, underlining, and italics that might be problematic in e-mail messages. For résumés submitted by fax, send the same cover message you would send by surface mail. For résumés submitted as PDF files, send the cover message as a PDF also.

13-6f Final Tips for Successful Cover Messages

As you revise your cover message, notice how many sentences begin with *I*. Although it is impossible to talk about yourself without using *I*, you can reduce "I" domination with a number of thoughtful techniques. Make activities and outcomes, and not yourself, the subjects of sentences. Sometimes you can avoid "I" domination by focusing on the "you" view. Another way to avoid starting sentences with *I* is to move phrases from within the sentence to the beginning.

Poor:	I took classes in business communication and computer applications.
Improved:	Classes in business communication and computer applications prepared me to. . . . (Make activities the subject.)

Figure **13.19** E-Mail Cover Message

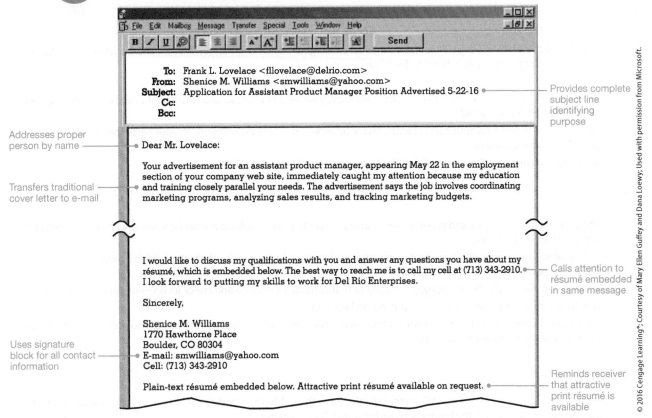

Provides complete subject line identifying purpose

Addresses proper person by name

Transfers traditional cover letter to e-mail

Calls attention to résumé embedded in same message

Uses signature block for all contact information

Reminds receiver that attractive print résumé is available

© 2016 Cengage Learning®; Courtesy of Mary Ellen Guffey and Dana Loewy; Used with permission from Microsoft.

To: Frank L. Lovelace <fllovelace@delrio.com>
From: Shenice M. Williams <smwilliams@yahoo.com>
Subject: Application for Assistant Product Manager Position Advertised 5-22-16
Cc:
Bcc:

Dear Mr. Lovelace:

Your advertisement for an assistant product manager, appearing May 22 in the employment section of your company web site, immediately caught my attention because my education and training closely parallel your needs. The advertisement says the job involves coordinating marketing programs, analyzing sales results, and tracking marketing budgets.

I would like to discuss my qualifications with you and answer any questions you have about my résumé, which is embedded below. The best way to reach me is to call my cell at (713) 343-2910. I look forward to putting my skills to work for Del Rio Enterprises.

Sincerely,

Shenice M. Williams
1770 Hawthorne Place
Boulder, CO 80304
E-mail: smwilliams@yahoo.com
Cell: (713) 343-2910

Plain-text résumé embedded below. Attractive print résumé available on request.

Other examples illustrate how to avoid starting too many sentences with *I*:

Poor:	I enjoyed helping customers, which taught me to. . . .
Improved:	Helping customers was a real pleasure and taught me to. . . . (Make outcomes the subject.)
Poor:	I am a hardworking team player who. . . .
Improved:	You are looking for a hardworking team player who. . . . (Use the "you" view.)
Poor:	I worked to support myself all through college, thus building. . . .
Improved:	All through college, I worked to support myself, thus building. . . . (Move phrases to the beginning.)

However, strive for a comfortable style. In your effort to avoid sounding self-centered, don't write unnaturally.

Like your résumé, your cover message must look professional and suggest quality. This means using a traditional letter style, such as block format. Also, be sure to print it on the same quality paper as your résumé. As with your résumé, proofread it several times yourself; then have a friend read it for content and mechanics. Don't rely on spell-check to find all the errors. Just like your résumé, your cover message must be perfect.

SUMMARY OF LEARNING OBJECTIVES

13-1 Prepare to search for a job in the digital age by understanding the changing job market, identifying your interests, assessing your qualifications, and exploring career opportunities.

- Searching for a job in this digital age has dramatically changed. Search engines, job boards, and social networks have all become indispensable tools in hunting for a job.
- Emphasis today is on what the employer wants, not what the candidate wants.
- Begin the job-search process by learning about yourself, your field of interest, and your qualifications. How do your skills match what employers seek?
- Search the Web, visit a campus career center, take a summer job, interview someone in your field, volunteer, or join professional organizations.
- Identify job availability, the skills and qualifications required, duties, and salaries.

13-2 Develop savvy search strategies by recognizing job sources and using digital tools to explore the open job market.

- The primary sources of jobs today are networking (46 percent), Internet job boards and company websites (25 percent), and agencies (14 percent).
- In searching the open job market—that is, jobs that are listed and advertised—study the big job boards, such as CareerBuilder, Monster, and CollegeGrad.
- To find a job with a specific company, go directly to that company's website and check its openings and possibilities.
- Nearly all serious candidates today post profiles on LinkedIn.
- For jobs in specialized fields, search some of the many niche sites, such as Accountemps for temporary accounting positions or Dice for technology positions.

13-3 Expand your job-search strategies by using both traditional and digital tools in pursuing the hidden job market.

- Estimates suggest that as many as 80 percent of jobs are in the hidden job market—that is, never advertised. Successful job candidates find jobs in the hidden job market through networking.
- An effective networking procedure involves (a) developing a contact list, (b) reaching out to these contacts in person and online in search of referrals, and (c) following up on referrals.
- Because electronic media and digital tools continue to change our lives, you should use social media networks—especially LinkedIn—to extend your networking efforts.
- Effective networking strategies include building a personal brand, preparing a professional business card with a tagline, composing a 30-second elevator speech that describes what you can offer, and developing a strong online presence.

13-4 Organize your qualifications and information into effective résumé segments to create a winning, customized résumé.

- Because of intense competition, you must customize your résumés for every position you seek.
- Chronological résumés, which list work and education by dates, rank highest with recruiters. Functional résumés, which highlight skills instead of jobs, may be helpful for people with little experience, those changing careers, and those with negative employment histories.
- In preparing a résumé, organize your skills and achievements to aim at a particular job or company.
- Study models to effectively arrange the résumé main heading and the optional career objective, summary of qualifications, education, work experience, capabilities, awards, and activities sections.
- The most effective résumés include action verbs to appeal to human readers and job-specific nouns that become keywords selected by applicant tracking systems.
- As you complete your résumé, look for ways to strengthen it by polishing, proofreading, and checking for honesty and accuracy.

13-5 Optimize your job search and résumé by taking advantage of today's digital tools.

- To increase the probability of having your résumé selected by an automated tracking system, include specific keywords, especially nouns that name job titles, technical skills, and tools used or specific experience.
- Consider preparing a career e-portfolio to showcase your qualifications. This collection of digital files can feature your talents, accomplishments, and technical skills. It may include examples of academic performance, photographs, multimedia files, and other items beyond what can be shown in a résumé.

- A video résumé enables you to present your experience, qualifications, and interests in video form.
- A hot trend among creative candidates is the infographic résumé, which provides charts, graphics, and time lines to illustrate a candidate's work history and experience.
- Most candidates, however, should start with a basic print-based résumé from which they can make a plain-text résumé stripped of formatting to be embedded within e-mail messages and submitted online.

13-6 Draft and submit a customized cover message to accompany a print or digital résumé.

- Although cover messages are questioned by some in today's digital world, recruiters and hiring managers overwhelmingly favor them.
- Cover messages help recruiters make decisions, and they enable candidates to set themselves apart from others.
- In the opening of a cover message, gain attention by addressing the receiver by name and identifying the job. You might also identify the person who referred you.
- In the body of the message, build interest by stressing your strengths in relation to the stated requirements. Explain what you can do for the targeted company.
- In the body or closing, refer to your résumé, request an interview, and make it easy for the receiver to respond.
- If you are submitting your cover message by e-mail, shorten it a bit and include your complete contact information in the signature block.

CHAPTER REVIEW

1. When preparing to search for a job, what should you do before writing a résumé? (Obj. 1)

2. What are the current trends in sources of new jobs? Which sources are trending upward and which are trending downward? (Obj. 2)

3. Although one may not actually find a job on the Internet, how can the big job boards be helpful to job hunters? (Obj. 2)

4. What is the hidden job market, and how can candidates find jobs in it? (Obj. 3)

5. In searching for a job, how can you build a personal brand, and why is it important to do so? (Obj. 3)

6. What is a customized résumé and why should you have one? (Obj. 4)

7. How do chronological and functional résumés differ, and what are the advantages and disadvantages of each? (Obj. 4)

8. What is an ATS, and how does it affect the way you prepare a résumé? (Obj. 5)

9. How can you maximize the keyword hits in your résumé? What three categories are most important? (Obj. 5)

10. What are the three parts of a cover message, and does each part contain? (Obj. 6)

CRITICAL THINKING

11. How has job searching for candidates and job placement for hiring managers changed in the digital age? In your opinion, have the changes had a positive or a negative effect? Why? (Obj. 1)

12. The authors of *Guerrilla Marketing for Job Hunters*[37] claim that every year 50 million U.S. jobs are filled, almost all without a job posting. Why do you think businesses avoid advertising job openings? If jobs are unlisted, how can a candidate locate them? (Obj. 3)

13. Some employment authors claim that the paper résumé is dead or dying. What's behind this assertion, and how should current job candidates respond? (Obj. 4)

14. Why might it be more effective to apply for unsolicited jobs than for advertised jobs? Discuss the advantages and disadvantages of letters that "prospect" for jobs. (Obj. 6)

15. Some jobs are advertised even when a leading candidate has the position nailed down. The candidate could be an internal applicant or someone else with an inside track. Although not required by law, management policies and human resources departments at many companies demand that hiring managers list all openings on job boards or career sites. Often, hiring managers have already selected candidates for these "phantom" jobs. Do you believe it is ethical to advertise jobs that are not really available?[38]

RADICAL REWRITES

Note: Radical Rewrites are provided at **www.cengagebrain.com** for you to download and revise. Your instructor may show a suggested solution.

13.1 Radical Rewrite: Rescuing a Slapdash Résumé (Obj. 4)

The following poorly organized and written résumé needs help to remedy its misspellings, typos, and inconsistent headings.

YOUR TASK. Analyze Isabella's sad résumé. List at least eight weaknesses. Your instructor may ask you to revise sections of this résumé before showing you an improved version.

Résumé of Isabella R. Jimenez

1340 East Phillips Ave., Apt. D Littleton, CO 80126

Phone 455-5182 • E-Mail: Hotchilibabe@gmail.com

OBJECTIVE

I'm dying to land a first job in the "real world" with a big profitable company that will help me get ahead in the accounting field.

SKILLS

Word processing, Internet browsers (Explorer and Google), Powerpoint, Excel, type 40 wpm, databases, spreadsheets; great composure in stressful situations; 3 years as leader and supervisor and 4 years in customer service

EDUCATION

Arapahoe Community College, Littleton, Colorado. AA degree Fall 2013

Now I am pursuing a BA in Accounting at CSU-Pueblo, majoring in Accounting; my minor is Finance. My expected degree date is June 2015; I recieved a Certificate of Completion in Entry Level Accounting in December 2012.

I graduated East High School, Denver, CO in 2009.

Highlights:

- Named Line Manger of the Month at Target, 08/2009 and 09/2010
- Obtained a Certificate in Entry Level Accounting, June 2012
- Chair of Accounting Society, Spring and fall 2013
- Dean's Honor List, Fall 2014
- Financial advisor training completed through Primerica (May 2014)
- Webmaster for M.E.Ch.A, Spring 2015

Part-Time Employment

Financial Consultant, 2014 to present
I worked only part-time (January 2014-present) for Primerica Financial Services, Pueblo, CO to assist clients in refinancing a mortgage or consolidating a current mortgage loan and also to advice clients in assessing their need for life insurance.

Target, Littleton, CO. As line manager, from September 2008-March 2012, I supervised 22 cashiers and front-end associates. I helped to write schedules, disciplinary action notices, and performance appraisals. I also kept track of change drawer and money exchanges; occasionally was manager on duty for entire store.

Mr. K's Floral Design of Denver. I taught flower design from August, 2008 to September, 2009. I supervised 5 florists, made floral arrangements for big events like weddings, send them to customers, and restocked flowers.

List at least eight weaknesses.

13.2 Radical Rewrite: Inadequate Cover Letter (Obj. 6)

The following cover letter accompanies Isabella Jimenez's résumé (**Radical Rewrite 13.1**). Like her résumé, the cover letter needs major revision.

YOUR TASK. Analyze Isabella's cover letter and list at least eight weaknesses. Your instructor may ask you to revise this letter before showing you an improved version.

To Whom It May Concern:

I saw your internship position yesterday and would like to apply right away. It would be so exiting to work for your esteemed firm! An internship would really give me much needed real-world experience and help my career.

I have all the qualifications you require in your add and more. I am a junior at Colorado State University-Pueblo and an Accounting major (with a minor in Finance). Accounting and Finance are my passion and I want to become a CPA and a financial advisor. I have taken Intermediate I and II and now work as a financial advisor with Primerica Financial Services in Pueblo. I should also tell you that I was at Target for four years. I learned alot, but my heart is in accounting and finance.

I am a team player, a born leader, motivated, reliable, and I show excellent composure in stressful situation, for example, when customers complain. I put myself through school and always carry at least 15 units while working part time.

You will probably agree that I am a good candidate for your internship position, which should start July 1. I feel that my motivation, passion, and strong people skills will serve your company well.

Sincerely,

List at least eight weaknesses.

ACTIVITIES AND CASES

13.3 Beginning Your Job Search With Self-Analysis (Obj. 1)

⟨ **E-mail** ⟩

YOUR TASK. In an e-mail or a memo addressed to your instructor, answer the questions in the section "Beginning Your Job Search With Self-Analysis" on page 427. Draw a conclusion from your answers. What kind of career, company, position, and location seem to fit your self-analysis?

13.4 Evaluating Your Qualifications (Obj. 1–3)

YOUR TASK. Prepare four worksheets that inventory your qualifications in these areas: employment; education; capabilities and skills; and awards, honors, and activities. Use active verbs when appropriate and specific nouns that describe job titles and skills.

a. **Employment.** Begin with your most recent job or internship. For each position list the following information: employer; job title; dates of employment; and three to five duties, activities, or accomplishments. Emphasize activities related to your job goal. Strive to quantify your achievements.

b. **Education.** List degrees, certificates, and training accomplishments. Include courses, seminars, and skills that are relevant to your job goal. Calculate your grade point average in your major.

c. **Capabilities and skills.** List all capabilities and skills that qualify you for the job you seek. Use words and phrases such as *skilled, competent, trained, experienced,* and *ability to*. Be sure to include **nouns** that describe keywords relevant to your career field. Also list five or more qualities or interpersonal skills necessary for success in your field. Write action statements demonstrating that you possess some of these qualities. Empty assurances aren't good enough; try to show evidence (*Developed teamwork skills by working with a committee of eight to produce a . . .*).

d. **Awards, honors, and activities.** Explain any awards that the reader might misunderstand. List campus, community, and professional activities that suggest you are a well-rounded individual or possess traits relevant to your target job.

13.5 Choosing a Career Path (Obj. 1)

⟨ **Web** ⟩

Many people know amazingly little about the work done in various occupations and the training requirements.

YOUR TASK. Use the online *Occupational Outlook Handbook* at **http://www.bls.gov/ooh**, prepared by the Bureau of Labor Statistics (BLS), to learn more about an occupation of your choice. This is the nation's premier source for career information. The career profiles featured here cover hundreds of occupations and describe what people in these occupations do, the work environment, how to get these jobs, salaries, and more. You can browse categories including highest paying, fastest growing, and most new jobs.

Find the description of a position for which you could apply in two to five years. Learn about what workers do on the job, working conditions, training and education needed, earnings, and expected job prospects. Print the pages from the *Occupational Outlook Handbook* that describe employment in the area in which you are interested. If your instructor directs, attach these copies to the cover letter you will write in **Activity 13.9**.

13.6 Searching the Job Market (Obj. 1)

⟨ **Web** ⟩

Where are the jobs? Even though you may not be in the market at the moment, become familiar with the kinds of available positions because job awareness should be an important part of your education.

YOUR TASK. Clip or print a job advertisement or announcement from (a) the classified section of a newspaper, (b) a job board on the Web, (c) a company website, or (d) a professional association listing. Select an advertisement or announcement describing the kind of employment you are seeking now or plan to seek when you graduate. Save this advertisement or announcement to attach to the résumé you will write in **Activity 13.8**.

13.7 Posting a Résumé on the Web (Obj. 2)

E-mail Web

Learn about the procedure for posting résumés at job boards on the Web.

YOUR TASK. Prepare a list of three websites where you could post your résumé. In a class discussion or in an e-mail to your instructor, describe the procedure involved in posting a résumé and the advantages for each site.

13.8 Writing Your Résumé (Obj. 4)

YOUR TASK. Using the data you developed in **Activity 13.4**, write your résumé. Aim it at the full-time job, part-time position, or internship that you located in **Activity 13.6**. Attach the job listing to your résumé. Also prepare a list of references. Revise your résumé until it is perfect.

13.9 Preparing Your Cover Message (Obj. 6)

E-mail

YOUR TASK. Using the job listing you found for **Activity 13.6**, write a cover message introducing your résumé. Decide whether it should be a letter or an e-mail. Again, revise until it is perfect.

13.10 Using LinkedIn to Assist You in Your Job Search (Obj. 2)

Social Media

LinkedIn is the acknowledged No. 1 site for job seekers and recruiters. It's free and easy to join. Even if you are not in the job market yet, becoming familiar with LinkedIn can open your eyes to the kinds of information that employers seek and also give you practice in filling in templates such as those that applicant tracking systems employ.

YOUR TASK. To become familiar with LinkedIn, set up an account and complete a profile. This consists of a template with categories to fill in. The easiest way to begin is to view a LinkedIn video taking you through the steps of creating a profile. Search for *LinkedIn Profile Checklist*. It discusses how to fill in information in categories such as the following:

- **Photo.** Your photo doesn't have to be fancy. Just take a cell phone shot in front of a plain background. Wear a nice shirt and smile.

- **Headline.** Use a tagline to summarize your professional goals.

- **Summary.** Explain what motivates you, what you are skilled at, and where you want to go in the future.

- **Experience.** List the jobs you have held and be sure to enter the information precisely in the template categories. You can even include photos and videos of your work.

You can fill in other categories such as Organizations, Honors, Publications, and so forth. After completing a profile, discuss your LinkedIn experience with classmates. If you already have an account set up, discuss how it operates and your opinion of its worth. How can LinkedIn help students now and in the future?

13.11 Tweeting to Find a Job (Obj. 5)

Web Social Media Team

Twitter résumés are a new twist on job hunting. While most job seekers struggle to contain their credentials on one page, others are tweeting their credentials in 140 characters or fewer! Here is an example from TheLadders.com:

> RT #Susan Moline seeks a LEAD/SR QA ENG JOB http://bit.ly/1ThaW @TalentEvolution - http://bit.ly/QB5DC @TweetMyJobs.com #résumé #QA-Jobs-CA

Are you scratching your head? Let's translate: (a) RT stands for retweet, allowing your Twitter followers to repeat this message to their followers. (b) The hashtag (#) always means *subject;* prefacing your name, it makes you easy to find. (c) The uppercase abbreviations indicate the job title, here *Lead Senior Quality Assurance Engineer.* (d) The first link is a "tiny URL," a short, memorable Web address or alias provided free by TinyURL.com and other URL-shrinking services. The first short link reveals the job seeker's Talent Evolution profile page; the second directs viewers to a job seeker profile created on TweetMyJobs.com. (e) The hashtags indicate the search terms used as seen here: name, quality assurance jobs in California, and the broad term *résumé.* When doing research from within Twitter, use the @ symbol with a specific Twitter user name or the # symbol for a subject search.

YOUR TASK. As a team or individually, search the Web for *tweet résumé*. Pick one of the sites offering to tweet your résumé for you—for example, TweetMyJobs.com or Tweet My Résumé. Describe to your peers the job-search process via Twitter presented on that website. Some services are free, whereas others come with charges. If you select a commercial service, critically evaluate its sales pitch and its claims. Is it worthwhile to spend money on this service? Do clients find jobs? How does the service try to demonstrate that? As a group or individually, share the results with the class.

13.12 Analyzing and Building Student E-Portfolios (Obj. 5)

Communication Technology · Web · Team

Take a minute to conduct a Google search on your name. What comes up? Are you proud of what you see? If you want to change that information—and especially if you are in the job market—think about creating a career e-portfolio. Building such a portfolio has many benefits. It can give you an important digital tool to connect with a large audience. It can also help you expand your technology skills, confirm your strengths, recognize areas in need of improvement, and establish goals for improvement. Many students are creating e-portfolios with the help of their schools.

YOUR TASK NO. 1. Before attempting to build your own career e-portfolio, take a look at those of other students. Use the Google search term *student career e-portfolio* to see lots of samples. Your instructor may assign you individually or as a team to visit specific digital portfolio sites and summarize your findings in a memo or a brief oral presentation. You could focus on the composition of the site, page layout, links provided, software tools used, colors selected, or types of documents included.

YOUR TASK NO. 2. Next, examine websites that provide tutorials and tips on how to build career e-portfolios. One of the best sites can be found by searching for *career e-portfolios San Jose State University*. Your instructor may have you individually or as team write a memo summarizing tips on how to create an e-portfolio and choose the types of documents to include. Alternatively, your instructor may ask you to actually create a career e-portfolio.

13.13 Exploring Infographic Résumés (Obj. 5)

E-mail · Web

The latest rage in résumés is infographics. However, are they appropriate for every field?

YOUR TASK. Using your favorite browser, locate 10 to 15 infographic résumés. Select your favorite top three. Analyze them for readability, formatting, and color. How many use time lines? What other similarities do you see? What career fields do they represent? Do you find any in your career field? In terms of your career field, what are the pros and cons of creating an infographic résumé? Do you think an infographic résumé would improve your chances of securing an interview? In an e-mail to your instructor, summarize your findings and answer these questions.

GRAMMAR/MECHANICS CHECKUP—13

Number Style

Review Sections 4.01–4.13 in the Grammar/Mechanics Handbook. Then study each of the following pairs. Assume that these expressions appear in the context of letters, reports, or memos. Write *a* or *b* in the space provided to indicate the preferred number style, and record the number of the G/M principle illustrated. When you finish, compare your response with those at the end of the book. If your responses differ, study carefully the principles in parentheses.

a _____ (4.01a)	EXAMPLE	(a) three cell phones	(b) 3 cell phones
_____	1.	(a) fifteen employees	(b) 15 employees
_____	2.	(a) Third Avenue	(b) 3rd Avenue
_____	3.	(a) twenty-one new phone apps	(b) 21 new phone apps
_____	4.	(a) September 1st	(b) September 1
_____	5.	(a) thirty dollars	(b) $30
_____	6.	(a) on the 15th of July	(b) on the fifteenth of July
_____	7.	(a) at 4:00 p.m.	(b) at 4 p.m.
_____	8.	(a) 3 200-page reports	(b) three 200-page reports

_____ 9. (a) over fifty years ago   (b) over 50 years ago

_____ 10. (a) 2,000,000 people   (b) 2 million people

_____ 11. (a) fifteen cents   (b) 15 cents

_____ 12. (a) a thirty-day warranty   (b) a 30-day warranty

_____ 13. (a) 2/3 of the e-mails   **(b) two thirds of the e-mails**

_____ 14. (a) two printers for 15 employees   (b) 2 printers for 15 employees

_____ 15. (a) 6 of the 130 messages   (b) six of the 130 messages

EDITING CHALLENGE—**13**

To fine-tune your grammar and mechanics skills, in every chapter you will be editing a message. This résumé has problems with number usage, capitalization, spelling, proofreading, and other writing techniques. Study the guidelines in the Grammar/Mechanics Handbook as well as the lists of Confusing Words and Frequently Misspelled Words to sharpen your skills.

YOUR TASK. Edit the following message (a) by correcting errors in your textbook or on a photocopy using proofreading marks from Appendix A or (b) by downloading the message from the premium website at **www.cengagebrain.com**.

Amanda J. Copeland

3010 East 8th Avenue   acopeland@charter.com
Monroe, Mich. 48162

SUMMARY OF QUALIFICATIONS

- Over three years experience in working in customer relations
- Partnered with Assistant Manager to create mass mailing by merging three thousand customers names and addresses in ad campaign
- Hold AA Degree in Administrative Assisting
- Proficient with MS Word, excel, powerpoint, and the internet

EXPERIENCE

Administrative Assistant, Monroe Mold and Machine Company, Munroe, Michigan
June 2015 to present
- Answer phones, respond to e-mail and gather information for mold designers
- Key board and format proposals for various machine Platforms and Configurations
- Help company with correspondence to fulfill it's guarantee that a prototype mold can be produced in less than 1 week
- Worked with Assistant Manger to create large customer mailings
- Use the internet to Research prospective customers; enter data in Excel

Shift Supervisor, Monroe Coffee Shop, Monroe, Michigan
May 2014 to May 2015
- Trained 3 new employees, opened and closed shop handled total sales
- Managed shop in the owners absence
- Builded satisfied customer relationships

Server, Hostess, Expeditor, Busser, Roadside Girll, Toledo, Ohio
April 2012 to April 2014
- Created customer base and close relationships with patrons of resterant
- Helped Owner expand menu from twenty to thirty-five items
- Develop procedures that reduce average customer wait time from sixteen to eight minutes

AWARDS AND ACHEIVEMENTS

- Deans List, Spring, 2015, Fall, 2014
- Awarded 2nd prize in advertise essay contest, 2014

EDUCATION

- AA degree, Munroe Community College, 2015
- Major: Office Administation and Technology
  GPA in major: 3.8 (4.0 = A)

COMMUNICATION WORKSHOP

Fudging the Facts on Résumés: Worth the Risk?

Given today's brutal job market, it might be tempting to puff up your résumé. You certainly wouldn't be alone in telling fibs or outright whoppers. A CareerBuilder survey of 8,700 workers found that 8 percent admitted to lying on their résumés; however, the same study found that of the 3,100 hiring managers surveyed, 49 percent caught a job applicant lying on some part of his or her résumé. Worse, 57 percent of employers will automatically dismiss applicants who misrepresent any part of their résumés.[39] It's a risky game, warns recruiter Dennis Nason. Background checks are much easier now, he says, with the Internet and professionals who specialize in sniffing out untruths.[40]

After they have been hired, candidates may think they are safe—but organizations often continue the checking process. If hiring officials find a discrepancy in a GPA or prior experience and the error is an honest mistake, they meet with the new-hire to hear an explanation. If the discrepancy wasn't a mistake, they will likely fire the person immediately.

No job seeker wants to be in the unhappy position of explaining résumé errors or defending misrepresentation. Avoiding the following actions can keep you off the hot seat:

- **Enhancing education, grades, or honors.** Some job candidates claim degrees from colleges or universities when in fact they merely attended classes. Others increase their grade point averages or claim fictitious honors. Any such dishonest reporting is grounds for dismissal when discovered.

- **Inflating job titles and salaries.** Wishing to elevate their status, some applicants misrepresent their titles or increase their past salaries. For example, one technician called himself a programmer when he had actually programmed only one project for his boss. A mail clerk who assumed added responsibilities conferred upon herself the title of supervisor.

- **Puffing up accomplishments.** Job seekers may inflate their employment experience or achievements. One clerk, eager to make her photocopying duties sound more important, said that she assisted the *vice president in communicating and distributing employee directives*. Similarly, guard against taking sole credit for achievements that required many people. When recruiters suspect dubious claims on résumés, they nail applicants with specific—and often embarrassing—questions during their interviews.

- **Altering employment dates.** Some candidates extend the dates of employment to hide unimpressive jobs or to cover up periods of unemployment and illness. Although their employment histories may have no gaps, their résumés are dishonest and represent potential booby traps.

CAREER APPLICATION. Cassidy M. finally got an interview for the perfect job. The big problem, however, is that she padded her résumé a little by making the gaps in her job history a bit smaller. Oh, yes, and she increased her last job title from administrative assistant to project manager. After all, she was really doing a lot of his work. Now she's worried about the upcoming interview. She's considering coming clean and telling the truth. On the other hand, she wonders whether it is too late to submit an updated résumé and tell the interviewer that she noticed some errors. Of course, she could do nothing. A final possibility is withdrawing her application. In groups, discuss Cassidy's options. What would you advise her to do? Why?

ENDNOTES

1 Adams, S. (2011, June 7). Networking is still the best way to find a job, survey says. Retrieved from http://www.forbes.com/sites/susanadams/2011/06/07/networking-is-still-the-best-way-to-find-a-job-survey-says; see also Stevens-Huffman, L. (2012, August 9). Networking is still the best way to find a job. Retrieved from http://news.dice.com/2012/08/09/networking-most-effective-way-find-job

2 Waldman, J. (2012, February 26). 10 differences between the job search of today and of yesterday. Retrieved from http://www.careerrealism.com/job-search-differences

3 Bureau of Labor Statistics. (2010, September 14). Economic news release: Employee tenure summary. Retrieved from http://www.bls.gov/news.release/tenure.nr0.htm. See also Kimmit, R. M. (2007, January 23). Why job churn is good. *The Washington Post*, p. A17. Retrieved from http://www.washingtonpost.com/wp-dyn/content/article/2007/01/22/AR2007012201089.html

4 Adams, S. (2012, July 25). Odds are your internship will get you a job. Retrieved from http://www.forbes.com/sites/susanadams/2012/07/25/odds-are-your-internship-will-get-you-a-job

5 Adams, S. (2011, June 7). Networking is still the best way to find a job, survey says. Retrieved from http://www.forbes.com/sites/susanadams/2011/06/07/networking-is-still-the-best-way-to-find-a-job-survey-says

6 Mathison, D., & Finney, M. I. (2009). *Unlock the hidden job market: 6 steps to a successful job search when times are tough.* Upper Saddle River, NJ: Pearson Education, FI Press. See also Poplinger, H., as reported by Jessica Dickler (2009, June 10) in The hidden job market. Retrieved from CNNMoney.com at http://money.cnn.com/2009/06/09/news/economy/hidden_jobs

7 Adams, S. (2013, February 5). New survey: LinkedIn more dominant than ever among job seekers and recruiters, but Facebook poised to gain. Retrieved from http://www.forbes.com/sites/susanadams/2013/02/05/new-survey-linkedin-more-dominant-than-ever-among-job-seekers-and-recruiters-but-facebook-poised-to-gain

8 Mathison, D., & Finney, M. I. (2009). *Unlock the hidden job market: 6 steps to a successful job search when times are tough.* Upper Saddle River, NJ: Pearson Education, FI Press. See also Poplinger, H., as reported by Jessica Dickler (2009, June 10) in The hidden job market. Retrieved from CNNMoney.com at http://money.cnn.com/2009/06/09/news/economy/hidden_jobs

9 Richardson, V. (2011, March 16). Five ways inside the 'hidden job market.' Retrieved from http://www.dailyfinance.com/2011/03/16/five-ways-inside-the-hidden-job-market

10 Adams, S. (2012, March 27). Make LinkedIn help you find a job. Retrieved from http://www.forbes.com/sites/susanadams/2012/04/27/make-linkedin-help-you-find-a-job-2

[11] Ibid.

[12] Williams, N. (2013, December 12). How to strategically use buzzwords on LinkedIn. *U.S. News & World Report*. Retrieved from http://money.usnews.com/money/blogs/outside-voices-careers/2013/12/12/how-to-strategically-use-buzzwords-on-linkedin

[13] Doyle, A. (n.d.). Facebook and professional networking. Retrieved from http://jobsearch.about.com/od/networking/a/facebook.htm

[14] Ibid.

[15] Swallow, E. (2011, October 23). How recruiters use social networks to screen candidates. Retrieved from http://mashable.com/2011/10/23/how-recruiters-use-social-networks-to-screen-candidates-infographic

[16] Hansen, K. (n.d.). From *Tell me about yourself: Storytelling that propels careers* (Ten Speed Press). Excerpt appearing in Heather Huhman's blog at http://www.personalbrandingblog.com/how-to-write-your-60-second-elevator-pitch

[17] Isaacs, K. (2012). How to decide on résumé length. Retrieved from http://career-advice.monster.com/resumes-cover-letters/resume-writing-tips/how-to-decide-on-resume-length/article.aspx

[18] Green, A. (2012, June 20). 10 things to leave off your résumé. Retrieved from http://money.usnews.com/money/blogs/outside-voices-careers/2012/06/20/10-things-to-leave-off-your-resume

[19] Diaz, C. (2013, December). Updating best practices: Applying on-screen reading strategies to résumé writing. *Business Communication Quarterly, 76*(4), 427–445.

[20] Korkki, P. (2007, July 1). So easy to apply, so hard to be noticed. *The New York Times*. Retrieved from http://www.nytimes.com/2007/07/01/business/yourmoney/01career.html

[21] Berrett, D. (2013, January 25). My GRE score says I'm smart. Hire me. *The Chronicle of Higher Education*, A4.

[22] Diaz, C. (2013, December). Updating best practices: Applying on-screen reading strategies to résumé writing. *Business Communication Quarterly, 76*(4), 427–445. See also Nielsen, J. (2006, April 17). F-shaped pattern for reading web content. Retrieved from http://www.nngroup.com/articles/f-shaped-pattern-reading-web-content.

[23] Struzik, E., IBM expert quoted in Weber, L. (2012, January 24). Your résumé vs. oblivion. *The Wall Street Journal*, p. B6.

[24] Harris, C. (2012, February 15). Why applicant tracking systems are the weakest link. Retrieved from http://www.unrabble.com/blog/why-applicant-tracking-systems-are-the-weakest-link

[25] Optimalresume.com. (n.d.). Optimizing your résumé for scanning and tracking. Retrieved from http://www.montclair.edu/CareerServices/OptimalsScannedresumes.pdf

[26] Ibid.

[27] Krum, R. (2012, September 10). Is your résumé hopelessly out of date? Retrieved from http://infonewt.com/blog/2012/9/10/infographic-resumes-interview-by-the-art-of-doing.html

[28] Larsen, M. (2011, Nov. 8). Infographic résumés: Fad or trend? Retrieved from http://www.recruiter.com/i/infographic-resumes

[29] Ibid.

[30] Balderrama, S. (2009, February 26). Do you still need a cover letter? Retrieved from http://msn.careerbuilder.com/Article/MSN-1811-Cover-Letters-Resumes-Do-You-Still-Need-a-Cover-Letter

[31] Quoted in Doyle, A. (2012, July 14). Do you need a cover letter? Retrieved from http://jobsearch.about.com/b/2012/07/14/do-you-need-a-cover-letter.htm

[32] Quoted in Balderrama, S. (2009, February 26). Do you still need a cover letter? Retrieved from http://msn.careerbuilder.com/Article/MSN-1811-Cover-Letters-Resumes-Do-You-Still-Need-a-Cover-Letter

[33] Needleman, S. E. (2010, March 9). Standout letters to cover your bases. *The Wall Street Journal*, p. D4.

[34] Balderrama, S. (2009, February 26). Do you still need a cover letter? Retrieved from http://msn.careerbuilder.com/Article/MSN-1811-Cover-Letters-Resumes-Do-You-Still-Need-a-Cover-Letter

[35] Grant, A. (2011, March 1). Proactive Job-Search Strategy: Pitch Your Dream Company. *U.S. News & World Report*. Retrieved from http://money.usnews.com/money/careers/articles/2011/03/01/proactive-job-search-strategy-pitch-your-dream-company

[36] Korkki, P. (2009, July 18). Where, oh where, has my application gone? *The New York Times*. Retrieved from http://www.nytimes.com/2009/07/19/jobs/19career.html?_r=1&scp=1&sq=Where,%20oh%20where,%20has%20my%20application%20gone&st=cse

[37] Levinson, J. C., & Perry, D. (2011). *Guerrilla marketing for job hunters 3.0*. Hoboken, NJ: John Wiley & Sons.

[38] Weber, L., & Kwoh, L. (2013, January 9). Beware the phantom job listing. *The Wall Street Journal*, pp. B1 and B6.

[39] Zupek, R. (2008, March 27). Honesty is the best policy in résumés and interviews. Retrieved from Careerbuilder.com at http://msn.careerbuilder.com/Article/MSN-1854-Cover-Letters-Resumes-Honesty-is-the-Best-Policy-in-R%C3%A9sum%C3%A9s-and-Interviews

[40] Quoted in Purdy, C. (n.d.). The biggest lies job seekers tell on their résumés—and how they get caught. Retrieved from http://career-advice.monster.com/resumes-cover-letters/resume-writing-tips/the-truth-about-resume-lies-hot-jobs/article.aspx

ACKNOWLEDGMENTS

p. 430 Office Insider based on quotation in Giang, V. (2013, September 14). 3 reasons why the paper resume isn't dead. Retrieved from http://www.businessinsider.com/why-the-paper-resume-isnt-dying-any-2013-9#ixzz2sDbs8OYV
Figure 13.2 based on Right Management survey. Most Expect to Get New Job by Networking (2013). Retrieved from http://www.right.com/news-and-events/press-releases/2013-press-releases/item24727.aspx?x=24727

p. 435 Office Insider based on Vaas, L. (n.d.). Customize your résumé for that plum job. Retrieved from http://www.theladders.com/career-advice/customize-resume-for-plum-job

p. 439 Office Insider based on Matuson, R. C. (n.d.). Recession-proof your career. Retrieved from http://www.hcareers.com/us/resourcecenter/tabid/306/articleid/522/default.aspx

p. 448 Office Insider based on quotation in Needleman, S. (2010, February 2). Job hunters, beware. *The Wall Street Journal*. Retrieved from http://online.wsj.com/news/articles/SB10001424052748704107204575039361105870740

p. 449 Office Insider based on Bersin, J. (2013, July 4). The hottest trends in corporate recruiting. Retrieved from http://www.forbes.com/sites/joshbersin/2013/07/04/the-9-hottest-trends-in-corporate-recruiting/2

p. 455 Office Insider based on quotation in Needleman, S. (2010, March 9). Standout letters to cover your bases. *The Wall Street Journal*, p. D4.

Appendix A: Correction Symbols and Proofreading Marks

In marking your papers, your instructor may use the following symbols or abbreviations to indicate writing weaknesses. Studying these symbols and suggestions will help you understand your instructor's remarks. Knowing this information can also help you evaluate and improve your own memos, e-mails, letters, reports, and other writing. These symbols are keyed to your Grammar/Mechanics Handbook and to the text.

Adj	Hyphenate two or more adjectives that are joined to create a compound modifier before a noun. See G/M 1.17e.
Adv	Use adverbs, not adjectives, to describe or limit the action. See G/M 1.17d.
Apos	Use apostrophes to show possession. See G/M 2.20–2.22.
Assgn	Follow the assignment instructions.
Awk	Recast to avoid awkward expression.
Bias	Use inclusive, bias-free language. See Chapter 2, page 50.
Cap	Use capitalization appropriately. See G/M 3.01–3.16.
CmConj	Use a comma before the coordinating conjunction in a compound sentence. See G/M 2.05.
CmDate	Use commas appropriately in dates, addresses, geographical names, degrees, and long numbers. See G/M 2.04.
CmIn	Use commas to set off internal sentence interrupters. See G/M 2.06c.
CmIntr	Use commas to separate introductory clauses and certain phrases from independent clauses. See G/M 2.06.
CmSer	Use commas to separate three or more items (words, phrases, or short clauses) in a series. See G/M 2.01.
Coh	Improve coherence between ideas. Repeat key ideas, use pronouns, or use transitional expressions. See Chapter 3, pages 75–76.
Cl	Improve the clarity of ideas or expression so that the point is better understood.
CS	Avoid comma-splice sentences. Do not use a comma to splice (join) two independent clauses. See Chapter 3, page 70.
CmUn	Avoid unnecessary commas. See G/M 2.15.
:	Use a colon after a complete thought that introduces a list of items. Use a colon in business letter salutations and to introduce long quotations. See G/M 2.17–2.19.
Direct	Use the direct strategy by emphasizing the main idea. See Chapter 3, pages 66–68.
Dash	Use a dash to set off parenthetical elements, to emphasize sentence interruptions, or to separate an introductory list from a summarizing statement. See G/M 2.26.
DM	Avoid dangling modifiers by placing modifiers close to the words they describe or limit. See Chapter 3, page 74.

Filler	Avoid fillers such as *there are* or long lead-ins such as *this is to inform you that*. See Chapter 4, page 92.
Format	Choose an appropriate format for this document.
Frag	Avoid fragments by expressing ideas in complete sentences. A fragment is a broken-off part of a sentence. See Chapter 3, page 70.
GH	Use graphic highlighting (bullets, lists, indentions, or headings) to enhance readability. See Chapter 4, pages 100–101.
MM	Avoid misplaced modifiers by placing modifiers close to the words they describe or limit. See Chapter 3, page 74.
Num	Use number or word form appropriately. See G/M 4.01–4.13.
Ob	Avoid stating the obvious.
Org	Improve organization by grouping similar ideas.
Par	Express ideas in parallel form. See Chapter 3, pages 73–74.
Paren	Use parentheses to set off nonessential sentence elements such as explanations, directions, questions, or references. See G/M 2.27.
Period	Use one period to end a statement, command, indirect question, or polite request. See G/M 2.23.
Pos	Express an idea positively rather than negatively. See Chapter 2, page 47.
PosPro	Use possessive-case pronouns to show ownership. See G/M 1.07 and 1.08d.
Pro	Use nominative-case pronouns as subjects of verbs and as subject complements. Use objective-case pronouns as objects of prepositions and verbs. See G/M 1.07 and 1.08.
ProAgr	Make pronouns agree in number and gender with the words to which they refer (their antecedents). See G/M 1.09.
ProVag	Be sure that pronouns such as *it, which, this*, and *that* refer to clear antecedents.
?	Use a question mark after a direct question and after statements with questions appended. See G/M 2.24.
Quo	Use quotation marks to enclose the exact words of a speaker or writer; to distinguish words used in a special sense; or to enclose titles of articles, chapters, or other short works. See G/M 2.28.
Redun	Avoid expressions that repeat meaning or include unnecessary words. See Chapter 4, page 93.
RunOn	Avoid run-on (fused) sentences. A sentence with two independent clauses must be joined by a coordinating conjunctions (*and, or, nor, but*) or by a semicolon (;). See Chapter 3, page 70.
Sp	Check misspelled words.
Self	Use *self*-ending pronouns only when they refer to previously mentioned nouns or pronouns. See G/M 1.08h.
;	Use a semicolon to join closely related independent clauses. A semicolon is also an option to join separate items in a series when one or more of the items contain internal commas. See G/M 2.16.
Shift	Avoid a confusing shift in verb tense, mood, or voice. See G/M 1.15c.
Trans	Use an appropriate transition. See Chapter 3, page 76.
Tone	Use a conversational, positive, and courteous tone that promotes goodwill. See Chapter 2, page 47.
You	Focus on developing the "you" view. See Chapter 2, page 45.

VbAgr	Make verbs agree with subjects. See G/M 1.10.
VbMood	Use the subjunctive mood to express hypothetical (untrue) ideas. See G/M 1.12.
VbTnse	Use present-tense, past-tense, and part-participle forms correctly. See G/M 1.13.
VbVce	Use active- and passive-voice verbs appropriately. See G/M 1.11.
WC	Focus on precise word choice. See Chapter 4, page 98.
Wordy	Avoid wordiness including flabby expressions, long lead-ins, unnecessary *there is/are* fillers, redundancies, and trite business phrases. See Chapter 4, pages 91–94.

Proofreading Marks

Proofreading Mark	Draft Copy	Final Copy
⸗ Align horizontally	TO: Rick Munoz	TO: Rick Munoz
‖ Align vertically	166.32 132.45	166.32 132.45
☰ Capitalize	Coca-cola sending a pdf file	Coca-Cola sending a PDF file
⊂ Close up space	meeting at 3 p. m.	meeting at 3 p.m.
⌐⌐ Center	Recommendations	Recommendations
℘ Delete	in my final judgement	in my judgment
⌄ Insert apostrophe	our companys product	our company's product
⌃ Insert comma	you will of course	you will, of course,
⌃ Insert hyphen	tax free income	tax-free income
⊙ Insert period	Ms Holly Hines	Ms. Holly Hines
⌄⌄ Insert quotation mark	shareholders receive a bonus.	shareholders receive a "bonus."
# Insert space	wordprocessing program	word processing program
/ Lowercase (remove capitals)	the Vice President HUMAN RESOURCES	the vice president Human Resources
⊏ Move to left	I. Labor costs	I. Labor costs
⊐ Move to right	A. Findings of study	A. Findings of study
○ Spell out	aimed at 2 depts	aimed at two departments
¶ Start new paragraph	Keep the screen height of your computer at eye level.	Keep the screen height of your computer at eye level.
····· Stet (don't delete)	officials talked openly	officials talked openly
∿ Transpose	accounts recievable	accounts receivable
bf Use boldface	Conclusions	**Conclusions**
ital Use italics	The Perfect Résumé	*The Perfect Résumé*

Appendix B: Document Format Guide

Business communicators produce numerous documents that have standardized formats. Becoming familiar with these formats is important because business documents actually carry two kinds of messages. Verbal messages are conveyed by the words chosen to express the writer's ideas. Nonverbal messages are conveyed largely by the appearance of a document and its adherence to recognized formats. To ensure that your documents carry favorable nonverbal messages about you and your organization, you will want to give special attention to the appearance and formatting of your e-mails, letters, envelopes, and fax cover sheets.

E-Mail

E-mail continues to be a primary communication channel in the workplace. Chapter 5 presents guidelines for preparing e-mails. This section provides additional information on formats and usage. The following suggestions, illustrated in Figure B.1 and also in Figure 5.1 on page 124, may guide you in setting up the parts of any e-mail. Always check, however, with your organization to ensure that you follow its practices.

***To* Line.** Include the receiver's e-mail address after *To*. If the receiver's address is recorded in your address book, you just have to click it. Be sure to enter all addresses very carefully since one mistyped letter prevents delivery.

***From* Line.** Most mail programs automatically include your name and e-mail address after *From*.

Figure **B.1** Typical E-Mail

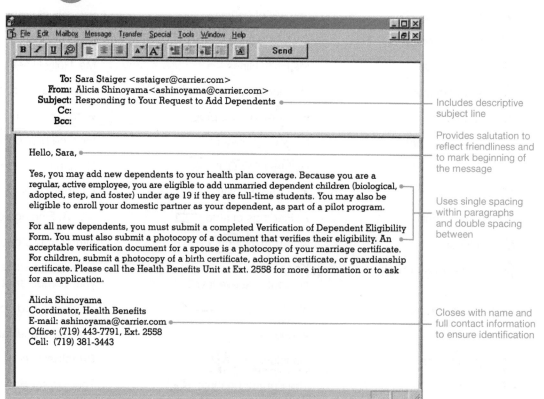

Cc and Bcc. Insert the e-mail address of anyone who is to receive a copy of the message. *Cc* stands for "carbon copy" or "courtesy copy." Don't be tempted, though, to send needless copies just because it is easy. *Bcc* stands for "blind carbon copy." Some writers use *bcc* to send a copy of the message without the addressee's knowledge. Writers also use the *bcc* line for mailing lists. When a message is sent to a number of people and their e-mail addresses should not be revealed, the *bcc* line works well to conceal the names and addresses of all receivers.

Subject. Identify the subject of the e-mail with a brief but descriptive summary of the topic. Be sure to include enough information to be clear and compelling. Capitalize the initial letters of main words. Main words are all words except (a) the articles *a, an,* and *the*; (b) prepositions containing two or three letters (such as *at, to, on, by, for*); (c) the word *to* in an infinitive (*to work, to write*); and (d) the word *as*—unless any of these words are the first or last word in the subject line.

Salutation. Include a brief greeting, if you like. Some writers use a salutation such as *Dear Sara* followed by a comma or a colon. Others are more informal with *Hi, Sara; Hello, Sara; Good morning;* or *Greetings.*

Message. Ideally, cover just one topic in your message, and try to keep your total message under three screens in length. Single-space and be sure to use both upper- and lowercase letters. Double-space between paragraphs.

Closing. Conclude an e-mail, if you like, with *Cheers, Best wishes,* or *Warm regards,* followed by your name and complete contact information. Some people omit their e-mail address because they think it is provided automatically. However, programs and routers do not always transmit the address. Therefore, always include it along with other identifying information in the closing.

Attachment. Use the attachment window or button to select the path and file name of any file you wish to send with your e-mail. You can also attach a Web page to your message.

Business Letters

Business communicators write business letters primarily to correspond with people outside the organization. Letters may go to customers, vendors, other businesses, and the government, as discussed in Chapters 6, 7, and 8. The following information will help you format your letters following conventional guidelines.

Conventional Letter Placement, Margins, and Line Spacing

To set up business letters using conventional guidelines, follow these guidelines:

- For a clean look, choose a sans serif font such as Arial, Calibri, Tahoma, or Verdana. For a more traditional look, choose a serif font such as Times New Roman. Use a 10-point, 11-point, or 12-point size.
- Use a 2-inch top margin for the first page of a letter printed on letterhead stationery. This places the date on line 12 or 13. Use a 1-inch top margin for second and succeeding pages.
- Justify only the left margin. Set the line spacing to single.
- Choose side margins according to the length of your letter. Set 1.5-inch margins for short letters (under 200 words) and 1-inch margins for longer letters (200 or more words).
- Leave from two to ten blank lines following the date to balance the message on the page. You can make this adjustment after keying your message.

Formatting Letters With Microsoft Word 2007, 2010, and 2013

If you are working with Microsoft Word 2007, 2010, or 2013, the default margins are set at 1 inch and the default font is 11-point Calibri. The default setting for line spacing is 1.15, and the paragraph default is 10 points of blank space following each paragraph or each tap of the Enter key. Many letter writers find this extra space excessive, especially after parts of the letter that are normally single-spaced. The model documents in this book show conventional single-spacing with one blank line between paragraphs.

To format your documents with conventional spacing and yet retain a clean look, change the Microsoft defaults to the following: Arial font set for 11 points, line spacing at 1.0, and spacing before and after paragraphs at 0.

Spacing and Punctuation

For some time typists left two spaces after end punctuation (periods, question marks, and so forth). This practice was necessary, it was thought, because typewriters did not have proportional spacing and sentences were easier to read when two spaces separated them. Professional typesetters, however, never followed this practice because they used proportional spacing, and readability was not a problem. Influenced by the look of typeset publications, many writers now leave only one space after end punctuation. As a practical matter, however, it is not wrong to use two spaces.

Business Letter Parts

Professional-looking business letters are arranged in a conventional sequence with standard parts. Following is a discussion of how to use these letter parts properly. Figure B.2 illustrates the parts of a block style letter. See Chapter 6 for additional discussion of letters and their parts.

Letterhead. Most business organizations use 8½ × 11-inch paper printed with a letterhead displaying their official name, street address, Web address, e-mail address, and telephone and fax numbers. The letterhead may also include a logo and an advertising message.

Dateline. On letterhead paper you should place the date one blank line below the last line of the letterhead or 2 inches from the top edge of the paper (line 12 or 13). On plain paper place the date immediately below your return address. Because the date goes on line 12 or 13, start the return address an appropriate number of lines above it. The most common dateline format is as follows: *June 9, 2016.* Don't use *th* (or *rd, nd* or *st*) when the date is written this way. For European or military correspondence, use the following dateline format: *9 June 2016.* Notice that no commas are used.

Addressee and Delivery Notations. Delivery notations such as *E-MAIL TRANS-MISSION, FEDEX, MESSENGER DELIVERY, CONFIDENTIAL,* or *CERTIFIED MAIL* are typed in all capital letters two blank lines above the inside address.

Inside Address. Type the inside address—that is, the address of the organization or person receiving the letter—single-spaced, starting at the left margin. The number of lines between the dateline and the inside address depends on the size of the letter body, the type size (point or pitch size), and the length of the typing lines. Generally, one to nine blank lines are appropriate.

Be careful to duplicate the exact wording and spelling of the recipient's name and address on your documents. Usually, you can copy this information from the letterhead of the correspondence you are answering. If, for example, you are responding to *Jackson & Perkins Company*, do not address your letter to *Jackson and Perkins Corp.*

Always be sure to include a courtesy title such as *Mr., Ms., Mrs., Dr.,* or *Professor* before a person's name in the inside address—for both the letter and the envelope. Although many women in business today favor *Ms.,* you should use whatever title the addressee prefers.

Figure B.2 Block and Modified Block Letter Styles

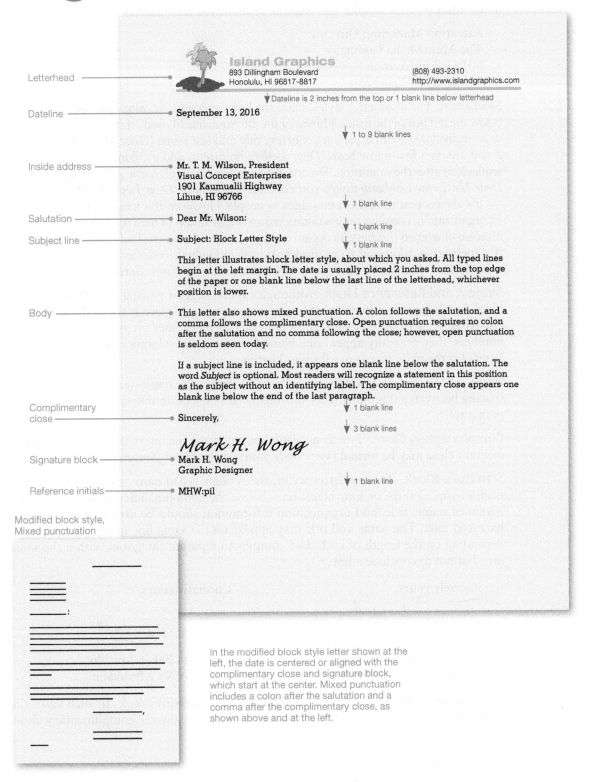

Letterhead

Island Graphics
893 Dillingham Boulevard
Honolulu, HI 96817-8817

(808) 493-2310
http://www.islandgraphics.com

▼ Dateline is 2 inches from the top or 1 blank line below letterhead

Dateline

September 13, 2016

▼ 1 to 9 blank lines

Inside address

Mr. T. M. Wilson, President
Visual Concept Enterprises
1901 Kaumualii Highway
Lihue, HI 96766

▼ 1 blank line

Salutation

Dear Mr. Wilson:

▼ 1 blank line

Subject line

Subject: Block Letter Style

▼ 1 blank line

This letter illustrates block letter style, about which you asked. All typed lines begin at the left margin. The date is usually placed 2 inches from the top edge of the paper or one blank line below the last line of the letterhead, whichever position is lower.

Body

This letter also shows mixed punctuation. A colon follows the salutation, and a comma follows the complimentary close. Open punctuation requires no colon after the salutation and no comma following the close; however, open punctuation is seldom seen today.

If a subject line is included, it appears one blank line below the salutation. The word *Subject* is optional. Most readers will recognize a statement in this position as the subject without an identifying label. The complimentary close appears one blank line below the end of the last paragraph.

▼ 1 blank line

Complimentary close

Sincerely,

▼ 3 blank lines

Signature block

Mark H. Wong

Mark H. Wong
Graphic Designer

▼ 1 blank line

Reference initials

MHW:pil

Modified block style, Mixed punctuation

In the modified block style letter shown at the left, the date is centered or aligned with the complimentary close and signature block, which start at the center. Mixed punctuation includes a colon after the salutation and a comma after the complimentary close, as shown above and at the left.

In general, avoid abbreviations such as *Ave.* or *Co.* unless they appear in the printed letterhead of the document being answered.

Attention Line. An attention line allows you to send your message officially to an organization but to direct it to a specific individual, officer, or department.

However, if you know an individual's complete name, it is always better to use it as the first line of the inside address and avoid an attention line. Placing an attention line first in the address block enables you to paste it directly onto the envelope:

Attention Marketing Director
The MultiMedia Company
931 Calkins Avenue
Rochester, NY 14301

Salutation. For most letter styles, place the letter greeting, or salutation, one blank line below the last line of the inside address or the attention line (if used). If the letter is addressed to an individual, use that person's courtesy title and last name (*Dear Mr. Lanham*). Even if you are on a first-name basis (*Dear Leslie*), be sure to add a colon (not a comma or a semicolon) after the salutation. Do not use an individual's full name in the salutation (not *Dear Mr. Leslie Lanham*) unless you are unsure of gender (*Dear Leslie Lanham*).

It's always best to address messages to people. However, if a message is addressed to an organization, consider these salutations: an organization of men (*Gentlemen*), an organization of women (*Ladies*), an organization of men and women (*Ladies and Gentlemen*). If a message is addressed to an undetermined individual, consider these salutations: a woman (*Dear Madam*), a man (*Dear Sir*), a title (*Dear Customer Service Representative*).

Subject and Reference Lines. Although experts suggest placing the subject line one blank line below the salutation, many businesses actually place it above the salutation. Use whatever style your organization prefers. Reference lines often show policy or file numbers; they generally appear one blank line above the salutation. Use initial capital letters for the main words or all capital letters.

Body. Most business letters and memorandums are single-spaced, with double-spacing between paragraphs. Very short messages may be double-spaced with indented paragraphs.

Complimentary Close. Typed one blank line below the last line of the letter, the complimentary close may be formal (*Very truly yours*) or informal (*Sincerely* or *Cordially*).

Signature Block. In most letter styles, the writer's typed name and optional identification appear three or four blank lines below the complimentary close. The combination of name, title, and organization information should be arranged to achieve a balanced look. The name and title may appear on the same line or on separate lines, depending on the length of each. Use commas to separate categories within the same line, but not to conclude a line.

Sincerely yours,   Cordially yours,

Jeremy M. Wood   Casandra Baker-Murillo

Jeremy M. Wood, Manager   Casandra Baker-Murillo
Technical Sales and Services   Executive Vice President

Some organizations include their names in the signature block. In such cases the organization name appears in all caps one blank line below the complimentary close, as shown here:

Cordially,

LIPTON COMPUTER SERVICES

Shelina A. Simpson

Shelina A. Simpson
Executive Assistant

Reference Initials. If used, the initials of the typist and writer are typed one blank line below the writer's name and title. Generally, the writer's initials are capitalized and the typist's are lowercased, but this format varies.

Enclosure Notation. When an enclosure or attachment accompanies a document, a notation to that effect appears one blank line below the reference initials. This notation reminds the typist to insert the enclosure in the envelope, and it reminds the recipient to look for the enclosure or attachment. The notation may be spelled out (*Enclosure, Attachment*), or it may be abbreviated (*Enc., Att.*). It may indicate the number of enclosures or attachments, and it may also identify a specific enclosure (*Enclosure: Form 1099*).

Copy Notation. If you make copies of correspondence for other individuals, you may use *cc* to indicate courtesy copy, *pc* to indicate photocopy, or merely *c* for any kind of copy. A colon following the initial(s) is optional.

Second-Page Heading. When a letter extends beyond one page, use plain paper of the same quality and color as the first page. Identify the second and succeeding pages with a heading consisting of the name of the addressee, the page number, and the date. Use the following format or the one shown in Figure B.3:

Ms. Sara Hendricks	2	May 3, 2016

Both headings appear six blank lines (1 inch) from the top edge of the paper followed by two blank lines to separate them from the continuing text. Avoid using a second page if you have only one line or the complimentary close and signature block to fill that page.

Plain-Paper Return Address. If you prepare a personal or business letter on plain paper, place your address immediately above the date. Do not include your name; you will type (and sign) your name at the end of your letter. If your return address

Figure **B.3** Second-Page Heading

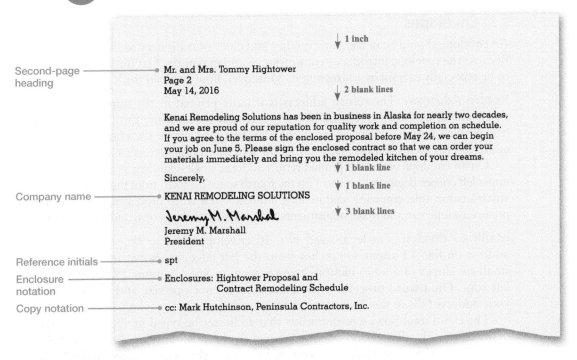

contains two lines, begin typing so that the date appears 2 inches from the top. Avoid abbreviations except for a two-letter state abbreviation.

580 East Leffels Street
Springfield, OH 45501
December 14, 2016

Ms. Ellen Siemens
Escrow Department
TransOhio First Federal
1220 Wooster Boulevard
Columbus, OH 43218-2900

Dear Ms. Siemens:

For letters in the block style, type the return address at the left margin. For modified block style letters, start the return address at the center to align with the complimentary close.

Letter and Punctuation Styles

Most business letters today are prepared in either block or modified block style, and they generally use mixed punctuation.

Block Style. In the block style, shown in Figure B.2, all lines begin at the left margin. This style is a favorite because it is easy to format.

Modified Block Style. The modified block style differs from block style in that the date and closing lines appear in the center, as shown at the bottom of Figure B.2. The date may be (a) centered, (b) begun at the center of the page (to align with the closing lines), or (c) backspaced from the right margin. The signature block—including the complimentary close, writer's name and title, or organization identification—begins at the center. The first line of each paragraph may begin at the left margin or may be indented five or ten spaces. All other lines begin at the left margin.

Mixed Punctuation Style. Most businesses today use mixed punctuation, shown in Figure B.2. This style requires a colon after the salutation and a comma after the complimentary close. Even when the salutation is a first name, a colon is appropriate.

Envelopes

An envelope should be of the same quality and color of stationery as the letter it carries. Because the envelope introduces your message and makes the first impression, you need to be especially careful in addressing it. Moreover, how you fold the letter is important.

Return Address. The return address is usually printed in the upper left corner of an envelope, as shown in Figure B.4. In large companies some form of identification (the writer's initials, name, or location) may be typed above the company name and address. This identification helps return the letter to the sender in case of nondelivery.

On an envelope without a printed return address, single-space the return address in the upper left corner. Beginning on line 3 on the fourth space (½ inch) from the left edge, type the writer's name, title, company, and mailing address. On a word processor, select the appropriate envelope size and make adjustments to approximate this return address location.

Mailing Address. On legal-sized No. 10 envelopes (4⅛ × 9½ inches), begin the address on line 13 about 4¼ inches from the left edge, as shown in Figure B.4. For small envelopes (3⅝ × 6½ inches), begin typing on line 12 about 2½ inches from the left edge. On a word processor, select the correct envelope size and check to be sure your address falls in the desired location.

The U.S. Postal Service recommends that addresses be typed in all caps without any punctuation. This Postal Service style, shown in the small envelope in Figure B.4, was originally developed to facilitate scanning by optical character readers. Today's OCRs,

A-10

Appendix B: Document Format Guide

Figure (B.4) Envelope Formats

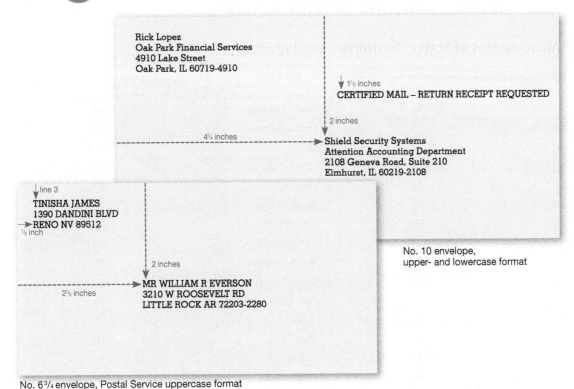

Rick Lopez
Oak Park Financial Services
4910 Lake Street
Oak Park, IL 60719-4910

↓ 1½ inches
CERTIFIED MAIL – RETURN RECEIPT REQUESTED

4¼ inches

↓ 2 inches
Shield Security Systems
Attention Accounting Department
2108 Geneva Road, Suite 210
Elmhurst, IL 60219-2108

No. 10 envelope,
upper- and lowercase format

↓ line 3
TINISHA JAMES
1390 DANDINI BLVD
➤ RENO NV 89512
½ inch

↓ 2 inches
MR WILLIAM R EVERSON
3210 W ROOSEVELT RD
LITTLE ROCK AR 72203-2280

2½ inches

No. 6³/₄ envelope, Postal Service uppercase format

however, are so sophisticated that they scan upper- and lowercase letters easily. Many companies today do not follow the Postal Service format because they prefer to use the same format for the envelope as for the inside address. If the same format is used, writers can take advantage of word processing programs to copy the inside address to the envelope, thus saving keystrokes and reducing errors. Having the same format on both the inside address and the envelope also looks more professional and consistent. For those reasons you may choose to use the familiar upper- and lowercase combination format. However, you should check with your organization to learn its preference.

In addressing your envelopes for delivery in this country or in Canada, use the two-letter state and province abbreviations shown in Figure B.5. Notice that these abbreviations are in capital letters without periods.

Folding. The way a letter is folded and inserted into an envelope sends additional nonverbal messages about a writer's professionalism and carefulness. Most businesspeople follow the procedures shown here, which produce the least number of creases to distract readers.

For large No. 10 envelopes, begin with the letter face up. Fold slightly less than one third of the sheet toward the top, as shown in the following diagram. Then fold down the top third to within ⅓ inch of the bottom fold. Insert the letter into the envelope with the last fold toward the bottom of the envelope.

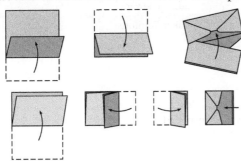

For small No. 6¾ envelopes, begin by folding the bottom up to within ⅓ inch of the top edge. Then fold the right third over to the left. Fold the left third to within ⅓ inch of the last fold. Insert the last fold into the envelope first.

Figure **B.5** Abbreviations of States, Territories, and Provinces

State or Territory	Two-Letter Abbreviation	State or Territory	Two-Letter Abbreviation
Alabama	AL	North Carolina	NC
Alaska	AK	North Dakota	ND
Arizona	AZ	Ohio	OH
Arkansas	AR	Oklahoma	OK
California	CA	Oregon	OR
Canal Zone	CZ	Pennsylvania	PA
Colorado	CO	Puerto Rico	PR
Connecticut	CT	Rhode Island	RI
Delaware	DE	South Carolina	SC
District of Columbia	DC	South Dakota	SD
Florida	FL	Tennessee	TN
Georgia	GA	Texas	TX
Guam	GU	Utah	UT
Hawaii	HI	Vermont	VT
Idaho	ID	Virgin Islands	VI
Illinois	IL	Virginia	VA
Indiana	IN	Washington	WA
Iowa	IA	West Virginia	WV
Kansas	KS	Wisconsin	WI
Kentucky	KY	Wyoming	WY
Louisiana	LA	**Canadian Province**	
Maine	ME	Alberta	AB
Maryland	MD	British Columbia	BC
Massachusetts	MA	Labrador	LB
Michigan	MI	Manitoba	MB
Minnesota	MN	New Brunswick	NB
Mississippi	MS	Newfoundland	NF
Missouri	MO	Northwest Territories	NT
Montana	MT	Nova Scotia	NS
Nebraska	NE	Ontario	ON
Nevada	NV	Prince Edward Island	PE
New Hampshire	NH	Quebec	PQ
New Jersey	NJ	Saskatchewan	SK
New Mexico	NM	Yukon Territory	YT
New York	NY		

Appendix C: Documentation Formats

For many reasons business writers are careful to properly document report data. Citing sources strengthens a writer's argument, as you learned in Chapter 10 on page 316, while also shielding the writer from charges of plagiarism. Moreover, good references help readers pursue further research. As a business writer, you can expect to routinely borrow ideas and words to show that your ideas are in sync with the rest of the business world, to gain support from business leaders, or simply to save time in developing your ideas. To be ethical, however, you must show clearly what you borrowed and from whom.

Source notes tell where you found your information. For quotations, paraphrases, graphs, drawings, or online images you have borrowed, you need to cite the original authors' names, full publication titles, and the dates and facts of publication. The purpose of source notes, which appear at the end of your report, is to direct your readers to the complete references. Many systems of documentation are used by businesses, but they all have one goal: to provide clear, consistent documentation.

Rarely, business writers use content notes, which are identified with a raised number at the end of the quotation. At the bottom of the page, the number is repeated with a remark, clarification, or background information.

During your business career, you may use a variety of documentation systems. The two most common systems in the academic world are those of the American Psychological Association (APA) and the Modern Language Association (MLA). Each organization has its own style for text references and bibliographic lists. This book uses a modified MLA style. However, business organizations may use their own documentation systems.

Before starting any research project, whether for a class or in a business, inquire about the preferred documentation style. For school assignments ask about specifics. For example, should you include URLs and dates of retrieval for Web sources? For workplace assignments ask to see a previous report either in hard-copy version or as an e-mail attachment.

In your business and class writing, you will usually provide a brief citation in parentheses that refers readers to the complete reference that appears in a references or works-cited section at the end of your document. Following is a summary of APA and MLA formats with examples.

American Psychological Association Format

First used primarily in the social and physical sciences, the American Psychological Association (APA) documentation format uses the author-date method of citation. This method, with its emphasis on current information, is especially appropriate for business. Within the text, the date of publication of the referenced work appears immediately after the author's name (Rivera, 2014), as illustrated in the brief APA example in Figure C.1. At the end of the report, all references appear alphabetically on a page labeled "References." The APA format does not require a date of retrieval for online sources, but you should check with your instructor or supervisor about the preferred format for your class or organization. For more information about the APA format, see the *Publication Manual of the American Psychological Association*, Sixth Edition (Washington, DC: American Psychological Association, 2009).

APA In-Text Format. Within your text, document each text, figure, or personal source with a short description in parentheses. Following are selected guidelines summarizing the important elements of APA style.

Figure C.1 Portions of APA Text Page and References

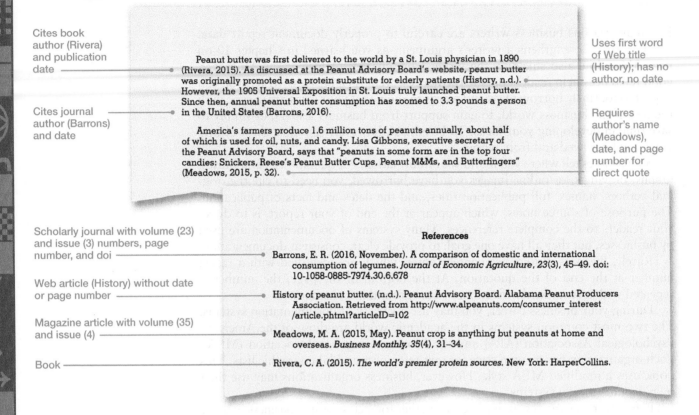

Cites book author (Rivera) and publication date

Cites journal author (Barrons) and date

Scholarly journal with volume (23) and issue (3) numbers, page number, and doi

Web article (History) without date or page number

Magazine article with volume (35) and issue (4)

Book

Uses first word of Web title (History); has no author, no date

Requires author's name (Meadows), date, and page number for direct quote

Peanut butter was first delivered to the world by a St. Louis physician in 1890 (Rivera, 2015). As discussed at the Peanut Advisory Board's website, peanut butter was originally promoted as a protein substitute for elderly patients (History, n.d.). However, the 1905 Universal Exposition in St. Louis truly launched peanut butter. Since then, annual peanut butter consumption has zoomed to 3.3 pounds a person in the United States (Barrons, 2016).

America's farmers produce 1.6 million tons of peanuts annually, about half of which is used for oil, nuts, and candy. Lisa Gibbons, executive secretary of the Peanut Advisory Board, says that "peanuts in some form are in the top four candies: Snickers, Reese's Peanut Butter Cups, Peanut M&Ms, and Butterfingers" (Meadows, 2015, p. 32).

References

Barrons, E. R. (2016, November). A comparison of domestic and international consumption of legumes. *Journal of Economic Agriculture, 23*(3), 45–49. doi: 10-1058-0885-7974.30.6.678

History of peanut butter. (n.d.). Peanut Advisory Board. Alabama Peanut Producers Association. Retrieved from http://www.alpeanuts.com/consumer_interest /article.phtml?articleID=102

Meadows, M. A. (2015, May). Peanut crop is anything but peanuts at home and overseas. *Business Monthly, 35*(4), 31–34.

Rivera, C. A. (2015). *The world's premier protein sources.* New York: HarperCollins.

- For a direct quotation, include the last name of the author(s), if available, and the year of publication; for example, *(Meadows, 2015, p. 32).* If no author is shown in the text or on a website, use a shortened title or a heading that can be easily located on the References page; for example, *(History, n.d.).*

- If you mention the author in the text, do not use the name again in the parenthetical reference. Just cite the date; for example, *According to Meadows (2015).*

- Search for website dates on the home page or at the bottom of Web pages. If no date is available for a source, use *n.d.*

APA References Format. At the end of your report, in a section called "References," list all references alphabetically by author, or by title if no author is available. To better understand the anatomy of an APA scholarly journal article reference, see Figure C.2.

Figure C.2 Anatomy of an APA Journal Article Reference

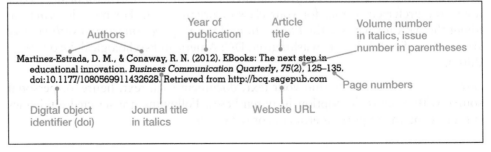

Authors

Year of publication

Article title

Volume number in italics, issue number in parentheses

Martinez-Estrada, D. M., & Conaway, R. N. (2012). EBooks: The next step in educational innovation. *Business Communication Quarterly, 75*(2), 125–135. doi:10.1177/1080569911432628. Retrieved from http://bcq.sagepub.com

Digital object identifier (doi)

Journal title in italics

Website URL

Page numbers

As with all documentation methods, APA has specific capitalization, punctuation, and sequencing rules, some of which are summarized here:

- Include the last name of the author(s) followed by initials. APA is gender neutral, so first and middle names are not spelled out; for example, *(Martinez-Estrada, D. M.)*.

- Show the date of publication in parentheses immediately after the author's name. A magazine citation will also include the month and day in the parentheses.

- Use sentence-style capitalization for all titles except journal article titles. Do not use quotation marks.

- Italicize titles of magazines, newspapers, books, and journals.

Figure C.3 APA Sample References

References

Online article, no author (Ignore "The" when alphabetizing)
→ The art of investment economics. (2000). Retrieved from http://www.becon.cornell.org

Online magazine with volume, issue, and page numbers
→ Balcazar, W. (2010, March 2). The imminent problem in investing. *Fortune 62*(5), 26–28. Retrieved from http://www.fortune.com

Online journal
→ Bray, U., Onkussi, P., & Genessee, R. (2003). The behavior of Thailand's stock market. *Web Journal of Applied Topics in Business and Economics.* Retrieved from http://www.westga.edu

Annual report
→ C. H. Robinson. *2011 Annual Report.* Retrieved from http://investor.chrobinson.com/phoenix.zhtml?c=97366&p=irol-reportsannual

Journal with DOI
→ Cox, A. T., & Followill, R. (2012). The equitable financing of growth: A proportionate share methodology for calculating individual development impact fees. *The Engineering Economist: A Journal Devoted to the Problems of Capital Investment, 57*(3), 141–156. doi: 10.1080/0013791X.2012.702195

Journal with two authors
→ Fernandez, A. A., & Nickels, R. (2010). Globalization and the changing nature of the U.S. economy's influence in the world. *Economic Letters, 3*(11), 1–4.

Book
→ Gurati, F. (2011). *Basic econometrics* (4th ed.). New York: McGraw-Hill.

Magazine, no author
→ How to: Communicate with investors. (2010, May). *Inc., 32*(4), 55–58.

Online newspaper with URL
→ Killebrew, M. (2011, January 24). Keeping up with global money changes. *International Herald Tribune.* Retrieved from http://www.nytimes.com/2012/09/27/world/unitednations-general-assembly.html

Newspaper article with author
→ Schwartz, J. (2009, September 21). The global economy changes investment patterns. *The New York Times,* p. B9.

Blog post
→ Turner, M. (2013, January 12). Tricky interview questions and how to nail them. [Blog post]. Retrieved from http://blogs.vault.com/blog/interviewing/tricky-interview-questions-and-how-to-nail-them

Magazine article with volume, issue, and page numbers
→ Zahamen, C. (2009, August). Ten unfriendly states for investment. *Kiplinger's Personal Finance Magazine (42)*2, 44–45.

Note: Although APA style prescribes double spacing for the references page, we show single spacing to conserve space and to represent preferred business usage.

- Include the digital object identifier (DOI) when available for online periodicals. If no DOI is available, include the home page URL unless the source is difficult to retrieve without the entire URL.
- Break a URL or DOI only before a mark of punctuation such as a period or slash.
- If the website content may change, as in a wiki, include a retrieval date; for example, *Retrieved 7 July 2016 from http://www.encyclopediaofmath.org /index.php/MainPage*.
- Please note, however, that many instructors require that all Web references be identified by their URLs.
- For articles easily obtained from an online college database, provide the print information only. Do not include the database name or an accession number unless the article is discontinued or was never published.

For a comprehensive list of APA documentation format examples, see Figure C.3.

Modern Language Association Format

Writers in the humanities and the liberal arts frequently use the Modern Language Association (MLA) documentation format, illustrated briefly in Figure C.4. In parentheses close to the textual reference, include the author's name and page cited (Rivera 25). At the end of your writing on a page titled "Works Cited," list all the sources alphabetically. Some writers include all of the sources consulted. Differing from APA, MLA style does not require the URL if the source can be located with a keyword search. However, it's wise to check with your instructor or organization

Figure **C.4** Portions of MLA Text Page and Works Cited

Cites book author (Rivera) and page number

Cites journal author (Barrons) and page number

Peanut butter was first delivered to the world by a St. Louis physician in 1890 (Rivera 25). As discussed at the Peanut Advisory Board's website, peanut butter was originally promoted as a protein substitute for elderly patients ("History"). However, the 1905 Universal Exposition in St. Louis truly launched peanut butter. Since then, annual peanut butter consumption has zoomed to 3.3 pounds a person in the United States (Barrons 47).

America's farmers produce 1.6 million tons of peanuts annually, about half of which is used for oil, nuts, and candy. Lisa Gibbons, executive secretary of the Peanut Advisory Board, says that "peanuts in some form are in the top four candies: Snickers, Reese's Peanut Butter Cups, Peanut M&Ms, and Butterfingers" (Meadows, 32).

Lists first word of Web title ("History") when no author or page number is available

Places period outside of author, page reference

Scholarly article with volume (23) and issue (3) numbers, page number, and medium (Print)

Web article without date or page number; medium (Web) and acquisition date (2016) appear last

Magazine article

Book

Works Cited

Barrons, Elizabeth R. "A Comparison of Domestic and International Consumption of Legumes." *Journal of Economic Agriculture*, 23.3, (2016): 45–49. Print.

"History of Peanut Butter." *Peanut Advisory Board*. Alabama Peanut Producers Association, n.d. Web. 19 Jan. 2016.

Meadows, Mark A. "Peanut Crop Is Anything but Peanuts at Home and Overseas." *Business Monthly*, May 2015: 31–34. Print.

Rivera, Carlos A. *The World's Premier Protein Sources*. New York: HarperCollins, 2015. 25–26. Print.

to see what is required. Another notable way MLA differs from APA is in the identification of the publication medium such as *Print* or *Web*. For more information, consult the *MLA Handbook for Writers of Research Papers*, Seventh Edition (New York: The Modern Language Association of America, 2009).

MLA In-Text Format. Following any borrowed material in your text, provide a short parenthetical description. Here are selected guidelines summarizing important elements of MLA style:

- For a direct quotation, enclose in parentheses the last name of the author(s), if available, and the page number without a comma; for example, *(Rivera 25)*. If a website has no author, use a shortened title of the page or a heading that is easily found on the works-cited page; for example, ("History").

- If you mention the author in the text, do not use the name again in parentheses; for example, *According to Rivera (27) . . . .*

- Search for website dates on the home page or on each Web page for use in the in-text citation. If no page number is available, use a paragraph number; for example, *(Killebrew par. 4)*. If neither a page number nor a paragraph number is available, cite the website in your text; for example, *The Inc. website about how to communicate with investors says that. . . .*

MLA Works-Cited Format. In a section called "Works Cited," list all references alphabetically by author or, if no author is available, by title. As with all documentation methods, MLA has specific capitalization and sequencing rules. Some of the most significant are summarized here:

- Include the author's last name first, followed by the first name and initial; for example, *(Rivera, Charles A.)*.

- Enclose in quotation marks the titles of articles, essays, stories, chapters of books, pages in websites, individual episodes of television and radio broadcasts, and short musical compositions.

- Italicize the titles of books, magazines, newspapers, and journals.

- Include the medium of the publication, such as *Web, Print, Radio, Television, Film*.

- Include the URL only if the online site cannot be located by a keyword search. However, for class assignments, check to learn whether your instructor requires URLs, database names, and retrieval dates.

  To better understand the anatomy of the format of an MLA scholarly journal article reference, see Figure C.5. For a comprehensive list of MLA documentation format examples, see Figure C.6.

Figure **C.5** Anatomy of an MLA Journal Article Reference

Figure **C.6** MLA Sample References

Online magazine article. *Note:* Include date and page numbers but not volume or issue, even if available

Annual report from website

Journal article with two authors

Magazine article without author. No period after magazine title unless part of title

Newspaper article with author and edition

Blog post

Works Cited

Balcazar, William. "The Imminent Problem in Investing." *Fortune* 2 March 2010: 26–28. Web. 5 Jan. 2013.

Bray, Unoki, Peter Ohkussi, and Ronni Genessee. "The Behavior of Thailand's Stock Market." *Web Journal of Applied Topics in Business and Economics* (2003): n. pag. Web. 22 Dec. 2012.

C. H. Robinson. *2011 Annual Report*. Web. 22 Dec. 2012.

Cox, Arthur T., and Robert Followill. "The Equitable Financing of Growth: A Proportionate Share Methodology for Calculating Individual Development Impact Fees." *The Engineering Economist: A Journal Devoted to the Problems of Capital Investment* 57.3 (2012): 141–156. Web. 6 Jan. 2013.

Fernandez, Anthony A., and Roberto Nickels. "Globalization and the Changing Nature of the U.S. Economy's Influence in the World." *Economic Letters* 3.11 (2010): 1–4. Print.

Gurati, Fredrik. *Basic Econometrics*. 4th ed. New York: McGraw-Hill, 2011. Print.

"How to: Communicate with Investors." *Inc.* May 2010: 55–58. Print.

Killebrew, Matthew. "Keeping Up with Global Money Changes." *International Herald Tribune* 24 Jan. 2011: 22+. Web. 24 Dec. 2012.

Schwartz, John. "The Global Economy Changes Investment Patterns." *The New York Times* 21 Sept. 2009, late ed.: B9. Print.

"The Art of Investment Economics." (2000): 1. Web. 24 Dec. 2012. <www.becon .cornell.org>.

Turner, Michelle. "Tricky Interview Questions and How to Nail Them." *Vault Blogs*. Vault Career Intelligence. Blog post. 12 Jan. 2013.

Zahamen, Cecil. "Ten Unfriendly States for Investment." *Kiplinger's Personal Finance Magazine* Aug. 2009: 44–45. Print.

Online journal without page, volume, or issue numbers

Online journal with volume (57) and issue (3) numbers

Book

Online newspaper

Unsigned online article with URL if required

Magazine article. Include date but not volume or issue numbers

Note: Check with your instructor about whether to cite URLs. Although MLA suggests using them only if necessary, many schools require students to include all URLs in their research papers.